The Politics of the Environment
Ideas, Activism, Policy

The rising profile of the environment in politics reflects growing public concern that we may be facing a large-scale ecological crisis. This unique textbook surveys the politics of the environment, providing a comprehensive and comparative introduction to ideas, activism and policy. Part I explores environmental philosophy and green political thought, assessing the relationship between 'green ideas' and other political doctrines. Part II considers parties and movements, including the development of green parties from protest parties, the response of established political parties to the environmental challenge, and the evolution of the environmental movement. Part III analyses public policy-making and environmental issues at the international, national and local levels. As well as considering a wide variety of examples from around the world, this important new textbook includes a glossary, lists of key issues, chapter summaries and guides to further study.

NEIL CARTER is Senior Lecturer in the Department of Politics, University of York. He is the author of *How Organisations Measure Success: The Use of Performance Indicators in Government* (with R. Klein and P. Day, 1992) and Joint Editor of the journal *Environmental Politics*.

The Politics of the Environment
Ideas, Activism, Policy

Neil Carter

Department of Politics, University of York

CAMBRIDGE
UNIVERSITY PRESS

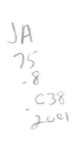

PUBLISHED BY THE PRESS SYNDICATE OF THE UNIVERSITY OF CAMBRIDGE
The Pitt Building, Trumpington Street, Cambridge, United Kingdom

CAMBRIDGE UNIVERSITY PRESS
The Edinburgh Building, Cambridge CB2 2RU, UK
40 West 20th Street, New York NY 10011–4211, USA
477 Williamstown Road, Port Melbourne, VIC 3207, Australia
Ruiz de Alarcón 13, 28014 Madrid, Spain
Dock House, The Waterfront, Cape Town 8001, South Africa

http://www.cambridge.org

© Cambridge University Press 2001

First published 2001

Printed in the United Kingdom at the University Press, Cambridge

Typeface Swift (*Typeface vendor*) 9.5/12.5pt   *System* QuarkXPress® [TK]

A catalogue record for this book is available from the British Library

Library of Congress Cataloguing in Publication data
Carter, Neil, 1958–
The politics of the environment: ideas, activism, policy / Neil Carter.
    p.   cm.
Includes bibliographical references and index.
ISBN 0 521 47037 4 – ISBN 0 521 46994 5 (pb.)
1. Green movement.   I. Title.
JA75.8 .C38 2001   320.5 – dc21   2001035638

ISBN 0 521 47037 4 hardback
ISBN 0 521 46994 5 paperback

To my mother, Molly Carter

Contents

Figures

Tables

Boxes

Acknowledgements

In writing a book that has been as long in gestation as this one, I have inevitably accrued many debts. Andy Dobson, Meg Huby, Andy Jordan, Sue Mendus and Chris Rootes have each read several chapters, and I know that the book is much better for their wise and helpful comments. Brian Doherty, Mat Paterson and Andrew Williams have each commented on a chapter. A wide range of people have helped in small but important ways, including Keith Alderman, Riley Dunlap, Katarina Eckerberg, Dave Humphreys, Janet Jenkins, Arthur Mol and Ben Seel. Many others, too numerous to mention, have contributed in a less formal manner. I should, however, like to make a special fond mention for Dick Richardson, with whom I shared many discussions about green politics and whose enthusiasm and good humour are greatly missed by his many friends. My colleagues at the University of York have provided a friendly, supportive and stimulating working environment. Several cohorts of students who have taken my courses in 'Green Politics' and 'Environmental Policy' have also helped me to develop my ideas. I am also grateful to Nuffield College, Oxford, where I spent Autumn 1997 as a Visitor. John Haslam has been a remarkably patient, supportive and encouraging editor throughout.

Finally, Charlie Burns has been an unfailing source of emotional and intellectual support throughout the often painful process of writing this book. She has read every chapter, usually several times, and offered excellent, constructive advice. I cannot thank her enough.

Abbreviations

ACF	Advocacy Coalition Framework
APP	Anti-party party
BSE	Bovine spongiform encephalopathy
CBA	Cost–benefit analysis
CDU	Christian Democrat Union (Germany)
CFC	Chlorofluorocarbons
CITES	Convention on International Trade in Endangered Species
COP	Conference of the Parties
CSD	Commission on Sustainable Development
DDT	Dichlorodiphenyltrichloroethane (insecticide)
EAP	Environmental Action Plan
EEA	European Environment Agency
EIA	Environmental Impact Assessment
EMAS	Eco-Management and Audit Scheme
EPA	Environmental Protection Agency (USA)
EU	European Union
FDP	Free Democrats Party (Germany)
FoE	Friends of the Earth
GEF	Global Environment Facility
GMO	Genetically modified organism
HCFC	Hydrochlorofluorocarbons
HFC	Hydrofluorocarbons
IFF	Intergovernmental Forum on Forests
IMF	International Monetary Fund
IPCC	Intergovernmental Panel on Climate Change
IWC	International Whaling Commission
LA21	Local Agenda 21
LCV	League of Conservation Voters (USA)
LETS	Local employment and trading system
LRTAP	Long-range transboundary air pollution
LULU	Locally unwanted land-use
MBI	Market-based instrument
ME	Ministry of the Environment
MEP	Member of the European Parliament

MP	Member of Parliament
NAFTA	North American Free Trade Agreement
NATO	North Atlantic Treaty Organisation
NGO	Non-governmental organisation
NIMBY	Not in my back yard
NSM	New social movement
OECD	Organisation for Economic Co-operation and Development
POS	Political opportunity structure
PPP	Polluter Pays Principle
RSPB	Royal Society for the Protection of Birds (UK)
SPD	Social Democratic Party (Germany)
UNCED	United Nations Conference on Environment and Development
UNDP	United Nations Development Programme
UNEP	United Nations Environment Programme
UNGASS	United Nations General Assembly Special Session
WCED	World Commission on Environment and Development
WWF	World Wide Fund for Nature
WTO	World Trade Organisation

Glossary

Anthropocentrism A way of thinking that regards humans as the source of all value and is predominantly concerned with human interests.

Biodiversity The number, variety and variability of living organisms; sometimes refers to the total variety of life on Earth.

Bioregionalism An approach that believes that the 'natural' world (specifically, the local bioregion) should determine the political, economic and social life of communities.

Climate change Any change in climate over time, whether due to natural variability or to human activity.

Conservationism An approach to land management that emphasises the efficient conservation of natural resources so that they can later be developed for the benefit of society.

Corporatism A system in which major organised interests (traditionally, capital and labour) work closely together within the formal structures of government to formulate and implement public policies.

Cost–benefit analysis A study that compares the costs and benefits to society of providing a public good.

Decentralisation The expansion of local autonomy through the transfer of powers and responsibilities away from a national political and administrative body.

Deep ecology The pre-eminent radical ecocentric moral theory which has the primary aim of preserving nature from human interference.

Ecocentrism A mode of thought that regards humans as subject to ecological and systems laws and whose ethical, political and social prescriptions are concerned with both humans and non-humans.

Ecological modernisation A policy strategy which aims to restructure capitalist political economy along more environmentally benign lines based on the assumption that economic growth and environmental protection can be reconciled.

Ecologism A distinctive green political ideology encompassing those perspectives that hold that a sustainable society requires radical changes in our relationship with the non-human natural world and our mode of economic, social and political life.

Eco-tax A tax levied on pollution or on the goods whose production generates pollution.

Environmental impact assessment A systematic non-technical evaluation, based on extensive consultation with affected interests, of the anticipated environmental impact of a proposed development such as a dam or road.

Genetically modified organism New organisms created by human manipulation of genetic information and material.

Green consumerism The use of environmental and ethical criteria in choosing whether or not to purchase a product or service.

Holism The view that wholes are more than just the sum of their parts, and that wholes cannot be defined merely as a collection of their basic constituents.

Intrinsic value The value which something has, independently of anyone finding it valuable.

Issue attention cycle The idea that there is a cycle in which issues attract public attention and move up and down the political agenda.

Limits to growth The belief that the planet imposes natural limits on economic and population growth.

Market-based instrument A policy instrument which internalises into the price of a good or product the external costs to the environment of producing and using it.

Modern environmentalism The emergence, from the late 1960s, of growing public concern about the state of the planet, new political ideas about the environment and a mass political movement.

Moral extensionism Ethical approaches which broaden the 'moral community' to include non-human entities such as animals, based on the possession of some critical property such as sentience.

New politics The view that since the late 1960s the rise of postmaterial values, a new middle class and new social movements has changed the political agenda and led to a realignment of established party systems.

New social movement A loose-knit organisation which seeks to influence public policy on an issue such as the environment, nuclear energy or peace, and which may use unconventional forms of political participation, including direct action, to achieve its aims.

Ozone depletion Depletion of ozone in the Earth's upper atmosphere which leaves the surface of the Earth vulnerable to harmful ultraviolet radiation.

Party politicisation A process whereby the environment ascends the political agenda to become electorally salient and the subject of party competition.

Pioneer states Those countries, mostly in Northern Europe, that have taken the lead in developing progressive environmental policies and setting high standards of environmental protection.

Policy paradigm A framework of ideas and standards that specifies the nature of a problem and the policy goals and instruments needed to address it.

Political opportunity structure The dimensions of the political environment that either encourage people to use collective action or discourage them from doing so, and which shape the development of movements and parties.

Postmaterialism The theory that, as material affluence spreads, 'quality of life' issues and concerns tend to replace material ones, fundamentally changing the political culture and values of industrialised countries.

Precautionary principle The principle states that the lack of scientific certainty shall not be used as a reason for postponing measures to prevent environmental degradation.

Preservationism An approach based on an attitude of reverence towards nature, especially wilderness, that advocates the protection of a resource from any form of development.

Regime The principles, norms, rules and decision-making procedures which form the basis of co-operation on a particular issue in international relations.

Regulation Any direct ('command and control') attempt by the government to influence the behaviour of businesses or citizens by setting environmental standards (e.g. for air quality) enforced via legislation.

Renewable energy Energy sources, such as wind, geothermal and hydro-electric, that never run out.

Resource mobilisation An approach to collective action which focuses on the way groups mobilise their resources – members, finances, symbols – in turning grievances into political issues.

Risk assessment An evaluation of the potential harm to human health and the environment from exposure to a particular hazard such as nitrates in drinking water.

Sentience The capacity to suffer or to experience enjoyment or happiness.

Social justice The principles that should govern the basic structure of a society, focusing on the distribution of rights, opportunities and resources among human beings.

Survivalism Approaches characterised by an overriding preoccupation with human survival, a sense of urgency about an impending ecological crisis and drastic, often authoritarian, solutions.

Sustainable development The ability of the present generation to meet its needs without undermining the ability of future generations to meet their needs.

Technocentric A mode of thought which optimistically believes that society can solve all environmental problems, using technology and science, and achieve unlimited material growth.

Traditional policy paradigm An approach to the environment that treats each problem discretely, gives priority to economic growth and results in reactive, piecemeal and tactical policies and end-of-pipe solutions.

1

Introduction

Before the late 1960s, the environment had a relatively insignificant place on the political agenda; today, it is one of the most challenging, contested and important subjects in politics. This rise to prominence reflects a widespread public concern about the state of the environment; indeed, the idea that the planet is confronting an eco-crisis that may threaten the very existence of life as we know it has wide currency. The lifestyle choices of many people are increasingly shaped by environmental considerations: they eat organic produce, they cycle to work and they invest their savings 'ethically'. As citizens, by joining environmental groups or voting for green parties, they put pressure on governments to protect the environment. The mainstream environmental movement is an important actor in national and international politics, while the dramatic stunts of eco-warriors have become a familiar part of the political repertoire. Green parties, particularly in Europe, are now an established feature of party politics and have even joined coalition governments in several of the most powerful countries in the world. Established parties have also adopted greener policies because every government, irrespective of political hue, is obliged to address a wide range of environmental problems. Most countries are, at least formally, committed to the principles of **sustainable development**, and the search for international co-operation to resolve global environmental problems such as **climate change** has become a central concern of international diplomacy. In short, the environment is now firmly on the political agenda in most industrialised countries.

Nevertheless, environmentalists frequently despair over how little actually seems to have changed. The overall state of the environment in most countries continues to deteriorate, despite some successes such as the reduction of some forms of air pollution. Not least, evidence suggests that climate change, probably the most serious contemporary global environmental problem, is gathering pace (IPCC 2001), while other global problems, such as **biodiversity** loss, rainforest depletion and desertification rapidly deteriorate. The litany of eco-disasters – ranging from natural disasters such as floods and droughts, through oil-tanker spillages and nuclear accidents, to the indirect effects of NATO bombing in Serbia – rolls inexorably on. Meanwhile, global capitalism and consumerist

Sustainable development: The ability of the present generation to meet its needs without undermining the ability of future generations to meet their needs.

Climate change: Any change in climate over time, whether due to natural variability or to human activity.

Biodiversity: The number, variety and variability of living organisms; sometimes refers to the total variety of life on Earth.

1

lifestyles grow ever more demanding on the environment. People want more goods, they maintain a love affair with their cars and they are wedded to a 'throwaway' culture that results in landfill sites piled high with plastic bottles and obsolete computers. Compared to entrenched business interests and technocratic elites, the environmental movement wields only a marginal influence over key policy decisions. Despite the growing **party politicisation** of environmental issues, electoral politics is still dominated by economic and materialist issues. Governments frequently talk 'green' but, in practice, usually give priority to economic growth over environmental protection. It seems that the sustainable society is still a distant dream.

Party politicisation: A process whereby the environment ascends the political agenda to become electorally salient and the subject of party competition.

It is a fascinating – and frustrating – feature of environmental politics that both the above perspectives contain a good deal of truth. There is no doubt that environmental issues have had a big impact on contemporary politics, and yet the frequency with which governments adopt a business-as-usual response to environmental problems raises the cynical thought that perhaps nothing much has really changed. This puzzle is one of many challenges confronting environmental politics, which has rapidly become an established subject of political enquiry and a regular part of the university curriculum.

The rationale behind this book is that environmental politics is a distinctive subject that is worthy of study both in its own right and also for the challenges it poses for the wider discipline of politics. Environmental politics is a wide-ranging subject with three core components:

1.   the study of political theories and ideas relating to the environment;
2.   the examination of political parties and environmental movements;
3.   the analysis of public policy-making and implementation affecting the environment at international, national and local levels.

The broad aim of this book is to provide an introduction to environmental politics that covers all three aspects of this rapidly expanding subject. The primary focus of the book is on environmental politics in the industrialised world. It is the affluent industrialised countries of Europe and North America that are largely responsible for causing contemporary environmental problems and it is essential that they take the lead in solving them. Much of the substance of environmental politics – ideas and theories, parties and movements, policy initiatives – is rooted in the industrialised world too. Although North–South issues and development themes regularly surface in the book, for reasons of substance, practicality and space, the book has a primary focus on advanced industrialised countries.[1] The rest of this introduction identifies the distinctive features of environmental politics and explains the structure of the book.

So, in what ways is environmental politics distinctive? One distinguishing characteristic is that it has a primary concern with the relationship between human society and the natural world. This human–nature relationship connects the extraordinarily diverse set of issues encompassed by environmental politics, which include wilderness preservation and nature conservation, numerous forms of air, water and land pollution, the depletion of scarce resources such as fish stocks, rainforests and endangered species, the use of nuclear power and biotechnology, and 'global' issues such as biodiversity loss, climate change and **ozone depletion**. Traditionally, many of these issues were (and often still are) treated discretely as separate policy problems. The increasing tendency to conceptualise these problems as 'environmental' reflects the emergence of an environmental discourse, or way of thinking about the world, which has given coherence and political significance to the notion of 'the environment'. Underpinning this discourse is a **holistic** perspective which, rather than examining individual issues in isolation, focuses on the interdependence of environmental, political, social and economic issues and the way in which they interact with each other.

At this point it is important to provide some historical context because the emergence of this wider environmental discourse is a relatively recent development. Of course, many of the problems that we now regard as environmental, such as pollution, deforestation and land degradation, are not new. In the classical world, Plato, Lucretius and Caesar all commented on the problem of soil erosion (Wall 1994: 2–3). The collapse of the Mayan civilisation hundreds of years ago can probably be attributed to deforestation and soil erosion (Ponting 1992). Much later, however, it was the industrial and scientific revolutions of the eighteenth and nineteenth centuries that really created the conditions for contemporary concern about the environment. In particular, the process of industrialisation contributed to environmental degradation by accelerating resource consumption, urban development and pollution. One of the earliest examples of what we would now call environmental legislation was the 1863 Alkali Act in Britain, whilst in the USA the first legal action against air pollution occurred in 1876 in St Louis (Paehlke 1989: 23). The first wave of concern about environmental issues can be traced to the emergence of conservation and nature protection groups in the latter part of the nineteenth and the early twentieth centuries, reflecting a growing middle-class interest in the protection of wildlife, wilderness and natural resources (Lowe and Goyder 1983). Several leading pressure groups, including the Sierra Club in the USA, the Royal Society for the Protection of Birds in the UK, and the Naturschutzbund Deutschland in Germany, date from this period. The **conservationist** movement established a firm base through the twentieth century as most countries saw a gradual accumulation of policies affecting various 'environmental' issues, ranging from the regulation of industrial pollution to the creation of national parks. Nevertheless, it was not until the emergence of '**modern environmentalism**' – the wave of popular concern about environmental issues that swept across the developed world during the 1960s – that the environmental discourse became widespread (Pepper 1996) (see Box 1.1).

Ozone depletion: Depletion of ozone in the Earth's upper atmosphere which leaves the surface of the Earth vulnerable to harmful ultraviolet radiation.

Holism: The view that wholes are more than just the sum of their parts, and that wholes cannot be defined merely as a collection of their basic constituents.

Conservationism: An approach to land management that emphasises the efficient conservation of natural resources so that they can later be developed for the benefit of society.

Modern environmentalism: The emergence, from the late 1960s, of growing public concern about the state of the planet, new political ideas about the environment and a mass political movement.

1.1 Evolution of environmental issues

First generation: preservation and conservation (pre-1960s)
Protection of wildlife and habitats
Soil erosion
Local pollution

Second generation: 'modern environmentalism' (from 1960s)
Population growth
Technology
Desertification
Pesticides
Resource depletion
Pollution abatement

Third generation: global issues (late 1970s onwards)
Acid rain
Ozone depletion
Rainforest destruction
Climate change
Loss of biodiversity
Genetically modified organisms

Preservationism:
An approach based on an attitude of reverence towards nature, especially wilderness, that advocates the protection of a resource from any form of development.

The rise of modern environmentalism highlights a second distinctive feature of the environment as a political subject which is that, unlike most other single issues, it comes replete with its own ideology and political movement (Jacobs 1997: 1). An awareness of historical context is again important, for neither a green ideology nor an environmental movement existed before the late 1960s. Modern environmentalism differed from the earlier **preservationist** and conservationist movements in two important ways (McCormick 1989: ch. 3). First, it was driven by the idea of a global ecological crisis that threatened the very existence of humanity. The atomic age had brought home the fragility of planet Earth. This perception was nurtured by a series of well-publicised eco-disasters, notably the massive oil spillages from the wrecked *Torrey Canyon* tanker off the Cornish coast in 1967, the blow-out of an oil platform at Santa Barbara, California, two years later, and the mercury poisoning of Minamata Bay in Japan. Following Rachel Carson's 1962 best-seller, *Silent Spring*, which alerted the world to the danger posed by the synthetic chemicals used in pesticides such as DDT, advances in scientific knowledge were increasingly catapulted from closed academic circles into the public arena. Fierce public debates about the consequences of population growth, technology and resource depletion encouraged people to think increasingly in global terms about the environment (Ehrlich 1968; Commoner 1971; Meadows et al. 1972). Secondly, modern environmentalism was a political and activist mass movement which demanded a radical transformation in the values and structures of society. It was influenced by the broader 'politics of affluence' and the general upsurge in social movement protest at that time. Modern environmentalism came of age on 22 April 1970 when millions of Americans celebrated and protested on Earth Day, which remains the largest environmental demonstration in history. The burgeoning environmental movement certainly helped to popularise the environmental discourse. Governments set up environmental ministries and agencies and introduced swaths of new legislation to protect the environment. The watershed 1972 UN Stockholm conference, which examined how a range of global environmental problems affected human life, marked the entry of the environment onto the international agenda. Thus, by the early

1970s, the component parts of environmental politics had started to take shape: the appearance of new political ideas and ways of thinking about the environment; the rise of a mass environmental movement; and the creation of a new policy agenda.

These three core components of environmental politics provide the framework for this book, which is divided into three parts to reflect the distinctive contribution made by each area of study: ideas; parties and movements; and policy.

Part I explores different ways of thinking about the environment. A major theme of the book is to explore whether there is now a sufficiently comprehensive and distinctive view of environmental issues to talk in terms of a green political ideology, or '**ecologism**' (Dobson 2000). In particular, green political thought offers two important insights. One is the belief that we need to reconceptualise the relationship between humans· and nature, which prompts many important questions about which parts of nature, if any, have value, on what basis that value may be attributed and whether such value is equal to that of humans. A further critical insight is the conviction that the Earth's resources are finite and that there are ecological **limits to growth** which, unless we change our ways, will sooner rather than later be exceeded. Radical greens draw the conclusion that we need a fundamental reassessment of our value systems and a restructuring of existing political, social and economic systems in order to achieve an ecologically sustainable society. Part I assesses this claim that ecologism is a distinctive ideology. Chapter 2 provides an introduction to environmental philosophy by exploring ethical questions about how humans ought to think about and act towards nature. Chapter 3 outlines and analyses the green political programme and assesses the relationship between green ideas and other political ideologies.

Part II turns to the question of how we get to a sustainable society, with a focus on collective action. Environmental activism is now a very broad church. Green parties have become established in several countries and there are many 'environmentalists' operating with established political parties. Beyond parties, the contemporary environmental movement now encompasses mass membership pressure groups such as the Sierra Club, international non-governmental organisations (NGOs) such as Greenpeace and Friends of the Earth, thousands of local grassroots groups and radical protest groups such as Earth First! Whether by directly influencing the policy process or indirectly raising public consciousness about environmental issues through media campaigns and protest activities, the environmental movement has become a significant political actor and agent of change. In Chapter 4 the rise of green parties is examined in the context of the claim that they represent a '**new politics**'. A range of structural and institutional factors is explored to explain why green parties have achieved electoral success in some countries, but failed elsewhere, with a particular focus on Germany, France and Britain. Chapter 5 investigates

Ecologism: A distinctive green political ideology encompassing those perspectives that hold that a sustainable society requires radical changes in our relationship with the non-human natural world and our mode of economic, social and political life.

Limits to growth: The belief that the planet imposes natural limits on economic and population growth.

New politics: The view that since the late1960s the rise of postmaterial values, a new middle class and new social movements has changed the political agenda and led to a realignment of established party systems.

the impact of environmental issues on party politics. It looks first at the way green parties, notably the German Greens, have dealt with the transition from pressure politics to parliamentary respectability and now into government; it then assesses the impact of environmentalism on established parties, through case studies of Germany, Britain and the USA. Chapter 6 explores the development and achievements of environmental groups, particularly in the USA and Britain, using the dynamic tension between the large, mainstream environmental lobby and grassroots action as a means of exploring some central questions of green agency, or how to achieve political change.

Finally, Part III is concerned with environmental policy; specifically, it examines progress towards the implementation of sustainable development. Whilst governments may be deaf to the radical message of ecologism, many have been influenced by the alternative **policy paradigms** of sustainable development and **ecological modernisation** which offer the promise of protecting the environment by reforming capitalism. As a result, radical ideas like the '**precautionary principle**', and innovative policy instruments such as **eco-taxes**, have begun to appear on the policy agenda. At an international level, the search for solutions to global environmental problems has engendered unprecedented efforts to secure widescale international co-operation between independent sovereign states to solve problems such as ozone depletion. However, policy-makers have discovered that environmental issues pose distinctive and pressing problems. Chapter 7 explores the environment as a policy problem, identifying its distinguishing characteristics and outlining the **traditional policy paradigm**, which has proved unable to cope with the range and intensity of contemporary environmental problems. The resilience of this traditional paradigm is explained by the structural power that capitalism gives to producer interests and by the segmentation of the policy process, but the chapter also explores a range of policy models and frameworks that can help make sense of environmental policy-making and show how change is possible. Chapter 8 analyses the strengths and weaknesses of the alternative policy paradigms of sustainable development and ecological modernisation, and the remaining chapters evaluate how far they have been implemented. Chapter 9 looks at the emergence of international co-operation between nation states intended to address problems of the global commons, with detailed studies of climate change and ozone depletion. Chapter 10 investigates progress towards greener government by examining how far environmental policy considerations have been integrated into routine policy-making processes. Chapter 11 analyses the strengths and weaknesses of different policy instruments, concentrating on the key debate between the competing claims of **regulatory** and **market-based instruments**, with particular studies of climate change policies in the energy and transport sectors.

Policy paradigm: A framework of ideas and standards that specifies the nature of a problem and the policy goals and instruments needed to address it.

Ecological modernisation: A policy strategy which aims to restructure capitalist political economy along more environmentally benign lines based on the assumption that economic growth and environmental protection can be reconciled.

Precautionary principle: The principle that the lack of scientific certainty shall not be used as a reason for postponing measures to prevent environmental degradation.

Eco-tax: A tax levied on pollution or on the goods whose production generates pollution.

Throughout Parts II and III an informal comparative approach is employed. It is informal in the sense that it makes no attempt to follow a rigorous comparative methodology; but it is comparative in that it uses examples and case studies from several different countries, mostly from Europe, the USA and Australasia, to illustrate the arguments.

Another key theme of the book is that environmental politics, in addition to being a distinctive and fascinating subject worthy of study in its own terms, is also interesting and important because it challenges established political discourses, political behaviour and policy agendas. Thus the growing significance of environmental politics has seen political philosophers extend mainstream theories of justice to consider whether non-human nature or future generations of humans have interests or rights or are owed obligations. Political ideologies, including conservatism, liberalism, socialism, anarchism and feminism, have had to respond to the environmental challenge, giving rise to several new hybrid concepts, such as ecosocialism and ecofeminism. Where green parties have achieved electoral success, they have destabilised long-standing party alliances and voting patterns. The growing legitimacy and influence of environmental groups has frequently disrupted established policy networks and challenged the influence of producer interests over the policy process. The sustainable development paradigm forces governments to rethink the way they make policy. Traditional Realist accounts of international relations struggle to account for the growth of co-operation and collective action to prevent environmental degradation. The book will show how the rise of environmental politics has therefore been responsible for a widespread re-examination of established assumptions, interpretations and beliefs about contemporary political ideas and behaviour.

Conversely, core political ideas inform our understanding of environmental politics. Concepts such as justice, democracy and equity are central to green political theory. For example, an analysis of the green commitment to participatory democracy can draw on a rich literature on democratic theory and practice. The political science literature on new politics and **postmaterialism** offers important insights about the development of the environmental movement. The study of environmental policy-making is incomplete without concepts and frameworks drawn from the public policy literature, such as agenda-setting theory or policy network analysis.

Some familiar political dichotomies also resurface. Is the state or the market the more effective means of achieving environmental policy outcomes? Are centralised or decentralised political structures better at dealing with environmental problems? Most importantly, in debating how to achieve a sustainable society, greens confront the familiar dilemma of reformism versus radicalism. Should environmental activists pursue an evolutionary reform of the capitalist system by getting elected to parliament, or should they seek nothing less than a radical transformation

Traditional policy paradigm: An approach to the environment that treats each problem discretely, gives priority to economic growth and results in reactive, piecemeal and tactical policies and end-of-pipe solutions.

Regulation: Any direct ('command and control') attempt by the government to influence the behaviour of businesses or citizens by setting environmental standards (e.g. for air quality) enforced via legislation.

Market-based instrument: A policy instrument which internalises into the price of a good or product the external costs to the environment of producing and using it.

Postmaterialism: The theory that, as material affluence spreads, 'quality of life' issues and concerns tend to replace material ones, fundamentally changing the political culture and values of industrialised countries.

Green consumerism: The use of environmental and ethical criteria in choosing whether or not to purchase a product or service.

Social justice: The principles that should govern the basic structure of a society, focusing on the distribution of rights, opportunities and resources among human beings.

of the system? Should groups adopt conventional or unconventional forms of protest? Is collective action (through green parties and pressure groups) or individual action (by changing lifestyles and **green consumerism**) more effective? In returning to some of these themes in the concluding chapter, I argue that, as the environment has become an increasingly mainstream issue, so the centre of gravity in environmental politics has shifted from a *radical* rejection of contemporary society and a relatively *narrow* concern with ecological issues, to a *reformist* acceptance of capitalist liberal democracy accompanied by a *broader* **social justice** agenda.

Further reading and websites

Ponting (1992) is a very readable environmental history of the world. Grove (1995) offers a fascinating account of the early history of environmentalism as part of colonial expansion. Wall (1994a) provides an interesting anthology of early green writings. For a history of the rise of environmentalism, see McCormick (1989). For a balanced assessment of the state of the environment, see the annual publications by the World Resources Institute (*http://www.wri.org/*), the wide range of publications by the United Nations Environment Programme, notably its State of the Global Environment Report (*http://www.unep.org/SGE/*) and, for Europe, the excellent reports from the European Environment Agency (see *www.eea.eu.int*). There are also countless books and articles outlining and seeking to explain the environmental crisis, including Pickering and Owen (1994), McMichael (1995), Barrow (1995) and Lester Brown's annual State of World reports for new developments.

Note

1. Bryant and Bailey (1997) is a good introduction to environmental issues in less developed countries. Escobar (1995) offers an interesting and provocative analysis of development issues. See Miller (1995) for the role of third world countries in international environmental politics.

PART I THEORY:
THINKING ABOUT THE ENVIRONMENT

Part I examines how political theorists think about environmental issues. Specifically, it asks the question: is there a sufficiently comprehensive, coherent and distinctive view of environmental issues to justify talking about a green political ideology which, following Dobson (2000), can be called ecologism?

There has been a phenomenal growth in the literature on environmental philosophy and political thought in recent years. The distinction between *reformist* and *radical* approaches provides a useful shorthand means of categorising two quite different ways of thinking about environmental problems. Broadly speaking, reformist approaches adopt 'a managerial approach to environmental problems, secure in the belief that they can be solved without fundamental changes in present values or patterns of production and consumption' whereas radical positions (i.e. ecologism) argue that 'a sustainable and fulfilling existence pre-supposes radical changes in our relationship with the non-human natural world, and in our mode of social and political life' (Dobson 2000: 2).[1] In short, reformist and radical approaches represent qualitatively different interpretations of environmental problems.

Dobson also makes the bigger and bolder claim that ecologism should be regarded as a distinct political ideology. To cohere as an ideology, ecologism must have three basic features: (1) a common set of concepts and values providing a critique of the existing social and political systems; (2) a political prescription based on an alternative outline of how a society ought to look; (3) a programme for political action with strategies for getting from the existing society to the alternative outline. Ecologism, according to Dobson, passes the test on all three counts. First, it is characterised by two core ideas: a rethinking of the ethical relationship between humans and the natural world, and the belief that there are natural limits to growth. Secondly, it offers an alternative political prescription for a sustainable society. Thirdly, it identifies various strategies for reaching the sustainable society. By contrast, reformist approaches clearly do not add up to an ideology. They offer no distinctive view of the human condition or the structure of society. They are embedded in and 'easily accommodated by other ideologies' (p. 7) such as conservatism, liberalism or socialism.

It is because ecologism encapsulates the most interesting, challenging and distinctive contributions made by environmental political theorists that Part I focuses on its arguments and examines the veracity of the claim that it represents a distinct ideology. Chapter 2 identifies some of the key issues in environmental philosophy by exploring ethical questions about the relationship between humans and the natural world. Chapter 3 outlines the core features of green political thought and examines the relationship between green ideas and traditional political ideologies. There is often a close, and sometimes confusing, relationship between theory and practice in any discussion of political ideology. One further question underlying the discussion in Part I concerns the implications of ecologism for practical political arrangements: what impact has it had on the development of green parties and the wider environmental movement, and what lessons does it have for policy-makers?

Note

1. Dobson actually uses the term 'environmentalism' rather than 'reformism', but his is a very particular use of the term which can give rise to confusion, for example, when discussing 'modern environmentalism' or the 'environmental movement'.

2

Environmental philosophy

Contents

- What are the main theories and debates in environmental philosophy?
- Does nature have value independent of human needs?
- Are some parts of nature more valuable than others?
- On what grounds might humans have duties towards the natural world?
- Can environmental philosophy provide the moral basis for a green ideology?

KEY ISSUES

Deep ecology: The pre-eminent radical ecocentric moral theory which has the primary aim of preserving nature from human interference.

Anthropocentrism: A way of thinking that regards humans as the source of all value and is predominantly concerned with human interests.

Ecocentrism: A mode of thought that regards humans as subject to ecological and systems laws and whose ethical, political and social prescriptions are concerned with both humans and non-humans.

Moral extensionism: Ethical approaches which broaden the 'moral community' to include non-human entities such as animals, based on the possession of some critical property such as sentience.

> The central and most recalcitrant problem for environmental ethics is the problem of constructing an adequate theory of intrinsic value for nonhuman natural entities and for nature as a whole.
>
> (Callicott 1985: 257)

Environmental politics is suffused with ethical dilemmas. Should we reduce the employment prospects of poor people in order to save an endangered species? Are draconian controls on population growth justified if we are to reduce the pressure on the natural environment? Is it wrong to eat meat? Should we ban commercial seal-hunting in order to preserve the Inuit way of life in Canada? Environmental ethics, by examining questions about how humans ought to think about and act towards nature, provides a link between theory and practice. It is primarily concerned with values. Does nature have value separate from its role in meeting human needs? If so, why? Which parts of nature possess value and are some parts more valuable than others?

There is a strong normative element to environmental philosophy. Many leading contributors are also committed activists whose main objective is to develop a robust environmental ethical theory to underpin green activism. Radical perspectives such as **deep ecology** question the existence of a clear divide between humans and nature and even push humans off their pedestal at the top of the ethical hierarchy. If ecologism is a separate ideology, then the way the human–nature relationship is conceptualised provides arguably its most distinctive and radical feature.

This chapter provides an introduction to the key debates in environmental philosophy. It considers whether an environmental ethic that attributes value and moral significance to nature is defensible, and whether it is a necessary component of a green political theory. The opening sections stake out the territory covered by environmental philosophy by distinguishing three different types of value, explaining the **anthropocentric–ecocentric** dichotomy and setting out a simple typology categorising the main approaches within environmental philosophy. The core of the chapter consists of a critical analysis of environmental theories of value under the two broad categories of holism and **moral extensionism**. The final section suggests that the search for a pure non-anthropocentric perspective may be fruitless. Ecologism is, and perhaps *should be*, informed by a wide range of value theories – a form of value eclecticism – each of which can contribute constructively to the development of an ethical framework to guide human behaviour towards the environment.

STAKING OUT THE TERRITORY

Types of value

A key concept in environmental philosophy is *value*. Unfortunately, not only are there several different *kinds* of value, but there is also little consistency in the way key terms, such as instrumental, inherent and **intrinsic value**, are used. The distinctions between these terms are contested and key writers use them differently.[1] Rather than becoming embroiled in arcane debates about these distinctions, the three definitions used in this chapter are simply set out in Box 2.1. These terms are not mutually exclusive; being valuable in one way does not preclude something also being valuable in another way.

2.1 Defining value

1. *Instrumental value* is the value which something has *for someone* as a *means to an end* which they desire. So, a word processor is valuable to me in so far as it enables me to write, when writing is something I want to do.
2. *Inherent value* is the value something has *for someone,* but *not* as a means to a further end. A beautiful landscape has value for me, but not because it enables me to do something further. It is something which I find valuable in itself.
3. *Intrinsic value* is simply the value which something has. No appeal need be made to those for whom it has value. It simply is valuable and is so independently of anyone finding it valuable.

The anthropocentric–ecocentric divide

Why is value a key concept in environmental philosophy? A central tenet of green thinking is the belief that the current ecological crisis is caused by human arrogance towards the natural world which legitimates its exploitation in order to satisfy human interests. Human arrogance towards nature is rooted in *anthropocentrism*: the belief that ethical principles apply only to humans and that human needs and interests are of highest, perhaps exclusive, significance – humans are placed at the centre of the universe, separated from nature, and endowed with unique values (see Box 2.2). Anthropocentrism regards only humans as having intrinsic value, a claim usually based on their capacity either to experience pleasure and pain or to reason; and, furthermore, that only humans have interests. The rest of nature is of instrumental value; it has value and deserves moral consideration only in so far as it enhances human well-being. Non-human nature – the koala bear or brown rat, the field of tulips or tract of wilderness – is simply a 'storehouse of resources' for the satisfaction of human ends (Eckersley 1992: 26). An anthropocentric case for environmental protection will therefore be justified instrumentally in terms of the consequences that pollution or resource depletion might have for human interests. Lead is removed from petrol because it harms human health and fishing grounds are protected because of the threat to a vital economic and food resource. Although there are undoubtedly many powerful instrumental arguments for defending the environment, many greens believe that they are not sufficiently robust to support a strong environmental ethic. For example, anthropocentric arguments generally place the onus on those wishing to protect the environment to make their case, rather than on those wishing to intervene in nature to justify their actions.

One of the key themes in environmental ethics has been the attempt to develop a non-anthropocentric, or *ecocentric* ethic (Eckersley 1992). Ecocentrism rejects the 'human chauvinism' of anthropocentrism and

Intrinsic value: The value which something has, independently of anyone finding it valuable.

2.2 The roots of anthropocentrism

1. *The Bible*

The 'historical roots of our ecological crisis' can be located in the despotic Judaeo-Christian world-view which interpreted Genesis as regarding nature as existing solely to serve mankind and therefore ripe for exploitation (White 1962).

A different reading of the Bible identifies a strong tradition of stewardship, conservation and concern for non-humans that is 'at least as representative of Christian history as any despotic view' (Attfield 1983: 45). Nor can the Judaeo-Christian thesis explain why a non-Christian country, such as Japan, has an equally strong technocratic-industrial culture and similar levels of environmental damage as Europe and North America.

2. *The Enlightenment*

Many greens blame the dominance of anthropocentrism in western culture on the Enlightenment ideas and the scientific revolution of the sixteenth and seventeenth centuries. Francis Bacon, for example, argued that by analysing nature atomistically – breaking it into parts and reducing it to basic components – scientific knowledge could give us mastery over nature which could then be manipulated for our own ends. Greens are critical of the Enlightenment legacy for encouraging the misconceived belief that humans can master nature and for the apparent lack of concern towards nature that it has engendered; attitudes that, for example, inform scientific enthusiasm for genetically modified products.

A contrary view points to the great achievements of the Enlightenment: the triumph of reason over traditional authority and the ascendancy of liberal values such as rights, freedom and justice. There is nothing wrong with a disinterested scientific attempt to master nature in order to understand how it works. Without science, how would we even know about global environmental problems such as climate change and ozone depletion? The problem arises when scientific achievements and technologies are misused through ignorance or for immoral reasons.

See Hayward (1995: ch. 1) for a discussion of ecology and the Enlightenment tradition.

Sentience: The capacity to suffer or to experience enjoyment or happiness.

argues that non-human entities also have intrinsic value. Precisely which entities or categories in the non-human world have value varies according to the writer, ranging through animals, trees, plants and other non-**sentient** living things (both individuals and species), and even inanimate objects such as rivers or mountains. A common thread linking all ecocentric arguments is the belief that to show that some or all of nature has intrinsic value may prove a powerful instrument for defending the environment.

The anthropocentric/ecocentric dualism is a key conceptual distinction in environmental philosophy.[2] For many observers and activists, an acceptance of a non-anthropocentric perspective is the litmus test for being green; it is what distinguishes ecologism from other political ideologies (Eckersley 1992). However, it will be argued below that the attempt to draw a sharp conceptual distinction between anthropocentrism and ecocentrism is at best misguided, at worst, untenable. For now, it is sufficient to note that this simple twofold typology fails to capture the rich complexity and variation within environmental philosophy. Several commentators have found it helpful to distinguish an intermediate area of environmental concern located between the two poles of shallow (anthropocentric) and deep (ecocentric) environmental ethics (Vincent 1993; Sylvan and Bennett 1994). The threefold typology outlined in Box 2.3 categorises the different approaches within environmental ethics.

2.3 A typology of environmental philosophy

1. *Shallow* perspectives such as 'resource conservationism' and 'preservationism' (see Box 2.6) express considerable concern about the treatment meted out to the environment, but environmental protection remains subordinate to other human interests. Shallow perspectives accept the Sole Value Assumption – that humans are the sole items of value.

2. *Intermediate* perspectives argue that moral consideration should be extended to include certain non-human entities, although the categories included (animals? plants?) and the reasons for extension (sentience? capacity to flourish? protection of diversity?) differ. A large part of environmental philosophy falls within this category, notably 'moral extensionist' positions based on sentience (Singer 1976) and rights (Regan 1983), and the 'ethical holists' (Callicott 1985, 1986; Rolston 1988, 1991).

Intermediate positions remain wedded to some version of the 'Greater Value Assumption': that human interests always outvalue other considerations and the value of non-humans (Sylvan and Bennett 1994), or, slightly differently, that the value of normal members of a species will never exceed that of humans (Attfield 1993: 22).

3. *Ecocentric* perspectives reconceptualise ethical positions around a non-human-centred attitude to the environment which involves the rejection of both the Sole and Greater Value Assumptions. Ecocentrics see value residing in the ecosphere as a whole rather than in humans or in individual entities, and that value exists independently of humans. Deep ecology is the most prominent ecocentric position (Naess 1973, 1989; Devall and Sessions 1985), although other 'deep' positions exist, such as 'transpersonal ecology' (Fox 1990).

Adapted, with amendments, from Vincent (1993: 256).

A green theory of value?

A major concern in environmental ethics has been to construct a green, or environmental, theory of value, based on a concern for the whole environment, not just individual parts of it. A 'theory of value', as Goodin (1992) puts it, is 'a theory of the Good . . . [which] should tell us both *what* is to be valued and *why*' (p. 19). It should provide a set of principles, or a code of conduct, to guide the way we behave towards the environment. However, this ethical enterprise draws on a range of concepts from moral philosophy which raise various issues that should be flagged up here, as they will keep surfacing in the subsequent discussion.

First, what are the implications of showing that nature, or parts of nature (e.g. animals or plants), possesses intrinsic or inherent value? Greens hope it will encourage us to change our behaviour towards nature, but others might say that it means nothing: just because nature has value does not imply that someone has a moral duty to behave towards it in certain ways. These different interpretations point to two distinct questions which are often run together in the literature: one is a philosophical question about the kind of value that inheres in nature; the other is a more political question about how to motivate people to act on the recognition of that value. It is often difficult to maintain the distinction between the two questions, but this chapter focuses on the former, although the latter issue will also be discussed, especially in the conclusion.

Secondly, some writers argue that if, say, animals do have intrinsic or inherent value, then they also have *interests* (perhaps in living a full life?) or, stronger still, that they possess certain *rights* (a right to life?). They then try to show that the possession of interests or rights creates obligations or *duties* concerning the way we should behave towards animals. However, there is a tendency to make some big jumps here. Consequently, in assessing such claims, it is important to distinguish between the possession of interests or rights and the existence of duties. So, just because a chimpanzee might have an interest in living a full life does not necessarily mean that I have a duty to ensure that it can flourish. Similarly, I might concede that a chimpanzee has a right to life but deny that this right gives me an obligation to do all in my power to protect it. Conversely, I might deny that the chimpanzee has a right to life yet still acknowledge that I have duties not to do certain things to it (e.g. not to treat it cruelly). In short, there is no necessary symmetry between rights and duties.

More broadly, without assessing the validity of claims about the interests or rights of animals, it is important to be aware that terms such as interests, rights and duties carry considerable conceptual baggage from moral philosophy. For example, one common approach in political philosophy would argue that only those creatures which are capable of making a contract can be moral agents with corresponding rights and duties. As animals clearly cannot carry out responsibilities or duties, according to this contractarian view, they cannot have rights (Rawls 1973). Of course, there are objections to this interpretation: for example, on what grounds do we ascribe rights to babies or the senile who cannot carry out such duties or responsibilities? The simple point being made here is that debates about the appropriateness and accuracy of applying this kind of human moral discourse to the non-human world lie at the heart of environmental ethics.

To summarise, this section has shown that greens object to the anthropocentric basis of most traditional ethical and political theory. They argue that value should be accorded not simply to humans but also to nature. We now need to know what *kind* of value (instrumental, inherent or intrinsic) can be ascribed to nature, what *parts* of nature have value and on *what grounds* that value is accorded (see Figure 2.1). There are two dominant ways of approaching these questions in environmental ethics – 'holism' and 'moral extensionism' – which are critically analysed in the following sections.

CRITICAL QUESTION 1

Why is it important to environmentalists to show that nature has value independent of human needs?

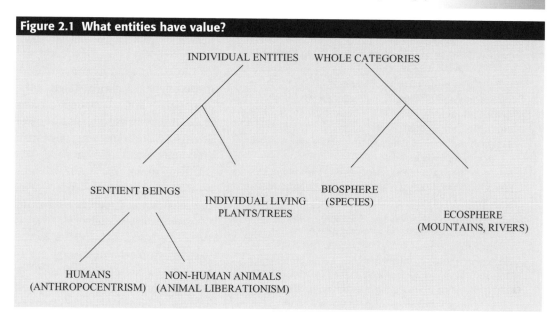

Figure 2.1 What entities have value?

INDIVIDUAL ENTITIES   WHOLE CATEGORIES

SENTIENT BEINGS
INDIVIDUAL LIVING
PLANTS/TREES

BIOSPHERE
(SPECIES)

ECOSPHERE
(MOUNTAINS, RIVERS)

HUMANS
(ANTHROPOCENTRISM)

NON-HUMAN ANIMALS
(ANIMAL LIBERATIONISM)

HOLISTIC PERSPECTIVES

The most radical ecological approaches adopt an holistic analysis of the human–nature relationship: they include all ecocentric perspectives, notably deep ecology, and the group of intermediate approaches known as 'ethical holism' (see Box 2.3). Holism is concerned with the way the different parts of nature interact with each other in ecosystems and the biosphere – the interdependence and reciprocity that make up the 'whole' – rather than atomistic accounts of nature that focus on individual parts in isolation (see Box 2.4). Broadly speaking, holistic theories are prepared to extend the boundaries of moral consideration well beyond individual humans by according intrinsic value to a range of non-human entities (to include animals, plants and even rocks) and to 'whole' categories, such as species and ecosystems.

Holists are engaged in two kinds of exercise: a quest for an ethical code of conduct based on the existence of intrinsic value in nature and the development of an ethics based on a changed ecological consciousness or 'state of being' (Dobson 2000: ch. 2). Both approaches can be found in the work of Arne Naess, one of the

2.4 Mechanistic v. holistic perspectives

Mechanism
1. Matter is composed of atomic parts.
2. The whole is equal to the sum of the parts (law of identity).
3. Knowledge is context-independent.
4. Change occurs by the rearrangement of parts.
5. Dualism of mind and body, matter and spirit.

Holism
1. Everything is connected to everything else.
2. The whole is greater than the sum of the parts.
3. Knowledge is context-dependent.
4. The primacy of process over parts.
5. The unity of humans and non-human nature.

Source: Merchant (1992: 65).

founders of deep ecology, whose ideas have shaped the development of ecocentrism.

The claim that nature possesses intrinsic value is clearly stated in the eight-point platform for deep ecology drawn up by Naess and Sessions (see Box 2.5): 'The flourishing of human and non-human life on Earth has intrinsic value. The value of non-human life forms is independent of the usefulness these may have for narrow human purposes' (Naess 1989: 29). Naess is informed by the idea of symbiosis: that every entity has value because it is needed by at least one other entity. Nothing and no one is entirely independent, so everything has value. He also extracts a principle of equality from the holistic thesis that everything is interdependent. This principle – Naess calls it 'biocentric egalitarianism' – states that all forms of life have 'the equal right to live and blossom'.[3] Naess does not attempt to produce a scientific case for intrinsic value; instead, biocentric egalitarianism is justified as simply an 'intuitively clear and obvious value axiom'. Thus, with this first theme, Naess seems to be offering the basis for a green theory of value.

The second theme in Naess's work, which underpins the first claim that nature has intrinsic value, is a metaphysical argument about how the closer identification of the human self with nature could provide a rationale for nurturing a higher ecological consciousness. This argument rejects the Enlightenment view that humans are separate from nature and that 'man' is controller of nature. Instead, Naess adopts a position that is rather similar to the ancient Greek view of 'man' as part of nature (Nussbaum 1986). Naess favours '*the relational, total-field image*' (1989: 28) which regards the 'relational self' as having a wider understanding of identity based on the perceived continuity between self and nature. He argues that by seeing ourselves as part of nature and by identifying more closely with it, to the extent that the other (nature) becomes part of our self, a self-realisation emerges upon which we can develop obligations to non-human nature. Thus the second theme emphasises the importance of developing an 'ecological consciousness'; only by changing the way we perceive and think about nature can we overcome the current ecological crisis.

Although both these themes were of central importance in early eco-centric theory (in the 1970s and 1980s), there has been a distinct shift within deep ecology from the quest for an ethical code of conduct, in favour of the second, 'state of being' approach. This shift is revealing because it represents an implicit acknowledgement that the pursuit of intrinsic value theory may be misplaced (Dobson 2000: 46). Efforts to construct a holistic theory of value have encountered three notable obstacles.

First, many writers express their unease about the explicitly intuitive basis upon which Naess accords intrinsic value right across the ecosphere, to include mountains, rivers and cultures. Other holistic theorists have sought to construct a more robust case based on scientific arguments.[4] Callicott (1986), for example, draws on Hume and Darwin to elaborate a 'bio-empathetic' theory based on the claim that moral sentiments are a product of the evolutionary process. A holistic interpretation of sociobiology and quantum physics holds that there is no significant distinction between the individual self and the environment. If humans could identify more closely with other organisms in the biosphere, they would recognise that they have common interests with non-humans and may then develop moral sentiments towards them. The continuity of self and nature means that, if the individual self is intrinsically valuable, then nature must also be intrinsically valuable. Rolston (1991) similarly draws heavily on ecological science to support his belief that nature has intrinsic value.

One criticism of this type of argument is that holistic theorists draw rather selective lessons from modern scientific discoveries. For example, contrary to the claims of the holists, the science of ecology does not deny the existence of differences between the self and nature. Its study of individual organisms 'entails no radically holistic ontology' in which 'I and nature are one' (O'Neill 1993: 150). Brennan (1988) offers the even more fundamental objection that ecosystems do not operate according to the principles of holism and interdependence. Either way, the point is that holistic arguments depend on highly contestable scientific interpretations.

However, putting aside any concerns about the validity of these scientifically based claims, the idea that someone might have reason to act because they are part of a wider entity which can itself flourish or perish is not so strange. Many people think that their well-being depends, in part, upon the success of a group of which they are a part, such as their nation, local community or fellow workers. The crucial *political* question is membership. Just because every academic whose name, like mine, begins with the letter C writes well or badly in no way bears on my own well-being. Even if holistic arguments are admissible in principle, they may not serve green purposes unless their proponents can show that my interests are related not merely to some living entities but to a wide array of such entities.

Secondly, a key feature of holism is that moral consideration is given to whole categories (species, ecosystems, the cosmos) or ecological concepts (diversity, complexity), rather than (or in addition to) individual entities, such as an individual human being. Holistic accounts perceive the whole to be greater than the sum of its parts: 'Intrinsic value is a part in a whole and is not to be fragmented by valuing it in isolation' (Rolston 1991: 95). Here, Naess, and ethical holists such as Callicott and Rolston, draw on Aldo Leopold's (1949) 'land ethic' thesis which holds that 'a thing is right when it tends to preserve the integrity, stability and beauty of the biotic community' (pp. 224–5).[5] Large 'wholes', such as the biotic community or ecosphere, are sufficiently organised and integrated to have a good of their own and to possess intrinsic value. Thus, in holistic accounts, intrinsic value resides in the general process, rather than the individual expressions, of life (Taylor 1992: 114).

One objection to these arguments holds that a collective entity, such as a species or a system, cannot have intrinsic value because it does not have interests, at least none over and above the sum of those of its individual members (Attfield 1983: 150). Brennan (1986) argues that these wholes are not even wholes in their own right but mere aggregations of individuals. However, even if we accept that a species cannot have interests, the view that the possession of interests is not necessarily a condition for the possession of intrinsic value – even if it is necessary for the attribution of rights – is quite respectable in mainstream moral philosophy (Dworkin 1993).

Perhaps a more powerful criticism is Regan's (1983: 361–2) charge that the holistic focus on the whole species or biosphere is essentially 'environmental fascism' because it ignores or suppresses the rights of individual entities. Eckersley (1992: 60–1) suggests that this problem can be overcome through the concept of 'autopoiesis', or self-renewal – the idea that all entities continuously strive to reproduce their own organisational activity and structure – which attributes value both to the collective whole (species, ecosystem) and to the individual organisms that make it up. Yet the task of producing an ethical code of conduct based on autopoiesis would hardly be straightforward, not least because the idea that 'wholes' have value would have serious implications in any conflict between the interests of the ecosystem and individuals within it. Suppose, for example, it was generally agreed that the good of the biotic community (which would include humanity as a whole) required a drastic reduction in human population to lessen pressure on scarce resources. Would infanticide therefore be justified, or would the rights of individual babies be upheld against the good of the larger biotic community? Some system for reconciling the competing claims of wholes and individual parts would be essential. The absence of any satisfactory method for resolving these trade-offs is a major obstacle to the development of any code of conduct based on holistic assumptions.

Thirdly, perhaps the most controversial feature of all these ethical claims concerns the distribution of value between morally considerable entities. In short, do holders of intrinsic value possess equal amounts of it? Naess's concept of 'biospherical egalitarianism – in principle' appears to be both radical and ecocentric in rejecting the 'differential imperative'

(Rodman 1980), whereby human attributes are valued as higher than, rather than simply different from, those of other species. The inference is that humans possess no greater moral significance than koalas, rats or mosquitoes. To avoid one obvious objection, Naess (1989) appended the clause 'in principle' because 'any realistic praxis necessitates some killing, exploitation and suppression' (p. 28). Nevertheless, the doctrine has still, not surprisingly, provoked enormous controversy.[6] How much killing, exploitation and suppression is acceptable? Of whom? By whom? On what grounds? In response to an array of withering attacks on the unworkability of the principle, Naess tried to clarify his position:

> The principle of biospherical egalitarianism defined in terms of equal right, has sometimes been misunderstood as meaning that human needs should never have priority over non-human needs. But this is never intended. In practice, we have for instance greater obligation to that which is nearer to us. This implies duties which sometimes involve killing or injuring non-humans.

(Naess 1989: 170)

However, this qualification denudes the principle of its radicalism; it now merely provides a guideline to help adjudicate when the needs of different species conflict. For example, 'You shall not inflict unnecessary suffering upon other living beings' (ibid.: 171); but what is unnecessary? In his defence, Fox (1990: 223–4) makes clear that Naess is not in the business of producing moral 'oughts'; rather, he is simply making 'a statement of non-anthropocentrism'. Yet there are further problems with Naess's reformulation.

It seems that Naess believes we owe a greater duty to those closest to us (family? friends? pets?) than to someone (a starving Ethiopian?) or something (a Brazilian rainforest?) far away. If so, it seems rather strange that a holistic thinker should focus on one 'local' ecosphere, as opposed to the entire planet. There is also a broader issue here concerning the way that the 'community' is privileged by those holistic theories influenced by the 'land ethic'. The claim seems to be that the community possesses intrinsic value because we are all parts of the same 'whole' (the biosphere or ecosphere). It was argued above that, even if we recognise our interdependence with the natural world, it does not also imply acceptance of a moral relationship. Conversely, we often recognise obligations to those with whom we share no sense of interdependence or community, such as Ethiopian famine victims. In this sense, the community argument may even erect barriers that prevent us from fulfilling obligations to the needy in poorer countries because of the primary obligations we might owe to those in our own community. Consequently, community may be both too exclusive (of those suffering elsewhere) and too inclusive (of those in the community with a lesser claim on grounds of need or well-being) to provide the basis of an ethical code.

Another implication of the reformulated principle is that Naess clearly regards humans as having priority over non-humans, which seems to place him in the anthropocentric camp. Most other holists adopt a similar position.[7] Typically, they construct hierarchies of value-holders – humans, higher mammals, animals, plants and so on – in which humans always seem to come out on top. Mathews (1991), for example, defines 'the degree of power of self-maintenance' (i.e. complexity) as the criterion for determining priority in conflicting moral claims, a characteristic that (coincidentally?) humans possess in abundance. Put differently, in adjudicating conflicts between values, it seems that ecocentric writers ultimately fall back on arguments that privilege humans. Alternatively, they avoid the challenge of providing moral codes of conduct altogether.

Thus, to summarise, Naess does little more than stipulate that nature possesses intrinsic value; many writers would simply deny this claim. The 'scientific' grounds on which nature is accorded intrinsic value are also strongly contested. Even if we accept that nature does have intrinsic value, it is not clear what that implies. Holistic arguments provide little guidance about how we are to resolve dilemmas when different parts of nature conflict with one another. So, in practice, the claim that nature has intrinsic value simply sits there; it does not tell us how we should behave towards nature.

Consequently, it is not surprising that deep ecologists have focused increasingly on developing the second key theme in Naess's work – the concept of the 'relational self'. Warwick Fox (1990), with his concept of 'transpersonal ecology', is one of the more sophisticated exponents of this approach.[8] Fox explicitly rejects intrinsic value theory and the entire enterprise of issuing moral 'oughts'. Transpersonal ecology bears the heavy imprint of psychology.[9] Fox argues that the 'self' should be extended beyond the egoistic, biographical or personal sense of self to produce 'as expansive a sense of self as possible' (Fox 1990: 224). Instead of regarding ourselves atomistically – as separate and isolated from everyone and everything else – we should seek to empathise with others, particularly with animals, plants and wider nature. Humans should try to experience a lived sense of identification with other beings; if someone's sense of self can embrace other beings, then there is little need for moral exhortation to behave in a caring way towards those beings (Eckersley 1992: 62). This 'state of being' approach therefore focuses on the normative question of how people might be motivated to develop a higher ecological consciousness.

Fox deliberately rejects the practice of issuing moral injunctions, preferring an 'experiential invitation' to individuals to experience our oneness with the world, to engage in wider identification and move towards a more expansive sense of self (pp. 244–5).[10] He believes that the exercise of providing moral 'oughts' simply reinforces the traditional idea of an atomistic volitional self (and reinforces the belief that 'man' is the controller of nature, rather than a part of it). Yet this dismissal of ethical codes may be a little disingenuous; in reality, as Fox himself concedes, it partly reflects the failure of deep ecologists to make a robust case for intrinsic value, without which moral injunctions may lack normative force. Consequently, Fox (and other exponents of the 'state of being' school) choose to avoid the issue: 'Rather than convince us through logic and morals, they try to convert us through their example and experience' (Lucardie 1993: 31). In practice, humans may need a code of conduct to help them make choices between different courses of action. Human actions constantly and unavoidably involve intervention in the natural world, but a greater capacity to identify with that world will not itself resolve tricky conflicts of interest. On the contrary, a higher ecological consciousness would be more likely to sharpen and intensify the range and complexity of conflicts, which would increase the need for some form of ethical code of conduct.

There may also be a paradox at the heart of transpersonal ecology in the way it allocates a central role to the 'individual', who can only reach complete self-fulfilment by choosing to live a life at one with nature, yet the essence of holism is the importance of whole systems and species, which surely implies a downgrading, or even a denial, of the autonomous individual? It seems that there is a strong anthropocentric flavour to the quest for 'self-realisation'. Although Fox is genuinely searching for a different ecological conception of the self – a means of raising ecological consciousness – the psychological language and the emphasis on the experiential convey the impression that personal (human) transformation is the ultimate goal (Taylor 1991; Sylvan and Bennett 1994: 110). Put differently, transpersonal ecology looks more like a form of enlightened self-interest – a criticism Fox himself directs at the ethical holists – which is driven by the belief that individuals have an interest in and a duty to protect and preserve nature because they are at one with it.

A sympathetic interpretation of the two themes running through holistic approaches, although perhaps not one that Fox would accept, is that they separate justificatory questions about why it is right to do something from motivational questions about how to persuade people to do what is right. Thus it might be argued that holists are claiming that: (a) it is right to respect nature because it has intrinsic value; and (b) what will motivate us to respect nature is a recognition of our own relational status, or interdependence, with nature. So the appeal to self-interest comes in only at the level of motivation, not at the level of justification.

Although this approach might be philosophically legitimate, it still confronts some of the difficulties outlined above. For example, this synthesis still has to convince us of the intuitive stipulation that nature has intrinsic value. In practical terms, it is also not clear that the individualistic focus on the self can provide a basis for the broader political transformation of society that greens seek. If the aim is to reach out to a wider human audience – to educate and persuade people of the need to raise their ecological consciousness – then holistic perspectives may not be doing a good job. One of the characteristics of deep ecology writing is that it is often couched in mystical or spiritual language. Indeed, Devall (1990) explicitly describes the experiential approach as evocative of what he admits is 'primarily a spiritual-religious movement' (p. 160); we are encouraged 'to think like mountains'. Whilst this mysticism may appeal to some people, many are likely to find it off-putting. There are also numerous examples of deep ecologists making bold or radical claims, such as Naess's principle of biocentric egalitarianism, but then backtracking. Together, these two characteristics may have alienated many uncommitted sympathisers.

Overall, holistic arguments have potentially far-reaching implications: removing narrow human interests from centre-stage, attributing value to non-human entities and nurturing a new ecological consciousness. They represent a radical enterprise that is seeking to push back the boundaries of conventional political philosophy by replacing anthropocentric moral reasoning with an ecocentric moral sensibility. Whether or not we judge them successful in this task, these writers draw our attention to the importance of developing a higher ecological consciousness that will encourage us to adopt different attitudes and behaviour towards the natural world. Holism also shows that concepts developed in traditional liberal moral philosophy do not always serve us well when we are considering non-human nature. Each attempt to develop an ethical code of conduct has foundered badly. Yet green political theory might benefit from identifying a clear set of ethical principles to provide a framework for laws and policies which, in turn, could act as a powerful legitimating force to change attitudes and behaviour towards nature. 'Moral extensionism' is a different approach to producing such a code.

CRITICAL QUESTION 2

Is the quest for an ethical code of conduct based on the interdependence of nature doomed?

MORAL EXTENSIONISM

'Moral extensionism' broadens the 'moral community' to include non-human entities, such as animals, based on the possession of some critical property such as sentience or the capacity to reason. The 'expanding circle' of moral concern is usually justified on the grounds that the morally relevant property – sentience, consciousness, rationality – is a capacity that humans share with non-humans.[11]

Animal liberationism

Animal liberationism is the best known example of moral extensionism. It might appear surprising that the animal liberation literature is at the margins of green political thought.[12] After all, an advocate of animal rights explicitly traverses the anthropocentric–ecocentric divide by granting moral consideration to non-humans. Yet animal liberationists employ ethical arguments that have set them apart from ecocentric theory. In part this divergence can be explained by the origins of the animal rights movement. Whereas contemporary environmentalism is rooted in early conservationist and preservationist movements (see Box 2.6), animal liberationism emerged from the separate animal protection tradition. Animal liberationists have mobilised their arguments in support of vegetarianism, and in opposition to hunting, the fur trade, modern farming practices and vivisection. The animal liberation literature has focused on protecting individual creatures (rather than

---

2.6 Preservationism and conservationism

Conservationism and preservationism were two early currents of environmental thinking that gave birth to the first wave of 'environmental' pressure groups in the nineteenth and early twentieth centuries.

'Resource conservationism' refers to the ideas of modern land management popularised by Gifford Pinchot early in the twentieth century. His doctrine of conservation abhorred the wasteful exploitation of nature. Pinchot commended the use of scientific management techniques in developing land for the wider benefit of society rather than for a privileged few.

'Preservationism' represents an attitude of reverence towards nature, especially for the wilderness of the USA and Australia. Its leading exponent was John Muir of the Sierra Club, whose writings had a greater emphasis on the interrelation of humanity and nature.

Both approaches were clearly anthropocentric, although in preservationism humans were not the sole source of value. Conservation involves managing a resource for later consumption whereas preservation will protect a resource from any interference. Or, as Eckersley (1992) puts it, 'whereas Pinchot was concerned to *conserve* nature *for* development, Muir's concern was to *preserve* nature *from* development' (p. 39).

For further discussion see Eckersley (1992: ch. 2) and Oelschlaeger (1991).

---

whole species or ecosystems) by employing prevailing moral discourses to argue that the moral consideration shown to humans should also be extended to a range of non-human creatures. The two main approaches within animal liberationism – utilitarianism and animal rights – are represented by the leading theorists, Peter Singer and Tom Regan.

Singer (1976, 1979) proposes a utilitarian argument in which actions should be judged by their consequences, i.e. the pleasure or pain, happiness or well-being they produce. He develops Jeremy Bentham's observation that to determine which creatures should receive moral consideration, the question we should ask is 'not, Can they *reason*? nor Can they *talk* but, *Can they suffer?*' (in Singer 1979: 50). Singer argues that *sentience* – 'the capacity to suffer or experience enjoyment or happiness' (ibid.: 50) – is 'a prerequisite for having interests at all'. What he broadly means by 'interests' here is the opportunity for creatures to live their lives to the full. Without sentience, Singer argues, we can have no interests. A stone has no feelings and cannot suffer, so a boy kicking it along the street is not harming its interests. Conversely, a mouse does have an interest in not being treated in this way because it will suffer. Singer argues that the principle of equal consideration of interests should consequently be applied to all creatures that can suffer: sentience 'is the only defensible boundary of concern for the interests of others' (ibid.: 50). Singer's definition of sentience includes a range of life-forms such as birds, reptiles, fish and some crustaceans, drawing the line 'somewhere between a shrimp and an oyster' (Singer 1976: 188).

Regan (1983) prefers a rights-based approach to animal protection. All 'subjects-of-a-life' – individuals who have beliefs, desires, perception, memory and a sense of the future, an emotional life and a psychophysical identity over time (p. 243) – are either 'moral agents' or 'moral patients' possessing equal intrinsic value.[13] Thus he extends the moral community from humans to include many animals. Everyone within that moral community is entitled to respectful treatment. Just as human moral agents should respect the rights of, and have a prima-facie duty not to harm, individual human moral patients (the handicapped, senile and infants), so individual non-human moral patients (mentally normal mammals over the age of one year) have an inviolable right to be treated with respect and allowed to 'live well'.

Thus animal liberationists differ from holists in two important respects. First, they extend the moral community to include a range of sentient creatures, but they do not venture as far into nature as the holists. Secondly, both Singer and Regan focus on the intrinsic value that resides in the capacities and interests of *individual* creatures rather than in wholes (ecosystems, species). The key difference between the two writers is that Singer employs utilitarianism whereas Regan uses a rights-based argument. The work of both writers has been subjected to extensive review and, for reasons of space, the following critical discussion focuses on the writings of Singer as probably the most well-known exponent of animal liberationism.[14]

One form of criticism exposes Singer's argument to some of the familiar criticisms of utilitarianism. For example, although animal liberation is concerned with the welfare of individual animals, ironically one of the weaknesses of utilitarianism is that it is not always very good at defending the individual (Williams 1973). A consequentialist argument such as utilitarianism places intrinsic value only in 'states of affairs' – suffering or enjoyment – rather than in the individuals who are experiencing that suffering or enjoyment. So the principle of maximising aggregate pleasures over pains in a given population of individuals might result in significant harm being inflicted on one or two individuals in order to improve the net welfare of a larger group of individuals. Hence utilitarian calculations may provide the individual creature with only a limited, rather than an absolute, obligation that its interests be respected by humans.

A different response is to reject sentience as a sufficient criterion to be a rights-holder, or to receive equal consideration, and instead to argue that other attributes, notably the ability to reason or to talk, set humans apart from other species. Many political philosophers argue that the inability to reason means that animals cannot enter into reciprocal agreements or discharge moral obligations, so they cannot be the subject of moral rights or obligations. Singer acknowledges that animals are unable to comprehend the requirements of acting as moral agents, but points out that the same is true of various groups of human moral patients, such as those with learning difficulties, the senile or infants, who can neither reason nor talk – so why are their interests still protected? Singer argues that the implicit grounds on which such moral patients receive moral consideration is due to their capacity to suffer (i.e. sentience). Consequently, logically we should therefore extend equal consideration to the suffering of other sentient creatures, such as factory-farmed livestock. Indeed, Singer (1979: ch. 3) condemns as 'speciesists' those who would treat the suffering of humans as more important than the suffering of other species.

Another set of criticisms focuses on the internal consistency of the arguments. In particular, does sentience imply *equal treatment* for all sentient creatures? Equality across species might suggest that rats, cats and humans should all be accorded equal treatment, but few humans would be happy with the idea that a drowning cat, let alone a rat, should be pulled from a pond before a human. In practice, Singer says that all sentient creatures should receive equal consideration, but that does not imply that they should receive equal treatment. As a utilitarian, Singer is concerned with the total or aggregate consequences in each particular situation. He argues, perhaps a little conveniently, that the capacity for human suffering is generally of a higher order than for other creatures (Singer 1979: 52–3). For example, the human capacity to anticipate oncoming death, perhaps through a terminal illness, often makes our suffering much greater. In particular, human capacities such as self-awareness, intelligence and planning for the future make human life more valuable than that of creatures not possessing those capacities.[15] Singer consequently anticipates that human suffering will receive greater weight in the utilitarian calculus. On a straight choice, a human life will, almost always, outweigh that of an animal. It may also be legitimate, for example, to use mice in medical experiments if the outcome is to relieve suffering for even a small group of humans.

This line of argument suggests a weakness in Singer's claim that all sentient creatures have an interest. By attributing greater weight to capacities such as self-awareness and planning, one inference could be that Singer shows that humans have interests whilst other sentient creatures simply feel pain. It suggests that a stronger definition, by which 'having an interest' involves plans, projects and purposes, is more valid. Creatures which lack those capacities are, arguably, creatures which do not have interests. Applying this definition would rein back attempts to extend value to a wide range of species, but it would not necessarily confine it solely to humans. Certainly apes have some of these superior capacities,[16] whilst other sentient creatures, such as mice, may not possess such capacities – and therefore do not have interests. Of course, it does not necessarily follow, therefore, that humans can treat creatures such as mice in whatever way they please. Whilst these creatures might not have interests or rights, it could be argued that humans still have a duty to treat them in certain ways.

Putting aside the above objection, if human suffering or well-being is always given more weight, what practical benefits for animals flow from the sentience thesis? According to Singer, quite a lot, as the requirement to stop inflicting 'unnecessary' suffering on animals would result in radical changes to human diets, farming methods, scientific experimental procedures, hunting, trapping and wearing of furs, and areas of entertainment like circuses, rodeos and zoos (Singer 1979: 53). The outcome of this dramatic change in attitudes and behaviour would be a massive reduction in the quantity of suffering.

Rights-based arguments have received particularly stern treatment from traditional ethical theorists, notably because they seek to ascribe a liberal principle, which was developed to fit uniquely human attributes, to animals. Nash (1989), for example, suggests that extending rights to animals is simply a logical progression of liberal ethical theory which historically has gradually extended its reach to slaves, women, blacks and other excluded groups. Critics counter that this argument founders on a faulty analogy between humans and animals: to extend equal consideration to non-white humans on the grounds of their common humanity (i.e. denying the relevance of skin colour as an indicator of moral standing in society) is qualitatively different from arguments about our relationship with animals (Taylor 1992: 60–1). Indeed, it might be regarded as morally offensive to compare the struggle for animal rights with the women's emancipation, civil rights and anti-slavery movements. Clearly, an acceptance of Regan's argument very much depends on the persuasiveness of his 'subject-in-a-life' criterion as the basis for attributing intrinsic value to some animals.

From holistic perspectives, animal liberationism does not go nearly far enough and cannot alone provide the framework for a broad environmental, or ecological, ethic.[17] Ecocentrics condemn the focus on the individual creature because it ignores the holistic message that solutions to environmental problems should be sensitive to the interdependence of the natural world. Certainly, animal liberationism offers no prima-facie case for extending moral consideration beyond individual animals. Utilitarian and rights-based arguments attribute no moral standing to non-sentient entities such as insects, plants and rocks. By focusing on the well-being of individual creatures, animal liberationists deny that any value can reside in collectives, such as a species. Thus, the loss of the last two members of a species, perhaps the last two giant pandas, would be regarded as no more morally significant than the loss of two stray mongrel dogs. Ecocentrics also point out that animal liberationist arguments may encounter the 'problem of predation' – the logical, if absurd, argument that humans should intervene in the food chain to turn non-human carnivores, such as cats, into vegetarians, or at least to minimise the suffering of their prey (Eckersley 1992: 45).

It is certainly hard to see how either the sentience or the 'subject-in-a-life' argument could be used to justify the existence of *intrinsic* value in species or ecosystems, let alone the wider biotic community or ecosphere. Attfield argues that sentience is a sufficient but not a necessary condition for moral consideration. He claims that trees and plants also have a good of their own, defined as their flourishing, or capacity to flourish, which gives them moral standing (Attfield 1983: 154). Yet biological science suggests that a tree is incapable of having any experience. Moreover, Attfield tempers the potentially 'devastating' ethical implications of this view by pointing out that moral *standing* should not be confused with moral *significance*, as they involve quite separate judgements (Attfield 1983: 154). An organism may have intrinsic value (standing), but that value may be extremely low (significance). Thus Attfield constructs a hierarchy of supremacy based on attributes, such as sentience, consciousness and cognition, that privilege human interests over all others, with plants sitting at the bottom of the pile. In practice, like animal liberationism, this weak anthropocentric ethic might do little more than hasten the demise of factory farming and similar 'unnecessary' practices.

It might be possible to build an *instrumental* case in support of environmental protection on the grounds that the interests of a sentient creature demand that its natural habitat – nesting sites, breeding grounds, food sources – should be protected (Eckersley 1992: 43–4). In a similar vein, Benton (1993) draws on both socialist and ecocentric theory to develop the rights-based approach. Although he retains an analytical focus on the individual as the bearer of rights, Benton rejects the disembodied, atomistic individual of liberal thought for a wider view of the individual in relationship with other persons (the socialist focus on the individual in society) and with ecological conditions (the ecocentric view). He argues that if priority is attributed to individual (human and non-human) autonomy, then the same moral priority must be given to the material conditions – notably protection of the environment – which enable that individual autonomy to be exercised (see Chapter 3). However, at root, this argument appears to be qualitatively similar to other instrumental anthropocentric arguments that support environmental protection (see below, pp. 34–5).

Nevertheless, animal liberation arguments are often dismissed too easily by ecocentrics. Utilitarian and rights-based arguments for animal liberation have undoubtedly made an important contribution to environmental ethics. A major strength of both approaches is the way they build a case for animal protection by extending a familiar moral discourse beyond humans. The language and the form of argument employed in this liberal discourse is less likely to alienate the reader, although their radical conclusions might. Singer's claim that the moral community should be based on the capacity for sentience rather than the capacity to reason or talk is powerfully made and conforms with the intuitions of many people – especially the pet owner or lover of wildlife. Regan's strategy of employing rights as a means of protecting and furthering the interests of animals also sits comfortably within the traditions of liberal thought. Both approaches have tapped the widespread contemporary unease about the treatment of animals, as in factory farming or vivisection, and the way it offends our 'humanitarian' sensibilities. They also suggest many practical policies – bans on hunting for sport, the regulation of factory farming, the abolition of veal crates – that have widespread appeal. Admittedly, these same strengths, couched as they are in a conventional anthropocentric individualist moral discourse, limit the potential of animal liberationism to underpin a broader environmental ethic. Nevertheless, one knock-on effect might be that once people accept that some animals are worthy of moral consideration, the more radical claim that further parts of the natural world also have value may become more acceptable.

CRITICAL QUESTION 3
Are animal liberationists necessarily environmentalists?

Moral extensionism as an environmental ethic

The flourishing of environmental ethics in recent years has produced a wide range of moral extensionist theories. Most have been developed by academic political philosophers who straddle the divide between the primary and secondary literature (Brennan 1988; Norton 1991; Goodin 1992; Benton 1993; O'Neill 1993; Hayward 1995; Dobson 1998; Wissenberg 1998; Barry 1999a, *inter alia*). These are generally intermediate perspectives which accept the greater value assumption that humans are the only creatures able to value, but that humans are not the only bearers of value (see Box 2.3).

One interesting approach involves the use of intuitive arguments about 'naturalness' and the special significance of nature to humans, as grounds for ascribing inherent value to nature. Goodin (1992) outlines a green theory of value based on the idea of 'naturalness'. He argues that natural objects have value because they are the product of a natural process rather than an artificial, human process.[18] Naturalness has value (i) because humans want 'some sense and pattern to their lives'; (ii) people want their own lives set in some larger context (to which they are connected); (iii) it is the products of natural processes, untouched (or lightly touched) by human hands which provides that larger context (p. 37).[19] Similarly, Dworkin (1993) talks of the 'sacredness' of nature and the importance of respecting 'nature's investment' as grounds for his claim that nature has intrinsic value. He argues that people wish animal species to be preserved because of 'respect for the way they came into being rather than for the animals considered independently of that history . . . we consider it wrong, a desecration of the inviolable, that a species that evolution did produce should perish through our acts' (ibid.: 78). Consequently, the extinction of a species is 'an intrinsically bad thing to do . . . a waste of nature's investment' (ibid.: 78).

There are weaknesses in this approach. Dworkin (1993) concedes that there is inconsistency in what we regard as sacred and inviolable. We might regard a rare species of exotic bird or the Siberian tiger as sacred, whilst not overly regretting the extinction of pit vipers or sharks. Nor do we treat everything produced by nature as inviolable; we are happy to dig up coal or chop down trees to build a house. In short, this kind of intuitive argument is necessarily selective. Similarly, Goodin's (1992) theory of value rests heavily on the intuitive claim that humans have a psychological need for something larger than themselves, yet that intuition is open to dispute. Even if we do have such a need, is 'nature' the only means of satisfying it? Many people would say that religion provides this larger context. Others would say that phenomena which touch nature neither lightly nor lovingly – feats of technological wizardry such as huge skyscrapers in Los Angeles, or atomic bombs – may also inspire us to contemplate something larger than ourselves. What makes the village preferable to the city is not that it is in better balance with nature but that it required less human intervention in nature. Put differently, for Goodin, value resides not in protecting nature from harm for its own sake, but in humans deriving 'satisfaction from reflection upon its larger setting' (ibid.: 52). In this sense, it appears that nature has inherent value (see Box 2.1).

Another theme in several intermediate approaches involves drawing an important distinction between constitutive and instrumental value in a flourishing human life. John O'Neill (1993) constructs an environmental ethic around Aristotle's idea of objective human good. The Aristotelian objective is the flourishing of human life. The constitutive parts of this 'good life' include a range of liberal values, notably autonomy, and a range of positive relationships with contemporaries, across generations and, crucially, with nature. The flourishing of non-human creatures, therefore, 'ought to be promoted because they are constitutive of our own flourishing' (ibid.: 24). Despite the prima-facie anthropocentrism, O'Neill claims that this involves no reversion to narrow instrumentalism. Rather, just as Aristotle taught us to care for our friends for their own sake, and not for the benefits it may bring to us (such as self-satisfaction or anticipated reciprocity), so we should promote the flourishing of non-human living things as an end in itself. Thus, 'care for the natural world is constitutive of a flourishing human life' (ibid.: 24). Similarly, Raz (1986) offers the example of a close relationship between a man and a dog. The man's life is richer and better because of that relationship. So the dog has value not just because it causes feelings of security and comfort in the man (instrumental value) but because of the constitutive role it plays in enhancing the quality of his life (inherent value)[20] (see Box 2.1). Raz suggests that this kind of inherent value is insufficient to justify according rights to dogs, although it may still be sufficient to create duties to protect or promote their well-being (Raz 1986: 178).

The above approaches are just two examples selected from a range of moral extensionist frameworks. Neither is complete, but both have something interesting to offer. The existence of these intermediate theories of value suggests that the search for a single definitive value system to underpin an environmental ethic may be doomed. Instead, green political theorists might be better advised to accept familiar intuitive arguments, like Dworkin's, that a plurality of value theories exist and that there is no hierarchy between them. This notion of a plurality in value theories is not controversial in itself. However, while many writers argue that we need to determine which is the 'right' or 'best' theory, the suggestion here is that there may be some advantage in accepting an eclecticism of theories.[21]

First, it allows for the fact that different considerations might apply in different cases. A single value theory may be good at dealing with one type of ethical problem but less helpful for another. An eclectic approach recognises the virtue of drawing on a range of value theories – utilitarian, rights-based, ecocentric and so on – to help deal with different types of problem. Thus Brennan (1992: 28) argues that the value systems we use to justify (a) killing a badly injured animal to put it out of its suffering; (b) preserving the life of a human in severe pain; (c) protecting a (non-sentient) tree by forcibly restraining a vandal from damaging it, might involve different moral considerations. Secondly, the sheer complexity of many environmental issues suggests that there may be more than one way of viewing the same problem, as is often the case in public policy. Perhaps no single value system provides an exhaustive framework for dealing with a problem. Indeed, an environmental ethic might also draw on a range of *anthropocentric* arguments about how humans should treat other humans, such as the need for intragenerational justice and the obligations we owe to future generations (see Chapter 3). Such explicitly anthropocentric debates are often excluded from green political theory, but with the increasing importance of the sustainable development discourse in public policy they have gained in significance (Dobson 1998).

This observation resonates with the 'convergence thesis' outlined by Norton (1991).[22] He argues that the differences between opposing wings of the environment movement are more apparent than real; in particular, although ecocentric and anthropocentric defences of the non-human world may come from different starting points and apply different value systems, they can end up producing more or less similar solutions. Norton emphasises the importance of anthropocentric arguments that act in the interests of future generations:

> introducing the idea that other species have intrinsic value, that humans should be 'fair' to all other species, provides no operationally recognizable constraints on human behaviour that are not already implicit in the generalized, cross-temporal obligations to protect a healthy, complex, and autonomously functioning system for the benefit of future generations of human beings. Deep ecologists, who cluster around the principle that nature has independent value, should therefore not differ from longsighted anthropocentrists in their policy goals for the protection of biological diversity.

(Norton 1991: 226–7)[23]

The policy convergence that Norton perceives between ecocentrics and future generation anthropocentric perspectives on biodiversity provides a good illustration of value eclecticism in practice. One further observation might be that from this perspective, rather than regarding the ecocentric challenge as an attempt to replace conventional human-centred moral principles with a new, wide-ranging framework that encompasses the natural world, it might be treated as a new *supplementary* dimension that can contribute to a richer, more informed moral synthesis.

CRITICAL QUESTION 4

Is 'value eclecticism' a firm basis for a green political theory?

CONCLUSION: BREAKING DOWN THE ANTHROPOCENTRIC–ECOCENTRIC DIVIDE

One of the distinguishing features of ecologism is the view that humans are not necessarily seated at the top of the ethical hierarchy. Holistic arguments that draw attention to the interdependence of ecosystems have forced philosophers to reappraise the human–nature relationship and to think seriously about the duties we owe to the natural world.

Nevertheless, it has been argued here that all ecocentric accounts ultimately employ some form of anthropocentric argument – the idea that human needs and interests are of highest, and even exclusive, value and importance. Attempts to develop an ethical code of conduct based on the existence of intrinsic value in nature have struggled to apply traditional ethical concepts to unfamiliar entities and categories, such as species and ecospheres, and they have fallen back onto hierarchies of value which always concede priority to human interests in all critical inter-species conflicts.[24] Although 'state of being' ecocentrics have resisted the path of issuing ethical injunctions, the centrality in their work of the individual self also fails to avoid the trap of anthropocentrism, and they too concede priority to humans in conflicts of interest. Indeed, a pure ecocentric position which tried to deny the existence of a clear and morally relevant dividing line between humankind and the rest of nature is, arguably, untenable. Certainly, any principle along the lines of biocentric egalitarianism would be impossible to implement. Taking it to the extreme, how could a human justify killing any animal or fish, or consuming a vegetable, bean or berry? All involve some restraint on another entity's capacity to live and to flourish. Humans must place themselves above other species and entities 'simply to live' (Luke 1988: 521). No ecocentric denies that humans have the right to live and to flourish, but to do so inevitably involves the denial of other entities that same right. If it is accepted that a pure non-anthropocentric position is impossible or, at the very least, that every deep ecologist employs some form of anthropocentric argument, then it is a nonsense to talk about an ecocentric–anthropocentric dichotomy in such stark terms.

A more fruitful approach regards the debates in environmental philosophy as 'between relative positions concerning the moral weight we should give to the natural environment in relation to human interests' (Taylor 1991: 580). It is helpful also to distinguish between 'strong anthropocentrism', which retains the Sole Value Assumption, and 'weak anthropocentrism', which concedes that nature may have some non-instrumental value.[25] Thus weak anthropocentrism means that the human–nature relationship need not always be reduced to purely human interests (Barry 1999a). Rather than define different perspectives according to which side of the ecocentric/anthropocentric divide they lie, they can be located along a *continuum* which moves from ecocentrism through various gradations of anthropocentrism to 'strong anthropocentrism'.

If the ecocentric/anthropocentric divide is redundant, where should the boundary of ecologism lie? Which perspectives fall within ecologism, and which fall outside? The obvious division would include within ecologism all weak anthropocentric or intermediate perspectives that reject the Sole Value Assumption. This delineation would encompass all those perspectives that make the qualitatively significant step of conceding some intrinsic or inherent value to the non-human world. Thus a crucial defining feature of ecologism might be that it includes all perspectives which concede *humans will always be the distributors of value, but they are not necessarily the only bearers of value*. In other words, only humans can accord value, but humans and their interests are not the only things that possess value. Of course, it is not always clear what practical implications flow from the attribution of value to non-human entities. Do animals or (parts of) nature have interests and/or rights? If so, what does that mean in practical terms? What duties do we owe towards nature? This chapter has shown the difficulties encountered in trying to develop environmental codes of conduct. None is entirely convincing (although the same is true of all codes of conduct), but many have something interesting to offer. If any conclusion can be drawn from these debates, it is that perhaps too much emphasis has been placed on the need for a robust case for intrinsic value or for rights. There may be most mileage in those intermediate approaches that recognise the existence of inherent value in non-human forms – from which it can then be argued that, whilst non-human entities may not have rights, humans do have duties not to do certain things to them. Whatever position is adopted, the advantage of the broad definition of ecologism proposed here is that it includes a wide range of perspectives, all of which seek to generate a higher ecological consciousness that 'will turn the tables in favour of the environment, such that the onus of persuasion is on those who want to destroy, rather than those who want to preserve' (Dobson 2000: 59).

There are also *political* advantages in adopting this broad definition because it might help to open up environmental philosophy to a wider audience and even to influence the behaviour of politicians and citizens. One inference frequently drawn from the conventional dichotomy is that ecocentrism represents the boundary of ecologism. Much ink has been spilt discussing this point, often in the form of a polarised debate about doctrinal purity – about being 'greener than thou' – reminiscent of the fratricidal conflicts associated with other 'isms' such as socialism, anarchism and feminism. Ecocentrics tend to dismiss other positions for being insufficiently 'deep' and, in so doing, have claimed the moral high ground: 'After all, who would embrace a shallow view of any subject which one genuinely cares about, when a deeper view is available?' (Goodin 1992: 43). Such exclusive attitudes would be harder to sustain once it is accepted that a pure ecocentric position is untenable and that a wider range of ideas can be incorporated within the ambit of ecologism. The inclusion of intermediate perspectives, such as moral extensionism, does not denude ecologism of its radicalism; rather, deep ecology would colonise the most extreme ecocentric wing of a broad church of philosophical and political positions. After all, the boundaries of all ideologies display a plasticine-like quality, being both malleable and movable, as illustrated by the breadth of different positions within socialism (from Marxism to social democracy). If ecologism is an ideology, then, within the wider boundary identified above, value eclecticism suggests we should expect it to contain a wide range of perspectives.

However, an ideology also needs a coherent political dimension, including a strategy for political change and a policy programme. Ecocentrics have been criticised for being more concerned with getting the philosophy right by, for example, elevating the anthropocentric–ecocentric debate into a litmus test for greenness, rather than developing a practical political programme for change (Dobson 2000; Taylor 1991; Barry 1999a). In so far as ecocentrics do think 'politically', they emphasise the need to change individual consciousness, with a heightened awareness of our proper place in nature as the preferred path to ecological salvation.[26] This interest in personal transformation is reflected in an apparent lack of interest in wider issues of political change in society. The message seems to be: 'if you cannot change the world, change yourself' (Barry 1994: 390). The next chapter examines attempts to develop a broader political dimension to ecologism.

Further reading

The collections edited by Gruen and Jamieson (1994), Elliot and Gare (1983), Elliot (1995), Botzler and Armstrong (1998) and Smith (1999) provide an introduction to the sheer breadth and variety of environmental philosophical writing. The Sessions (1995) reader is a good introduction to deep ecology; see also Devall and Sessions (1985) and Naess (1989). Fox (1990) is, arguably, the most sophisticated ecocentric analysis. Eckersley (1992) offers the best sympathetic survey of ecocentric writing. Good discussions of environmental philosophy can be found in Dobson (2000), Hayward (1995), Barry (1999a) and Pratt et al. (2000). The specialist journals *Environmental Ethics* and *Environmental Values*, as well as the more general *Environmental Politics*, provide a good coverage of contemporary developments and debates.

Notes

1. Some writers use 'extrinsic value' in preference to 'instrumental value'. Some use either 'inherent value' or 'intrinsic value', but not both; others distinguish 'inherent' and 'intrinsic' value, but with little consistency in meaning. Intrinsic value is a particularly tricky concept. O'Neill (1993: 9) distinguishes three different uses of the term:
   1. An object has intrinsic value if it is an end in itself, not a means to an end.
   2. Intrinsic value is used to refer to the value an object has solely in virtue of its 'intrinsic properties'.
   3. Intrinsic value is used as a synonym for 'objective value', i.e. value that an object possesses independently of the valuations of valuers.
2. Several alternative typologies stake a similar territory in environmental philosophy, notably the shallow/deep ecology cleavage formulated by Arne Naess (1973).
3. Naess (1989) later acknowledged that instead of the 'biosphere' a more accurate term would be 'ecosphere' to indicate that 'life' refers also 'to things biologists may classify as non-living: rivers, landscapes, cultures, ecosystems, "the living earth"' (p. 29).
4. A common criticism of holistic arguments is that they commit the 'naturalistic fallacy' of deriving an 'ought' from an 'is', i.e. they shift from a description of the way nature works (how it 'is') to a prescription for an ethical system (how we 'ought' to behave). Whilst a familiarity with scientific developments might inform a debate about ethics, it cannot in itself justify a philosophical or political theory: 'appealing to the authority of nature . . . is no substitute for ethical argument' (Eckersley 1992: 59). See Taylor (1992); Lucardie (1993); Hayward (1995). For a defence from deep ecology, see Fox (1990: 188–93).
5. Barry (1999a: 12–5) points out that this sentence is usually taken out of context and that Leopold's land ethic does not support a deep ecology perspective based on the intrinsic value of nature.
6. The populist accusation that ecocentrics are misanthropic does them an injustice. Ecocentrics object to human chauvinism, not to humans; they want humans and human culture to blossom and flourish, just as they do other species. Their emphasis on the welfare of the non-human world is an attempt to correct an imbalance in philosophical and social science theory (Eckersley 1992: 56–7).

7. •Ethical holists, such as Rolston and Callicott, can be placed in the intermediate category (Box 2.3) anyway, because they explicitly or implicitly concede ultimate moral superiority to humans (Vincent 1993). The question here is whether all or most 'ecocentrics' also fall back on anthropocentric arguments.

8. Other prominent deep ecologists include Drengson (1989), McLaughlin (1993) and Mathews (1991).

9. Fox is particularly influenced by Maslow (1954), whose work has also shaped the postmaterialist thesis of Ronald Inglehart (see Chapter 4).

10. There is some slippage in Fox's use of the concepts of the 'self' and 'identification'. Plumwood (1993: 176) detects three 'shifting, and not always compatible' types of self – indistinguishability, expansion of self and transcendence of self – a lack of clarity that contributes to confusion.

11. The ethical holists are extensionists in so far as they seek to extend moral consideration based on intrinsic value, but their reliance on holistic arguments distinguishes them from the animal liberationist focus on individual living entities (Vincent 1993).

12. The term 'animal liberation' is preferred to 'animal rights' because the latter may be used in a narrow sense to refer to specifically rights-based approaches (e.g. Regan), whilst the former also includes utilitarian perspectives (e.g. Singer).

13. Regan actually uses the term 'inherent value' where here 'intrinsic value' is preferred (see Box 2.1).

14. The discussion focuses on those issues with most relevance to the development of an environmental ethic. For a broader discussion of animal liberation issues, see Clark (1977); Benson (1978); Midgley (1983); Benton (1993); Garner (1993); Gruen (1993).

15. Singer (1979: ch. 3) does distinguish between pain and death. Whilst 'pain is pain' and pain of similar intensity will be equally bad for all sentient creatures, the various 'superior' capacities for self-awareness and so on mean that the life of humans is more valuable than that of those creatures which do not possess those capacities.

16. Recent research, for example, has shown a chimpanzee picking up a stick en route to rooting out a termite nest, and an orangutan using a piece of cardboard to pick a lock on its cage (Goodall 1986). See also Benton (1993).

17. Not that animal liberationism, which is rooted in a specific concern for the suffering of individual animals, claims to do so.

18. Goodin (1992) locates his theory halfway between intrinsic and instrumental value theories: only humans can impart value to nature, but the characteristics of nature that give value 'must necessarily be separate from and independent of humanity' (p. 45).

19. Goodin recognises the obvious conflict between the idea of humans being part of nature and the concept of naturalness. He argues that we cannot expect nature to be 'literally' untouched, rather it should be touched 'lightly' or 'lovingly' (Goodin 1992: 53). He illustrates this idea of the 'modesty of creation' by comparing a small English village with Los Angeles, where humanity has ridden roughshod over nature.

20. Raz talks of 'derivative' intrinsic value, which roughly corresponds to the definition of 'inherent value' used here and he uses 'ultimate value' where 'intrinsic value' is used here.

21. Here value eclecticism bears some similarity to Brennan's (1992) case for 'moral pluralism' – that we should 'think in terms of a plurality of values, and an associated plurality of principles' (p. 27) – and draws on some of his arguments.

22. This is the point where value eclecticism diverges from moral pluralism because the latter assumes that there are many values and that they will not converge, so any choice between values will involve a loss of value. Put differently, an argument for convergence is an argument against pluralism.

23. Also quoted in both Barry (1999a: 223) and Dobson (1998: 255).

24. See discussion of the 'Great Chain of Being' in Barry (1999b: 40–3).

25. Several writers make a similar distinction between weak/strong, soft/hard and human-centred/human-instrumental anthropocentrism (Luke 1988; Dobson 2000; Norton 1991; Barry 1999a).

26. Bill Devall's (1990) book title, *Simple in Means, Rich in Ends*, underlines how deep ecologists also make the normative plea for a simple lifestyle not just in terms of its being *necessary* to save the planet, but because it is *morally superior* to our current consumerist existence.

3

Green political thought

Contents

- Is there a distinct and coherent green ideology?
- What would a 'green' society look like?
- What are the distinguishing principles of green political theory?
- How have traditional political doctrines responded to the green challenge?
- Where does green politics lie on the left–right spectrum?

KEY ISSUES

Is ecologism a distinct and coherent ideology? Do the two core ideas underpinning the ecological imperative – the need to reassess human–nature relations (discussed in Chapter 2) and the existence of ecological limits to growth – supplemented by a set of principles drawn from other doctrines, justify talking about ecologism as an ideology in its own right? If so, can it accommodate the broad range of competing perspectives and discourses within contemporary green political thought?

This chapter is divided into two parts. The first part examines the central themes of ecologism. It starts by assessing the significance of the 'limits to growth' thesis as a green principle. As all ideologies need a vision of the 'good society' different from our own, the next section outlines the main features that characterise the dominant model of a green sustainable society. The following sections assess whether the driving idea behind green politics – the ecological imperative that we need to save the planet – requires that a green polity be built on the core political principles that characterise most versions of a green society, namely grassroots democracy, **decentralisation**, social justice and non-violence. The second part of the chapter focuses on the way traditional political doctrines have responded to the environmental challenge. The concluding section draws these themes together by arguing that ecologism does represent a new and distinct ideological tradition that is broad enough to encompass several, often competing, green perspectives.

> **Decentralisation:** The expansion of local autonomy through the transfer of powers and responsibilities away from a national political and administrative body.

THE CENTRAL IDEAS OF ECOLOGISM

The limits to growth

The publication of *The Limits to Growth* (Meadows et al. 1972) provoked a massive international debate about the existence of ecological limits to economic and population growth.[1] The report used systems theory and computer modelling techniques (a new concept in the early 1970s) to analyse the complex interdependencies between five key variables: industrial output, resource depletion, pollution, food production and population growth. The computer simulations charted predicted outcomes up to 2100 if each variable continued growing at existing rates, and then six permutations based on different assumptions about the growth of each variable. However, the interconnectedness of each variable meant that every attempt to address a single problem (e.g. resource depletion) simply pushed problems elsewhere (technical developments that double resource availability increase output, resulting in higher pollution).[2] The authors concluded that if existing growth trends in each variable continued, 'the limits to growth on this planet will be reached sometime within the next one hundred years' (Meadows et al. 1972: 23).

The *Limits to Growth* report was enormously significant in the development of environmental thought.[3] The immediate impact of its apocalyptic message was to catapult environmental issues into the public eye and onto the political agenda. Its pessimism also resonated with the contemporary '**survivalist**' concern (see Box 3.1) about population growth (see Box 3.2). In the longer term, 'the belief that our finite Earth places limits on industrial growth' has become a 'foundation-stone of radical green politics' (Dobson 2000: 62). Specifically, greens draw several lessons from the 'limits to growth' thesis (Martell 1994: 27–33; Dobson 2000: 63). First, the concept of *finitude* which underpins the 'limits to growth' thesis is unique to ecologism; it implies that any future sustainable world will be characterised by material scarcity rather than abundance. Secondly, by plotting the combined impact of the five variables, the report underlined the *interdependent* relationship between humans and nature, which teaches us that problems cannot be separated and treated in isolation. Thirdly, the current pace of economic growth is *exponential*, so that the gradual build-up of environmental problems may produce a sudden catastrophic outcome. This point is often illustrated by the following riddle. On what day will a pond be half covered with lilies, if the coverage doubles every day and will cover the entire pond on the thirtieth day? The answer is the twenty-ninth day. The message is that policy-makers need foresight to act early enough to prevent

> **Survivalism:** Approaches characterised by an overriding preoccupation with human survival, a sense of urgency about an impending ecological crisis and drastic, often authoritarian, solutions.

3.1 Survivalism: leviathan or oblivion?

Many environmental theorists in the early 1970s had an overriding preoccupation with human survival. The leading environmental 'doomsayers' were driven by a sense of urgency about the impending ecological crisis which prompted them to recommend drastic – often authoritarian – solutions.

Garrett Hardin's (1968) famous essay on the 'Tragedy of the Commons' (see Box 7.1) warned that, in a world of finite resources, freedom in the unregulated commons brings ruin to all. He proposed the illiberal solution of 'mutual coercion, mutually agreed upon by the majority of people affected'. His 'lifeboat ethic' (Hardin 1977) callously recommended that 'developed' countries should abandon 'less developed' countries if their governments refused to control population growth and prevent ecological destruction. Thus rich countries in the North would be the 'lifeboats' loaded with survivors, cutting off aid to the poor nations of the South, who would 'drown' (even though the North consumes most resources and places most pressure on fragile ecosystems).

Robert Heilbroner (1974) and William Ophuls (1977) concluded reluctantly that the management of the commons required a strong central authority to persuade self-interested people to change their ways. For Heilbroner, only a centrally planned, authoritarian state – ruled by a monastic government that combined religious orientation and military discipline – could force the required sacrifices and restructure the economy along ecologically sustainable lines. Ophuls envisaged a strong central authority dominated by 'ecological mandarins' who would govern by the application of ecological principles. If self-restraint was not forthcoming, then mildly coercive methods were needed in the short term to avoid resorting to more draconian methods in the longer term.

The illiberal recommendations of survivalism have been attacked from all sides: by capitalists and socialists, and by the Catholic church and ecofeminists. Ironically, despite the emphasis on practical solutions, the draconian, authoritarian prescriptions of survivalism seem impractical in a modern world dominated economically by global capitalism and politically by liberal democracy.

See Dryzek (1997) and Eckersley (1992) for a wider discussion of survivalism.

3.2 Population growth

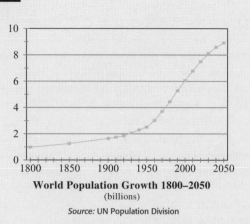

World Population Growth 1800–2050
(billions)

Source: UN Population Division

The flourishing of human life and cultures is compatible with a substantial decrease of the human population. The flourishing of non-human life requires such a decrease.

(Fourth principle of the deep ecology platform)

World population grew dramatically during the twentieth century, reaching 6 billion in October 1999. The rate of growth has, however, slowed and global population is expected to peak at 9 to 10 billion around 2060, with most growth in less developed countries.

Population control has been a key issue in environmental writing since the publication of Paul Ehrlich's bestseller *The Population Bomb* in 1968 with its neo-Malthusian thesis that population growth was exponential. Many greens believe that only by reducing the world's population can global consumption be cut to sustainable levels.

Population control is controversial because many suggested solutions are authoritarian and/or appear to discriminate against poorer countries, as illustrated by Hardin's 'lifeboat ethic' (see Box 3.1), and by proposals to cut off food aid to poor countries unless their governments introduce compulsory sterilisation programmes or to impose stronger immigration controls to protect rich countries from refugees from the South. There is also enthusiasm among some environmentalists for the Chinese 'one child per family' policy.

Green parties today, well aware of the sensitivities surrounding population issues, tend to downplay it and pointedly reject coercive methods. After all, most evidence suggests that economic and social development – reducing poverty, providing for basic needs, improving female literacy and entry to the workforce – are the most effective means of slowing population growth (Sen 1994; Harrison 1993).

the catastrophic outcome predicted by limits to growth. Lastly, short-term technological fixes are insufficient because they do not address the underlying economic, social and political causes of the environmental crisis; they may delay destruction, but they will not prevent it. Overall, *Limits to Growth* suggests that ecological destruction is inextricably linked to prevailing economic, social and political systems. Greens have concluded that only if these arrangements are radically transformed can environmental apocalypse be averted.

Subsequently, the 'limits to growth' thesis has been subjected to widespread criticism (Cole et al. 1973; Martell 1994; Beckerman 1995, *inter alia*). Many of the empirical claims, particularly about resource depletion, have proved inaccurate because new reserves of oil, gas, coal and other minerals have been discovered (Beckerman 1995). It is now commonly agreed that the prediction of crisis by 2100 was overly pessimistic. The computer modelling used was very primitive, many of the assumptions were inaccurate and much of the data was flawed. Perhaps most important, little account was taken of human technological and political capacity to adapt. These are serious weaknesses. At the very least they show that the sense of urgency that the 'limits to growth' thesis provoked, particularly in survivalist writing, now seems misplaced. Nevertheless, the basic idea that there are ecological limits to growth remains potent, particularly with the emergence since the 1970s of a new range of global problems such as climate change and ozone depletion. Indeed, an updated version of the *Limits to Growth* report tries to meet some of these criticisms (Meadows et al. 1992) and in 1995 a group of leading economists declared that economic growth must sooner or later encounter limits imposed by the Earth's environmental carrying capacity (Arrow et al. 1995). If the great and the good of a discipline known more for its hostility to environmentalism are calling for institutional redesign to deal with pending ecological crisis, then there must be something in the idea (Dryzek 1997). Perhaps greens need not be too defensive about drawing lessons from the 'limits to growth' thesis.

Finally, the 'limits to growth' debate also acted as a catalyst for an important debate in political philosophy about intergenerational justice, for it suggested that our actions now are likely to have a dramatic impact on the kind of world that we pass on to future generations of people not yet born. If so, do we have an obligation to future generations to protect the environment – to conserve resources, prevent pollution, avoid environmental degradation – so that the world they inherit is no worse (or even better) than today? Future-generations arguments provide a powerful anthropocentric case for environmental protection that can supplement the ecocentric arguments discussed in Chapter 2 (see Box 3.3).[4]

CRITICAL QUESTION 1
Must green politics be based on the idea of limits to growth?

A green programme for a sustainable society

If ecologism is a distinct ideology, then it should be possible to identify a vision of the good society based on ecological principles that is fundamentally different from other ideologies. This section outlines the central characteristics of a green sustainable society. Of course, just as any definitive list of the core principles of socialism, liberalism or conservatism would be open to dispute, there is also considerable variation between the

3.3 Obligations to future generations

The concept of intergenerational justice provides a powerful *anthropocentric* case for sustainability. Environmental protection is justified because our actions now will clearly have an effect on those still to be born; climate change, resource depletion, nuclear waste and biodiversity loss will all pose problems for future generations. However, there are problems inherent in the attempt to extend moral considerations to future generations.

(i) The problem of *reciprocity*: why should we consider the interests of future people, who cannot offer us anything in return? This difficulty is acute for those who see justice as a matter of mutual advantage (e.g. Gauthier 1986), but such theories also have difficulty explaining obligations to existing people: for example, the poor and needy. So, while theories of mutual advantage pose problems for future generations, they are also problematic in other, independent, ways.

(ii) The problem of *knowledge*: it may be objected that we cannot know what future generations will want or need (Golding 1972). However, against this, Barry (1991) argues that, whatever their wants, 'they are unlikely to include a desire for skin cancer, soil erosion, or the inundation of all low-lying areas as a result of the melting of the ice-caps' (p. 248).

(iii) The problem of *scope*: it is sometimes argued that people who do not yet exist cannot have rights or interests. This consideration raises very complex issues about the possibility of benefiting or harming those who do not yet exist – and may never exist (see Parfitt 1984).

If we conclude that we do have obligations to future generations, many practical issues arise, including:

1. How strong is the obligation? Is it the same as that which is owed to people living now? Is it stronger for the immediate next generation than for later generations? Does the obligation diminish as it gets further away (in time) perhaps because we can share it with intervening generations? Does the satisfaction of future *needs* trump current *wants*?

2. What kind of obligation might we have towards future generations? Are we obliged to ensure they are no worse off than us or should we seek to improve their welfare?

In short, how much sacrifice is needed today?

---

contrasting interpretations or discourses (Dryzek 1997) of ecologism. This account builds on the so-called 'four pillars', or core principles, of green politics identified by the German Greens in the 1980s – ecological responsibility, social justice, grassroots democracy and non-violence (see Box 3.4) – supplemented by the writings of green theorists, activists and academics.[5]

Ecological responsibility, or sustainability, is the primary aim of green politics and flows directly from the idea of limits to growth. A sustainable society has the capacity to last because the ecological carrying capacities of the planet are not exceeded. If the planet (and human society) is to survive, then development – economic, social, political – must be self-sufficient and geared towards the satisfaction of basic needs. Development must be guided by the principle of futurity so that the impact of economic activities on natural resources today does not prevent future generations of humans from meeting their needs and will allow non-human nature to flourish; thus futurity mixes the anthropocentric aim of protecting future generations of humans with the ecocentric aim of preserving the well-being of non-human nature.

The sustainable economy will require a fundamental transformation in attitudes to economic growth, consumption, production and work.[6] The relentless pursuit of economic growth that characterises the existing

3.4 The 'four pillars' of green politics

The 1983 political programme of Die Grünen, the German green party, set out four core political principles which have subsequently been adopted by most green parties elsewhere:
1. Ecological responsibility
2. Grassroots democracy
3. Social justice
4. Non-violence

The concept of ecological responsibility, or sustainability, is informed by the two core ideas of ecologism: (i) the need to recast human–nature relations; (ii) the limits to growth. However, it is less clear how the *practical* political commitments to grassroots democracy, social justice and non-violence reflect these two ideas. If the primary aim of ecologism is to achieve a sustainable society, does it really matter how we get there and what the green polity looks like?

capitalist economic system creates a range of environmental problems, notably resource depletion, destructive production and pollution. In contrast, greens advocate 'an economic system oriented to the necessities of human life today and for future generations, to the preservation of nature and a careful management of natural resources' (Die Grünen 1983: sect. 1, p. 7). If we aim to satisfy 'needs not wants', the pressure for continual economic growth would be removed. Many greens advocate a steady-state economy in which the levels of population and wealth are kept constant (Daly 1992), or dramatically scaled back (Georgescu-Roegen 1971).

Greens identify consumption, in particular 'unnecessary' consumption, as a major problem. They argue that the rate of economic growth is maintained by the creation of artificial wants, through advertising, fashion and peer pressure, that generate the unnecessary and wasteful levels of economic activity characteristic of the consumer society. The 'needs not wants' principle poses an explicit challenge to the supremacy of the profit motive. Greens believe that the pursuit of profit stimulates activities which create unnecessary consumer wants and encourages wasteful production strategies such as built-in obsolescence. Instead, a green economy would be based on production primarily for use rather than profit, and would thereby rule out such frivolous consumption. In this *conserver* society people would be educated to consume less, thereby reducing production, conserving resources and cutting pollution. Where production is necessary, environmental damage can be minimised through good 'green' practices such as using renewable resources, reusing goods, recycling materials and adopting cleaner technologies.

Greens also believe that the rejection of the consumer society will improve the quality of life because a society based on material acquisition is, at best, undesirable, at worst, ethically wrong. As Trainer (1985) puts it: 'Our main problem is that most people hold the disastrously mistaken belief that affluence and growth are possible – and worse still that they are important. Our chief task is to spread the understanding that being able to buy and use up more and more expensive things is hollow and senseless' (p. 249). Another view is that, in a society dominated by the pursuit of economic growth and consumption, there is little time for active citizen participation in the democratic activities of the polity (Barry 1999a: 175). Thus consumerism restricts the opportunity for liberty and self-determination. On either count, greens believe that any quantitative reduction in the overall material standard of life in the sustainable economy will be more than compensated for by the resulting benefits: both material, such as improved craftsmanship, healthier food products and safer communities, and 'spiritual' in terms of personal happiness, individual fulfilment and a more co-operative society.

Greens are firmly committed to the 'small is beautiful' philosophy of Fritz Schumacher (1975). The sheer size and complexity of large-scale production and modern technologies damage the environment in many ways (see Box 3.5). For example, pollution is concentrated in one area so that 'hotspots' stretch the carrying capacity of the local ecosystem to the limit. There is also an indirect impact on traffic volume from the spatial separation of workplace and home: employees travel long distances to work and the finished product is then transported nationally or internationally to consumers. Thus the price of economic efficiency from economies of scale is massive resource consumption and traffic pollution. Instead, the green economy would be characterised by decentralised, small-scale production within a self-sufficient local community. Production would be for local needs rather than for commercial trade further afield. Agricultural production would use less intensive, organic farming methods and serve the local community. Consequently, traffic volume would fall, as fewer journeys would be made and people would travel shorter distances to work, probably by foot, bicycle or public transport. Overall, resource consumption would drop dramatically.

The green economy would not dispense with money, but it would be a non-capitalist market economy with less trading activity. It might look like the local employment and trading systems (LETS) that have gained some popularity in recent years. In LETS, goods, skills and services are exchanged or bartered within a closed local network of individuals. No money changes hands. The aim is exchange and trade, not accumulation (see Barry 1999a: ch. 6). There would be less

3.5 Greens and technology

Greens believe that the *control of technology* is a prerequisite for effective environmental protection. A suspicion of modern 'high' technology has been a constant theme of modern environmentalism: from Rachel Carson's (1962) warnings about poisonous synthetic chemicals and pesticides, through fears about nuclear power, to contemporary concern about genetically modified organisms. Greens question the widespread assumption that technological solutions will always be found to environmental problems and that the benefits of technology always outweigh its costs.

Greens are not simply Luddite opponents of all forms of technological progress. They recognise that some technologies, such as medical advances, have dramatically improved the quality of life. Some greens see modern information technology playing a key role in a green society characterised by small, high-tech cottage industries, although others point out that the production and use of these technologies massively deplete resources and generate pollution.

What all greens seek is greater democratic control over the development and use of technology. So, consistent with their commitment to economic and political decentralisation, greens would remove the control of technology from central government and big corporations and place it in the hands of the community. Following the ideas of Gandhi and Schumacher, they advocate wider use of intermediate and appropriate technologies, such as wind power and other forms of renewable energy, which are congruent with the needs, skills, culture and environment of local communities.

emphasis on paid work in the formal economy. Greater value and social recognition would be attributed to the wide range of tasks that currently do not normally count as paid labour, such as parenting, housework and community voluntary work. Greens support basic income schemes in which everyone would receive a non-means-tested income, partly to help remove the stigma attached to unemployment, but primarily to ensure economic security for all and to allow people to adopt a more fulfilling lifestyle less dependent on the whims of the market place (Robertson 1985).

What kind of political institutions would be needed to support the sustainable society? The clarion call of the greens – 'Think global, act local' – underpins the principle of political *decentralisation*. Political power would be located at the lowest 'appropriate' level to encourage what Kirkpatrick Sale (1980) has called 'politics on a human scale'. In its most radical deep ecology and ecoanarchist forms, the green polity would consist of small self-governing communities. Sale even proposes that the basic unit of the sustainable society should be the 'bioregion': an area of land defined by the natural, biological and geological features that give an area its identity, such as watersheds or mountain ranges, rather than the human political boundaries represented by towns, states or countries (Sale 1980, 1991; Tokar 1992). Social and economic life within that community should be self-sufficient, requiring no more than the resources available within that bioregion.

Green politics is not, however, confined to the concept of sustainability. As we have seen, greens identify moral as well as environmental reasons for cutting back on consumption and changing our lifestyles. The fact that we over-consume and degrade the environment is not just bad for the environment, it is also evidence that we are 'bad people'. Green politics has a view on how a 'good person' should behave in the 'good (green) society', as illustrated by the centrality of the three remaining pillars to green politics. First, green party organisations are typically modelled on *participatory democracy*. The green state would be a grassroots democracy; indeed, participatory democracy would extend beyond political institutions into the economic arena, where the basic form of collective work organisation would be the worker co-operative or commune. Secondly, green politics emphasises *social justice*. A principle of intragenerational equity regards distributional equity, particularly between the rich North and the poor South but also within each country, as a prerequisite of sustainability. A principle of intergenerational justice requires justice towards unborn future generations (see Box 3.3). The need to protect biodiversity leads greens to favour diversity in human relations, specifically opposing all forms of discrimination based on race, gender, sexual orientation or age. Thirdly, greens espouse *non-violence*, opposing international violence (war, armies, nuclear weapons), and are committed to non-violent civil protest.

Thus greens have a broad and radical vision of what a sustainable society might look like. Inevitably, this programme has attracted extensive criticism. Few people would deny that the economic and social prescriptions outlined here would help reduce environmental destruction, but many sympathisers question whether such wholesale reform of economic activity and individual lifestyles is really necessary or desirable, let alone feasible. Unease about the radical prescriptions proposed by many greens has contributed to the popularity of *sustainable development* (see Chapter 8), which outlines an alternative policy paradigm based on the reform of the existing capitalist system, rather than the more fundamental transformation of society outlined above.

However, this chapter is concerned with the content and coherence of ecologism as a radical and distinct green ideology. This section has shown that, although sustainability is the central imperative of ecologism, greens have yoked it to a more general understanding of what a good society and a good person will be like. This begs a fundamental question: does a commitment to sustainability *necessarily* imply a commitment to the principles of participatory democracy, social justice, non-violence and decentralisation – or is the relationship merely contingent?

CRITICAL QUESTION 2

Is the radical green vision of the sustainable society an unattainable utopia?

Does sustainability require specific political arrangements?

The primacy of the ecological imperative is the driving feature of green ideology. If the objective is to save the planet, does it matter how we do it? Suppose the 'survivalist' prescription of an authoritarian, centralised and inequitable society were the most effective means of achieving sustainability. Put differently, how can greens be certain that the principles of democracy, decentralisation, social justice and non-violence are the best means of reaching the sustainable society?

Goodin (1992) provides the best formulation of this problem with his distinction between the green *theory of value* and the green *theory of agency*. He argues eloquently that the significance greens attribute to the theory of agency – the means of getting there – is wrongheaded. Instead, the green theory of value, which underpins the case for sustainability, should take priority (Goodin's own theory of value is outlined in Chapter 2). It is this ecological imperative which provides the unified moral vision that binds the green agenda together; without it the green message lacks legitimacy, coherence and direction. Goodin's vision is consequentialist: 'it is more important that the right things be done than that they be done in any particular way or through any particular agency' (ibid.: 120). In any irreconcilable conflict between the two, the theory of agency will always be subordinate to the green theory of value. It may be desirable that Good actions coincide with Right actions – that democratic, non-violent methods achieve the sustainable society – but it is not essential. Put simply (and simplistically), green ends justify the means.[7]

Most radical greens recoil at the consequentialist implications of Goodin's thesis, for, in theory, it might justify using authoritarian or coercive measures to reach a sustainable society. However, are there good grounds for rejecting Goodin's claim that ecological outcomes trump procedures? It is not enough for greens, rooted as many activists are in the emancipatory new social movements and New Left of the 1960s and 1970s (see Chapter 4), simply to express a preference for participatory democracy, non-violence and egalitarianism. They also need to show that without them an ecologically sustainable society is unattainable. More provocatively, if they cannot do so, then greens must either drop their radical political and moral agenda, or concede that environmental outcomes are less important to them than doing things the 'right' way.

The force of Goodin's argument stems from distinguishing between the theories of value and agency. Eckersley (1996a) argues that such a sharp delineation is flawed, and that greens are right to say that the means are as important as the ends. She criticises Goodin's own theory of value for being too narrowly based on the non-human world, and therefore providing an insufficient grounding for a green political theory. Instead, the green theory of value should be expanded to incorporate the value of autonomy and self-determination: 'the freedom of human and non-human beings to unfold in their own ways and live according to their "species life"' (Eckersley 1996a: 223). If moral priority is attributed to autonomy, then it is essential to establish political arrangements that will allow human (and non-human) autonomy to flourish, such as social justice, non-violence and grassroots democracy. This emancipatory interpretation of green politics suggests a blurring of the Right and the Good so that the *way* something is done is part of what makes it the *right* thing to do – a clear rejection of Goodin's consequentialist position. In short, a green theory of agency can be grounded in a green theory of value.

Whether this interpretation enriches ecologism is open to debate. Eckersley's argument, despite the reference to enhancing the autonomy of 'non-humans', appears self-consciously anthropocentric. It is also explicitly individualistic, since autonomy is precisely the value made paramount in liberal individualism.[8] At the very least, giving moral priority to individual autonomy seems odd in an environmental theory. It may be that encouraging individual human autonomy is the best *means* to the sustainable society because it can contribute to changing the way people behave.[9]

Alternatively, greens might argue that change should be justified to further the wider *social* good, rather than to allow *individual* autonomy to flourish. Thus a 'green' riposte to Goodin might hold that ecologism is not only about sustainability, it is also about creating the good society in which, for example, self-interested materialism is rejected as morally unacceptable.

We return to these two arguments below in examining whether participatory democracy, decentralisation and social justice and (briefly, in Box 3.6) non-violence are the political arrangements most suitable to bring about sustainability.

CRITICAL QUESTION 3

Do green 'ends' justify the 'means'?

Must green politics be democratic?

The uneasy relationship between ecological concerns and democracy is a central issue in green political theory, and a good example of the means/ends debate. Most greens declare that democracy, specifically participatory democracy, is a core principle of ecologism. However, if Goodin is correct, the primacy of the ecological imperative might justify sacrificing democratic principles to protect the planet. This kind of consequentialist thinking underpins the eco-authoritarian argument of the survivalists that ecological imperatives such as population growth and resource depletion demanded swift, decisive and drastic government action (see Box 3.1). A strong authoritarian government, unhampered by the need to win elections or protect liberal rights, might coerce self-interested individuals into acting in the collective interest by, for example, producing fewer children and living more frugal lifestyles.

Most contemporary greens find these solutions repugnant and they want to rule authoritarian solutions out of court for contravening the ecological principle of democracy. Yet on what grounds is democracy a core green principle? After all, it is obvious that democratic procedures may not always generate environmentally beneficial outcomes. For example, most experts agree that climate change prevention requires tough restrictions in car use and high petrol taxes. Yet governments are reluctant to implement such unpopular policies because an angry electorate might vote them out of office. As Goodin (1992) puts it: 'To advocate democracy is to advocate procedures, to advocate environmentalism is to advocate substantive outcomes: what guarantee can we have that the former procedures will yield the latter sort of outcomes?' (p. 168). He is not suggesting that democratic procedures are illegitimate or undesirable; it is just that when it comes to choosing between procedures, the ecological imperative should always trump democracy.

However, Goodin simply asserts that the theory of value takes priority without properly discussing how policies will be derived from it (Hayward 1995). One practical argument for democracy is that infallible green policies will not simply drop like apples from a theory of value, so the means of reaching decisions do matter. Those arguments that defend the use of non-democratic methods often contain an implicit technocratic

3.6 Is non-violence a green principle?

Green politics is informed by a concern not to harm the natural environment, yet there is no entirely satisfactory distinctive *green* justification for non-violence.

War is clearly bad for the environment. The use of Agent Orange in Vietnam, the burning Kuwaiti oilfields in the Gulf War and the pollution of the River Danube after the NATO bombing of Serbia all illustrate the devastation that modern warfare wreaks on the environment. Yet war is an extreme case. Within civil society, it is important to distinguish between violence against people and violence against property. Almost all greens reject the former, but many would regard the latter as legitimate and there are certainly numerous examples of environmental activism directed against property, whether it is spiking bulldozers, pulling up GM crops or smashing up McDonald's outlets (see Chapter 6). Thus it is important to be clear about what is meant by 'violence'.

The green commitment to non-violent protest in civil society has a practical explanation arising from the close links between the green movement and the peace, anti-nuclear and women's movements, which all rejected the use of violence against people. The use of well-rehearsed, *anthropocentric* arguments against non-violence that originated in other political struggles – anti-militarism, fear of nuclear accidents, the links with male violence – explains why non-violence has not figured prominently in debates within green political theory.

At the level of green *principle*, where there is a trade-off between non-violence and other green ends, such as achieving a sustainable society, greens need to show that non-violence is a prerequisite for achieving that end. Otherwise it will be trumped by the ecological imperative. However, at the level of *strategy*, a principle of non-violence places the onus on opponents to show why coercive or violent methods might be superior.

See Doherty (1996) for a wider discussion of non-violence and green politics.

assumption that a governing elite of politicians, scientists and professionals knows best; Ophuls (1977) even talks of a 'priesthood of technologists' (p. 159). The implication is that certain ecological decisions should be made by those people possessing this 'superior knowledge' (Saward 1996: 80) and not left to the whims of democratic procedures. This argument effectively privileges science over other forms of knowledge and understanding of ecological issues, and gives power to an elite minority. Whilst technical knowledge is, of course, critical in many ecological decisions, it provides only part of the picture. A wide range of alternative perspectives and considerations – non-technical, local, ethical, social, political – should also be included in the decision-making process to ensure a more informed decision that can attract widespread support (Barry 1999a: 199–201). Greens argue that participatory democracy offers the best means of including these factors in the decision process.

The case for participatory democracy starts from a critique of liberal democracy. Greens argue that liberal democracy is unable to produce the best decisions because it is characterised by hierarchy, bureaucracy, individualism and material inequalities. It offers limited opportunities to participate in the public sphere. For example, Porritt (1984) complains that 'The representative element of the system has insidiously undermined the element of participation, in that turning out to vote now and then seems to have become the be-all and end-all of our democracy' (p. 166).

Consequently, liberal democracy nurtures an atomised individualistic focus on the private sphere which, greens argue, makes it a poor breeding ground for the ecological consciousness and responsible citizenship needed to bring about a sustainable society. Greens want to replace representative democracy with participatory democratic procedures based on a deliberative or communicative model.[10] These radical forms of democracy presume active citizen participation in governance through a range of decentralised bodies such as workplace organisations, political parties, local government, neighbourhood assemblies and voluntary associations. The green case thus plugs into a much broader tradition of radical democratic theorising in seeking a society where widespread participatory democracy means citizens are fully, freely and actively involved in the decisions that shape their lives (Pateman 1970; Barber 1984). Greens frequently invoke the ancient Greek city state, or more contemporary examples such as the New England town meeting (Tokar 1992: 104), to argue that face-to-face democracy would produce communities that are more in tune with, and therefore considerate towards, their natural environment.

Greens employ two related arguments to support the claim that participatory democracy will result in beneficial environmental outcomes. First, participatory democracy should produce more responsive government. Institutions would be more responsive and accountable because power would be shifted away from the hands of the few: from central government to local communities, from managers to workers, from the central party bureaucracy to the local branch (Goodin 1992: 127–8). Environmental protection would be improved if more people had a say because the decision-making process would draw on a wider range of interests (i.e. beyond the political, business and professional elites who currently dominate). The greater diffusion of information necessary for participatory democracy to operate will provide more ammunition for local communities to protect their environment and, conversely, may enhance the speed with which evidence of environmental damage is communicated to decision-makers.[11] By forcing the institutions of civil society to respond to popular demands, participatory democracy is more likely to produce, if not morally perfect outcomes, then at least morally better ones (ibid.: 128). There will always be the possibility that even a participatory democratic decision will still give greater priority to material well-being than to environmental protection, perhaps by keeping a polluting industry open to protect jobs in the local community. Nevertheless, by virtue of the improved responsiveness gained from drawing on a wider circle of interests, knowledge and skills, there is, on balance, a strong, if not overwhelming, instrumental case for saying that participatory democracy makes ecological outcomes more likely.

A second argument for participatory democracy is that it will create the conditions for the development of greater individual autonomy. In liberal democracy, material inequalities, bureaucratic hierarchies and divisions of labour in work and home deny the majority of citizens the opportunity to shape their own lives; they are unable to become self-determining agents. If democratic structures and opportunities to participate were prevalent in all walks of life – at work, at school, in neighbourhood assemblies – then people should learn to participate simply by participating (Pateman 1970). This involvement should nurture a 'democratic personality' which shows greater respect for, and more responsibility towards, fellow citizens (Gould 1988). Discursive democracy, by encouraging citizen involvement and deliberation, enables preferences to be altered and encourages behaviour that conforms to publicly agreed norms. Replacing the self-contained individual of liberal democracy whose identity is only occasionally expressed in the public sphere (notably by voting), the individual in the participatory democracy is more likely to be a public-spirited citizen keen to promote collective activities and community identity. At this point, greens give the arguments for participatory democracy an ecological twist by suggesting that this radical conception of democratic citizenship can also nurture 'an ecological citizenship capable of developing and giving expression to collective ecological concerns' (Plumwood 1996: 158). At the very least, active citizen participation will educate individuals about environmental issues because they will have access to more information and the opportunity to exchange knowledge and views with fellow citizens. Further, once the shift from 'self-regarding' individual to 'other-regarding' citizen has been made, it is a much smaller step to extend that public concern to foreigners, future generations and non-human nature (Eckersley 1996a; Barry 1999a). In short, participatory democracy can help nurture an ecological consciousness.

If so, this second argument substantially strengthens the first claim that participatory democracy improves institutional responsiveness: whereas better responsiveness is concerned with the *aggregation* of preferences, greater autonomy should also produce a *transformation* of preferences (Elster, quoted in Barry 1999a). Indeed, it is the aggregation of preferences which (in part) has contributed to ecological problems, such as mass consumerism or public resistance to measures to reduce car use. If participatory democracy takes preferences as given and simply provides a more effective way of aggregating them, then governments may be *less* likely to introduce progressive environmental policies. Instead, greens want to alter human preferences because the radical transformation to a sustainable society will be easier to achieve if people can be persuaded by the force of argument that it is right for them to change their beliefs, attitudes and behaviour, rather than being told to do so (Barry 1999a).

To return to the discussion at the end of the previous section: Eckersley argues that ecological ends justify democratic means because moral priority should be given to nurturing the autonomy of members of the human and non-human community. Participatory democracy is one of the conditions necessary to construct a society in which the conditions for human autonomy prevail. Thus the connection between ecology and democracy is no longer merely contingent. Moreover, authoritarianism is 'ruled out at the level of green principle' because it 'fundamentally infringes the rights of humans to choose their own destiny' (Eckersley 1996a: 223).

However, an alternative green riposte to Eckersley might justify participatory democracy on the different grounds that its communicative and deliberative procedures provide the best *means* of changing individual preferences and facilitating the ecological citizenship necessary for the good society. Hence participatory democracy is a core green principle because it contributes to the *common good*, not because moral priority should reside with individual autonomy.

Whichever justification is accepted, how practical is this vision of a participatory democracy polity? It is significant that green theorists and activists have become increasingly reconciled to the continued existence of the representative institutions of liberal democracy (see Doherty and de Geus 1996). Many greens now see deliberative democratic procedures as *supplementing*, rather than replacing, reformed liberal democratic institutions. Thus the provision of more opportunities for greater citizen participation could operate alongside attempts to encourage greater 'institutionalised self-criticism' and 'reflexiveness' in existing institutions by making them more open, transparent and accountable (Paehlke 1989; Beck 1992; Barry 1999a). The ascendancy of the sustainable development paradigm has been the catalyst for widespread democratic institutional innovation along these lines during the last decade, including round-tables, citizen juries and extended referenda (see Chapter 10). It is a moot point whether this 'downgrading' of participatory democracy undermines the case for democracy as a core green principle. However, the arguments made here could be used to reformulate a green principle of democracy which would require an extensive *democratisation* of existing institutions and procedures – even if this falls short of pure participatory democracy.

CRITICAL QUESTION 4
Can a sustainable society be a liberal democracy?

Must a green polity be decentralised?

Goodin (1992) observes that 'If there is anything truly distinctive about green politics, most commentators would concur, it must surely be its emphasis on decentralisation' (p. 147). Decentralisation is a constant, oft-repeated theme in party programmes and theoretical tracts. The green case for political decentralisation, as with participatory democracy, draws on a range of intellectual traditions, most notably anarchism, but greens again add a distinctive ecological slant.[12] Greens follow the anarchist tradition in favouring decentralisation because it creates 'human-scale' political institutions. The underlying assumption is that only in a small community can individuals regain a sense of identity lost in the atomised, consumerist society. This idea informs, for example, the 'small is beautiful' philosophy of Schumacher (1975), the **'bioregionalism'** of Sale (1980, 1991) and the 'libertarian municipalism' of Bookchin (1989: 179–85). As Goldsmith et al. (1972) put it: 'it is probable that only in the small community can a man or woman be an individual. In today's large agglomerations he is merely an isolate' (p. 51). The basic argument is that individuals need to feel attached to their community if they are to participate meaningfully. Citizens need to be able to meet face to face to discuss issues openly, suitably informed about the issues affecting their community, able to understand the implications of their decisions and knowing that their participation may have some influence (Goodin 1992: 149).[13] Thus a decentralised community is a precondition for a flourishing participatory democracy. Greens hope that the combination of decentralisation and participatory democracy will produce fulfilled, other-regarding autonomous citizens prepared to accept the material sacrifices required of a low-consumption sustainable society.

> **Bioregionalism:**
> An approach that believes that the 'natural' world (specifically, the local bioregion) should determine the political, economic and social life of communities.

Greens make a further distinctive ecological argument for political decentralisation which holds that policy decisions made at the level of the local community should be more sensitive to the environment. Sale (1980) takes this line furthest by arguing that we should learn from nature by basing the decentralised community on the natural boundaries of the bioregion such as mountain ranges and watersheds. In the bioregion, human communities will become 'dwellers in the land': closer to nature and more respectful of it, more knowledgeable about the capacities and limits of the immediate physical surroundings and, therefore, able to cohabit more harmoniously with natural landscapes.[14]

Decentralisation may be a necessary condition for participatory democracy, but there is no guarantee that a decentralised society will be democratic. Sale (1980) concedes that a society based on a natural bioregion may not always be characterised by democratic or liberal values because another 'natural' principle, diversity, implies that bioregional societies should boast a wide range of political systems, some of which, presumably, might be authoritarian. Even if the political system is democratic, there may be drawbacks about life in a small community. Social control mechanisms may prove oppressive if, as Goldsmith et al. (1972) suggest, offenders are brought to heel by the weight of public opinion. Discrimination against minorities or non- conformist opinion may be rife. Small parochial societies may also be intellectually and culturally impoverished, perhaps reducing innovation in clean technologies (Frankel 1987). So, ironically, the homogeneous decentralised society may lack the diversity that ecologists value.

Another difficulty with decentralisation is that many environmental problems are best dealt with at the national or international level. Global commons problems do not respect the political boundaries between existing nation states, let alone small bioregions. Problems such as climate change and ozone depletion require co-ordinated action across communities and nations. In practice, this effectively means international co-operation between centralised nation states (see Chapter 9). The green slogan 'Think global, act local' may therefore offer an inadequate strategy for dealing with problems of the global commons which cannot be disaggregated into component parts. Relying on local communities to deal with problems properly assumes, first, that the local community has full knowledge about the causes, impact and solutions to a particular problem and, second, even then it 'makes sense only when the locals possess an appropriate social and ecological consciousness' (Eckersley 1992: 173).

Greens counter this criticism by stressing that they advocate decentralisation to the lowest 'appropriate' level of government (Schumacher 1975; Porritt 1984). If local communities need to co-ordinate action to deal with transboundary problems, greens insist they must do so 'as independent agents negotiating arrangements that are mutually agreeable to all concerned' (Goodin 1992: 152). Underpinning most 'ecoanarchist' accounts is a deep distrust of the state (Bookchin 1989; see also Barry 1999a: ch. 4) which leads them to reject a central co-ordinating agency that could encroach on the sovereignty of the autonomous decentralised community. Thus Bookchin (1989) talks of a 'humanly scaled, self-governing municipality freely and confederally associated with other humanly scaled, self-governing municipalities' (p. 182).

There are many reasons why this response is flawed. What if the communities are unwilling to act? Co-operation *within* a community may not result in a benevolent attitude towards the outside world. Small parochial communities often define themselves by reference to those outside, so they may be quite averse to considering wider questions, such as the possibility of environmental damage elsewhere. They may even try to free-ride on other communities by producing pollution that damages those living downstream or downwind. Hostility or indifference between communities may be accentuated by the existence of economic inequalities between them; perhaps a poor community might feel less co-operative towards a richer neighbour. It is not difficult to imagine a community being highly sensitive towards its own local environment but unconcerned by damage further afield. It may, therefore, require a central agency (the state?) to persuade localities to change their behaviour. Even if all communities were willing to act collectively to protect the environment, there would still be a role for a central agency to co-ordinate their actions. Yet, resolute in its rejection of such a central agency, the green anarchist model gives no adequate explanation of how the necessary co-ordination might take place (Goodin 1992; Martell 1994).

On balance, the problem lies not with decentralisation *per se*, but with the way the dominant ecoanarchist model, characterised by its distrust of the state, narrowly defines it. Decentralisation does not mean that there should be no central state, let alone no state at all, yet that is what many greens seem to imply. Indeed, where international co-ordination is required, green distrust of the state seems to override the ecological imperative. This ecoanarchist model of decentralisation has come under strong attack from writers sympathetic to green politics (Barry 1999a; Eckersley 1992; Goodin 1992; Martell 1994, *inter alia*). Rather than rejecting the state, they argue for a green theory of the state; they want to transform rather than to abolish the state.[15] These writers seek a radical democratisation of the bureaucratic, hierarchical liberal democratic state. They concede that there are good ecological arguments for greater decentralisation to 'appropriate' levels (rather like the principle of *subsidiarity* which states that responsibility should be allocated to the 'lowest appropriate level' of government). However, they stress that the (democratised) centralised nation state is the appropriate level for many tasks, including co-ordinating international co-operation, regulating the market and administering social justice. These pragmatists recognise that a reformed centralised state is one of the few institutions with the capacity and legitimacy to implement the radical changes that greens demand (Barry 1999a: 113). This reformed model of the green state would involve a considerable decentralisation of powers compared to current practice, with the onus resting on the proponent of centralisation to argue that specific powers or responsibilities should reside at a higher level. This reinterpretation would leave decentralisation as a core principle of ecologism, but the kind of state it would produce would look very different from the bioregional utopia envisaged by ecoanarchists.

To summarise, sustainability may not always be best achieved by political decentralisation. However, greens need not abandon decentralisation because ecologism is not simply concerned with achieving the right (short-term) outcomes. The case for decentralisation can also be based on its contribution to achieving a good society; although centralisation might sometimes produce better outcomes, if the long-term aim is to create people with the dispositions most likely to be conducive to sustainability, then decentralisation should make this more likely. As with democratisation, decentralisation is not just about getting the right outcomes now; it is also concerned with nurturing a good society inhabited by ecologically concerned citizens.

Must a green society be egalitarian?

Green theorists generally attribute great importance to 'social justice', but their treatment of the complex relationship between social justice and environmental issues has, until recently, been rather undeveloped (see Box 3.7). Social justice is a highly contested concept. The definition used by greens locates them firmly within the camp of those who link justice with equality. Greens seek a sustainable society characterised by social and economic

3.7 Defining social justice

Social justice is concerned with the principles that should govern the basic structure of a society, including the regulation of the legal system, the economy and welfare policy. Theories of social justice generally deal with the distribution of rights, opportunities and resources among human beings.

There are many competing accounts of justice with distribution based variously on principles such as needs, desert, entitlement, utility and equality. A broad division can be identified in modern theories of justice between those which link justice to some notion of equality and those which link it to entitlements, or rights. By defining social justice in terms of social and economic equality, greens adopt a socialist or welfare state liberal conception of justice. By contrast, Nozick (1974) argues that justice requires that we get the things that we are entitled to – because we have, say, a right to property. If that means some people get more than others, then so be it, because Nozick does not think that inequalities are *in themselves* unjust. However, not all who define justice by reference to rights are anti-egalitarian (e.g. Benton 1993).

Theories of social justice have, until recently, been largely silent about environmental issues. This is partly explicable by reference to the individualism inherent in, for example, liberal theories of justice. The problem here is that environmental goods – the reduction of acid rain or preservation of an endangered species – are not normally distributed to individuals. Yet most policies intended to protect the environment will have distributional implications, perhaps because they will require public expenditure or involve restrictions on the behaviour of individuals (car drivers or hunters), and they will certainly affect some people more than others (Miller 1999).

However, modern theories of justice also face a deeper difficulty, which is that, even when not individualistic, they are nevertheless anthropocentric in that they explicate value as value for and to human beings (whether individually or collectively). They therefore have difficulty in explaining the intuition that nature might have either inherent or intrinsic value.

equality, but why should this be good for the environment? Is there a causal relationship between social justice and sustainability so that, for example, the alleviation of poverty will benefit the environment? Or will inequitable policies sometimes be compatible with sustainability? Is equality a necessary condition for effective participatory democracy and political decentralisation? This section identifies three arguments supporting the claims of social justice to be a core green principle.[16]

First, some greens base their commitment to equality on a lesson from nature (Dobson 2000: 22). The holistic message is that nature consists of a mass of interdependent entities with each part having some value to other parts. Therefore no part is independent of, or superior to, any other part: hence the principle of equality (Dobson 2000: 24). Aside from the weaknesses in the holistic case discussed in Chapter 2, it is hard to see why interdependence necessarily implies equality. After all, there are many interdependent human relationships (employer/employee, landlord/villein, teacher/pupil) where equality would not normally exist. In short, the argument from nature is fundamentally flawed.

Secondly, social injustice contributes to environmental degradation. There is little doubt, for example, that poverty in less developed nations, by encouraging over-intensive farming and the cultivation of marginal land, results in environmental problems such as desertification and deforestation. Economic inequality between North and South is under-pinned by an international trading system that encourages less developed countries to produce cash crops for Northern consumption (rather than developing a self-sufficient economy), primarily to pay off debts to those same countries and their financial institutions. In affluent nations it is lower income groups who lack the financial resources to afford less environmentally damaging goods or to invest in energy conservation. The view that the alleviation of poverty will contribute to sustainability can be illustrated by the issue of population growth because most evidence links declining population rates with economic and social development. In particular, greater social and economic equality for women, improved female education and literacy, universal access to family planning programmes and the provision of quality maternal and child health care are the best means of controlling population growth (Harrison 1993; Sen 1994) (see Box 3.2).

Yet the relationship between social justice and sustainability is more complex than this simple conclusion suggests. In the first place, many environmental problems are the result of affluence. Major global problems – climate change, ozone depletion, acid rain – have been caused primarily by development in the advanced industrialised nations of the North. Conspicuous consumption, high levels of car ownership and the extensive use of air conditioning, for example, are key characteristics of rich nations and all massively damaging to the environment. Of course, the redistribution of wealth from the affluent North to the less developed South, and from rich to poor within individual nations, might have an overall positive impact on the environment, simply by cutting out the extremes of wealth and poverty. It is not axiomatic, however, that greater economic equality will reduce damage to the environment; it might just lead to different types of degradation, or a sharing out of the responsibility for causing it as poorer nations are able to increase consumption. Moreover, a key issue in North–South environmental diplomacy is that of 'catch-up': poorer Southern countries want the material benefits of development – refrigerators, washing machines, cars – that the affluent North has experienced. Why should they be denied these opportunities by accepting a steady-state economy? Yet catch-up for the South is certain to have some negative consequences for sustainability because it will inevitably result in higher levels of consumption.

It is also important to consider the impact of sustainability on social justice. Every policy aimed at resolving an environmental problem will have a distributional impact. The closure of a heavily polluting factory or nuclear power station will have a negative distributional impact on the employees who will lose their jobs. A policy to reduce petrol consumption through fuel taxes or restrictions on car use may discriminate more heavily against someone who is dependent on a car, because they need it for work or they live in a remote rural area, than someone who has no car or who can easily switch to public transport. When the British Conservative government raised value-added tax on domestic energy in an attempt to reduce consumption, it proved unpopular because of the disproportionate impact on poor – especially old – people who could not afford to heat their homes or invest in insulation. In short, there will be many occasions when a choice has to be made between social justice and sustainability.

A third argument suggests that social justice may have a close functional relationship with other components of the green programme, notably the steady-state economy, participatory democracy and decentralisation. Thus a more egalitarian society may be an essential condition of the transition to a steady-state economy. Currently, the gross economic and social inequalities that are integral to capitalist accumulation and wealth creation are legitimated politically by a trickle-down effect that raises the absolute standard of living of low-income groups (even though relative poverty increases) and a costly welfare state that provides a safety net for the very poorest members of society. This situation is made possible by continued economic growth and an ever-expanding economic pie, but would these inequalities still be acceptable if economic growth were static? People may accept inequality when their own material lot is improving, but they are likely to resent it deeply if they are getting poorer. Moreover, the greater transparency of a democratic, decentralised sustainable society would make the persistence of inequality more obvious. Any shift to more frugal consumption patterns and simpler lifestyles is likely to prove more acceptable where everyone is seen to be making similar sacrifices; if not, inequality is likely to be a potential source of social conflict. If this argument holds true at the level of an individual country, it is even more valid on the international stage. Without a major reduction in intragenerational inequality between North and South, by means of debt relief, aid, technology transfer and reform of international trading agreements, there is likely to be only limited progress towards resolving global environmental problems (see Chapter 9).

The radical forms of participatory democracy and decentralisation desired by greens may also be unworkable without something approximating to equality of wealth and income. It is hard to envisage participatory democracy functioning effectively if the face-to-face interactions that it requires bring individuals of vastly different wealth (and hence power?) together on a regular basis. Indeed, the extension of participatory democracy across society, especially in the workplace, where it should result in narrower income differentials, will in itself contribute to greater equality, partly by making the many sources and forms of inequality more transparent to ordinary people and fuelling demands for their removal (Carter 1996). Similarly, it is more likely that decentralised communities would co-ordinate environmental policies and accept reductions in consumption if the standard of living in each was reasonably similar. The existence of significant disparities in material wealth might encourage poorer communities to seek economic parity with their neighbours.

Overall, there are good reasons for regarding social justice as a core green principle. Admittedly, the relationship between social justice and sustainability is complex and uncertain. Not least, many policies intended to protect the environment will inevitably have a negative impact on social justice (it is therefore the responsibility of government to ensure that disadvantaged groups are compensated in other ways). Nevertheless, on balance, greater equality should benefit sustainability both by alleviating poverty and by facilitating democratisation and decentralisation. Underpinning both arguments is the powerful pragmatic political imperative: 'no justice, no cooperation; no cooperation, no solution' (Connelly and Smith 1999: 23). This mantra of poor Southern nations has catapulted equity issues to the forefront of international environmental diplomacy (see Chapter 9). Similarly, equity considerations are critical in persuading individual citizens to support sustainable policies and become ecological citizens. In short, the pursuit of social justice is a core green principle because it should ease the transition to a sustainable society.

It has been argued in the preceding sections that participatory democracy, decentralisation and social justice (or reformed versions of these concepts) can be regarded as essential components of a sustainable society (and of the means of getting there), although the case for non-violence seems less persuasive (see Box 3.6). The discussion has also brought out the importance of *green citizenship* as a critical, yet often neglected, ingredient of a green theory of agency.[17] The need for green citizenship is founded on the belief that the transition to a sustainable society requires more than institutional restructuring: it also needs a transformation in the beliefs, attitudes and behaviour of individuals. Greens recognise that the radical changes necessary for sustainability are only possible if undertaken willingly by individual citizens. As Barry puts it, 'Citizenship . . . emphasizes the duty of citizens to take responsibility for their actions and choices – the obligation to "do one's bit" in the collective enterprise of achieving sustainability' (1999a: 231). Green citizenship needs to be nurtured at the level of the (reformed) state, through the deliberative processes engendered by democratisation, decentralisation and egalitarianism, but its effect would spill over from the political sphere into the realms of economic and social activity. This belief that human nature can be changed and preferences transformed – making people less individualistic and materialistic – is an important defining characteristic of ecologism which, as the following section shows, shapes its relationship with other ideologies. Indeed, the above discussion shows how ecologism has been informed by contributions from different ideological traditions. This infusion of ideas raises questions about the distinctiveness of ecologism and its relationship with other political traditions.

TRADITIONAL POLITICAL IDEOLOGIES AND THE GREEN CHALLENGE

Ecologism is an ideology built on two main ideas: a reconceptualisation of the human–nature relationship away from strong anthropocentrism and an acceptance of the idea of limits to growth. It draws its subsidiary principles, such as participatory democracy, decentralisation and social justice, from other political traditions, but the relationship is not all one way. Ideas developed by ecologism have begun to influence established political ideologies. So, whereas the first part of this chapter showed how ecologism has given a green slant to concepts borrowed from other traditions, this second part shows how those other traditions have responded to the challenge posed by ecologism. The discussion starts with those political traditions based on individualism and a belief in social order – conservatism, liberalism, authoritarianism – followed by those traditions that seek human emancipation through political, economic and social change – socialism, feminism, anarchism. It is argued that this second group of ideologies is closest to ecologism.

Conservatism and neo-liberalism

There seems little in common between ecologism and the neo-liberal and conservative New Right with its enthusiasm for the market and the defence of the individual. Indeed, the New Right has been particularly hostile towards environmentalism (e.g. Ridley 1995; see also Paehlke 1989: ch. 8; Rowell 1996). Environmentalists are dismissed as 'doomsayers' and environmental regulations attacked for constraining free trade. The emergence of 'free market environmentalism' (Anderson and Leal 1991; Moran et al. 1991) reflects less a concern for the environment *per se* than an extension of a set of economic canons – the hegemony of the market and the sanctity of property rights – to incorporate a new problem. Environmental problems are blamed on the 'Tragedy of the Commons' which, it is argued, arises from the absence of clear, enforceable and tradeable property rights; put differently, the market solution is to privatise public goods, such as endangered species. The libertarian notion of justice based on entitlements contrasts sharply with the green conception of justice based on equity (see Box 3.7). In short, there is nothing that cannot be solved by the market; if there is an environmental problem, then trust the market to sort it out.[18]

Traditional conservative writing, although less overtly hostile, has also been critical of environmentalism: quick to condemn greens as dangerous radicals or socialists in disguise. Typically, green parties are compared to a water melon: 'green on the outside; red on the inside'. Yet there are many similarities between traditional conservatism (see Scruton 1984) and green principles. Both share a deep suspicion of Enlightenment ideas of progress and rationality, whilst drawing comfort from Romantic and nostalgic visions of a pre-industrial past. The principle of conservation – common to both doctrines – represents a desire to protect our historical inheritance and maintain the existing order for ourselves and our descendants. The conservative philosopher Edward Burke stressed the importance of partnership between past, present and future generations. This idea informs the conservative notion of 'stewardship' – holding land in trust for the next generation and for the wider nation – which has something in common with future generation arguments. Both doctrines display respect for stability and tradition. Change, where necessary, should involve organic, gradual adaptation, not revolution. The green 'precautionary principle' resonates with the conservative scepticism about radical technical or social experimentation. Both doctrines reject liberal individualism, believing that individuals flourish best when embedded within strong, supportive communities. Overall, Gray observes that 'Concern for the integrity of the common environment, human as well as ecological, is most in harmony with the outlook of traditional conservatism' (1993: 124).

Despite these affinities between conservatism and ecologism, the attempt by Gray (1993) to appropriate environmentalism for conservatism represents a rare exercise in linking the two doctrines.[19] This omission reflects a fundamental difference between the two traditions that Gray, in his attempt to 'rescue' environmentalism from its radicalism, rather misrepresents. Put simply, conservatism tends to see human nature as fixed and immutable whilst ecologism, as the discussion above showed, believes it is both possible and desirable to transform people. More broadly, whereas conservatism seeks to protect the status quo, ecologism seeks the radical transformation of the economic, political and social system. Core green principles such as participatory democracy, egalitarianism and non-violence contrast sharply with the conservative preference for authority, hierarchy and (where necessary) coercion. Conservatism has little to say about limits to growth and dismisses any attempt to extend value beyond humans. Not surprisingly, despite certain common ideas, ecologism and conservatism have drawn few explicit lessons from each other.

Classical liberalism

The discussion of environmental ethics in the previous chapter showed how many green theorists have employed a liberal rights discourse and, following Bentham, mobilised utilitarian ideas to justify extending obligations to non-humans. It was John Stuart Mill, in his *Principles of Political Economy*, who first developed the idea of the steady-state economy, whilst several key liberal ideas such as toleration, deliberation and the civic society have all informed ecologism. However, there is also much in liberalism that seems incompatible with green theory. In particular, liberal individualism contrasts sharply with the holistic arguments about interdependence. Liberal ideas such as representative government, market freedom and the pursuit of individual private gain sit uneasily alongside the green acceptance of collective solutions to environmental problems, intervention and the need for constraints on individual lifestyles (Martell 1994: 141). On balance, many aspects of classical liberalism conflict with the core tenets of ecologism. Nevertheless, there is evidence that liberalism is exercising a growing influence in green political theory as contemporary (academic) theorists seek to develop concepts such as a green theory of justice or ecological citizenship that inevitably draw on the discourse of liberal political philosophy (see Wissenburg 1998).

Authoritarianism

The legacy of survivalism suggests that ecologism has more in common with authoritarian thinking, although this is a linkage that is distressing to most greens and seized upon by opponents to berate environmentalism.

It is important, first, to dismiss any suggestion that green politics can be linked to fascism, despite the best efforts of Anna Bramwell, one of whose polemics is entitled *Blood and Soil: Walter Darré and Hitler's 'Green Party'*. The Nazi enthusiasm for biological metaphors and spiritualism was reflected in their view of man as at one with nature, which is embodied in the idea of 'blood and soil', i.e. human attachment to land and place. The Nazis also set up nature reserves and experimented in deciduous reforestation, organic farming and alternative forms of energy. However, the vast bulk of Nazi ideas, principles and policies directly conflict with those of ecologism. The existence of a few 'ecological ideologues' does no more than show that National Socialism was open to ecological ideas; indeed, 'the ecologists were eventually seen as hostile to Germany's national interests' (Bramwell 1989: 205). The few similarities should not be over-exaggerated. As Vincent (1993) observes, just because the Nazis employed 'socialist methods or favoured ancient German traditions does not mean that either socialism or conservatism are eternally besmirched' (p. 266).

There is a stronger case for identifying an authoritarian wing within ecologism dating from the survivalist writings in the 1970s (see Box 3.1). Driven by their overriding preoccupation with human survival and strong sense of urgency, the survivalists were prepared to recommend strict government controls on individuals and organisations, even if it meant suppressing liberal values. Nevertheless, it has been argued above that the centrality of green principles of democracy and social justice effectively place these authoritarian perspectives outside the ambit of ecologism. Ironically, the main impact of survivalism was to provoke a reaction against this authoritarian strand of thinking which gave green politics its powerful emancipatory character. Contemporary green theorists now go out of their way to distinguish themselves from the authoritarian tradition.

Socialism and Marxism

Ecologism has an ambivalent relationship with socialism. Many greens emphasise the sharp differences between the two doctrines, in particular the socialist commitment to unconstrained economic growth, and they point to the poor environmental record of countries in the former Soviet bloc as evidence that socialist central planning is no better for the environment than capitalism. Indeed, Porritt (1984) regards both capitalism and socialism as forms of the 'super-ideology' of *industrialism*. Conversely, socialists condemn environmentalists for failing to recognise capitalism as the source of environmental ills and for seeking to protect middle-class privileges such as access to the countryside, whilst ignoring basic social issues such as poverty (Enzensberger 1974). In recent years, however, several theorists have sought to build links between the opposing camps – often for reasons of practical politics – and the manifestation of this convergence is a body of writing known as *ecosocialism* (Gorz 1980; Frankel 1987; Ryle 1988; Benton 1993; Pepper 1993; Hayward 1995; Sarkar 1999).[20]

There are, of course, several distinct traditions of socialism which can be broadly divided into revolutionary doctrines, such as Marxism, and reformist approaches, such as social democracy. Most versions are characterised by two related features that seem to set socialism apart from ecologism: its anthropocentrism and its commitment to economic expansion. First, socialism, like capitalism, sits firmly in the Enlightenment tradition in striving for human mastery over nature and assuming that greater freedom will be achieved through material accumulation. Thus Marx believed that alienated humans could attain freedom by mastering, transforming and manipulating nature, none of which was tempered by any great concern for the non-human world. Contemporary Marxists have condemned green ideas such as the steady-state economy as regressive and anti-working class. However, some socialists point out that mastery does not have to result in environmental destruction; it might imply a more ecologically benevolent notion of stewardship (Pepper 1993: 221). Others have tried to 'rescue' Marxism for ecology by, for example, reinterpreting his early writings on the dialectical theory of human–nature relations (Dickens 1992; Benton 1993).[21] Nevertheless, the socialist tradition, including ecosocialism, bases its concern for the environment firmly on human-centred motives, so there seems to be little scope for reconciling the contrasting views of human–nature relations.

Secondly, socialism is committed to the pursuit of economic growth. Marxism anticipates human emancipation occurring in a communist utopia characterised by material *abundance* where the economic pie is sufficiently large to satisfy everyone's needs. By contrast, the utopian green sustainable society would experience some degree of material *scarcity*. Whereas socialists have little problem with economic growth and wealth creation *per se*, greens believe that in a finite planet unconstrained economic growth is simply unsustainable. Socialists argue that environmental ills should be blamed specifically on capitalism, not industrialism (and they dismiss the record of the former state socialist countries as irrelevant because they were never truly socialist). It is capitalism, characterised by the dominance of the competitive and dynamic market, the need to accumulate capital, the unbridled pursuit of profit, the use of destructive technologies and the hegemony of economic interests, which has created the contemporary ecological crisis. By creating new goods and wants, capitalism nurtures the consumerist ethos, whilst contributing to wider and deeper poverty, which socialists see as the underlying cause of environmental problems: 'It is the accumulation of wealth and its concentration into fewer and fewer hands which creates the levels of poverty that shape the lives of so many people on our planet, thus making it a major determinant of the environment which people experience' (Weston 1986: 5). Socialists despair that the greens' 'naive' analysis of society leads them to miss the real target, namely the capitalist system, its institutions and power relations.

It is on this second point that ecosocialism has started to build a bridge between socialism and ecologism. In particular, some writers in the ecosocialist tradition concede that there may be ecological limits to growth, and that unrestrained economic expansion is unsustainable (Ryle 1988; Benton 1993; Hayward 1995).[22] If the central socialist goal of changing the ownership and control of the means of production is insufficient to prevent environmental degradation, then the assumption that material accumulation is the surest path to human emancipation is also brought into doubt. Ecosocialists argue that economic growth must take account of ecological limits and they challenge the 'productivity' ethos of industrial society (Ryle 1988). At a strategic level, the 'industrialism or capitalism' debate now has little immediate significance because the global hegemony of capitalism, especially since the collapse of the Soviet bloc, clearly makes it the main adversary for both greens and socialists. Thus ecosocialism encourages greens to focus their attention on capitalism as the root cause of ecological problems.

The emergence of ecosocialism has encouraged a process of mutual learning on other issues too. Socialism presses greens to consider how change might be achieved when confronted by the institutions and power relations associated with global capitalism, such as multinational corporations, international financial markets and trading systems. Ecologism is rather hazy about how the change to a sustainable society is to occur, and who will take the lead in bringing it about. Socialists question whether the green emphasis on changing individual values, lifestyles and consumption patterns, combined with a focus on micro-level community politics, is sufficient to overcome the might of global capital. Conversely, socialism has endured many setbacks since the 1980s which, combined with the declining importance of the industrial proletariat (the key agent for socialist change), have forced socialists to cast around for new allies. Not surprisingly, there seems to be considerable common ground with the ecological movement, as illustrated by the red–green coalitions that have emerged in several countries (see Chapter 5). The consensus between ecologism and socialism across a range of common core principles, notably social justice, equality and democratisation, has led theorists from both camps to explore the potential of new social movements and rainbow coalitions of issue movements – socialists, greens, feminists, anti-racists, gay rights – as agents for change (see Part II). Although most socialists might agree with Gorz (1980) that 'the ecological movement is not an end in itself, but a stage in a larger struggle. It can throw up obstacles to capitalist development and force a number of changes' (p. 3), for now they share a common foe: capitalism.

Ecosocialists have also encouraged some reassessment of the role of the state within green political theory (Hayward 1995). Whilst greens traditionally distrust the state, socialists see it as playing a central role in bringing about social change. Socialists' solutions to environmental problems mirror their approach to other problems: a reformist socialist approach to the environment uses a central interventionist state to regulate the market whilst pursuing a social programme based on a redistribution of wealth, equality and collective ownership. Although greens have not yet begun a similar romance with the state, the earlier discussion of decentralisation showed that many greens now attribute a key role to the state in co-ordinating international responses to environmental problems.

Finally, it would be wrong to over-emphasise the significance of ecosocialism within the socialist tradition. Ecosocialism tends to draw on a very narrow body of socialist ideas, namely, the 'decentralist, non-bureaucratic, non-productivist socialism' (Dobson 2000: 187) of utopian socialists such as William Morris, G. D. H. Cole and Robert Owen, and even anarchists such as Kropotkin and Proudhon. Their vision of a decentralised, self-sufficient community has much in common with ecologism, but it is not the dominant position within socialism, where the centralist, labourist heritage represents a sharp cultural barrier between the two movements. On balance, ecologism has been sharpened by the socialist critique of capitalism, whilst socialism has taken on board some of the lessons of ecologism, but there are still critical differences on key issues, such as attitudes to human–nature relations, and in the institutional and cultural manifestations of each movement.

Feminism

Ecofeminists are keen to correct the tendency for green politics to ignore feminist issues.[23] The deep ecology movement, and especially the US group Earth First!, is often criticised for 'misogynistic proclivities' and for being 'saturated with male bravado and macho posturing' (Seager 1993: 226–7). Yet women are very active within the green movement, especially green parties, and opinion polls frequently show that women are more concerned about environmental issues than are men. Just as there is no doubting the important contribution made by women to green politics, neither can the vibrancy of the burgeoning ecofeminist discourse be contested, with at least four broad approaches to ecofeminism identifiable: liberal, cultural, social and socialist (Merchant 1992). Nevertheless, the lack of agreement about the central message of ecofeminism has diluted its impact on ecologism. The main source of conflict has been the dominance within ecofeminism of the 'difference' approach, which has been widely attacked within mainstream feminism.

'Difference' feminism, rather than seeking equality within the existing patriarchal society, emphasises the virtues of attributes such as nurture, kindness and care that are specifically feminine in that they are generally possessed by women (King 1983; Collard 1988). 'Difference' ecofeminists claim that these feminine values and forms of behaviour are precisely what will be needed in a green society, as opposed to the individualistic, instrumental rationality of patriarchal society, which, ecofeminists argue, is primarily responsible for the current abuse of nature. In short, ecofeminists identify a set of female traits, value them positively, and argue that the environment would be better protected if everyone (men and women) developed these traits. Ecofeminists also draw parallels between the domination of nature and the domination of women. They claim that, as women are closer to nature, they can better empathise with and understand its problems 'because we recognise the many faces of oppression' (Collard 1988: 97). Combining these arguments, ecofeminists claim that to solve ecological problems we must first remove patriarchy.

The 'difference' approach has been attacked on a number of fronts. Many feminists shudder at the way ecofeminists celebrate precisely the kind of stereotypical female traits that most feminists blame for the subjugation of women in contemporary society. Feminists might sympathise with the sentiment that the traditional undervaluing of female characteristics such as motherhood needs to be rectified, and that men should be encouraged to develop female traits – 'feminising' men. Nevertheless, there is a danger that this may turn out to be a reactionary path which exposes women to strong social pressures to conform to those subservient female forms of behaviour which patriarchal society allocates to them. Moreover, the task of trying to identify gender-specific traits may be fruitless. After all, men often display so-called feminine traits and women exhibit 'masculine' traits. Even if we could identify male and female traits, not all female traits (submissiveness?) may be desirable, and not all male traits (courage?) undesirable (Dobson 2000: 191–2). Moreover, if feminine traits immutably belong to women because of their biological make-up, how can men be expected to develop them?

Underlying these criticisms is the fundamental objection that this entire exercise smacks of 'essentialism': that female traits are biologically derived and, therefore, the female character does not vary across time, culture, race or class. Evans objects that this essentialist celebration of the natural – the idea that women's biology is their destiny – 'could entrench more or less every aspect of the female condition many of us have fought to renounce. Having fought to emerge from nature, we must not go back' (Evans 1993: 187). Alert to the dangers of essentialism, several ecofeminists have qualified the nature–female link by arguing that gender roles are socially rather than biologically produced (King 1989; Plumwood 1993; Seager 1993). If femininity is a social construction, then it follows that men could learn female traits. Plumwood (1993) argues that we need a model of a 'degendered' human consisting of traits that are independently chosen rather than based on either male or female characteristics.

Alternatively, several ecofeminists, like ecosocialists, argue that female oppression and environmental degradation are both inextricably tied up with the power structures of capitalist society (Biehl 1991; Mellor 1992, 1997; Salleh 1997). These writers argue that it is women's gender – the nature of women's work and their roles in society – rather than their biology that brings women closer to nature. Both women and nature are materially exploited, by patriarchy and by capitalist institutions and mechanisms. It is through their social location that women frequently bear the brunt of ecological devastation, particularly in less developed nations where women's issues and poverty go hand in hand. Indeed, women have initiated many collective grassroots struggles to defend their environment, as illustrated by the protests of the Chipko women in India who famously used the non-violent strategy of 'tree-hugging' to protect their forests from multinational timber companies (Shiva 1989). Wider solutions to these problems would require the transformation of capitalist society, but ecofeminism, with its predominantly philosophical orientation, has only recently started to engage with these issues.

Ecofeminism highlights the need to incorporate feminist concerns into green theory and, 'by tapping into women's rage and despair at the destruction of our planet' (Seager 1993: 252), it may provide a catalyst for environmental activism. However, ecofeminism has made only a limited contribution to ecologism because it offers no coherent vision of a green society and no clear strategy for feminist environmental action.

Anarchism

The profound influence of anarchism on the development of ecologism has already been established.[24] Anarchist writers such as Bahro (1986), Bookchin and Sale have made a major contribution to the ecological critique of contemporary society, the model of a sustainable society and green theories of agency. Anarchism is, in many respects, the political tradition apparently closest to an ecological perspective and, conversely, anarchism is itself shaped by ecological concerns (Eckersley 1992: 145). Core green principles like decentralisation, participatory democracy and social justice are central features of the anarchist tradition, and many greens have inherited the anarchist distrust of the state. Anarchists have also helped shape the praxis of green politics by advocating grassroots democracy, extra-parliamentary activities and direct action.

Two main schools of ecoanarchism can be distinguished (Eckersley 1992; Pepper 1993): 'social ecology', which is primarily the product of Murray Bookchin's (1980, 1982, 1989) extensive writings, and ecocommunalism, which is a general category incorporating a range of more ecocentric positions, including the bioregionalism of Sale (1980, 1991). Ecocommunalism focuses on the relationship between society and nature and, in recommending greater integration of human communities with their immediate natural environment (for example, living within the carrying capacity of their bioregion), is closely linked with deep ecology and the ecocentric ideas discussed in Chapter 2. By contrast, social ecology attributes ecological degradation primarily to social causes. Bookchin's explicit linkage of social hierarchy and environmental problems has made a notable theoretical contribution to the emancipatory message of ecologism, so it is the focus of this section.

The core message of social ecology is that the human domination of nature stems from 'the very real domination of human by human' (Bookchin 1989: 44). Echoing the thinking of the nineteenth-century anarchist Peter Kropotkin, Bookchin has a benign view of nature based on the belief that it is interdependent and egalitarian – 'ecology recognises no hierarchy on the level of the ecosystem. There are no "kings of beasts" and no "lowly ants"' (Bookchin 1980: 59). Bookchin argues that humans are naturally co-operative and will flourish best in a decentralised, non-hierarchical anarchic society, such as early pre-literate societies, which, he claims, were organic and at one with nature, seeking neither to dominate nor be dominated by it. Subsequently, as social hierarchies developed based on age, gender, religion, class and race, so humans acquired the apparatus and aptitude for domination of other humans and, by extension, non-human nature. Today, domination and hierarchy characterise society and shape a range of related dualisms: intellectual over physical work, work over pleasure and mental control over the sensuous body. Social ecology seeks the replacement of domination and hierarchy with equality and freedom. In short, if social hierarchy can be removed, then environmental degradation will also disappear.

Bookchin's thesis is vulnerable to the empirical criticism that there have been many societies characterised by social hierarchy which have also lived in harmony with nature, such as feudalism. Conversely, a non-hierarchical egalitarian society, such as Marx's post-capitalist utopia, might still exploit nature (Eckersley 1992: 151). Nevertheless, Bookchin contributes an important social element to ecocentric thinking which is intended to rectify the mystical flavour of deep ecology. Indeed, Bookchin has engaged in a series of vicious attacks on deep ecology, which he describes disparagingly as 'mystical eco-la-la', for its insensitivity to social issues. He has little patience with the deep green belief that change will come about simply through a transformation of individual world-views stimulated by better spiritual connections with nature. He also despises the misanthropic flavour of some deep green writing, detecting support for coercive forms of population control, immigration and aid policy, and he has engaged in vitriolic debate with the former leading Earth First! activist Dave Foreman (Bookchin and Foreman 1991). Notwithstanding their mutual hostility, social ecology and ecocommunalism share important principles, notably their belief that the state is intrinsically inimical to green ecological and social values (Barry 1999a: 98). Despite the limitations of decentralisation and the growing acceptance of liberal democratic institutions amongst greens, the anarchist critique of the bureaucratic, centralised state and the commitment to local political action continue to wield a huge influence over green theory and practice.

CRITICAL QUESTION 5

Can green ideas be satisfactorily accommodated within established political ideologies?

NEITHER LEFT NOR RIGHT BUT IN FRONT?

Greens like to describe themselves as 'neither left nor right but in front' because they want to affirm their difference from other ideologies. What do they mean by this claim and is it accurate? Is ecologism a distinct ideology? If so, can it accommodate the many different green discourses discussed above, and where is ecologism located on the classic left–right ideological spectrum? Or is it necessary to use different criteria to categorise it?

Ecologism is characterised by two core ideas: the need to reconceptualise the human–nature relationship and the acceptance of the idea of limits to growth. At this point, consensus breaks down. Some writers hold that ecological imperatives require no specific political structures (Enzensberger 1974; Gorz 1980; Ryle 1988; Goodin 1992). Ryle, for example, believes that 'widely varying forms' of sustainable society are possible, including 'authoritarian capitalist' and 'barrack socialism', which would be a far cry from the green model outlined above (Ryle 1988: 7). Others believe that ecological imperatives do imply certain political forms and exclude others. Martell (1994: 160), for example, argues that intervention and central co-ordination are needed, thus ruling out markets, capitalism and decentralisation. By contrast, Dobson believes that 'there is something about ecologism . . . that pushes it irrevocably towards the left of the political spectrum' (Dobson 2000: 73) – a position that acknowledges the powerful influence of the emancipatory tradition over ecologism (Eckersley 1992).

It is helpful to illustrate the relationship between ecologism and other ideologies diagrammatically. Conventional political discourse is dominated by distributive issues: who gets what, when and how? Thus ideologies are typically categorised along the familiar left–right dichotomy according to the position they take on key political dualisms such as 'state v. market' or 'equality v. hierarchy'. In contrast, ecologism, whilst not denying the importance of distributional issues, is driven by an ecological imperative which is not picked up by the left–right dimension. By adapting O'Riordan's classic **technocentric**–ecocentric dichotomy (Box 3.8), it is possible to categorise different ideologies according to their perspective on environmental issues (see Figure 3.1).

> **Technocentric:** A mode of thought which optimistically believes that society can solve all environmental problems, using technology and science, and achieve unlimited material growth.

The technocentric–ecocentric dimension cuts across the left–right dimension, thus giving some force to the green claim to represent a fundamentally different approach to politics. This sharp distinction holds good as long as we focus on those two ideas of non-anthropocentrism and limits to growth. However, as soon as the broader set of green principles is introduced into the equation, the distinction becomes more blurred. In Figure 3.2 the relationship between ecologism and other ideologies is illustrated by superimposing the technocentric–ecocentric dimension onto the conventional left–right dimension (based on attitudes to state intervention in the market).[25] If ecologism consists of the core ecological imperative supplemented by green principles of democratisation, decentralisation and social justice, then the shaded area in Figure 3.2 represents the broad area covered by ecologism. On this reading, ecologism clearly has most in common with those

3.8 The technocentric–ecocentric dimension

Technocentric orientation
- ❏ an adherence to cornucopian assumptions that there are no limits to growth
- ❏ an unrestrained commitment to economic growth
- ❏ scientific and technological optimism that human ingenuity will find an answer to every ecological problem
- ❏ a strong emphasis on material values and resistance to widening public participation in decision-making
- ❏ an anthropocentric world-view

Ecocentric orientation
- ❏ a belief that there are both ecological and social limits to growth
- ❏ a development philosophy that seeks to minimise resource use and operate within the carrying capacity of ecosystems
- ❏ an appreciation of the complexities of ecosystems and the limits to human understanding and elitist expertise; i.e., we cannot solve every problem and we must adopt a cautious approach to the use of technology
- ❏ belief that materialism for its own sake is wrong, which results in an emphasis on non-material values such as education, fellowship, civic responsibility, democratic participation, community
- ❏ an ecocentric respect for nature and a belief that all lifeforms should be given the opportunity to pursue their own destinies

Modelled on O'Riordan (1981).

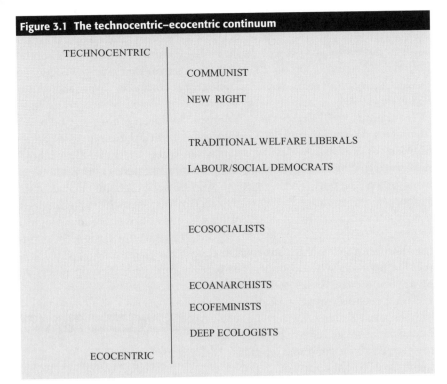

Figure 3.1 The technocentric–ecocentric continuum

TECHNOCENTRIC

COMMUNIST

NEW RIGHT

TRADITIONAL WELFARE LIBERALS

LABOUR/SOCIAL DEMOCRATS

ECOSOCIALISTS

ECOANARCHISTS

ECOFEMINISTS

DEEP ECOLOGISTS

ECOCENTRIC

Figure 3.2 Mapping ecologism

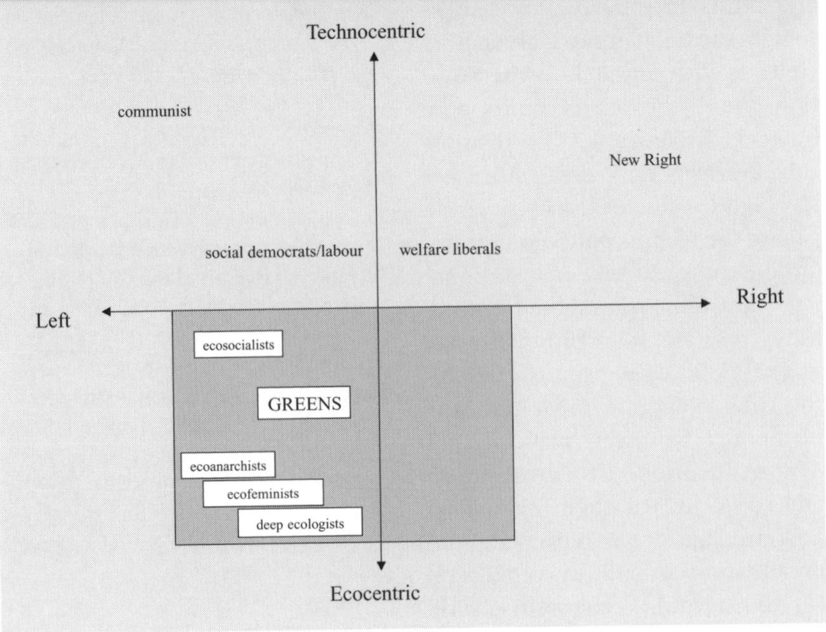

Technocentric

communist

New Right

social democrats/labour   welfare liberals

Left

Right

ecosocialists

GREENS

ecoanarchists

ecofeminists

deep ecologists

Ecocentric

doctrines (socialism, anarchism, feminism) that (1) are critical of capitalism and have sought to transform it and (2) believe that human nature can and should be changed to make us less individualistic and less materialistic, although it has also drawn on reformist doctrines that seek to dilute the worst aspects of the market, such as welfare liberalism and social democracy. Thus ecologism stretches leftwards from just right of centre, but it does not reach the far left because greens want to control the market rather than remove it and their suspicion of the state means they reject any form of command economy. Ecologism goes no further to the right because sustainability is incompatible with an unfettered market economy. Moreover, greater participatory democracy and decentralisation would be impossible in either a command economy, by definition, or in a free market, where each would be curtailed by economic inequality and the capitalist dynamics of accumulation, competition and concentration. The evidence suggests, therefore, a conclusion that is slightly broader than that of Dobson: yes, ecologism does occupy broadly left-of-centre territory, but it draws in a wider range of perspectives than the anarchist–emancipatory framework identified by Dobson. Although the model of a sustainable society outlined at the start of the chapter closely mirrored the ecoanarchist blueprint, the discussion of core green principles and the impact of other ideologies highlighted weaknesses at the heart of this model and, at the same time, indicated the existence of several alternative perspectives *within* the green political arena. After all, it seems reasonable to expect that, just as there are many varieties of socialism, feminism and conservatism, so within the territory staked out by ecologism there is space for a wide range of coherent green alternatives. For example, both the radical ecoanarchist model and the 'pro-state' ecosocialist models would fall within the boundary of ecologism.[26]

This relatively relaxed position on where the boundaries of ecologism lie is also sensitive to the view that attempts to pin down a definitive 'correct' version of ecologism not only close down discussion (and put off potential adherents) but they also understate the impact of green political theory on other political traditions. Connelly and Smith (1999) ask whether it is best 'to understand green political thought as a critical perspective which has forced existing traditions to undergo an internal analysis and re-think of their fundamental premises and concerns, as well as providing a critical space for convergence and debate between traditions' (p. 55). There is much to commend both this view and Barry's (1999a) attempt to delineate green political theory from the ideology of ecologism to enable a richer debate unencumbered by the need to adhere to a 'party line'.

Nevertheless, the central argument of this chapter is that, on balance, the two core themes that underpin the ecological imperative (a reassessment of human–nature relations and the finitude of the Earth's resources), supplemented by a coherent set of principles drawn from other doctrines, is sufficient for us to talk legitimately about ecologism as an ideology in its own right. One further inference to be drawn is that many green theorists and activists have been moving towards an acceptance that liberal democracy is here to stay and ecologism needs strategies for reforming it (Wissenburg 1998). It is this question that underpins the remainder of this book.

Further reading

Dobson (2000) is the best introduction to ecologism. Barry (1999a) complements Dobson with particularly good coverage of issues such as the green state, ecological citizenship and green political economy. See also Smith (1998) and Baxter (1999). Goodin (1992) is a clever and provocative book which demands attention. See also Radcliffe (2000) on green politics and democracy. Other important attempts to relate green politics to traditional political theory include Hayward (1995), Wissenburg (1998) and Dobson (1998, 1999), while Barry (1999b) locates it within broader social theory. For the relationship between green theory and other ideologies, see Paehlke (1989), Eckersley (1992), Hayward (1995) and Pepper (1993), while Dryzek (1997) identifies a wide range of environmental discourses. See the journals *Environmental Politics* and *Capitalism, Nature, Socialism*, the latter being an interesting forum for red–green debates regarding the links between ecology and Marxism, socialism, anarchism and feminism. Milbrath (1989) presents a fascinating vision of a sustainable society. Ernest Callenbach's novel *Ecotopia* offers one vision of a green 'utopia'.

Notes

1. The *Limits to Growth* report was sponsored by the Club of Rome, a group of affluent industrialists, academics and civil servants.
2. See Chapter 7 for further discussion of the interdependence of environmental policy problems.
3. The *Limits to Growth* report was so successful that it drew attention away from other important contemporary contributions, notably Georgescu-Roegen's (1971) work on the second law of thermodynamics. See Barry (1994).
4. Detailed discussions of future generations arguments include Golding (1972); Barry (1991); Laslett and Fishkin (1992); de-Shalit (1995); Dobson (1998, 1999).
5. Fuller discussions of the sustainable society can be found in Die Grünen (1983); Porritt (1984); Ekins (1986); Milbrath (1989); Goodin (1992); Tokar (1992); Dobson (2000); Pepper (1996); and Barry (1999a).
6. For a more detailed discussion of the green, or steady-state economy, see Ekins (1986); Daly and Cobb (1990); Barry (1999a).
7. Goodin's own theory of agency differs significantly from radical green perspectives in that he regards the liberal democratic central state as the best means of achieving green ends and rejects (rather disparagingly) the green predilection for living simple individual lifestyles as misconceived and likely to detract from reaching green outcomes (Goodin 1992: 78–83, 120–3).
8. This individualism underpins Eckersley's ambiguity about which principles contribute to autonomy. In Eckersley (1992) she equates autonomy with radical emancipatory politics, i.e. grassroots democracy, social justice and non-violence. Subsequently, she accepts the

continuing robustness of the nation state and liberal democracy which leads her towards a more reformist approach incorporating the development of an environmental rights discourse (Eckersley 1996a).

9. Although it is also by exercising our autonomy – allowing our self-interested materialism to consume and deplete resources – that we have caused the ecological problems we face today. If autonomy has been the cause of the problem, can it be the solution?

10. For example, 'discursive democracy' (Dryzek 1990) or 'communicative democracy' (Young 1990).

11. However, conversely, decision-making procedures based on careful deliberation in small face-to-face forums are very time-consuming, particularly if it is a requirement that decisions be consensual.

12. The discussion here focuses on political decentralisation rather than the potential ecological benefits of a decentralised economy arising from small-scale production, appropriate technologies and reduced trade and travel.

13. Sale (1991: 64), for example, anticipates that the population of a bioregion will not exceed 10,000 people.

14. McGinnis (1998) provides a useful introduction to bioregional writings.

15. For example, Barry (1999a) develops a theory of 'collective ecological management'.

16. In the limited space available, this section can provide only a brief introduction to the burgeoning literature on the relationship between sustainability and social justice. See Dobson (1998, 1999) and Wissenburg (1998) for some tentative steps towards a green theory of justice; note that Dobson (1998: ch. 1) argues *against* the claim that social justice is a core green principle.

17. Political theorists are increasingly turning their attention to the question of green citizenship: Barry (1996, 1999a); Christoff (1996a); Smith (1998).

18. For a critique of free-market environmentalism, see Eckersley (1993) and Barry (1999a: 150–5).

19. See also Wells (1978).

20. Although there are considerable differences within this list. For example, Pepper is primarily interested in what greens can learn from socialists, whereas Benton and Hayward see it as a two-way learning process.

21. For the relationship between Marxism and ecology see also Grundmann (1991), Barry (1998), Hughes (2000) and Foster (2000).

22. Although some ecosocialists remain unconvinced by this idea (Harvey 1993; Pepper 1993).

23. Good collections of ecofeminist writings include Caldecott and Leland (1983), Collard (1988), Plant (1989) and Warren (1994).

24. See Eckersley (1992), Pepper (1993) and Barry (1999a) for a wider discussion of ecoanarchism.

25. The contemporary blurring of left and right on their attitudes to the market undoubtedly reduces the usefulness of the state–market dimension, but it remains the dominant way of categorising ideologies. Alternative dimensions, such as equality v. hierarchy, or the different *futures* that left (an imagined future such as the communist utopia) and right (based on an idealised past Golden Age) each desire, are worthy of further exploration. See also Paehlke (1989: 190) and Eckersley (1990).

26. Of course, each perspective (especially the ecoanarchists) would claim to represent the one 'true' green position – but that is the nature of ideological debate.

PART II PARTIES AND MOVEMENTS: GETTING FROM HERE TO THERE

Part II examines the question of green agency; or how do we get from here to there? Whether we are pursuing the radical green utopias envisaged by ecocentrics or a more moderate environmentally benign world, it is important to examine how we might achieve that sustainable society. One distinction to be made is that between collective action and individual lifestyle politics. The focus in Part II is on the main forms of collective action in environmental politics, namely green parties, the 'greening' of established parties and environmental groups, leaving the discussion of selected individual strategies, such as green consumerism, to Part III.[1]

A second distinction arises from the familiar *reformist* versus *radical* dilemma that underpins environmental politics. A broad strategic choice facing any political movement is whether to seek change through legislative institutions and the use of conventional forms of political activity or whether to adopt a more confrontational strategy that breaks the law and challenges the dominant rules and values of the political system. This tension lies at the heart of practical environmental politics: it underpins debates within green parties, colours their relationships with established parties and cuts across the environmental movement.

It is also important to place the rise of environmental politics within broader debates in political science about the trend towards a 'new politics' in western industrialised societies. To understand the 'new politics', we need first to understand what is meant by the 'old politics' that the 'new politics' is supposedly replacing. In the old politics, support for established parties is characterised by stable political cleavages and differences based on class, religion or regional divisions, of which the left–right pattern of partisan alignment is pre-eminent (Lipset and Rokkan 1967). The traditional values underlying political discourse relate to material issues of economics and security, such as economic growth, stable prices, public order, national security and the protection of traditional lifestyles. Political participation is low; for most people it extends no further than voting in national elections. Those citizens who are more active generally join movements such as trade unions or political parties which pursue economic and political rights that will enhance the interests of their class.

Since the late 1960s, many observers have detected fundamental changes in the values and forms of political activity in industrialised nations. These changes, it is claimed, are transforming the issues that dominate the political agenda and creating new political cleavages which are contributing to a realignment of long-established party systems – the new politics (Dalton 1988; Inglehart 1990). There are three notable manifestations of this new politics. First, the emergence of **new social movements** (NSMs), such as the women's, peace, anti-nuclear and environmental movements, which have been prepared to use unconventional forms of political participation, including civil disobedience and direct action, to achieve their aims. Secondly, the supporters of NSMs are drawn predominantly from what some theorists call a 'new middle class', of educated, professional service workers in industrialised societies. Lastly, a growing minority of citizens holds a set of postmaterial values emphasising equal rights, environmental quality and alternative lifestyles which challenge the old materialist concerns of economic and physical security. If the new politics thesis is accurate, then it may help to explain contemporary environmental politics: from this perspective, green parties and environmental groups would be regarded as new social movements, environmental activists would probably be from this new middle class, and environmental problems would be defined as postmaterial, quality-of-life issues. In short, a new politics account would interpret environmentalism as simply one element of a wider structural and cultural transformation of contemporary politics. One problem with such an approach is that it tends to denude environmental politics of its distinctiveness – notably its specific concern with ecological issues – whilst the underlying 'objective' state of the environment is dismissed as almost incidental in explaining the emergence of environmental politics.

These 'new politics' explanations are examined in detail in Chapter 4 to see whether they can account for the rise of green parties; they also inform the analysis of party politics and environmental pressure groups in Chapters 5 and 6. It is argued that, whilst there is some mileage in the new politics thesis, it cannot alone provide an adequate explanation of contemporary environmental politics. Instead, Part II adopts a broad comparative approach to party politics and environmental groups in Europe and North America, with specific studies of Germany, Britain, France and the USA, to argue that a range of institutional and political factors need to be included in any comprehensive analysis of environmental politics.

> **New social movement:**
> A loose-knit organisation which seeks to influence public policy on an issue such as the environment, nuclear energy or peace, and which may use unconventional forms of political participation, including direct action, to achieve its aims.

Note

1. There is also the radical option of attempting to opt out of capitalist society by setting up alternative self-sufficient communities or green communes. Bahro (1986) makes the case for communes and Pepper (1991) is a study of commune experiments. See Dobson (2000: ch. 4) for a wider discussion of strategies for change.

4

Green parties: the rise of a new politics?

Contents

Green parties have rapidly become a familiar feature of the political landscape, particularly in Europe. The first green parties were formed in Tasmania and New Zealand in 1972, and the Swiss elected the first green to a national assembly in 1979. By the late 1990s, green parties were sufficiently established to have joined national coalition governments in Belgium, Finland, France, Germany and Italy, to have elected deputies in several other national parliaments and wide representation in sub-national government. In 1999, a record thirty-eight Green MEPs from eleven countries were elected to the European Parliament and the first Green European Commissioner was appointed. The greens have clearly arrived, and their message seems to have sufficient coherence and reso-nance to exert an electoral appeal that transcends national borders. How do we account for the rise of green parties? Do they simply reflect a spe-cific public concern about the state of the environment, or are they part of a general shift towards a postmaterialist 'new politics'? To whom does the green message appeal? Why have green parties performed better in some countries than in others? Are green parties here to stay or are they simply a 'flash party' that will soon disappear?

The chapter begins with a brief survey of green party electoral perfor-mance, identifying those countries where green parties have secured elec-toral success and those where they have not. The next section assesses three broad macro-level new politics explanations of green party develop-ment: new social movements, new class accounts and postmaterialism. These macro-level theories help explain the rise of green parties, but they cannot account for variations in green party success between countries. In the next section, the '**political opportunity structure**' **(POS)** framework, which combines these broad structural and cultural explanations with institutional factors such as the electoral system and party competition in individual countries, is applied to green party performance in Germany, France and the UK. Finally, although the POS framework does provide a more comprehensive and sensitive account, it can be criticised for down-playing the influence of the actual state of the environment in public sup-port for green parties.

Political opportunity structure:
The dimensions of the political envi-ronment that either encourage people to use collective action or discourage them from doing so, and which shape the development of movements and parties.

GREEN PARTY ELECTORAL PERFORMANCE: AN OVERVIEW

Green parties have achieved their main electoral successes in Northern and Western Europe (see Table 4.1). In four countries – West Germany, Belgium, Switzerland and Luxembourg – green parties averaged at least 5 per cent of the vote during the 1980s and regularly won seats in national parliaments. The German and Belgian greens have proved most successful. Germany boasts the largest and most well-known green party, Die Grünen: it was the third strongest German political party in both the 1994 and

Table 4.1　Electoral performance of green parties in EU member states

	First Green MP elected	Average % vote national elections		Number of MPs[1]
		1980s	1990–2001	
Austria	1986	4.0	6.0	14
Belgium[2]	1981	5.9	10.9	20
Finland	1983	2.8	6.9	11
France	1997	1.1	7.2	7
Germany	1983	5.1[3]	6.3	47
Ireland	1989	1.0	2.1	2
Italy	1987	2.5	2.6	18
Luxembourg	1984	6.8	8.9	5
Netherlands[4]	1990	–	5.0	11
Portugal[5]	1987			2
Spain[6]		0.9	0.6	0
Sweden	1988	2.9	4.3	16
UK		0.3	0.6	0

Source: Keesings Archives Note.

Notes: No green parties have contested recent elections in Denmark or Greece.

[1] At most recent election before September 2001.

[2] Combined results of Ecolo and Agalev.

[3] This figure refers to West German elections.

[4] The figures refer to Groen Links, not the tiny De Groenen.

[5] Os Verdes contests elections on a joint list with the Communists (CDU) – 9.0% in 2000 – so it is impossible to isolate their exact share of the vote.

[6] These figures report the results of several ecological groupings. One MP was elected in 1999 on a regional joint United Left (IU)/Catalonian Greens ticket.

1998 federal elections and its forty-seven MPs formed a coalition government with the Social Democrats in October 1998.[1] The two Belgian green parties, Agalev (Flemish-speaking) and Ecolo (French-speaking), mirror the duplication of other Belgian parties on linguistic lines. Since entering parliament in 1981 they have steadily increased support, gaining a notable success in the 1999 elections with a combined vote of 14.3 per cent and twenty MPs, and subsequently entering government coalitions at federal and sub-national levels.

In a second group of countries – Finland, France, Austria and the Netherlands – green parties did not average over 5 per cent of the vote in national elections until the 1990s. The Finnish Vihreä Liitto was the first green party to join a national government in 1995 and, after strengthening its position with 7.3 per cent of the vote and eleven MPs, it remained in the rainbow coalition government after the 1999 election. In France, Les Verts gained its first seven deputies in 1997, and they joined the Lionel Jospin socialist-led coalition government. The Austrian Alternative Grüne Österreich (ALÖ), having absorbed most members of the moderate ecological party Vereinigte Grüne Österreich (VGÖ) in 1986, is now well established, gaining 7.4 per cent and fourteen MPs in the 1999 election. In the Netherlands, a small 'dark' green party, De Groenen, has been completely eclipsed by the merger in 1990 of four small left-of-centre parties – communists, pacifists, radicals and an evangelical party – to form Groen Links (Green Left). Although slow to take off, in the 1998 Dutch election it gained 7.3 per cent of the vote and eleven MPs. In addition to these 'successful' parties, the Swedish Miljopartiet entered parliament in 1988 and whilst it fell below the 4 per cent threshold in 1991, it regained its position in 1994, holding on to it in 1998 with 4.5 per cent of the vote.

Elsewhere, other European green parties have struggled to secure a firm electoral platform. The Italian Greens, despite averaging only 2–3 per cent of the vote, secured twenty-eight MPs in 1996 as a member of the victorious broad-left Olivo coalition while the 'Sunflower' green list still won eighteen seats when Berlasconi's right-wing coalition triumphed in 2001. The Irish Comhaontas Glas doubled its representation to two MPs in 1997 with 2.8 per cent share of the vote. A final group of countries, including Britain, Norway and Denmark, have yet to elect a green MP. Progress has been particularly difficult in Southern Europe. A national green party, Los Verdes, was not formed in Spain until 1992, whilst a similar attempt was stillborn in Greece. It is debatable whether the Portuguese Os Verdes, which contests elections in coalition with the Communists, is a genuinely distinct party. Further afield, greens have been elected to national assemblies in a disparate range of countries including Armenia, Estonia, Georgia, Lithuania, Slovakia, Ukraine and Mexico. New Zealand boasts probably the most successful non-European green party, with seven MPs and 5.2 per cent of the vote in the 1999 general election. The absence of a single national green party in Australia has hampered progress, although a handful of Greens have been elected to the Senate and to state parliaments, notably in Tasmania. Green parties have had little success in North America; for example, in December 2000 there were just eighty greens holding minor elected office across twenty-two American states (Green Party 2001), although the veteran consumer campaigner Ralph Nader attracted almost 3 million votes (2.7 per cent) on a green ticket in the 2000 US presidential election (see Box 5.5).

This brief overview of green parties raises two main questions. How can the rise of green parties in recent years be explained? Why have they met with such variable electoral success? The following section assesses how far the broad 'new politics' thesis can account for the rise of green parties.

IS THERE A NEW POLITICS?

This section examines the three components of the new politics thesis outlined in the introduction to Part II: the rise of new social movements, the emergence of a new middle class and the flourishing of postmaterial values. It then assesses how much they contribute to explaining the rise of green parties.

New social movements?

'New social movements' (NSMs), notably the student, peace, anti-nuclear, women's and environmental movements, were responsible for a major part of the collective social protest that swept Western Europe during the late 1960s, 1970s and 1980s. Scott (1990) distinguishes NSMs from old social movements, such as trade unions, according to their location, aims, organisational form and medium of action. First, while trade unions are located within the polity and typically seek to influence social democratic and labour parties, NSMs bypass the state by operating outside the established parties. In short, NSMs try to mobilise civil society rather than seize power. Secondly, the aims of trade unions have been political integration, legislative political reform and economic rights for workers, whereas NSMs focus on defending civil society against excessive political power (particularly from the state) and seek cultural changes to values and lifestyles. NSMs question the material assumptions, such as economic growth, that underpin the ideology of the older movements representing capital or labour. Thirdly, trade unions adopt the bureaucratic and hierarchical forms of organisation prevalent in society, while NSMs are usually informal, decentralised and participatory organisations. Finally, trade unions generally work within the existing political institutions, whereas NSMs adopt innovative repertoires of action, including confrontation and direct action, often outside the law (see Box 4.1).

This characterisation of the NSM as a participatory, issue-specific movement, geared to the mobilisation of public opinions, is an ideal type based on the NSM in its most radical and fundamentalist form. One obvious problem therefore is that it presents a snapshot of the NSM at one moment – its initial stage – when it 'has all the optimism of a new movement grounded in recent mobilisation, before the movement must reflect upon how it is to affect the social and political environment' (Scott 1990: 154). Once established, movements make compromises, usually by gradually adopting conventional organisational structures and strategies.

4.1 New social movements

There are two broad approaches to the study of social movements, commonly termed the European and American approaches (Klandermans and Tarrow 1988).

The *European* approach focuses on the structural transformations underpinning the rise of NSMs; i.e. *why* people take action in this way. Some theorists have made grand claims about their significance, suggesting that NSMs represent a radical new form of class politics (Touraine 1981), or that, in the modern information age, NSMs have a symbolic resonance reaching far beyond the scale of their activities (Melucci 1989).

The *American* approach, notably Resource Mobilisation Theory, sees politics as the mobilisation of resources. It examines *how* groups pursue goals by focusing on the role of organisation and of political entrepreneurs in turning grievances into political issues.

The *political opportunity structure* framework attempts to integrate these contrasting approaches by combining broad structural and cultural arguments with institutional factors.

These compromises have been so far-reaching that, 'by the end of the eight-ies, most of the new social movements in Western Europe appeared to be pragmatic reformist movements . . . closely connected to established politics in various dimensions' (Kriesi et al. 1995: xxi). It seemed that some of the more grandiose claims about the radical potential of NSMs (e.g. Touraine 1981; Melucci 1989) were misplaced. Nevertheless, the existence of a dynamic NSM milieu may provide an important *institutional* factor shaping the development of green parties.

Environmentalism as middle-class elitism?

This explanation of the new politics focuses on fundamental changes in the economic and social *structures* of advanced capitalist societies in the post-war era. The contraction of traditional manufacturing industry and the growth of the service sector produced a major shift in occupational structures, with the decline in the traditional blue-collar working class mirrored by an expansion of the white-collar sector. Other factors, including improved material standards of living, the massive expansion of higher education and the information revo-lution, have also contributed to the blurring of traditional class divisions and loyalties in the 'postindustrial society' (Bell 1973). Some writers claim that a new middle class has emerged: highly educated, filling professional and wel-fare jobs and economically secure (Gouldner 1979; Kriesi 1993). It is argued that this new class is in some respects more alienated from the political system than the traditional working class and, crucially, more able and willing to criticise the established parties, the bureaucracy and the dominant materialist agenda.

The relevance of the 'new class' thesis to the study of environmental politics is the empirical claim that participants in new social movements generally, and environmentalists in particular, are predominantly drawn from the new middle class (Cotgrove 1982; Morrison and Dunlap 1986; Rootes 1995a). Offe (1985) adds that two other groups are also active in NSMs: first, 'decommodified' groups who are peripheral to the labour market, such as students, housewives, pensioners and the unemployed; second, members of the 'old' middle class who are independent and self-employed, such as farmers, shop-owners and artisans. Significantly, all these groups fall outside the two traditional classes of capital and labour (i.e. the industrial working class).

New class explanations of NSMs assume that, as classes have interests, the domination of environmentalism by the new middle class must rep-resent an attempt to further its own class interests. Indeed, some social-ists have sought to dismiss environmentalism as an expression of middle-class elitism (Enzensberger 1974). However, class interest arguments are fraught with problems. In the first place, why should environmentalism serve exclusively middle-class interests? All classes suffer the conse-quences of pollution; indeed, it is usually the poorest groups and ethnic minorities who suffer the most direct and worst problems of environmental degradation and pollution in the workplace and in inner-city communities (Bullard 1990). Cotgrove (1982) suggests that the location of the new middle class in the non-productive sector marginalises it from the processes of decision-making at the economic and productive core of society. Hence new middle-class frustration at its own powerlessness is manifested in protest activity and involvement in NSMs. It is not clear, however, why members of the new middle class feel alienated when, by definition, they are usually fully employed in professional and administrative jobs (Eckersley 1989). Alternatively, McAdams (1987) argues that they have an interest in the expansion of government, not least because it provides so many of the professional and welfare jobs they hold. Yet this argument cannot support the view that middle-class involvement in environmentalism is an expression of class interest because the interests of the new class would hardly be served by green arguments for slower economic growth that might threaten future expansion of the non-productive service sector which employs so many of them. In short, there is no convincing argument why new middle-class concern for the environment should be in the material interests of that particular class. Martell (1994) observes that this concern may be 'class-based, but does not seem to be class-driven' (p. 130); there may be a disproportionate number of new middle-class environmentalists, but there is little evidence that occupational position determines environmental concern. Instead, it may be that the new middle classes hold attitudes and values that encourage their concern for the environment.

Environmentalism as postmaterialism?

Another explanation for the rise of green parties focuses on changes in the political culture and values of industrialised countries. Inglehart (1977, 1990) is the main exponent of the postmaterialist thesis. He claims that there has been a 'silent revolution' involving 'the basic value priorities of Western publics ... shifting from a Materialist emphasis toward a Postmaterialist one – from giving top priority to physical sustenance and safety toward heavier emphasis on belonging, self-expression and the quality of life' (Inglehart 1990: 66). This argument contains two core components: the scarcity hypothesis and the socialisation hypothesis. The *scarcity* hypothesis, which is closely modelled on Maslow's (1954) psychological theory of human motivation, claims that people place a higher priority on things that are in short supply. Inglehart argues that the post-war period brought an era of steady economic growth and unparalleled affluence which produced a generation of young people who took their economic well-being for granted. When the lower-order needs of economic and physical security are satisfied, people direct attention to higher-order 'quality of life', or postmaterial, needs, such as the environment. According to Inglehart, the ascendancy of postmaterial values does not arise from individuals actually changing their values, but through the *socialisation* of a new generation that lives its formative, pre-adult, years in a time of affluence. Inglehart initially developed this theory to account for the student unrest that swept across the western world in the late 1960s. Subsequently, it has been used to explain the dealignment of traditional partisan voting patterns, the involvement of this postmaterial generation in NSMs and, crucially, the emergence of green parties: 'The rise of the West German Greens . . . reflects both the emergence of a Postmaterialist constituency whose outlook is not captured by the existing political parties and the emergence of a growing pool of voters who are politicized but do not feel tied to established parties' (Inglehart 1990: 369).

Although Inglehart's theory has gained many adherents, it has also been subjected to a barrage of criticisms, particularly aimed at the two hypotheses underpinning the model, and the methodology used to measure postmaterialism (see Box 4.2).[2] The scarcity hypothesis assumes that the satisfaction of material needs encourages individuals to shift attention to postmaterial values. Yet the hierarchy of needs adopts a static definition of those material needs – a roof over our heads, food on our plates, money in our pockets, the protection of law and order – when, in the modern consumer society, with greater affluence and an ever increasing range of available goods, our appetite for more and more material goods may be insatiable. Our definition of basic needs is steadily broadening: a washing machine was a luxury item in the 1960s, but many would now consider it a basic item – along with the dishwasher, microwave and

---

4.2 Measuring postmaterialism

Inglehart's methodology for measuring postmaterialism asks people to select their two most important goals from four options:
1. Maintain order in the nation
2. Give people more say in the decisions of government
3. Fight rising prices
4. Protect freedom of speech

Anyone choosing the third and fourth options is defined as a postmaterialist and those choosing the first and third options are defined as materialists. All other combinations were placed in a 'mixed' category.

Inglehart (1990) has produced extensive comparative research across twenty-four countries to support his claim that Americans and Western European publics have become substantially more postmaterialist since 1970 and he predicts that this trend will continue. A 1993 European survey found that postmaterialists are still in a minority and,

almost everywhere, are outnumbered by materialists.

% classifed as	Germany	Britain	Italy	Spain
Postmaterialist	23	11	12	12
Mixed	56	63	62	57
Materialist	21	26	25	31

Bryson and Curtice (1998: 130).

Methodological concerns
(i) Is it possible to make confident categorisations of individual value priorities on the basis of such a narrow battery of items?
(ii) The four-item battery contains no environmental item. Even Inglehart's expanded, but rarely used, twelve-item battery contains just one explicitly environmental item: 'trying to make our cities and countryside more beautiful'. How helpful is such a limited measure in evaluating why people vote green?

mobile phone. In short, greater affluence may simply encourage further materialism rather than nurture postmaterial values.

Inglehart bases the socialisation hypothesis on the critical pre-adult years, and largely dismisses the impact of any adult economic insecurity on values. His prediction that the proportion of postmaterialists will continue to rise rather downplays the impact of widespread economic insecurity during the 1970s and 1980s on subsequent cohorts. If we put methodological objections aside and accept that postmaterialism has increased, can this change be explained by the scarcity and socialisation hypotheses? Rather than NSMs being a product of postmaterialism, value change may actually be rooted in the NSM milieu. Instead of better living standards generating postmaterialism, perhaps the growth of welfare-oriented jobs in education and public health has engendered value change (Martell 1994: 125)? On the more specific question of the environment, several commentators have argued that the key variable linked to increased concern about the environment is the experience of higher education, presumably because it helps people to process more information, enhances their job prospects and material security, and encourages a wider critical perspective (Offe 1985; Eckersley 1989). A further problem with the postmaterialist thesis is that 'if environmentalism is simply a question of values, then environmental conflict is a conflict without interests' (Andersen 1990: 104–5). Yet the opponents of environmentalism are not individuals who simply hold different values, such as a preference for economic growth; rather, they are usually economic actors (employers, farmers, trade unions) who perceive their material interests (profits, jobs) as directly threatened by green measures. Notwithstanding these criticisms of Inglehart, there is sufficient empirical evidence of a spread of postmaterial values to treat it seriously as at least partially explaining the emergence of environmentalism.

The next section assesses how far these three 'new politics' arguments can account for the rise of green parties.

CRITICAL QUESTION 1
Is the environment a postmaterial or material issue?

Green parties as new politics?

New social movement activity was certainly a catalyst for the development of green parties in some countries. The broad coalition of environmental and leftist groups that formed the anti-nuclear movements of the 1970s and 1980s was particularly conducive to green party formation in Germany, France, Luxembourg and Finland, and in Austria and Sweden green parties emerged from referendum campaigns against nuclear power (Rootes

1995b). 'Eco-pax' coalitions between the environmental and the peace movements were also important, especially in Germany. The radical principles of NSM activists left a strong imprint on some green parties, notably the German Greens, which informed their reluctance to work with mainstream parties, the preference for participatory, decentralised organisational structures and a willingness to use extra-parliamentary action to achieve their aims. Nevertheless, although undoubtedly influenced by the counter-cultural NSM milieu, green parties cannot be regarded as NSMs. Simply by contesting elections and operating within the political system, green parties set themselves clearly apart from the ideal-type NSM. Internal tensions over the extent to which green parties should engage with established political parties and institutions (see Chapter 5) are essentially about the *degree* of compromise, when the real compromise was the decision to form a party in the first place. It is revealing that NSMs, including environmental movements, have tended to treat green parties with some ambivalence. Indeed, the fact that several green parties, notably in the UK, Ireland, Sweden and throughout Eastern Europe, are not rooted in the NSM milieu suggests that environmental concern may be qualitatively different from NSM concerns such as gender, race or peace (none of which has, with the odd exception, spawned its own political party).

It is, however, clear that most European green parties do attract support overwhelmingly from new middle-class voters. Academic studies and opinion polls show conclusively that, compared to supporters of other parties, green voters are younger, better educated, less likely to attend church and more likely to hold public sector and/or white collar jobs (Müller-Rommel 1989, 1990; Richardson and Rootes 1995). A detailed picture emerges from Germany which, because of the success of Die Grünen, has been subjected to intensive analysis. Here, until the mid-1990s, the majority of green voters were under thirty-six even though only one-third of the total German electorate was in that age group (Poguntke 1993; Scharf 1994; Dalton and Bürklin 1996). Die Grünen has always drawn a disproportionately large share of support, around 50 per cent, from students and white-collar workers; conversely, it continues to attract relatively few older voters and blue-collar workers (Poguntke 1993; Dalton and Bürklin 1996; Gibowski 1999). Greens are well educated: about half of green voters have gained an *Abitur* – which qualifies an individual to enter university – compared to a national average of around a quarter (Poguntke 1993). The profiles of green electorates elsewhere look remarkably similar; for example, the green vote is similarly youthful in Austria (Lauber 1995; Williams 2000), Sweden (Bennulf 1995) and Finland (Arter 1995; Kontinnen 2000).

Green party activists have an even more distinctive socio-economic profile. A 1990 survey of the UK Green Party reported that the typical member 'is 41 . . . has a university degree in an arts or social science subject (but not engineering, business or law), is an owner-occupier, and

works as a "professional" in the public sector, most likely in education'
(Rüdig et al. 1991: 30). Similar profiles were found in surveys of Dutch
(Voerman 1995), Belgian (Kitschelt 1989) and German (ibid.; Poguntke
1993) activists.

Greens, therefore, do seem to be drawn disproportionately from the
so-called new middle class but, if Inglehart is right, they should also hold a
wide range of postmaterial values. Thus, rather than give priority to material issues such as economic well-being and physical security, greens
should display a greater concern for postmaterial 'quality of life' issues
such as peace, minority rights, civil liberties and, of course, environmental
protection. However, whilst levels of postmaterialism are high among
party activists – 94 per cent of German Green Party delegates (Poguntke
1993: 93) and 74 per cent of Dutch Green Left delegates (Lucardie et al.
1995: 100) – the relationship is weaker in the wider electorate. German
(Poguntke 1993: 58) and Dutch green voters do display a clear postmaterial
orientation, but elsewhere green voters hold a broad spread of both material and postmaterial concerns, with the environment as the one theme in
common (Jehlicka 1994). Typically, the evidence is suggestive rather than
conclusive. In Sweden, for example, green voters are slightly more postmaterialist than those voting for other parties, but the statistical association is no more than 'modest' (Bennulf 1995: 135). More broadly, several
surveys raise serious doubts about the existence of a direct link between
postmaterial values and environmental concern (Nas 1995; Bryson and
Curtice 1998).

These findings hint at a deeper problem with postmaterialist accounts
of environmental politics: is it accurate to define a wide range of ecological hazards as postmaterialist concerns (Nas 1995: 288; Rootes 1997:
320–1)? Many environmental concerns – the threat posed by nuclear
power, the links between air pollution and asthma, fears about the safety
of GM foods – could all reasonably be defined as materialist problems
because they affect personal security and health. As Beck (1992) has
argued, people are increasingly motivated by the growing perception that
we live in a 'risk society'. If so, perhaps the attachment to green politics is
partly prompted by old-fashioned materialist values (albeit in a new guise),
rather than, as Inglehart claims, the emergence of a new set of value priorities. Not least, this interpretation might explain why many 'materialists' vote for green parties.

On balance, 'new politics' arguments do help explain the rise of green
parties; in particular, there is a remarkable cross-national uniformity in
the socio-economic profile of green support. However, Inglehart's cultural
explanation of green politics as reflecting the emergence of postmaterialist values remains unproven. Indeed, the socio-economic profile of green
support suggests possible alternative explanations for the rise of green
parties. The large number of greens with higher education lends support
to Eckersley's (1989) claim that this variable may be critical. Also, while

most greens do have reasonable economic security (or the prospect of future security), they tend to be located on the margins of society. This is not to say, as some have argued (Alber 1989; Bürklin 1987), that greens are profoundly alienated from society, for they clearly are not; teachers and social workers may not always represent the dominant values in society, but neither are they outsiders. However, many greens are shielded from the productive private sector of the economy where growth and its materialist spin-offs are central considerations. Whether this detachment is deliberately chosen by people already concerned by environmental issues, or whether it reflects the experiences of working in specific occupations and sectors of the economy, is difficult to ascertain. However, it bodes well for the future prospects of the greens that they draw heavily for support on sectors of society – higher education, the service sector, health and welfare – that are expanding.

Conversely, there is some tentative evidence that the green vote is gradually getting older, or 'greying' (Rootes 1995b). Whereas 70.5 per cent of German green voters were under thirty-five in 1980, by 1994 it was 51 per cent and in 1998 it was just 41 per cent (Hoffman 1999: 143). Voters seem to have remained loyal to Die Grünen as they have got older, but the party is now less successful at recruiting first-time voters; so the centre of gravity of the party has shifted into the 35–45 age bracket. Rhodes (1995) reports a similar trend in Italy. Perhaps there is a cohort of green voters working its way through the system who joined the student protests in the late 1960s and provided the NSM activists during the following two decades. If so, it would be bad for the long-term prospects of green parties. However, as yet there is insufficient evidence to confirm that greying is a common trend. Indeed, there are several reasons why green parties might expect to remain popular with young voters. Voting green, particularly where the greens have not yet entered government, still represents a protest vote against the established parties and values, as the success of the Belgian Greens in the 1999 national election and the popularity of Ralph Nader in the 2000 US presidential election both showed. The increasing integration of environmental issues into the public domain, especially through the educational curriculum, should ensure that younger generations have a higher level of knowledge and understanding than older generations. Consequently, one speculative hypothesis is that, while older green supporters may be predominantly postmaterial in outlook, the new generation of younger voters may be less postmaterialist, but influenced by a specific concern about the environment.

To summarise, new politics arguments identifying structural and cultural trends can provide only broad-brush, macro-level explanations for the rise of green parties. They do not account for differences between countries. This weakness can be illustrated by Inglehart's (1990: 93) own data. He reports that in the mid-1980s the three European countries with the highest proportion of postmaterialists were the Netherlands (25 per cent),

West Germany (24 per cent) and Denmark (18 per cent). Yet green party development in these countries contrasts sharply: while Die Grünen has long been the leading light of the green movement, the Dutch Green Left only made a significant breakthrough in the late 1990s while the Danish greens are so weak that they do not even contest national elections. Furthermore, there was an identical number of postmaterialists (15 per cent) in both Belgium and the UK, but while the Belgian green parties have been very successful, the Green Party in Britain has a dismal electoral record. So, why have green parties developed earlier in some countries than in others, and why is their electoral performance so variable?

CRITICAL QUESTION 2

Is green politics a middle-class issue?

THE POLITICAL OPPORTUNITY STRUCTURE AND GREEN PARTY SUCCESS

The political opportunity structure (POS) is a useful framework for analysing green-party development because it looks beyond the broad macro variables that underpin the new politics thesis. The POS is concerned with the 'dimensions of the political environment which either encourage or discourage people from using collective action' (Tarrow 1994: 18).[3] Each writer tends to use a different combination of variables. The discussion here employs a model of the POS based on the work of Kitschelt (1986, 1988, 1990), who has used it to study green parties. His model incorporates the broad structural factors underpinning the new politics thesis, such as the development of modern welfare capitalism and contemporary economic prosperity, but draws particular attention to the institutional and political factors that might determine the openness of a political system to green parties. These include NSM activity, the form of electoral system, the nature of party competition and the existence of precipitating issues, such as the anti-nuclear protests, that may act as a catalyst for the emergence and development of a green party. The following short case studies of green party development in Germany, France and Britain focus on these critical institutional and political factors in the political opportunity structure that help account for variations in green party performance.

Germany[4]

Die Grünen has played a pioneering role in the development of the green movement. After entering parliament in 1983, it rapidly established itself in the German political system. Despite a blip in the 1990 post-unification election, when no Greens were returned in the former West Germany, by the mid-1990s the party had become a serious political power broker. After the 1998 federal election the Greens joined the Social Democrats (SPD) in a red–green government coalition.

Die Grünen was rooted in social movement activity. Leading elements included a long-lasting student movement, citizen action groups (protesting about issues such as housing shortages, high rents and pollution), the anti-nuclear power and women's movements. Many green activists were involved in the large peace movement, which campaigned against the siting of Pershing and Cruise missiles in Europe, and their 'eco-pax' agenda shaped the development of green ideology and practice. The acid rain issue was an important precipitating condition for the general increase in public concern about the environment in the early 1980s.

The electoral rules have generally proved very helpful to the Greens. German electoral law refunds campaign costs to any party gaining more than 0.5 per cent of the votes. Thus, from its early days the party was able to develop a national organisational structure without needing to attract rich sponsors. The Additional Member electoral system gives representation to every party receiving at least 5 per cent of the votes. This threshold was sufficiently low to be attainable, yet high enough to act as a force for unity for the disparate collection of green groups that mushroomed throughout West Germany in the late 1970s before forming Die Grünen in 1980. Progress was so rapid that the Greens gained twenty-seven MPs with 5.6 per cent of the vote in the 1983 federal election, matched by similar successes in sub-national government. Subsequently, the party's progress was hampered by internal factionalism but, after the shock of losing all its deputies in the 1990 federal election, the discipline brought by the electoral rules enabled the moderate 'Realist' (see Box 5.2) wing of the party to win control of the party, resulting in a range of organisational reforms, a more moderate programme and a merger with the East German Bundnis 90. The federal structure of the German political system provided several access points for the Greens, enabling the party to win seats in the *Länder* (states) which gave the party publicity and credibility when it first emerged in the early 1980s, and later acted as a laboratory for red–green coalitions with the SPD. European parliamentary elections have provided further electoral opportunities, with the Greens usually polling more strongly than in federal elections. The presence of a large and vocal group of Green MEPs in the European Parliament since 1984 has given the party another important political platform (Bomberg 1998a). Ironically, for a party that is uneasy with the idea of leadership and suspicious of charismatic personalities, the Greens have produced two of the most popular and well-known German politicians of recent times: Petra Kelly and Joschka Fischer.

The Greens have also benefited from the political vacuum on the left of the German party system. The leading party of the left, the SPD, shifted to the centre after a series of electoral defeats in the 1950s. As the dominant party in government between 1969 and 1982 it largely eschewed its socialist roots, to the despair of NSM activists. Consequently, in the absence of a communist party the Greens were able to fill the space to the left of the SPD by offering a new home for a sizeable constituency of disenfranchised leftists. Since unification, the Greens have struggled in the old East Germany where the PDS (the former Communist Party) has staked out the territory to the left of the SPD.

The actions of the German Green Party itself have also played an important role in its electoral success – its ideological development, internal party struggles – and now that it has crossed the threshold into government it will be judged on its performance in office (see Chapter 5).

Finally, there are also some peculiarly German features to the success of the Greens. Markovits and Gorski (1993) stress the 'Holocaust effect', which covers a number of sensitive issues which have contributed to the significance of student politics and pacifism in post-war Germany. Although this last factor perhaps makes the German Greens untypical of green parties everywhere, it is clear that institutional and political factors have played a critical role in the electoral performance of the party.

France[5]

Although an ecological candidate contested the presidential election as far back as 1974 and Les Verts won eight seats in the 1989 European parliamentary elections, it was not until 1997 that the first Greens were elected to the French national assembly. During the 1970s, especially after the right-wing government launched a huge nuclear power programme in 1974, French environmentalism was dominated by the nuclear issue. When the newly elected socialist President Mitterand broke his promise to place a moratorium on building new nuclear plants in 1981, environmental activists concluded that they needed a unified party to exercise greater influence in French politics. Consequently, Les Verts was formed in 1984 from the amalgamation of a disparate array of environmental and movement groups. After the success of Les Verts in the 1989 European election, a second green party, Génération Ecologie, was formed in 1990 by Brice Lalonde, a former environment minister in the Socialist government. Riding the crest of a green wave, both parties performed well in the 1992 regional elections, getting several hundred councillors elected. Subsequently, they put aside intense ideological and personal differences to form an Entente des Ecologistes to contest the 1993 legislative elections. Despite buoyant pre-election polls, the Greens failed to win any seats, although they secured a respectable combined 7.8 per cent share of the vote. The Entente immediately collapsed. Factionalism prompted further fragmentation into a dozen small rival groups by 1995 (Faucher 1998). Yet, from this low point, Les Verts was able to re-establish itself as the

dominant force in French green politics. In March 1997, it agreed an electoral pact with the Socialists that resulted in the election of eight greens
in the 1997 legislative elections, after which Les Verts joined the governing
coalition with its National Speaker, Dominique Voynet, holding the environment portfolio.

The political opportunity structure in France has constrained the development of green politics. Although the anti-nuclear movement contributed to the rise of ecological politics in the 1970s, it lost momentum in
the 1980s because of conflict within the anti-nuclear movement and the
obduracy of the socialist government on this issue. Subsequently, no big
ecological issues have provided a catalyst for the green parties.

France has a distinctive electoral system for legislative and presidential
elections based on two rounds of voting: if no candidate achieves 50 per cent
of the vote in the first round, all candidates gaining at least 12.5 per cent
can progress to the second round, which is a straight contest for the highest vote. This second-ballot system discriminates against minority parties
as it is difficult even to reach the 12.5 per cent threshold necessary to stay
in the contest, let alone win an individual seat. It was only due to the electoral pact, which saw Socialists and Greens standing down in favour of
each other in around 100 key seats to allow one candidate a clear run, that
Les Verts was eventually able to overcome this obstacle (Faucher 1998: 60).
Significantly, in European and regional elections, where proportional representation is used, ecological candidates have achieved more success.

French party politics has been dominated by a left–right cleavage, with
a political discourse centred on class politics. A four-party system consisting of two right-wing parties, the RPR and the UDF, and two left-wing
parties, the Socialists and the Communists, distributed the preferences of
the electorate across the political spectrum. It was very difficult for new
parties to enter the political arena and, unlike Germany, there was no
vacant political space on the left for the greens to colonise. Nevertheless,
greater instability characterised the political system during the 1980s: the
rise of the far-right National Front suggested growing disillusionment
with the established parties, particularly on the right. The greens benefited from the decline of the Communists and the shift rightwards by the
Socialist government, giving them the opportunity to recruit disillusioned
left-wing voters.

The electoral prospects of French green politics have been dominated by
factionalism. For example, there have always been strong differences of
opinion about whether Les Verts should eschew any dealings with other
political parties or try building links with the left. These differences have
been intensified by fierce personality clashes between leading activists,
notably Voynet, Lalonde and Antoine Waechter, a deep green. It was the
ascendancy of Voynet, a keen advocate of closer links with the left, together
with the departure of key fundamentalist factions that had strongly
opposed them, that eventually led Les Verts to discard its opposition to

coalitions. This move coincided with an opening up of the POS when the Socialist leader, Lionel Jospin, decided to forge a broad centre–left alliance to contest the 1997 election.

Subsequently, Les Verts became a minor player in the Socialist-led government. Its next aim is to overtake the Communists to become the second strongest force on the French left. Whilst its success in the 1999 European election and 2001 local elections suggested Les Verts might be capable of doing so, its prospects in the immediate future will be closely tied to the fortunes of the Socialists. In short, Les Verts is probably dependent on the red–green pact to maintain a presence in the national assembly. Moreover, the green movement itself remains fragmented and always likely to throw up new challenges to Les Verts.

Great Britain[6]

Although Britain boasted the first green party in Europe, the party has struggled to achieve any real electoral success. The party, originally called People, was formed in 1973 by members of a small discussion group in the Midlands to campaign on environmental issues (McCulloch 1992).[7] It did not emerge from a NSM milieu and has remained quite separate from the broader environmental movement, although it did work closely with the new wave of direct action protesters in the mid-1990s (see Chapter 6).

Small parties find it difficult to break into the British plurality electoral system in which most individual constituency contests are dominated by the major parties. Electors are unwilling to 'waste' their votes on a party with little chance of winning a seat. Only where a party can concentrate its vote geographically, as with the Welsh and Scottish nationalists, is there a chance of gaining representation, but the greens have been unable to establish any regional base. Even the remarkable 15 per cent of the vote the Green Party won in the 1989 European election was insufficient to get any MEPs elected. Small parties are penalised by the need to pay a £500 deposit for each candidate in a general election, returnable only if they poll 5 per cent of the vote, and there is no state funding for political parties. The Green Party was left with a huge bill after the loss of all 253 deposits in the 1992 general election, so it contested just 95 seats in 1997, again losing every deposit.

Party competition has left little space for the greens to make their own. The two major parties have traditionally proved adept at providing a sufficiently broad church to incorporate a wide range of ideological positions. In particular, the relatively inclusive attitude of the Labour Party towards dissident social movements has encouraged leading NSMs, such as the Campaign for Nuclear Disarmament, to pursue their aims by trying to persuade the Labour Party to change its policy, rather than by building links with what is widely seen as a narrow, single-issue, green party (Rüdig and Lowe 1986). The Green Party faces tough competition from the centrist

Liberal Democrats and the Scottish and Welsh nationalists, who have all made some attempt to appeal to the environmentalist vote, for the quarter of the electorate that does not support the two major parties. The significance of party competition is illustrated by the atypically strong green performance in the 1989 European election when the POS briefly opened up. The Greens were able to piggy-back on growing public interest in the environment at the time and benefit from a strong protest vote (in a second-order election) against the incumbent Conservative government and the weakness of the newly formed Liberal Democrats (Rootes 1995c). Subsequently, as the environment was crowded out by growing public concern about traditional material issues, such as the poll tax and the deepening recession, and the Liberal Democrats became established, this window of opportunity closed again.

The closure of the British electoral and party systems has meant that the focus of environmental politics in the UK has been on the large environmental lobby (see Chapter 6) rather than the Green Party. The pressure groups make a virtue of their non-partisan status, believing they will exercise most influence by lobbying politicians from all the three major parties. They see little to gain from working with a weak Green Party; indeed, any partisanship might close the doors to government and risk alienating its membership. This vicious circle of exclusion has further weakened the Green Party.

The closed POS helps explain why the Green Party has performed so feebly in every general election. In 1997 it attracted just 65,997 votes. Subsequently, its fortunes improved somewhat as the political opportunity structure was opened up a little by the Labour government's programme of constitutional reform. The introduction of proportional representation in the European Parliament and new sub-national elections saw two Green MEPs elected and one Green in the first Scottish Parliament in 1999, and three members of the first Greater London Assembly in 2000. In the June 2001 general election, although no Green MP was elected, the party did for the first time save ten deposits and attracted a record 166,487 votes – an average of 2.8 per cent in each seat contested, but still just 0.7 per cent overall.

Political opportunity structures

The German, French and British examples illustrate how the institutional and political context influences the openness of a national political opportunity structure to green parties. In this section, drawing on the three case studies and using illustrative examples from green party experiences elsewhere, the critical institutional and political factors are identified.

Electoral and institutional systems

The most striking institutional difference between the three countries appears to be the electoral system. The experience of Germany suggests that green parties do better in electoral systems based on some form of proportional representation (PR). This hypothesis is supported by the relative success of green parties in Belgium, Finland, the Netherlands, Sweden and Switzerland, which all have PR systems, and their failure in the UK and North America, where non-proportional systems are used. Yet in several countries with PR systems, such as Norway, Denmark, Italy, Spain and Greece, green parties have had little or no success. The weakness of green parties in Southern Europe may reflect lower levels of economic development and, consequently, the presence of fewer postmaterialists, but Norway and Denmark are affluent, developed economies with large numbers of postmaterialists. Moreover, the breakthrough of Les Verts in France shows that a plurality system is not an insuperable barrier, although this success was dependent on a pact with the Socialists. On balance, a facilitative electoral system is probably a necessary, but not a sufficient, condition for green party success.

Specific electoral rules may also shape green party development. The 5 per cent threshold in West Germany initially helped a fragmented environmental movement to unite into a single green party and, after the electoral defeat in 1990, contributed to the electorally driven internal transformation of the party. Similarly, after the Swedish Greens slipped below the 4 per cent threshold in 1991 to lose all its MPs, the party took a pragmatic turn, introducing organisational reforms and, during the successful 1994 election campaign, 'did everything to promote the image of a conventional party' (Bennulf 1995: 117). In Austria, the failure of the two small green parties to reach the 4 per cent threshold in 1983 led to their partial merger in 1986. By contrast, while it is initially easier for a green party to win seats in PR systems with no artificial threshold and multiple parties, as in the Netherlands and Italy (pre-electoral reform), the highly competitive nature of these systems may make it difficult to build on this toehold, although it did not hold back the Finnish Greens.

Green parties have performed comparatively well in European Parliament and sub-national elections, where low turnouts and widespread protest voting can often reward smaller parties. The breakthrough election of thirty-one Green MEPs in 1989 was particularly significant, providing a major boost to the green profile across Europe. After a minor reversal in 1994 (Carter 1994), the successful 1999 election produced thirty-eight Green MEPs who joined with assorted regionalists to make the Green Group the fourth largest political grouping in the European Parliament (Carter 1999) (see Table 4.2). The green message may be particularly apposite for elections to a supra-national forum because environmental problems are widely regarded as requiring international solutions. Conversely, sub-national elections, where the green message 'Think global, act local' may resonate with voters, have also provided an important base for several green parties.

Table 4.2 The green vote in the European elections, 1999

	MEPs	% vote
Austria (Die Grünen)	2	9.2
Belgium Agalev	2	7.5
Ecolo	3	8.4
Finland (Vihreä Liitto)	2	13.4
France (Les Verts)	9	9.7
Germany (Bündnis 90/Die Grünen)	7	6.4
Ireland (Comhaontas Glas)	2	6.7
Italy (Federazione dei Verdi)	2	1.8
Luxembourg (Dei Greng)	1	10.7
Netherlands (Groen Links)	4	11.9
Spain (Los Verdes)	0	1.4
Sweden (Miljopartiet de Grona)	2	9.5
United Kingdom (Green Party)	2	6.3

Note: No separate green party contested the election in Denmark, Greece or Portugal (where no Greens were elected on the joint Communist/Green list).

Green parties seem to have benefited from federal systems, as in Germany, Switzerland and, recently, Belgium, which offer more points of access, and hence more electoral opportunities, for a small party to gain visibility and representation. Yet federalism can be a double-edged sword. In Australia, whilst the Tasmanian Greens attracted considerable attention when they held the balance of power after the 1989 state elections and agreed a governing 'Accord' with the Labour Party (Haward and Larmour 1993), the federal system has also discouraged inter-state co-operation between green parties and impeded the formation of a national Australian green party, thereby hampering electoral progress.

Electoral and institutional systems are relatively fixed institutional features of the POS that have clearly influenced the development of green parties, but they do not explain the lack of success of small green parties in Norway, Denmark or, until recently, the Netherlands. All three countries have structural and institutional conditions that might be expected to have facilitated the development of green parties: a relatively large number of postmaterialists, electoral systems based on PR, an active NSM sector and a high level of environmental consciousness.

Political competition, in particular Kitschelt's (1988) concept of the 'left-libertarian' party, may explain this puzzle. Kitschelt identifies a handful of 'left-libertarian' parties in Europe which accept core elements of the socialist agenda – notably an egalitarian distribution of resources and a mistrust of the market – but, unlike the traditional left, reject authoritarian and bureaucratic statist solutions in favour of libertarian institutions that enhance autonomy and participatory democracy. Kitschelt identifies two groups of left-libertarian party: first, a small group of left-socialist parties that emerged in the late 1950s/early 1960s in several countries; second, the green parties.[8] He argues that the emergence of left-libertarian parties is shaped by political opportunities, specifically the long-term incumbency of social democratic parties in government. When in opposition social democratic parties appear more radical and offer hope to radical supporters, but once in power they shift rightwards, disappointing their left-wing supporters. Thus the first group of left-libertarian parties, including the Socialist People's Party in Denmark and in Norway, and the Pacifist Socialists in the Netherlands, flourished where social democratic parties had ruled in the 1950s. Later, when the environmental movement emerged, these existing left-libertarian parties provided a sympathetic platform for green concerns. Consequently, when small green parties were formed, such as De Groenen in the Netherlands, they found themselves crowded out because their 'natural' political space was already occupied and the loyalties of the green electorate committed elsewhere. In Sweden, the communist Left Party (VPK) became increasingly left-libertarian during the 1970s and now competes strongly with the Greens for the environmental vote. Kitschelt concludes that green parties have been less successful in countries where another left-libertarian party was already firmly established. By contrast, where social democratic parties dominated government throughout the 1970s, as in West Germany, Austria and Belgium, but there was no established left-libertarian party, green parties were able to colonise vacant political territory. The persuasiveness of the left-libertarian thesis is underlined by the keenness of many green parties to stress that they are not simply 'environmental' parties, but are pledged to a wider left-libertarian political programme. One qualification to Kitschelt's thesis is that left-libertarian parties have generally done less well in countries, such as France, Italy, Greece, Portugal and Spain, where a strong Communist Party provided stiff competition for the left-wing electorate (Markovits and Gorski 1993: 17). Indeed, the advance of the French Greens may have benefited from a corresponding decline in the electoral fortunes of the Communists. Nevertheless, Kitschelt's left-libertarian thesis is important for underlining the significance of political competition in green party development.

The POS framework shows how the interplay between structural, institutional and political factors can explain variations in green party performance between countries. Yet the strength of the POS is also its weakness. Although it provides a much fuller account of green party development – no credible account of green parties in Germany, France or the UK could omit discussion of these institutional and political dimensions – by throwing everything into the melting pot, the POS can end up looking like a catch-all typology: 'Used to explain so much, it may ultimately explain nothing at all' (Gamson and Meyer 1996: 275). The POS also conflates durable structural features of the political system, such as the electoral system, with contingent features, such as the state of party competition at a particular moment (Rootes 1995b). Whilst electoral systems rarely change (although the introduction of proportional representation in some

British elections and the shift towards a plurality system in Italy show that they are not set in stone), the configuration of party competition can alter dramatically, as illustrated by the rightward shift of the German SPD and the thawing of traditional left–right party alignments in France since the 1980s. As long as these limitations are acknowledged, the POS provides a useful framework for testing how different institutional variables have influenced the development of green parties.

CRITICAL QUESTION 3

Is party competition the critical factor determining the electoral success of green parties?

WHATEVER HAPPENED TO THE ENVIRONMENT?

One danger of using broad structural developments or institutional variables to explain the rise of green parties is that the underlying issue – the objective state of the environment – may be forgotten. Is it simply coincidence that the rise of green parties coincided with growing public knowledge and concern about the state of the environment? Perhaps there is no need for 'new politics' accounts to explain why people worry about the environment. Admittedly, there is no straightforward relationship between high levels of environmental consciousness and green party success. The environment has consistently ranked high as a salient political issue in Denmark, Norway and Greece, but none even has a national green party. Conversely, Belgian green parties have been very successful despite confronting the lowest level of environmental consciousness of any EU member state (Eurobarometer 1999). Nevertheless, there is also evidence that green parties have flourished as a direct response to specific environmental concerns. When the Swedish Greens achieved their electoral breakthrough in 1988, they attracted highest support in areas that had been most damaged by fall-out from the Chernobyl nuclear accident (Affigne 1990). The upsurge in green support in the 1989 European parliamentary election came on the back of growing concern about environmental issues such as acid rain, climate change and ozone depletion. The success of the Belgian green parties in the 1999 elections was linked to a scandal involving the contamination of the poultry and dairy food chain with highly poisonous dioxins (Hooghe and Rihoux 2000). Thus in searching for sophisticated political science explanations for the rise of green parties we should not sacrifice the most straightforward interpretation: that in the 'risk society' (Beck 1992) support for the greens may be driven by a specific concern about the objective state of the environment, as much as it is a reflection of post-material values.

CONCLUSION

No single argument adequately explains the rise of green parties. There is some support for the claim that green parties are an expression of a new politics. Several green parties originally sprang from a vibrant new social movement milieu, with anti-nuclear protest acting as a critical mobilising condition. Green parties do draw support disproportionately from the 'new middle class', but this statistical relationship does not tell us very much as the majority of this group supports other parties. Although Inglehart's cultural thesis that affluence and early socialisation have produced a population whose values are increasingly postmaterial has important theoretical and methodological weaknesses, there is considerable evidence that green parties do attract a relatively large share of postmaterial supporters. However, educational attainment, particularly possession of a higher degree in an arts or social science subject, may provide the strongest causal link with green support. Suggestions that the green constituency is gradually 'greying' could imply that there is a one-off generational cohort passing through the system, although the evidence is again inconclusive. The political opportunity structure helps to explain variation in green party performance by directing attention to institutional factors, such as the electoral system, and political competition. However, all of these explanations tend to understate the importance of the real cause of all the fuss: the state of the environment itself.

While the fortunes of individual green parties may wax and wane, the overall movement has established a reasonably secure and increasingly important role in several countries. The next challenge for those green parties that have entered government will be to retain electoral support when they are no longer a party of protest but tainted by involvement in the dirty business of government. Electoral success also raises broader questions about how green parties have adapted to the constraints of working within the parliamentary system and government, and how established parties have responded to the green challenge; we turn to these issues in the next chapter.

Further reading and websites

See Richardson and Rootes (1995) for a good, if dated, comparative study of the development of green parties in Europe. O'Neill (1997) provides a detailed comparative description of green party development. See Müller-Rommel (1998) on green electoral success. The journal *Environmental Politics* provides regular profile articles updating green party electoral performance in individual countries and see its 2002 special issue on green parties. For a general discussion of social movement theories, see Scott (1990) and della Porta and Diani (1999).

The website of the European Federation of Green Parties (*http://www.europeangreens.org/*) provides links to most national green parties, including Bündnis 90/Die Grünen (*http://www.gruene.de*), Les Verts (*http://www.verts.imaginet.fr*), and the Green Party of England & Wales (*http://www.greenparty.org.uk*). See also, New Zealand (*http://www.greens.org.nz/*), Australia (*http://www.greens.org.au/*), Canada (*http://green.ca/english/index.htm*) and USA (*http://www.greenparty.org/*). The global green parties' worldwide page provides links to green parties elsewhere (*http://www.greens.org/*).

Notes

1. The party is formally known as Bundis 90/Die Grünen since merging with the East German alliance of greens and civic action groups in 1993.
2. See Abramson and Inglehart (1995) for a combative rebuttal.
3. The concept of the 'political opportunity structure' has been widely used in the social movement literature (Tarrow 1994; Kriesi et al. 1995; McAdam et al. 1996), although Rootes (1998) notes that several writers now prefer to use 'political opportunity' as the use of 'structure' undervalues the importance of 'agency'.
4. Detailed accounts of the development of the German Greens include Frankland and Schoonmaker (1992), Poguntke (1993), Markovits and Gorski (1993), Scharf (1994), and Mayer and Ely (1998).
5. See Cole and Doherty (1995) and Faucher (1998) for a fuller account of the development of the French green movement.
6. See McCulloch (1992) and Rootes (1995c) for fuller accounts of the development of the Green Party.
7. The party name was changed to the Ecology Party in 1975 and to the Green Party in 1985. There are two green parties in the UK: one in England and Wales, another in Scotland.
8. Kitschelt categorises all green parties, apart from the Swiss, as left-libertarian. However, there are several small 'dark green' ecological parties, including the Dutch De Groenen and various French green factions, with a narrow ecological programme rather than a broader left-libertarian programme, which do not fit this label.

5

Party politics and the environment

Contents

KEY ISSUES

- What has been the impact of the environment on party politics?
- What is distinctive about green party organisation and strategy?
- Has electoral success and entry to government changed green parties?
- Does support for environmentalism follow partisan lines?
- What factors influence the greening of established parties?

Chapter 4 charted the electoral appearance of green parties across Europe. Yet the simple fact of green representation does not guarantee any influence in the parliamentary arena, particularly as Green MPs frequently advocate radical policies and behave in unconventional ways. Where green parties gain electoral success, their political influence will partly be determined by the way they adapt to the pressures of conventional party politics. However, as green parties remain of marginal importance in most countries, for the foreseeable future much will depend on how the political elites respond to the broad environmental challenge. This chapter assesses the impact of environmental issues on party politics by looking at both these issues. The first part examines the experience of green parties in parliament by analysing how they have dealt with the transition from pressure politics to parliamentary opposition and, recently, into government, focusing primarily on the evolution of Die Grünen in Germany. The second half of the chapter uses case studies of Germany, Britain and the USA to assess how far established parties have absorbed environmental ideas and to identify the main factors shaping their responsiveness to the environmental agenda.

GREEN PARTIES IN PARLIAMENT

The 'anti-party party' in theory

Green parties place great importance on *agency*: the means of achieving the sustainable society. Die Grünen is often regarded as the paradigm green party because its programme, organisation and electoral success have provided the dominant model for green parties elsewhere. The founders of Die Grünen set out to create a unique kind of party which its leading activist, Petra Kelly, called the 'anti-party party' (APP). The APP has two core elements: a party organisation based on grassroots democratic principles, and a rejection of coalitions with established parties.

First, the principle of grassroots democracy, or *Basisdemokratie*, one of the four pillars of green politics discussed in Chapter 3 (see Box 3.4), underpins the organisational structure of Die Grünen (Frankland and Schoonmaker 1992; Poguntke 1993), in sharp contrast to most major political parties. Large, well-established parties are usually hierarchical, centralised, bureaucratic and professional: typically, they have a small, dominant parliamentary elite, a powerful professionalised national party machine, a rigid rule-bound organisational structure, and a weak, inactive party membership.[1] These parties seem to confirm the 'iron law of oligarchy' identified by Robert Michels (1959) which stated that all political parties – even those with strong democratic principles – would always fall under the oligarchical control of a small ruling elite (see Box 5.1).[2]

The organisational structure of Die Grünen was designed to avoid these oligarchical tendencies by preventing the emergence of a separate ruling class of professional politicians who might resist the radical demands of the grassroots membership (see Frankland and Schoonmaker 1992; Poguntke 1993). Party officers were elected and unsalaried. Enforced job rotation prevented anyone from being re-elected immediately to the same post. No one could hold a party post and a parliamentary seat simultaneously. There was no single party leader; instead, a principle of collective leadership produced three elected national speakers to share power and responsibility in tandem with the federal party executive. Similar rules prevented a class of professional parliamentarians accumulating power over the wider party. A system of mid-term rotation required parliamentarians to step down halfway through their term of office in favour of a colleague lower on the party list. MPs had to live on an income equivalent to that of a skilled labourer, donating the remainder of their parliamentary salary to environmental causes. The 'imperative mandate' principle bound Green deputies to the resolutions or instructions of the party congress and the federal council. By restricting the trappings of office, the period of service, the accumulation of bureaucratic posts and the focus on individual leaders, the greens hoped to prevent the personalisation of politics. The grassroots membership was also vested with a range of powers to enable it to keep a tight rein on the activities of party 'leaders'. Party meetings at every level, including the federal executive and the parliamentary party, were normally open to all members, as well as non-members. The party also pursued an aggressive policy of positive gender discrimination, with equal male/female representation on candidate lists and committees (Frankland and Schoonmaker 1992: 106–9).

The second element of the APP model, the rejection of coalitions, was intended to prevent the institutionalisation of the party into the established system of parliamentary politics. Activists wanted the party to act as the parliamentary arm of the new social movements and remain committed to a role of fundamental opposition. The idea of the 'movement-party' was captured in Petra Kelly's 'two-leg' soccer metaphor: the party in parliament was to be the free-moving leg and the extra-parliamentary movement was the more important supporting leg. Coalitions were rejected

5.1 Michels's theory of oligarchy

'Who says organisation, says oligarchy.'

(Michels [1915] 1959: 401)

The Swiss political scientist Robert Michels outlined an 'iron law of oligarchy' stating that all political parties will inevitably turn into oligarchies dominated by a small group of leaders. Three main factors contribute to these oligarchical tendencies:

1. Direct democracy is difficult to operate once an organisation grows beyond a certain size in terms of members and task differentiation, so hierarchy is more 'efficient'.
2. Individual rank-and-file party members lack the abilities, resources or motivation to participate effectively in complex organisations, so management is left to professionals.
3. Party leaders develop their own interests, notably a love of power and enjoyment of regular contacts with the ruling elite, so the oligarchical elite runs the party in its own interests, not those of the rank-and-file members.

because they involved compromises that might lead the party to sacrifice its radical principles for short-term electoral or political gains. As Kelly observed, 'I am sometimes afraid that the greens will suddenly get 13 per cent in an election and turn into a power-hungry party. It would be better for us to stay at 6 or 7 per cent and remain uncompromising in our basic demands. Better to do that than have green ministers' (quoted in Markovits and Gorski 1993: 124).

Die Grünen therefore set out to be an alternative kind of party that would resist oligarchical tendencies and the corrupting temptations of the parliamentary arena. It was also hoped that this distinctive approach to politics might encourage a more participatory political culture throughout society.

The 'anti-party party' in practice

Can the APP concept 'work', and is it essential for green politics that it does? The organisational development of all political parties, including the greens, is shaped by competition from other parties (Duverger 1954; Epstein 1967). Upon entering the parliamentary arena, a green party will immediately be subjected to strong pressure – the *logic of electoral competition* (Kitschelt 1990) – to replace the APP model with the hierarchical, bureaucratic and professional structures characteristic of established parties. However, vote maximisation is not the only factor shaping party organisation; in particular, the strength of ideological convictions of the party membership – the *logic of constituency representation* – might provide a counterbalance (Panebianco 1988). Die Grünen has faced the constant dilemma of choosing between radical strategies of fundamental opposition to conventional party politics and moderate strategies of compromise intended to achieve incremental policy change. Whilst the radical strategy may keep core green voters content, it is less likely to attract broader support; by contrast, whereas the moderate strategy may win more votes, the resulting dilution of the APP model could antagonise the grassroots membership.

This strategic tension has underpinned the internal conflict between the Fundamentalists (*fundis*) and Realists (*realos*) that has plagued the party throughout its existence (see Box 5.2).[3] Broadly speaking, the two perspectives share the same long-term aim – to achieve an ecologically sustainable world – but disagree over the best means of getting there. Fundamentalists are firmly wedded to the APP and suspicious of the benefits of working within the parliamentary system. Realists believe that Greens can win significant incremental changes within the parliamentary system. Die Grünen was formed in 1980 when movement politics was in full swing and activists were hopeful that growing public awareness of the immediacy of the ecological crisis would provide the catalyst for radical change both inside and outside the parliamentary arena. However, during the 1980s, movement politics went into decline, leaving the Greens as the main voice of ecological concern. No longer was a transformation of the political system on the horizon; radical ambitions had to be tempered. The Greens had to come to terms with being a small party which regularly attracted no more than 10 per cent of the vote. From the mid-1980s, leading Realists, such as Joschka Fischer, argued that the 'anti-party' phase was over and that the Greens should become a normal party with a conventional organisational structure and prepared to form coalitions. The *fundi–realo* debate raged to and fro until, eventually, the shock of the 1990 electoral defeat shifted the balance of power decisively in favour of the Realists, whose position was cemented after the merger in 1993 with Bundnis '90, the moderate East German citizen alliance.

The Realists instigated a series of organisational reforms, including the abolition of the rotation principle and reform of the federal executive (see Box 5.3). Rotation was rejected as impractical in a parliamentary arena where effective politicians need time to develop a strong personal presence and master the complex procedures of the legislature. The principle of amateur politics also proved unworkable: how could the 27 unpaid, part-time members of the federal executive hold the parliamentary group of almost 200 salaried, full-time staff to account (Poguntke 1993: 153)? Other reforms included the introduction of salaries for members of the federal executive and, soon after forming the red–green government, a new Party Council was formed to improve co-ordination between national and state MPs and the wider party (Rihoux 2000).

As for the second plank of the APP model, Die Grünen had already dropped its complete rejection of coalitions by 1985 when, after much internal wrangling, the first coalition with the Social Democrats (SPD) was formed in Hesse. The principle of fundamental opposition proved unworkable because, once in the parliamentary arena, politicians have to decide whether to support specific policies and party groups are obliged to work alongside opponents. When a party holds the balance of power it is particularly difficult to refuse to deal with other parties by hiding behind political principles. The Hesse experiment was followed by red–green coalitions in several states (including a three-party coalition with the liberal FDP) and, eventually, in the federal government.

Despite these reforms, the Greens are still very different from other parties. Not least, the gender parity rules encouraging women to participate at

---

5.2 The *fundi–realo* division

The *fundi–realo* divide reflects a strategic dispute over the role of green parties in achieving change.

Fundamentalists
- ❑ oppose the centralisation of the party organisation;
- ❑ reject coalitions with other parties;
- ❑ regard the state as the agent of the capitalist system;
- ❑ are therefore sceptical about the possibility of achieving radical change by parliamentary means;
- ❑ emphasise the grassroots extra-parliamentary base of the party.

Realists
- ❑ believe radical changes require a piecemeal parliamentary strategy;
- ❑ insist that some participatory principles must be sacrificed if the party is to become a credible force in electoral and parliamentary politics;
- ❑ are willing to build coalitions with other parties.

In short, the Fundamentalists have defended the 'anti-party party' model, the Realists have sought to reform it.

Does the 'anti-party party' contain a paradox? Do rules that were designed to create a dynamic participatory democratic party have the unintended consequence of hampering internal democracy?

The grassroots democratic APP was built on the assumption that members will be highly motivated, committed and active participants. Rules that institutionalise democratic values in the party structure, such as rotation and the ban on joint office-holding, mean that there will be lots of jobs available throughout the party. Electoral success meant that Die Grünen needed more members to fill the growing number of party jobs, but membership remained small at around 46,000. The principle of openness that allows non-members access to party meetings reduces the incentive to join the party. Many who do join, particularly the busy professional middle classes, leave quite

quickly, put off by the demands of collective decision-making on their time: 'The more people taking part in meetings, and the more meetings strive for unanimity, the longer – and the more meetings – it takes to make any decision' (Goodin 1992: 140). The limited material incentives to take on party work – frequent enforced turnover of party positions, low pay for party officials, continuous supervision by the grassroots membership – may have the perverse anti-democratic effects of reducing the willingness of members to participate and driving people out of the party. Ironically, the APP model may have the unintended consequence of denying power to one kind of elite by creating the conditions for the emergence of a new type of elite: the minority of people with the time, resources and endurance to play an active role in the party.

all levels of the party provide a very visible difference: for example, twenty-seven of the forty-seven Green MPs elected in 1998 were women. So, too, does the refusal to have a single leader. Other significant differences include the incompatibility rule forbidding dual post holding in party and parliament, the continued openness of party meetings and the left-libertarian values of the green membership (Poguntke 1993). The party retains a distinctive elite-challenging internal culture. Although the *logic of electoral competition* has seen the Realists triumph and the Greens enter government, the party remains structurally and temperamentally distinct from other parties, suggesting that the *logic of constituency representation* retains some influence. No single oligarchical elite of professional politicians dominates the party, although it is too early to declare Michels redundant.

The unique features of each national political context mean that the experiences of green parties elsewhere have not been identical to Die Grünen, but they do have much in common. Most green parties initially adopted elements of the APP organisational model, notably the principle of collective leadership and rotation (Rihoux 2000). The Swedish Greens, for example, elect two spokespersons (one man, one woman) who are regularly rotated; office-holders are discouraged from holding more than one post at a time and are expected to relinquish it after two parliamentary terms; and the central powers of the party are devolved to four functional party committees (Bennulf 1995). Doherty (1992) reported that green parties in Britain, France and Italy have experienced internal conflicts along similar lines to the *fundi–realo* divide. Other green parties have also found it difficult to square the radical principles of the APP with the demands of electoral politics. It is significant that a particularly sharp electoral setback, such as the disappointment of the French green *entente* at not winning any seats in the 1993 national assembly election or the removal of all West German and Swedish Greens from parliament after failing to reach the minimum electoral thresholds in the early 1990s (see Chapter 4), has acted as a catalyst for internal party reform. The prospect of power has also seen lingering opposition to coalitions dissolve, as greens have entered national and sub-national government coalitions right across Europe. Overall, it seems that the *logic of electoral competition* has persuaded most green parties to shift towards a more professional, centralised party organisation and to display a willingness to work with established parties (Rihoux 2000).

CRITICAL QUESTION 1

Must electoral success inevitably undermine the 'anti-party party' model?

Greens in power

As green parties have strengthened their presence in national and sub-national assemblies and in the European Parliament, they have been forced to confront the challenges of governance. By the late 1990s, green politicians were at the heart of government making tough policy decisions: Joschka Fischer was the German foreign minister authorising German support for NATO bombing of Serbs; Dominique Voynet was the French environment minister charged with the task of solving traffic pollution and congestion in Paris; and Magda Aelvoet was the green health minister with the responsibility for clearing up Belgium's food-contamination scandal. As greens have entered government, the nature of debate within green parties has shifted from whether we *should* govern (Should we become a professional party? Should we enter parliament? Should we join a coalition?) to *how* we should govern (How do we cope with power? How do we exercise leadership? How do we handle the rank-and-file?). Many of the old strategic dilemmas remain, but they take different forms. Although it is too soon for clear answers to these questions, some early observations are possible.

The primary test of green governance will be its policy impact. Coalition agreements always involve compromises. The Greens' demands for specific policies and ministerial posts as the price for joining the coalition will, as long as they remain junior partners, only be partly met; moreover, they may also have to accept unpalatable policies imposed by their senior coalition partners. Nevertheless, initial coalition negotiations in all five countries where the Greens have entered government have proceeded reasonably smoothly, although subsequent relations have sometimes, as in Germany, proved more rocky.

After the 1998 federal election the SPD–Green coalition negotiations underlined the importance of a broad left-libertarian agenda, rather than an exclusive concern with environmental issues, to the German Greens. The final programme outlined three broad areas of agreement:

1. reduction of unemployment by up to 1 million over four years;
2. rapid withdrawal from use of nuclear power and a parallel programme of eco-tax reform;
3. reform of citizenship laws to reflect the multicultural reality of German society.

The Greens were allocated three ministerial portfolios (of a total of fourteen) in a well-balanced division of spoils. The SPD controlled all the key economic ministries, but the Greens received one major ministry – Joschka Fischer was appointed foreign minister – as well as the environment and health ministries, giving them a platform from which to introduce a range of ecological and social reforms. The package was smoothly negotiated and comfortably ratified at a party membership assembly . . . it was only later that the problems started!

Source: Lees (1999: 174).

After the 1998 German federal election, the coalition agreement between the SPD (298 seats) and the Greens (47 seats) incorporated three core themes: these combined traditional social democratic concerns (jobs) and a left-libertarian agenda (anti-nuclear, eco-taxes, citizenship) (see Box 5.4). Only one of the three planks of the agreement was explicitly 'environmental'; the reform of the citizenship laws was a left-libertarian demand supported by Greens and many Social Democrats alike, and the SPD emphasis on job creation was consistent with Green social justice concerns. The coalition agreement reflected the long-standing commitment of Die Grünen to a broad left-libertarian programme and its resistance to being labelled as a purely environmental party. Indeed, the Greens declared that they wanted to be judged at the next election primarily by their contribution to reducing unemployment (Rüdig and Franklin 2000). While the Greens have moderated their more radical left-libertarian demands, such as their ambivalence about the state's monopoly on legitimate force and membership of NATO, it is interesting that the programme contained elements of both old and new green politics. Similarly, in France, Les Verts secured the closure of the Superphenix nuclear power station when it joined the Jospin coalition government in 1997 (although it was subsequently reopened for experiments with nuclear recycling and further efforts to scale back nuclear power have been rebuffed by its coalition partners), but it was also strongly committed to the introduction of a maximum 35-hour working week and better opportunities for women (Szarka 1999). The traditional anti-nuclear roots of green politics also influenced green negotiators in Belgium, where the coalition parties agreed a relaxed forty-year phasing-out plan. However, the general support of governing green parties for eco-tax reform implies an acceptance of the discourse of ecological modernisation (see Chapter 8) and reflects a willingness to engage constructively with capitalist institutions and the market.

Whatever policies are agreed between the coalition parties, it will clearly be important for a green party to identify some tangible achievements from its period in government in order to keep members and supporters happy. Problems may arise if coalition governments are unable to deliver their handful of 'green' commitments. The difficulties encountered by the German red–green government in implementing its promise to shut down the nuclear power programme posed a severe early test of the stability of the coalition (see Box 7.8). Unforeseen events also require governments to make unpopular decisions. The Kosovo crisis led Joschka Fischer, as German foreign minister, to support military policies that flouted the long-standing green principle of pacifism. Good communication and relations between the national and parliamentary parties are essential because it is inevitable that radical rank-and-file members will be disappointed by some of the compromises required by involvement in the coalition government. Fischer, for example, was flour-bagged by green activists at a party conference in 1999 because of his stance on NATO bombing. Yet Die Grünen's collective leadership has made the management of relations with coalition partners difficult, especially as the leaders often speak from different scripts. Not surprisingly, there has been growing internal pressure from parliamentary leaders such as Fischer for a single party leader.

Finally, the impact of green government incumbency on electoral fortunes remains uncertain. To some extent, all parties to a coalition place their electoral prospects in the hands of others, as much will depend on the general perception of the government. Green parties are likely to confront a particular tension: whilst the wider public may judge them by their ability to be reliable and respectable coalition partners, much of their electoral support comes from an anti-establishment protest vote. It may be impossible to satisfy both constituencies (Rüdig and Franklin 2000). Thus the dismal performance of the German Greens in European and *Länder* elections during 1999/2000 was not helped by the early unpopularity of the coalition government and the highly visible internal Green Party wrangling over strategy and policy. Conversely, the Finnish Greens, after four years in a coalition government, were able to improve their share of the vote and representation in national and European elections, whilst Les Verts, after two years in government, performed strongly in the 1999 European election. One thing, however, is clear: the emergence of environmentalism and green parties has posed a serious challenge to established parties.

CRITICAL QUESTION 2

Does the entry of green parties into government demonstrate the superiority of the reformist strategy?

THE 'GREENING' OF ESTABLISHED PARTIES

Historically, party systems in industrialised liberal democracies have proved adept at incorporating new political interests and denuding them of their radicalism. Political parties have appropriated new issues or cleavages by developing their own policies to address the problems identified by an emerging interest, such as race or gender. Yet the rise of environmentalism poses distinctive problems for established parties because, as shown in Chapter 3, the technocentric–ecocentric divide cuts across the left–right cleavage that underpins most party systems (see Box 3.8). Established parties, both left and right, share a technocentric commitment to maximising economic growth and are often linked closely to producer interests: generally, labour and social democratic parties are supported by trade unions, while conservative and liberal parties are closer to business groups. Despite their obvious differences, these producer interests are broadly united in supporting expansionary economic policies and opposing environmental interests. Political elites may also be nervous about adopting unpopular 'green' policies such as stringent eco-taxes or restrictions on consumerist lifestyles.

Nevertheless, in recent years, most established parties have adopted a more positive attitude towards environmental protection. Whilst this adjustment often involves little more than the use of greener rhetoric, some parties have developed a much more progressive environmental programme. Such differences raise several questions. Why have some parties responded more positively than others? How significant is the presence of a successful green party in shaping the responsiveness of established parties? Do partisan divisions over the environment follow traditional left–right lines? Such questions are explored here by examining the party politicisation of the environment in two countries already examined in some detail and frequently compared in the green politics literature, Germany and Britain, as well as the USA, which is often ignored in this literature.[4] There is considerable variety amongst these three rich industrialised nations: Germany has a strong green party and a relatively open political opportunity structure (POS); Britain has a weak green party and a relatively closed POS; while the USA has no national green party but a pluralistic political system that is reasonably open to new challenges. Finally, it is worth noting that 'party politicisation' is used here in a broad sense to refer to a process whereby the environment ascends the political agenda to become electorally salient and the subject of party competition, so that parties increasingly embrace environmental concerns, strengthen their policy programmes and attack their opponents for the inadequacy of their environmental record.

Germany

Many observers agree that, since the early 1980s, 'Germany has moved from a position of reluctant environmentalism to one in which it is now legislating some of the most stringent pollution control standards in Europe and pressing internationally for more vigorous action on a wide range of issues' (Weale 1992: 71). Under a succession of conservative CDU-led governments, German political and economic elites gradually accepted the core tenets of ecological modernisation (see Chapter 8) and implemented numerous progressive environmental policies.[5] Germany is widely regarded as one of the '**pioneers**' of European environmental policy (Andersen and Liefferink 1997b). Not surprisingly, therefore, all established parties seem to have accepted the central place of environmental issues on the political agenda.

Most commentators agree that the success of Die Grünen played a key role in this party politicisation of the environment (Markovits and Gorski 1993: 271–3; Jahn 1997: 176–8). It is even claimed that 'As a direct consequence of the Greens' engagement, the Federal Republic developed the strictest environmental protection laws anywhere in the world' (Joppke and Markovits 1994: 235). Nevertheless, other factors also played a part. Widespread public concern about the environment, stimulated by the specific problems of acid rain and nuclear power, forced all parties to strengthen their environmental commitments. The state of political competition was critical in an electoral system in which coalition government is the norm and small parties can exercise considerable influence. The established parties initially regarded the Greens as outsiders, but as the party grew stronger and the electoral strength of the FDP (the traditional liberal coalition partner of the CDU and SPD) waned, the established parties had to treat Die Grünen as a prospective coalition partner.

Political competition rendered the SPD particularly vulnerable to the electoral challenge of Die Grünen. The entry of the Greens into parliament in 1983 coincided with the electoral defeat of the SPD, followed by years of internal crisis that produced a transformation in its attitude towards the environment. The SPD seemed to be the victim of a long-term dealignment of the electorate. It was losing support both to the Right, as a shift within the working class towards values of individual achievement rather than social solidarity seemed to favour the CDU, and to the Left, with the Greens attracting the progressive postmaterialist middle classes. The need to reconcile the aspirations and interests of these different constituencies posed a fundamental dilemma for the SPD: should it move rightwards to win back its core working-class supporters, or leftwards to counter the threat from the Greens? These tensions produced shifting SPD attitudes towards the green challenge, fluctuating from periods of co-operation and assimilation to bouts of non-co-operation and active opposition towards a party that many in the SPD regarded as irresponsible and unreliable.

By the mid-1990s, the SPD could no longer rule out the prospect of a red–green coalition because it offered the most realistic means of halting the long CDU tenure under Chancellor Kohl. Apart from this electoral imperative, several other factors encouraged the SPD to stop treating the Greens as maverick outsiders (Smith 1996: 66–7; Lees 1999: 184). The success of SPD–Green coalitions in the *Länder*, where it became clear that the two parties could 'do business', encouraged a more cooperative approach. There was also considerable policy convergence between the two parties. Internal opposition in the SPD to environmental protection, particularly

Pioneer states: Those countries, mostly in Northern Europe, that have taken the lead in developing progressive environmental policies and setting high standards of environmental protection.

from the trade unions, weakened and the party adopted a stronger post-materialist programme, including policies on nuclear power, gender equality and reform of citizenship laws (Markovits and Gorski 1993: 268–71; Lees 1999). Meanwhile, the ascendancy of the Realists heralded a considerable moderation of Green policies and institutional practices. Even the CDU no longer regarded Greens as a dangerous anti-democratic left-wing sect, illustrated by its support for a Green candidate for Vice-President of the Bundestag in 1994. By 1998, the party programmes of the SPD and the Greens shared so much common ground on key policies that a red–green coalition was clearly preferable to a SPD–CDU 'grand coalition' (Lees 1999). Thus political competition was crucial to the success of the Greens in compelling established German parties, especially the SPD, to treat environmental (and left-libertarian) issues more seriously.

However, it is important not to over-estimate the extent of party politicisation of the environment. Ironically, the Greens entered office just when their electoral fortunes seemed to be in decline and the saliency of the environmental issue had diminished. The tumultuous impact of German unification and the economic recession had pushed the environment down the political agenda in the early 1990s. The established parties became more circumspect about advocating progressive environmental policies; both the CDU and SPD moderated their support for eco-taxes, such as a carbon tax, because of the possible threat they posed to jobs (Strübin 1997). As Box 5.4 shows, the red–green coalition agreement contained only a limited number of 'environmental' policies. A critical question for the future of environmental politics in Germany will be whether the period of red–green government disrupts the dynamics of political competition. If the experiment succeeds, the Greens may be able to use their privileged position to push their left-libertarian agenda. If it fails, the SPD may look to the CDU or a resurgent FDP as an alternative coalition partner, a move that would inevitably result in the dilution of the government's environmental programme. In short, the party politicisation of the environment in Germany remains fragile and heavily dependent on wider political developments.

The analysis of party politicisation in Germany has focused on the impact of the Greens on other parties, but in the following sections on Britain and the USA, where green parties have had little influence, the focus shifts to a broader discussion of the extent to which major parties have embraced environmental concerns.

Britain

The party politicisation of the environment in Britain has been slow, uneven and incomplete. The environment has gradually moved up the policy agenda since the late 1980s, with parties most responsive at the mid-term stage of the electoral cycle when public concern tends to be highest and leaders are more receptive to environmentalists within their parties (Flynn and Lowe 1992). Typically, a flurry of policy documents from the three established parties, each outlining a slightly tougher environmental programme than before, has usually appeared roughly half-way between general elections. By the 1997 general election, the programmes of all three major parties included extensive environmental rhetoric: the Conservatives published a separate green manifesto; the Labour manifesto promised 'to put concern for the environment at the heart of policy-making'; whilst the Liberal Democrat programme prompted Friends of the Earth to describe it as 'the greenest manifesto ever from a mainstream party'. Yet the environment was again hardly mentioned during the election campaign (Carter 1997). This 'mid-termism' suggests that, rather than fully embrace the green challenge, electoral factors and party competition have shaped party responses.

The principal reason for the limited party politicisation of the environment is that it is not yet a salient issue at general elections. The British public is certainly worried about environmental issues: millions belong to environmental pressure groups (see Table 6.2) and surveys show that environmental concern is about average for EU member states (Eurobarometer 1999).[6] Yet environmental considerations are insignificant in determining voting preferences. Nor is the environment generally perceived in party political terms. None of the established parties is regarded as significantly greener than its rivals. The *logic of electoral competition* suggests that as long as the Green Party remains insignificant, there is little incentive for the established parties to raise the profile of the environment. The Liberal Democrat Party has made most effort to capitalise on the environmental deficiencies of its opponents, primarily because it is the party most vulnerable to political competition from the Greens, as illustrated by the 1989 European election when many supporters deserted to the Greens (Rootes 1995c). Significantly, after the Green Party successes in elections for the Scottish and European Parliaments and in the London mayoral elections during 1999–2000, the new Liberal Democrat leader, Charles Kennedy, stated explicitly that the party 'must not cede ground to the Greens' and has adopted a more upbeat approach to environmental issues. However, the Labour and Conservative Parties seem to have concluded that for electoral purposes it is sufficient to adopt a slightly greener rhetoric and appropriate some 'safe' environmental policies, whilst resisting a deeper politicisation of the issue.

There are also deeper political obstacles impeding the 'greening' of established parties. Successive Conservative governments between 1979 and 1992, enthused by Thatcherite deregulatory zeal, were reluctant environmentalists; willing to act when necessary, but prepared to ignore, delay and dilute their responses whenever possible. Nevertheless, Labour showed a marked reluctance to attack Conservative governments on this issue, even when Britain was popularly dubbed the 'Dirty Man of Europe' in 1990 for its poor pollution record.[7] Crucially, both parties remain committed to economic policies and spending plans that are dependent on continued economic growth. Powerful producer groups – industrialists, farmers, trade unions – exert strong external and internal pressure on both parties to resist the demands of the environmental lobby (Robinson 1992; Carter 1992). Thus Conservative ambivalence about the environment – notably its public support for the fuel protesters during 2000 and the pro-hunting lobby – rather blunted its criticisms of the Labour government's record after 1997. The process of 'greening' the Labour Party has encountered the additional suspicion of environmentalism as the preserve of the middle classes who, as Crosland (1971) put it, want to 'kick the ladder down behind them' by focusing on threats to the countryside while displaying an indifference to urban decay and the material needs of the working classes. Such prejudices have been fuelled by the lack of interest in environmental issues shown by Labour leaders in opposition: Kinnock, Smith and Blair (Carter 1997).

It was surprising, therefore, to find the Labour government striking a markedly upbeat attitude towards the environment in the immediate aftermath of its 1997 election victory. John Prescott, deputy prime minister, declared, for example, that Labour would be the 'greenest government' yet, Tony Blair led a heavyweight delegation to the UNGASS summit in New York and the new government launched numerous environmental initiatives. Several factors could explain this change of heart. Party strategists hoped that a greener image might retain the support of women and the young, whose votes were important in its landslide electoral victory. The presence of several longstanding environmentalists within the senior leadership ranks, such as Robin Cook and Chris Smith, made Labour more sympathetic to the environmental lobby. Declining trade union influence within the party has weakened the traditional objection that environmental policies damage jobs.[8] However, Labour failed to sustain this new-found enthusiasm for the environment. The positive response from many environmentalists towards some of the government's early achievements, notably Prescott's critical role at the Kyoto climate change negotiations and the ambitious climate change commitments, was soon tempered by the government's willingness to back down when faced with entrenched opposition to its environmental proposals. Thus a new climate change levy was diluted in the face of heavy business lobbying before it was even implemented in 2001 and Labour's plans for a sustainable transport policy were disrupted by fears of upsetting the powerful road lobby and a nation of car drivers. In short, the Labour government, like its Conservative predecessor and its German counterpart, found itself ducking those environmental measures that might threaten competitiveness, jobs or the government's popularity. The environment was again largely ignored during the 2001 general election. Labour was very downbeat, outlining few new proposals. The Conservatives' promise to cut fuel taxes and drop the climate change levy projected a distinctly anti-environmental image. Only the Liberal Democrats offered a radical environmental programme.

So, although the established parties have undoubtedly become considerably greener since the mid-1980s, their commitment is half-hearted and environmental politics remains non-partisan. Labour's refusal to counte-nance proportional representation in Westminster elections means that most environmental activists will continue to look to pressure groups as the most effective force for environmental change.

The USA

There are many similarities between environmental politics in the USA and Britain, notably the absence of a successful green party, the low elec-toral saliency of environmental issues and a large environmental lobby (see Tables 6.1, 6.2). Although public concern about the environment increased from the mid-1980s, only about 5–6 per cent of the electorate – the environmental 'issue public' – include environmental considerations in deciding which way to vote. Notwithstanding the performance of Ralph Nader in 2000, the environment has generally been insignificant during presidential campaigns (Tatalovich and Wattier 1999: 173–5) (see Box 5.5).

One important difference from the UK is that environmental politics has taken a more partisan form in the USA, with the Democratic Party

---

5.5 Ralph Nader in the 2000 presidential election

Ralph Nader, the well-respected veteran consumer campaigner, contested the 2000 presidential election on a Green Party ticket. After a half-hearted effort in 1996, when he attracted under 1 per cent of the vote, this time he ran a much more high-profile and impressive campaign. He did not fight on a narrow ecological ticket but offered a broader political programme headed by a fierce critique of excessive corporate power, and demands for campaign finance reform and 'clean government'. The liberal elements of his manifesto included support for affirmative action, tougher gun controls and an end to the death penalty. Thus Nader presented a programme similar in many respects to the left-libertarianism of European green parties.

In the months leading up to the election Nader drew strong poll ratings, regularly scoring up to 10 per cent in some key states, which prompted the Gore camp to launch a negative 'A vote for Nader is a vote for Bush' campaign aimed at persuading liberals and environmentalists that by failing to support the Democrat, Gore, they might put a Republican, Bush, in the White House. In the event, Nader received a respectable 2,878,157 votes (2.73 per cent), a good result for a third-party candidate, but it fell below the 5 per cent threshold needed to receive federal funding at the next election. Nader drew most support in the East and down the West Coast, where he secured an impressive 10 per cent share in Alaska and 418,000 votes (3.9 per cent) in California.

Impact

1. Did Nader deliver a Bush victory? In a limited sense, the answer is yes. In both Florida and New Hampshire the size of Nader's vote far exceeded Bush's majority over Gore. Most polls reported that in the absence of Nader his supporters would have voted 2:1 for Gore. Victory in either state would have made Gore president. However, putting aside the unsavoury procedures that delivered Florida to Bush, Democrats can surely have only themselves to blame for not winning the presidency after the economic prosperity of the Clinton years.

2. Nader's performance means that the Democrats can no longer be assured of the support of the environmental 'issue public' (and the assortment of independents, liberals and left-wingers who supported Nader). Rather like the SPD in Germany, the Democrats may be forced to choose between chasing the median voter in the political centre and offering a more radical left-libertarian programme to keep their radical supporters on board.

5.6 Environmental partisanship in the USA

The League of Conservation Voters, a bi-partisan pressure group, keeps an annual 'environmental scorecard' recording how Republicans and Democrats in the Senate and House of Representatives vote on key pieces of legislation affecting the environment.

Records show clearly that Democrats are much more likely to support environmental protection measures than are Republicans.

	Average % supporting environmental measures					
	House			Senate		
	1998	1999	2000	1998	1999	2000
Democrats	72	78	77	84	76	79
Republicans	24	16	17	12	13	12

Not surprisingly, given his positive record on the environment, the LCV endorsed the candidature of Al Gore as 'the only choice for environmentally concerned voters' in the 2000 presidential election.

Source: http://www.lcv.org/index.htm

embracing environmentalism to a greater extent than the Republicans. Democrat Party platforms at presidential elections since 1976 have 'generally called for increased spending, additional government action, and overall stronger efforts to control pollution', whilst the Republicans have favoured 'little or no government intervention . . . and a relaxation of current pollution control restrictions so that economic growth is not impeded' (Kamieniecki 1995: 152). Admittedly, research shows that successful presidential candidates have a poor record in implementing their (limited) environmental pledges (Tatalovich and Wattier 1999). Nevertheless, studies of roll-call voting on environmental bills in Congress and state legislatures since the 1970s show that Democrat representatives are more likely to support tougher environmental measures than their Republican counterparts (Kamieniecki 1995: 156), with recent figures (see Box 5.6) showing the gap between the two parties widening.[9]

Partisan differences were probably sharpest during the Reagan presidency (1981–8) when the government enthusiastically pursued environmental deregulation through a combination of savage budgetary cutbacks and ideologically committed presidential appointees to key agency posts, including the Environmental Protection Agency (Kraft and Vig 1999: 17–18). Hostilities were renewed after the 1994 congressional elections, when the Republican 'Contract with America' manifesto identified environmental regulations as a prime target for its conservative 'revolution', leading to further budget cuts and deregulation. Between these two periods, President Bush (1989–92), after declaring initially that he would be an 'environmental president', had briefly tried to strengthen the Republicans' green credentials (Francis 1994). Yet, with the exception of the 1990 Clean Air Act, few new environmental initiatives were forthcoming. Moreover, Bush supported further deregulation, refused to sign the Earth Summit biodiversity convention and eventually resorted to condemning environmentalists as extremists who threatened American jobs. By contrast, Clinton, with the enthusiastic environmentalist Al Gore[10] as his running mate, contested the 1992 election on a pro-environment platform. Although it was not a major issue, Clinton again took a relatively strong environmental stance in his 1996 re-election campaign, as did the Democratic Party in the 1998 congressional elections (Bosso 1999: 67) and Al Gore in his unsuccessful bid to become president in 2000.

Why, given the limited saliency of environmental issues, have the Democrats proved greener than the Republicans? Institutional factors, notably the 'winner takes all' electoral system which characterises every level of the federal structure, make it extremely difficult for small (poorly funded) parties to gain electoral success. However, the federal system and the weak political parties provide multiple opportunities for interest groups to lobby representatives in the Senate, House and state legislatures, and to influence the relatively pluralistic policy process. As in the UK, rather than attempting to build a green party, environmentalists have focused on influencing the established parties. In particular, they have concentrated on the Democrats, who are generally seen as less dependent on the support of business interests and more sympathetic to environmental causes. Indeed, environmental groups have become a leading part of the Democratic coalition; in some districts, particularly in the western states, the endorsement of key environmental groups and activists can play a critical role in securing the Democratic Party nomination. This partial incorporation of environmental groups into the Democrat Party peaked in the second half of the 1980s when Reagan's attacks on environmental regulations coincided with escalating public concern about the environment. One reason for the less enthusiastic, even hostile, response of the Republicans may be their greater dependence on the financial backing of large corporations and polluting firms which have been most critical of the burden imposed by environmental regulations (Kamieniecki 1995: 164). It certainly appears that the huge financial contributions by the major energy producers to the Republican presidential campaign in 2000 encouraged the newly elected President Bush to waive a range of environmental regulations and to renounce the Kyoto Protocol.

Although the relative greenness of the Democratic Party presents American voters with a clearer choice than their British counterparts, the significance of this partisan cue should not be exaggerated. Most American voters, in fact, do not view the environment in strong partisan terms: over half of voters detect no difference between the two parties (Kamieniecki 1995: 163). The weakness of American parties undoubtedly dilutes the partisan cues communicated to the electorate. So, too, do the geographical and ideological differences encompassed by the loose coalitions that make up the Democrat and Republican Parties.[11] For example, there is little difference in congressional roll-call voting patterns for environmental legislation between Democrats and Republicans in the East (where Republicans are relatively moderate and liberal) or in state legislatures in the Deep South (where Democrats are very conservative) (ibid.: 158).[12] The Democrats have also found it easier to be greener in opposition than in power. Clinton, despite benefiting from Democratic majorities in both Houses between 1992 and 1994, found it difficult to give priority to environmental interests above other members of the Democratic coalition, such as African-Americans or trade unions. Ironically, after 1994, when confronted by a hostile Republican majority Congress that effectively blocked his efforts in all these areas, he was more willing to speak out – almost as a voice of opposition – against its anti-environmental measures.

Where partisan differences do matter is in attracting the small environmental issue public to the Democrat banner. These core environmentalists have traditionally been loyal and committed Democrats: they are much more likely to identify with and vote for that party (Tatalovich and Wattier 1999: 176–7). In the 1992 presidential election, for example, this group voted for Clinton over Bush by a ratio of more than 5:1 (Vig 1997). In short, they are a highly partisan subgroup compared to the electorate at large. Significantly, they seem to prefer the Democrats primarily as a reaction to the anti-environmentalism of the Republicans, rather than from a positive enthusiasm for or confidence in the Democrats. Before Nader's intervention in 2000, the implication was that as long as the Democrats remained *relatively* greener than the Republicans they would keep the loyalty of the environmental issue public, without having to adopt a radical programme that might alienate the wider Democrat constituency. Clinton's predilection for making grand symbolic gestures in favour of environmental protection, such as his support for the Kyoto Protocol (which he knew the Senate would reject), suggests that this was his strategy. However, Nader's success in drawing the support of part of this environmental issue public may force the Democrats to adopt a more radical environmental agenda in the future.

In the USA, as in the UK, the environment is not yet an electorally salient issue. The major political parties have only partially embraced the environmental challenge and, despite the relative greenness of the Democrats, most Americans still do not perceive the environment in partisan terms. The bottom line for environmental politics in the USA is that on several key issues, notably climate change, the opposition to environmental measures (especially increased fuel taxes) is so strong that both parties are wary about taking a potentially unpopular green stance.

CRITICAL QUESTION 3

Will the 'success' of the Nader green ticket in the 2000 presidential contest raise the political profile of environmental issues in the USA?

EXPLAINING PARTY POLITICISATION

This section draws a number of conclusions from the case studies about the nature and extent of the party politicisation of the environment.

First, there has been a limited party politicisation of the environment, particularly since the mid-1980s, in all three countries. The environment is now established on the political agenda and no party can afford to ignore it. A major factor driving this process everywhere has been the strength of public concern about environmental problems (Eurobarometer 1999; Dunlap 1995). Fluctuations in the level and intensity of public opinion help explain variation in the enthusiasm shown by parties for environmental issues. Broadly speaking, people are most agitated about the environment during periods of economic prosperity and least interested when economic recession draws attention back to materialist issues. Thus the upsurge of interest in the mid/late 1980s, fuelled by growing knowledge about global problems and accentuated by precipitating events, such as the Chernobyl and *Exxon Valdez* accidents, undoubtedly contributed to the greening of German, British and American political parties during this period. Elsewhere, the intensity of public concern seems to be strongest in Scandinavia, where several polls have suggested that at least a third of citizens believe environmental problems should get a higher priority than (not just equal with) economic growth (Aardal 1990; Eurobarometer 1995; Sairinen 1996). This finding may reflect higher numbers of postmaterialists amongst those populations, or a specific sensitivity to environmental issues. Either way, this deeper concern helps explain why established parties in Scandinavia have generally developed greener platforms than elsewhere (Lester and Loftsson 1993).

Secondly, nevertheless, the environment has only rarely been an issue of genuine electoral salience.[13] Typically, fewer than 10 per cent of voters – around 5 per cent in the USA and UK – regard it as one of the most important issues in national elections. Politicians are more likely to talk about the environment between elections – in party documents, or in the US president's 'State of the Union' speech (Tatalovich and Wattier 1999) – than in election campaigns, where it tends to disappear. This low saliency undoubtedly sets limits on the commitment of established parties to environmentalism.

Thirdly, the presence of a successful green party in Germany certainly acted as a catalyst for a broader politicisation of the environment, whereas the absence of one in the UK and USA helps explain the lower intensity of environmental politics in these countries. Nevertheless, a flourishing green party does not guarantee a positive response from established parties. In Belgium, despite the presence of two electorally successful green parties, the main parties remained locked into a left–right materialist discourse and made few concessions to environmentalism (Kitschelt 1994: 190). It is too early to say whether the breakdown of these frozen party cleavages in the late 1990s, which allowed the Greens to join the government coalition, will prompt a wider politicisation of environmental issues in Belgium. In Switzerland, Austria and Sweden, intense political competition in multi-party systems prompted established parties to develop comprehensive environment programmes before green parties gained electoral success, thereby preventing them from assuming a monopoly over environmental concern. The foundation of the Dutch Green Left in 1990 post-dated the wider greening of established parties which had stymied the progress of the small green party, De Groenen (Lucardie 1997: 187–8). Similarly, established parties in Norway and Denmark adopted progressive environmental platforms without any prompting from a green party, in the process nipping in the bud the prospects of the nascent green parties (Lester and Loftsson 1993). It seems that the significance of green parties will be closely linked to the state of political competition in a particular country.

Fourthly, following on from the previous point, Rohrschneider (1993) argues that the policy responses of the major 'Old Left' parties, mediated by electoral laws, is critical in shaping the way environmental orientations affect the partisanship of voters in each country. Where environmental cleavages mirror the traditional left–right dimension so that left-wing voters display stronger support for green issues than those on the right, environmentalism can pose a particularly strong threat to 'Old Left' parties. The vacillation of the German SPD between centrist and leftist strategies is just one example of an established leftist party threatened by the emergence of a green party. The Austrian and Danish Social Democrats have attempted to counter the threat from green or left-libertarian parties by adopting stronger environmental programmes. In the Netherlands, the social democratic PvdA was initially responsive to environmental demands but, subsequently, particularly after it joined a coalition government in 1989, it diluted its programme, creating political space for the moderately ecological Green Left to emerge.

However, the environmental cleavage does not always mirror the left–right divide. In the UK, environmentalism transcends party lines; even the active environmental lobby remains fiercely non-partisan. The absence of an effective green party makes the electorate less likely to link environmental issues with a wider left-libertarian programme. In a political system dominated by two broad church parties, both adept at absorbing factions and dissident opinion, the 'Old Left' Labour Party has remained relatively unresponsive to environmentalism. US party politics is not structured along clear left–right lines, and there is no equivalent 'Old Left' party, although the two-party system and the absence of a green party have probably contributed to the low salience of environmental issues. By contrast, in multi-party Norway and Sweden (Lester and Loftsson 1993) and Switzerland (Church 1995), social democrat, centrist and liberal parties have all competed equally vigorously for environmental votes; consequently, environmental issues are high on the agenda, but conflicts do not follow clear left–right lines.

To sum up, these conclusions suggest that key institutional features of the political opportunity structure in each country will shape the nature of environmental politics. In Germany, the openness of the POS contributed to a sharp politicisation of the environment during the 1980s, whereas the relatively closed POS in the UK has enabled the major parties to get by with a slightly greener rhetoric and some limited environmental initiatives. The POS in the USA has been sufficiently open for pressure to be placed on the Democrats to take a more partisan stance on the environment, but the low salience of the environment has placed firm limits on the overall response of the two major parties to environmentalism.

CRITICAL QUESTION 4

To what extent does the success of environmentalism depend on the 'greening' of established political parties?

CONCLUSION

As green parties move into government, it is appropriate to assess their impact on the conduct of party politics and, more broadly, to assess whether the rise of environmentalism has contributed to the emergence of a new politics.

Green parties remain distinctly different, both formally and culturally, from other parties; in particular, green parties have successfully resisted appointing a single leader. However, the 'normalisation' of most green parties, as illustrated by Die Grünen, has seen them moderate the anti-party model in order to gain (and retain) electoral success and influence policy. The willingness of green parties to join governing coalitions suggests that they have been incorporated and deradicalised by the existing political system. Not surprisingly, the APP model has had little discernible effect on the way other parties conduct themselves, apart from adding to the general pressure to improve the representation of women throughout party organisation.

More broadly, the environment still lacks electoral saliency and political discourse is dominated by materialist issues, such as the state of the economy, unemployment, inflation and taxation. Green electoral success has helped disrupt traditional party alignments in several countries. A strong green party presence can push the environment up the political agenda, forcing established parties to respond to this new agenda. Environmental politics is no longer – if it ever was – the exclusive preserve of green parties. Even where green parties are weak, as in the UK and USA, other parties often claim to be the 'true' green party. Established parties have adopted a greener rhetoric and promised countless new environmental initiatives, although this has led to the appropriation and deradicalising of parts of the environmental agenda. Consequently, it is vital that green parties, especially as they enter government, do not allow their broader role as agitators and protectors of a green conscience to be sacrificed on the altar of electoral success. The wider environmental movement outside Parliament is struggling with a similar dilemma between radicalism and reformism, which we turn to in the next chapter.

Further reading and websites (see Chapter 4 for green party websites)

Analysis of the development of the German Greens can be found in Frankland and Schoonmaker (1992), Poguntke (1993) and Markovits and Gorski (1993). Bomberg (1998a) provides a good assessment of the role of the Greens in the EU. Look out for a rush of studies evaluating the experience of the Greens in government (e.g. Rüdig and Franklin 2000; Rihoux 2000). There is surprisingly little analysis of the greening of established parties, but for Germany see Jahn (1997); Lees (1999); for Britain Robinson (1992); Carter (1992, 1997); the Netherlands Lucardie (1997); and the USA Tatalovich and Wattier (1999).

Germany

CDU (*http://www.cdu.de/*)
SPD (*http://www.spd.de/*)
Free Democratic Party (FDP) (*http://www.fdp.de/portal/index.phtml*)
Christian Social Union (CSU) (*http://www.csu.de/*)
Party of Democratic Socialism (PDS) (*http://www.pds-online.de/*)

UK

Labour Party (*http://www.labour.org.uk/*)
Conservative Party (*http://www.conservative-party.org.uk/*),
Liberal Democrat (*http://www.libdems.org.uk/*)
Scottish National Party (*http://www.snp.org.uk/*)
Plaid Cymru (Welsh Nationalists) (*http://www.plaidcymru.org/*)

USA

Democratic Party (*http://www.democrats.org/index.html*)
Republican Party (*http://www.rnc.org/*)

Notes

1. This oligarchical characterisation does not fit smaller established parties, such as the Liberal Democrats in Britain and the FDP in Germany. Indeed, several types of political party can be identified, including cadre, mass membership, catch-all and cartel parties (Ware 1996).
2. The Greens were greatly influenced by the earlier 'oligarchisation' of the socialist German movement-party, the SPD. See Beetham (1977) and Kitschelt (1989) for a detailed critique of the 'iron law of oligarchy'.

3. There have also been several other factions, such as ecosocialists, within the German Greens. See Doherty (1992) and Markovits and Gorski (1993) for a discussion of the *fundi–realo* debate.

4. No attempt is made here to judge which of these countries has the best environmental policies.

5. For an analysis of German environmental policy, see Pehle and Jansen (1998).

6. Dalton and Rohrschneider (1998), however, report that levels of concern about the environment are lower in Britain than in other EU countries.

7. The Conservative record on the environment was not all bad; in particular, there were some positive achievements when John Gummer was Secretary of State for the Environment (1992–7), including the creation of a new Environment Agency. See McCormick (1991) for a readable account of British environmental policy during the Thatcher years; Carter and Lowe (1998) take the story up to the end of Conservative rule; and Jordan (2000) and Young (2000) provide early assessments of Labour's record.

8. A donation of £1 million from the Political Animal Lobby – because of Labour's commitment to a free vote in Parliament on a bill to ban hunting – symbolised the declining significance of trade union control of the party purse strings.

9. See Soden (1999), Vig and Kraft (1999a) and Lester (1995) for a broad analysis of US environmental policy.

10. Al Gore had written a best-selling book, *Earth in the Balance*, which argued for environmental protection to be given high priority.

11. See LCV environmental scorecards for details of how voting records vary within as well as across party lines (Box 5.6).

12. When the League of Conservation Volunteers endorses 'pro-environment' candidates at elections, its list always includes some Republicans; for example, fifteen of the ninety-four candidates it endorsed in the 1998 congressional elections were Republicans.

13. One exception was the 1989 Dutch general election, when 45 per cent of voters regarded the environment as the most important issue; indeed, the election itself was prompted by the collapse of the coalition government over disagreement about an environmentally inspired proposal to abolish tax deductions for travel expenses (Lucardie 1997: 185).

6

Environmental groups

Contents

KEY ISSUES

- How powerful is the contemporary environmental movement?
- In what ways – size, organisation, strategy, tactics – do groups differ?
- How do groups exert influence? How has this changed over time?
- Why has there been a resurgence of grassroots activism?
- What impact have environmental groups had?

Environmental pressure groups (EPGs) are probably the most visible expression of contemporary environmental concern. The publicity-seeking stunts and daring deeds of the direct action protesters, whether tiny Greenpeace dinghies bobbing on the waves alongside ocean whalers or anti-road protesters perched at the top of trees, have attracted enormous public attention. Most pressure-group activity, however, involves rather more mundane conventional political activities such as lobbying and education. The rapid growth of the environmental movement since the mid-1980s has provided the resources for some groups to become highly professional organisations and to win regular access to policy elites. There is little doubt that environmental groups have been the most effective force for progressive environmental change, particularly in those countries such as the USA and UK where there is no successful green party and established parties have been largely unresponsive to environmental problems. Nevertheless, this process of institutionalisation has involved compromises that have blunted the radical edge of large groups such as Friends of the Earth and Greenpeace, and contributed to the resurgence of grassroots environmental groups, including the UK anti-roads protesters and the US environmental justice movement. The environmental movement now stands at a crossroads: should it maintain the reformist insider strategy of pressure politics, or should it pursue a radical outsider strategy of confrontational protest politics?

In this chapter, the development and achievements of the environmental movement are examined. The opening section provides an audit of environmental groups and outlines a typology that will be used to help make sense of this large and diverse movement. The following sections explore the dynamic tension between the *mainstream* environmental lobby and the less formally organised *grassroots* sector as a means of examining some central questions of green agency.[1] The main focus is on the strategic dilemmas facing any environmental group: should it adopt a professional or participatory organisational structure, and should it use conventional or disruptive forms of pressure? The next section considers whether the environmental movement represents the emergence of a new civil society. The final section offers a tentative evaluation of the impact of environmental groups. One theme running through the chapter is the extent to which the environmental movement represents a manifestation of the new politics.

THE ENVIRONMENTAL MOVEMENT: AN AUDIT

The environmental movement, if judged simply by its sheer size and the scale of its activity, has clearly become a significant force in most industrialised countries. The USA boasts at least 150 national environmental organisations, 12,000 grassroots groups and an estimated 14 million members in the USA (Sale 1993). There are around 200 national organisations and between 4 and 5 million members in the UK (Rootes and Miller 2000; Rawcliffe 1998) and about 900 organisations and 3.5 million members in Germany (Blühdorn 1995). The Dutch have the highest membership per capita with 3.7 million members out of a population of 16 million. Put differently, one survey found that 7 per cent of German, 8 per cent of British, 5 per cent of French, 4 per cent of Spanish, 20 per cent of Dutch and 16 per cent of Danish adults claimed to be members of an environmental organisation (Eurobarometer 1992).

Two distinct waves of pressure-group mobilisation can be identified in most industrialised nations (Lowe and Goyder 1983; Dunlap and Mertig 1992a; Dalton 1994; Brand 1999).[2] The first wave, from the late nineteenth century to the 1950s, saw the emergence of the conservation movement with its focus on wildlife protection and the preservation of natural resources (see Box 2.6). Many major conservation groups today, including the Sierra Club and the National Audubon Society in the USA, the National Trust and the Royal Society for the Protection of Birds (RSPB) in the UK, and the Naturschutzbund Deutschland (NABU) and the BUND in Germany, had their roots in this period. The founding in 1961 of the World Wildlife Fund (WWF) (now World Wide Fund for Nature), a conservationist organisation but international in form and outlook, represented a bridge to a new type of international organisation. The second wave was a manifestation of 1960s modern environmentalism which heralded an explosion in the number and size of groups. Reflecting the international nature of modern environmentalism, new groups such as Friends of the Earth (FoE) and Greenpeace rapidly became international organisations with national affiliates in many countries. They shared with new national groups, such

Table 6.1 Membership of selected US environmental groups (000s)					
	1970	1980	1990	1995	1998
Sierra Club (1892)	113	181	630	570	555
National Audubon Society (1905)	148	400	600	570	575
National Parks and Conservation Assoc. (1919)	45	31	100	450	500
Izaak Walton League (1922)	54	52	50	54	50
Wilderness Society (1935)	54	45	350	310	350
National Wildlife Federation (1936)	540	818	997	1,800	4,000
Defenders of Wildlife (1947)	13	50	80	122	243
Nature Conservancy (1951)	22	n.a	600	806	901
WWF (1961)	n.a	n.a	400	800	1,200
Environmental Defense Fund (1967)	11	46	200	300	300
Friends of the Earth (1969)	6	n.a	9	35	12
Natural Resources Defense Council (1970)	n.a	40	150	185	400
Greenpeace USA (1972)	n.a	n.a	2,350	1,600	350

Source: Bosso (1999: 64).

Table 6.2 Membership of selected UK environmental organisations (000s)

	1971	1981	1991	1995	1998
National Trust[1]	278	1,046	2,152	2,293	2,557
Royal Society for the Protection of Birds	98	441	852	890	1,012
Wildlife Trusts[2]	64	142	233	260	320
WWF	12	60	227	219	240
Greenpeace		30	312	279	194
Friends of the Earth[1]	1	18	111	110	114
Council for the Protection of Rural England	21	29	45	45	47

Notes

[1] Data are for England, Wales and Northern Ireland only.

[2] Includes the Royal Society for Nature Conservation.

Source: Office for National Statistics (2000).

as the Environmental Defense Fund and Natural Resources Defense Council in the USA, a broader environmental, rather than conservationist, agenda incorporating industrial pollution, nuclear power and an expanding range of global problems. The growth of environmental concern at this time also greatly boosted the membership of traditional conservation groups and encouraged them to broaden their agendas.

Tables 6.1 and 6.2 show that membership has grown dramatically since the 1970s, becoming increasingly concentrated in a small number of large groups. Membership growth patterns show a cyclical form: periods of growth have been interspersed by periods of consolidation and standstill. After the initial spurt during the late 1960s/early 1970s, a second period of expansion reflected the escalation of public concern about global environmental problems during the mid/late 1980s.[3] During the early 1990s, several environmental groups experienced a decline in membership; in particular, the membership of Greenpeace USA collapsed, resulting in the closure of regional offices and the reduction of salaried staff from 400 to 65 (Bosso 1999: 71). Nevertheless, the major environmental groups now command huge budgets owing to the massive increase in membership subscriptions and the development of professional fund-raising activities (Bosso 1999; Jordan and Maloney 1997; Rawcliffe 1998).

A TYPOLOGY OF ENVIRONMENTAL GROUPS

The environmental movement is extraordinarily diverse, encompassing traditional conservation organisations (e.g. RSPB and the Sierra Club), international NGOs (FoE and Greenpeace), radical direct action groups (Earth First!) and a mass of local grassroots groups. Indeed, some observers argue that it is wrong to talk of a single environmental movement because the differences between groups are more significant than the similarities

(Bosso 1999; Jordan and Maloney 1997). By contrast, Dalton (1994) refers to an all-inclusive 'green rainbow' in which differences between groups simply reflect tendencies along a continuum between a conservation orientation and an ecological orientation – ideal types that broadly correspond to the two historical waves of environmentalism. An inclusive approach to the environmental movement as encompassing all 'broad networks of people and organisations engaged in collective action in the pursuit of environmental benefits' (Rootes 1999a: 2) is also used here. Nevertheless, one problem with inclusivity is that it can produce strange bedfellows, so the typology designed by Diani and Donati (1999) provides a helpful framework for making sense of this eclectic movement.

Diani and Donati (1999: 15–17) claim that all EPGs have to respond to two key functional requirements: **resource mobilisation** and political efficacy. Resource mobilisation involves securing the resources needed for collective action (see Box 4.1).[4] There are two broad options: either to maximise support from the general public, through mass membership and fund-raising, in order to fund a professional organisation; or to mobilise human resources by encouraging member activism. The basic choice is between a professional and a participatory organisation. *Political efficacy* refers to the choice of strategy and tactics. Again, there are two broad options: a conventional approach to political negotiation that complies with the political rules of the game or a strategy that disrupts routinised political behaviour by breaking those established rules.

Two core dilemmas are therefore identified: between professional and participatory organisational models, and between disruptive and conventional forms of pressure (see Table 6.3). These choices produce four organisational types:

1. The *public interest model* is managed by professional staff, has low participation and uses traditional pressure tactics.
2. The *participatory protest organisation* emphasises participatory action, subcultural structures and disruptive protest.
3. The *professional protest organisation* combines professional activism and mobilisation of financial resources with use of confrontational tactics alongside conventional ones.
4. The *participatory pressure group* involves rank-and-file members and supporters but uses conventional pressure techniques.

> **Resource mobilisation:** An approach to collective action which focuses on the way groups mobilise their resources – members, finances, symbols – in turning grievances into political issues.

Table 6.3 A typology of non-partisan political organisations

	Forms of action	
	Conventional pressure	Disruption
Professional resources	Public interest lobby	Professional protest organisation
Participatory resources	Participatory pressure group	Participatory protest organisation

From Diani and Donati (1999:16).

The following sections use this typology to analyse two key trends in the development of the environmental movement: the institutionalisation of the mainstream movement and the revitalisation of the grassroots sector.

CRITICAL QUESTION 1

Is it accurate to refer to a single environmental movement?

THE INSTITUTIONALISATION OF THE ENVIRONMENTAL MOVEMENT

There is general agreement that the environmental movement in North America and Western Europe has become increasingly institutionalised (Mitchell et al. 1992; Gottlieb 1993; van der Heijden 1997, 1999; Brand 1999; Diani and Donati 1999) (see Box 6.1). Although there is considerable variation between countries, with institutionalisation most pronounced in Nordic countries, Germany and the Netherlands, and weakest in France and Southern Europe (Rootes 1999b), overall it seems that the mainstream environmental movement has chosen reform over revolution. It has cast off its radical social movement roots in order to work within the political system; thus participatory principles and unconventional tactics have been replaced by professionalisation and conventional methods. This section analyses the nature and extent of this institutionalisation, using the criteria laid out in Box 6.1 by focusing in particular on the development of Friends of the Earth and Greenpeace.

First, the experience of 'environmental' groups should be distinguished from that of traditional conservation groups for whom institutionalisation is an unquestionable sign of success. Most conservation groups were 'born institutionalised' (Doyle and McEachern 1998: 101). They started out as elitist associations seeking moderate reforms within the existing socio-political order. The modern, mass-membership conservation groups remain hierarchical organisations, with limited democratic rights granted to members, and have used their enormous income to turn themselves into highly professional *public interest*

6.1 Institutionalisation

The *institutionalisation* of the environment involves the growing acceptance of environmental values, concerns and organisations so that environmental collective action becomes a regular and normal feature of the established political system.

Van der Heijden (1997) identifies three aspects of institutionalisation:

1. *organisational growth* in membership and income;
2. *internal institutionalisation* – professionalisation and centralisation of the organisation;
3. *external institutionalisation* – a shift from unconventional actions (e.g. direct action) to conventional actions (e.g. lobbying) as groups gain regular access to policy process.

groups. Where administration, legal advice and lobbying once depended on volunteers, today they employ professionals – managers, lawyers, fund-raisers, lobbyists and scientists. Most conservation groups are wedded to conventional forms of pressure. Their political campaigning focuses on the dissemination of information, lobbying and using the legal system to protect the environment. Conservation groups have acquired growing influence within the policy process, engaging in regular dialogue with politicians and civil servants, and, by representing environmental inter-ests in standard-setting and enforcement, they often play a formal role in policy implementation (Mitchell et al. 1992: 20). Conservation groups are involved in a wide range of activities, from habitat protection to eco-labelling, often in partnership with state agencies, for which many groups receive significant public funding. Institutionalisation reaches its purest form where, as in Germany and the Netherlands, leading environmental groups are funded by the government 'with the declared objective to create a counter-lobby' (Brand 1999: 52). Conservation groups have become more institutionalised, therefore, in so far as they are now mass-membership organisations which have acquired greater legitimacy and better access to policy-makers. Apart from developing a wider environ-mental perspective, this process has involved no fundamental transforma-tion in the aims or strategies of conservation groups. Organisations like the Sierra Club and the RSPB have always been *public interest* groups; now they are simply bigger and better at it.

The process of institutionalisation has proved more difficult for groups like Greenpeace and FoE which started out as radical social movements. Both were products of the era of 'modern environmentalism'. FoE was formed in the USA in 1969 by David Brower, a former Sierra Club activist, who was critical of its unwillingness to use confrontational methods. Greenpeace was founded in 1971 by Canadians protesting against a planned US nuclear test on a Pacific island.[5] Both groups quickly established a repu-tation for innovative campaigning, well-publicised protests and direct action. Greenpeace, in particular, attracted international attention through its dangerous, dramatic high-profile actions at sea against nuclear testing, whaling and the killing of seal pups. Today, both groups are huge interna-tional organisations: FoE International federation has member groups in sixty-six countries (Friends of the Earth International 2001) and Greenpeace International has twenty-five national offices with a presence in forty-one countries (Greenpeace 1999). Membership and income have both mush-roomed.[6] Greenpeace International had 2,473,000 'supporters' (i.e. regular donors) and a net income of 96 million euros in 1999 (ibid.).[7] FoE International had between 700,000 and 1 million members with a combined annual budget of approximately $15 million in 1993 (Wapner 1996: 122). FoE (England and Wales), for example, grew from 8 local groups, 1,000 sup-porters, 6 staff and an annual budget of £10,000 in 1971 (Lowe and Goyder 1983: 133), to over 300 local groups, 112,000 supporters, 96 staff and an annual income of £5.3 million by 1994 (Jordan and Maloney 1997: 39–40).[8] Organisational growth of this order clearly satisfies the first category of institutionalisation (see Box 6.1), but can it be compatible with social movement aims and strategies?

The organisational structures of FoE and Greenpeace initially differed markedly. FoE, in its early days, resembled a social movement organisation in that in each country it started life as a small campaigning group, usually with a central office to co-ordinate strategies and autonomous local groups with independent control over budgets and campaigns. As FoE expanded it became increasingly centralised and professional, and the distance between the centre and local groups grew ever wider (Lowe and Goyder 1983). FoE (UK), for example, initially resisted demands from local groups for a greater say in the organisation but, under growing pressure from members and campaign staff, it introduced a more democratic structure in 1983. Nevertheless, although elected members hold a majority on the board and local groups can influence strategy through the annual conference, with the continued growth and further professionalisation of the organisation, it is a matter of some debate how democratic FoE is in practice (Rawcliffe 1998; Jordan and Maloney 1997). What is clear is that FoE has shifted from an informal social movement to a professional, centralised organisation.

By contrast, Greenpeace has never claimed to be democratic. Its founders had a very clear organisational blueprint of an elitist, hierarchical structure where control resided with full-time staff and professional activists. The intention was to free those activists from inefficient, time-consuming democratic controls to allow them to concentrate on direct action. Most Greenpeace 'members' are, in fact, supporters whose subscription fee gives them no formal organisational rights, and the involvement of local groups and individual supporters is largely limited to fund-raising. There are just a few hundred full members in each country. In Greenpeace Germany, for example, those members elect a management board which sets the agenda and appoints a directorate (one or two people) to head a management team that runs the national organisation (Blühdorn 1995: 191). This highly personalised and centralised executive structure has been described as 'authoritarian leadership' (Rucht 1995: 70).

The growing professionalisation of FoE and Greenpeace is reflected in the way that their national offices now employ, as well as campaigners and administrators, a significant number of marketing and fund-raising specialists, and they depend decreasingly on volunteers (Rawcliffe 1998: 82; Jordan and Maloney 1997). Both groups invest huge resources in mail-order recruitment. One study of twelve large American environmental groups (in Shaiko 1993) found that Greenpeace spent the largest proportion of its budget on fund-raising: 23 per cent compared to an average of 10.6 per cent of the remaining eleven organisations (although that still

leaves a large share for campaigning). Both FoE and Greenpeace purchase address lists of people with the demographic qualities – occupation, education, age, disposable income, political affiliations – likely to
make them sympathetic to environmental causes, and willing and able
to pay a membership subscription (FoE) or donation (Greenpeace). Thus
one British study found that the typical FoE member is 'A well-educated
middle-class female under 45 in a professional/managerial occupation
from a relatively affluent household, who is a member of other campaigning organisations (most notably Greenpeace) and votes for a centre-
left party' (Jordan and Maloney 1997: 121). Each new 'eco-crisis' is
cleverly exploited with carefully chosen high-profile campaigns or
stunts to draw media attention, combined with a massive mailshot to
existing and potential supporters. The effectiveness of this strategy is
illustrated by the fact that the majority of British FoE members are
recruited via some form of direct mail approach or advertisement,
rather than through a social network such as friends, colleagues or word
of mouth (Jordan and Maloney 1997). Former Greenpeace activist Paul
Watson has complained that Greenpeace has 'turned begging into a
major corporate adventure' (*Time*, 10 June 1996).

Greenpeace and FoE both have a predominantly 'couch' membership
that is quite willing to pay a subscription fee and let the leadership get
on with running the organisation. Supporters seem to have only a limited emotional bond with the group; most do not wish to become
activists and are unwilling to make major sacrifices to protect the environment. This passive support is probably no more than can be expected
from a marketing strategy that asks for little more than a limited financial involvement from supporters in return for feeling good about helping the cause. Far from being new social movements, Jordan and
Maloney (1997: 22) even describe Greenpeace and FoE as *protest businesses*
modelled on private business practice because they emphasise investment in recruitment and marketing, make policy centrally, leave campaigning to professional staff and regard supporters as a source of
income. This label may be more applicable to Greenpeace than to FoE as
the latter still places considerable value on its links with its grassroots
membership.

Further evidence of institutionalisation is found in the changes that
both FoE and Greenpeace have made to their campaigning strategies.
Whereas both groups were originally on the margins of the political
system and made wide use of unconventional tactics, in recent years
each has adopted a more conventional repertoire of actions. This shift
from outsider to insider is most marked for FoE. In its early years, FoE
frequently used direct action (usually within the law), such as the
well-publicised 1971 campaign to return non-returnable soft drink bottles to Schweppes depots in Britain. Nevertheless, FoE has always
employed a mixture of strategies; in particular, it pins great weight on

the technical rationality of its case and likes to 'win the argument'. It gained considerable respect in Britain for its performance in the public inquiry into nuclear fuel reprocessing at Windscale in 1977, a success that encouraged it to move closer to the mainstream environmental lobby (Lowe and Goyder 1983). As it grew, FoE was able to devote more resources to monitoring government activities, publishing technical reports, using the judicial system and lobbying politicians and civil servants. Over time, the balance of its activities has gradually shifted from criticism and confrontation to practical, advice-based campaigning (McCormick 1991: 118). Today FoE is regularly consulted by government and its representatives are frequently found on official committees. Consequently it eschews the grand confrontational gestures which helped build its reputation but that might now lose it the respectability needed for regular insider status. Where FoE once relished direct action, it is now hesitant to use it because as a large 'protest business' it cannot afford to break the law for fear of having its financial assets sequestered by the courts.

Greenpeace remains more firmly wedded to the principle of direct action. It has always recognised the power of the media image, and quickly became associated with dramatic stunts that captured the attention of millions of viewers. A key event was the *Rainbow Warrior* incident in 1985. This Greenpeace ship, which was used to protest against French nuclear testing, was blown up by French government agents while it was docked in a New Zealand port, killing a crew member. The resulting publicity contributed to the rapid growth of Greenpeace as an international organisation. Yet this transformation brought new strategic dilemmas. Greenpeace had developed a symbiotic relationship with the media, based on its ingenious use of 'guerrilla theatre' to dramatise environmental destruction (Shaiko 1993: 97). These high-profile direct actions undoubtedly helped push issues such as whaling, sealing and the Antarctic into the limelight. The problem was that the tactics upon which Greenpeace built its reputation seemed to have a limited shelf-life: stunts needed to be ever more extreme to attract the interest of a media that was becoming bored with repetition. As a rich international NGO, Greenpeace now had the resources to develop new strategies (and, like FoE, it became increasingly reluctant to break the law),[9] so it adopted a more constructive 'solutions-led' approach (Rose 1993). This strategy built on the scientific expertise that Greenpeace had always prided itself on, by commissioning research, disseminating findings and appointing more scientists to key posts (Jamison et al. 1990: 117). However, by using science to engage in a 'rational' debate with industry, Greenpeace was compromising its hostile attitude to its traditional 'enemy'. During the 1990s, the solutions-led strategy saw Greenpeace working closely with corporations in search of alternatives to environmentally damaging activities such as the use of chlorine-free paper for

6.2 The changing nature of environmental pressure: solution-led campaigning

The 'greenfreeze' refrigerator

In 1992 Greenpeace Germany commissioned a prototype refrigerator with a hydrocarbon cooling agent instead of the ozone-depleting CFC-substitutes, HFCs and HCFCs. Large chemical companies were highly sceptical, declaring that the development of such technology was many years off. Yet Greenpeace persuaded a struggling East German company, Foron, to start commercial production of the refrigerator in 1993 (with government financial aid). Sales in Germany took off rapidly and within months major manufacturers such as Bosch began shifting to the new technology. By 1997, almost 100 per cent of German and approaching 80 per cent of production in Northern and Western Europe was 'greenfreeze'.

See Greenpeace greenfreeze page: (*http://www.greenpeace.org/ ~climate/*).

newspapers and fuel-efficient cars. As the successful 'greenfreeze' refrigerator campaign illustrates, a key aim was to use market pressures to change the behaviour of business (see Box 6.2); it is a strategy widely used by other groups, such as the Environmental Defense Fund and FoE.

Greenpeace has not found the transition to greater respectability easy. Ironically, the shift to solutions-led campaigning upset both the old guard activists and marketing staff. Hardline activists, several of whom left or were forced out of the organisation, accused the leadership of selling out by engaging in dialogue with capitalist firms. Meanwhile, the marketing professionals were alarmed that the low profile of the solutions-led approach was not producing the racy headlines and evocative pictures necessary for fund-raising. Since the mid-1990s, these internal pressures have encouraged Greenpeace to show a renewed enthusiasm for direct action, including the occupation of the Brent Spar oil-rig (see Box 6.3), the campaign against oil exploration in the North Atlantic (which involved a 48-day occupation of the remote, unoccupied island of Rockall) and an attempt to disrupt French nuclear testing in the Pacific Ocean (Bennie 1998). Direct action did not replace the policy of working with industry; rather, the two approaches are used in parallel. Gray et al. (1999) show how Greenpeace, in its various North Sea fishing industry campaigns, has used a broad range of unconventional and conventional strategies, ranging from confrontation to dialogue, selecting whichever seems most appropriate to achieve a particular objective. Where Greenpeace once preferred to operate in isolation, now, like FoE, it frequently works with other EPGs, such as the Dolphin Coalition of forty groups which played a key role in securing legislation to protect the dolphin from tuna-fishing fleets in the Eastern Pacific Ocean (Wright 2001).

It is clear that, measured by all three criteria, FoE and Greenpeace have undergone extensive (if not complete) institutionalisation. FoE started out as something close to a *participatory protest* organisation but, whilst it retains elements of democracy and participation, FoE is now much closer to the *public interest* model, with its professionalisation and emphasis on conventional strategies of publicity, lobbying, litigation and expert testimony. Greenpeace has also become more institutionalised, but its continuing commitment to direct action places it closer to the *professional protest* model. It is not yet an insider public interest group: its reluctance to engage in formal lobbying or to accept invitations to serve on government committees means that Greenpeace is still not always trusted by government or, indeed, by the mainstream environmental lobby. Conversely, its new dialogue with industry and its greater circumspection about law-breaking suggest to many environmental activists that even Greenpeace has lost its radical edge, although its recent involvement in the destruction of genetically modified crop experiments across Europe may have restored some of its radical credentials. Nevertheless, many environmentalists have become increasingly disenchanted with the mainstream environmental movement, opting instead to get involved in grassroots activity.

6.3 Lessons of Brent Spar

Brent Spar was a redundant 14,500 tonne oil platform which Shell, with the permission of the British government and acting on best scientific advice, had planned to dispose of deep in the North Atlantic. A high-publicity Greenpeace campaign against the 'dumping' during 1995, which included the occupation of Brent Spar, resulted in Shell abandoning the proposal.

Lessons:

1. *Direct action can be effective:* the brilliantly engineered media campaign stopped the dumping of Brent Spar and made the entire policy of deep-sea disposal of old oil rigs politically unacceptable.
2. *The power of the moral message:* Greenpeace used a familiar, emotionally charged message – that dumping at sea was wrong and that the ocean should not be used as a dustbin – to take the moral high ground and project Shell and the government as the bad guys (Bennie 1998).
3. *The power of the market:* a key factor in Shell's climbdown was a European consumer boycott of Shell products which was particularly effective in Germany, where demand dropped by up to 30 per cent almost overnight.
4. *Lasting damage to Greenpeace's media image:* the subsequent admission that Greenpeace mistakenly overestimated the amount of pollutant material still in the platform lost it considerable respect in the media and undermined its reputation for scientific expertise. The media felt manipulated and have since become more critical of Greenpeace – a dangerous development for an organisation that is so dependent on media coverage.

CRITICAL QUESTION 2

Has the institutionalisation of Greenpeace and Friends of the Earth turned them into 'protest businesses'?

THE RESURGENCE OF GRASSROOTS ENVIRONMENTALISM

There has always been a grassroots sector alongside the major environmental organisations, but there has been a revitalisation of this sector in recent years. Bosso (1997) has even called it the 'third wave' of environmentalism, following the earlier 'conservationist' and 'environmentalist' waves, because grassroots activity is often a direct response to the failings of the mainstream environmental movement. The term 'grassroots' conceals many differences, but three broad categories can be identified: first, radical social movements such as the Sea Shepherd Society, Robin Wood

(Germany) and Earth First!; secondly, small local groups campaigning against a specific locally unwanted land use (or LULU); thirdly, broad coalitions of groups, such as the US Environmental Justice Movement and the UK anti-roads protesters, which may contain groups from both the other categories. This section assesses the significance of the grassroots sector by examining each of these three categories.

The first category of groups holds an explicitly ecological, countercultural orientation and makes up the most radical strand of the grassroots movement. Although many of these groups have developed a national, or even international, structure, they are grassroots in their commitment to participatory, decentralised structures and in their fierce rejection of all forms of institutionalisation. Many were set up by activists disillusioned with mainstream environmental groups. Robin Wood was formed by a breakaway group of fifty Greenpeace Germany activists who wanted a more participatory organisation with an explicitly German agenda focusing on acid rain and forest decline (Blühdorn 1995: 197–200). Ex-Greenpeace activist Paul Watson founded the Sea Shepherd Society which is notable for dramatic acts such as sinking two Icelandic whaling vessels in 1986 (Chatterjee and Finger 1994: 72). Probably the most radical group is Earth First! which was founded in the USA in 1980 by five activists critical of the bureaucratic structures and moderate stance of major conservation groups such as the Wilderness Society and the Sierra Club (Gottlieb 1993; Rucht 1995).

The founders of Earth First! were deep ecologists committed to confrontational direct action, including acts of civil disobedience and 'monkey wrenching', or 'ecotage' (illegal actions such as tree-spiking and sabotaging bulldozers.[10] Our knowledge of Earth First! (USA) is rather murky because secrecy veils much of its (often illegal) activity. It is profoundly anti-institutional, with a highly decentralised structure of around 100 groups, each with 15–20 activists, plus supporting groups, and around 14 operational centres co-ordinating national initiatives (Rucht 1995). Groups are autonomous, determining their own campaigns and raising their own finances. No one individual speaks for Earth First!. There are various organs of co-ordination and communication, including a magazine, an annual meeting and an activist conference. Earth First! has gained considerable attention and notoriety for its theatrical attention-seeking stunts, such as perching in trees destined to be chopped down for logging, and, most of all, for its acts of ecotage. Activists have gone far beyond the limits of civil disobedience by repeatedly destroying the technical equipment of companies engaged in logging, drilling, electricity supply and surveying. Whereas Greenpeace breaks the law infrequently, preferably where there is no moral ambivalence about the act and only when it has carefully calculated the impact on its public reputation, Earth First! is proud that it flouts the law and relishes any media backlash directed against it (Rucht 1995: 80). Indeed, it has attracted a highly critical response from the American media and from other environmental groups, and has even been the subject of terrorist counter-attacks, including a pipe bomb under the car of a leading activist. However, by the early 1990s, Earth First! was badly split by ideological divisions between the older generation activists such as Dave Foreman, who emphasised a narrow 'deep ecology' zeal for wilderness and biodiversity issues, and a younger generation who disliked some of the misanthropic sentiments of the first group, preferring to develop a broader social agenda (Gottlieb 1993: 197–8). Eventually, Foreman and his allies departed, allowing Earth First! to develop a wider environmental justice agenda. Earth First!, with its democratic, decentralised structure, its commitment to direct action and willingness to operate outside the formal political system, is a clear example of a *participatory protest* group. During the 1990s, Earth First! groups were formed in Britain, Ireland and the Netherlands.

Most groups fall within the second category of grassroots group. They are based in a local community and are usually formed by residents as a 'not in my back yard' (NIMBY) response to a proposed LULU, such as a new road or incinerator, or from concern about the health risks of an existing hazard, such as a polluting factory or pesticide spraying.[11] These groups are usually participative and rely heavily on voluntary action, membership subscriptions and fund-raising. Membership is likely to reflect the local base of the group: middle-class in an affluent area; working class in poorer communities. A notable feature of US grassroots groups is the prevalence of anti-toxic waste and environmental justice groups in many poor urban communities, with a sharply different membership profile from the predominantly middle-class mainstream environmental movement. In particular, women of all classes are heavily represented in the anti-toxics movement (Gottlieb 1993) and they contain a much larger proportion of African-Americans and Latinos (Freudenberg and Steinsapir 1992; Pulido 1996; Schlosberg 1999a).

NIMBY groups exist in all countries and employ a wide range of strategies. Some are *participatory pressure* groups employing conventional tactics, including lobbying, organising petitions, filing lawsuits or running candidates in local elections to publicise their case. However, conventional methods often prove fruitless, prompting frustrated and increasingly politicised activists to adopt more confrontational, unconventional tactics, such as demonstrations, sit-ins and blockades. A famous case involved the residents of Love Canal in New York holding two officials of the Environmental Protection Agency 'hostage' for several hours in 1978 in order to publicise the danger of local toxic chemical pollution. Two days later, President Carter declared the area a disaster zone, which made the residents eligible for relocation assistance (Gibbs 1982). Although grassroots campaigns have achieved many individual successes, causing projects to be abandoned, delayed or amended, there have also been countless failed campaigns where the LULU gets built regardless. More often than not, enthusiastic local campaigners are impotent against the combined power of profit-seeking corporations and governments anxious not to impede economic development (Gould et al. 1996). Where local campaigns are successful, it is usually because of external factors. One study of local campaigns in Britain shows how any limited success was largely 'dependent on action or inaction at other levels', such as national government, the European Commission, transnational corporations or the involvement of the mainstream environmental lobby (Rootes 1999c). Thus the conventional methods of the long-running (1979–96) local campaign against a proposed nuclear power station at Druridge Bay, Northumberland, finally succeeded when the British government introduced a moratorium on the building of all nuclear power stations (Baggott 1998).

Many local groups, recognising the limitations of operating in isolation, have built links with other like-minded grassroots groups. Consequently, the third category of grassroots group refers to the development of coalitions and networks amongst local environmental groups, which is particularly marked in the USA (Gould et al. 1996; Schlosberg 1999a). Two large national coalitions that co-ordinate campaigns against toxic hazards are the Citizens' Clearinghouse for Hazardous Wastes (CCHW)[12] and the National Toxics Campaign, which claim to be in contact with up to 10,000 and 7,000 local groups respectively (Dowie 1995: 133). There are also many regional groups, such as the Silicon Valley Toxics Coalition in California and the Work on Waste (anti mass-burn incinerators/pro-recycling) in New York State. These coalitions have arisen from a common wish to share scientific and technical information, learn from each other's experiences and pool resources in jointly run campaigns. An additional catalyst has been a widespread disenchantment with the smooth professionalism of mainstream environmental groups. Grassroots activists frequently criticise the ineffectiveness of public interest group campaigning, the refusal of the established groups to endorse direct action, their willingness to get into bed with big corporations and their focus on the Washington lobby.

The environmental justice movement is particularly condemnatory of the largely apolitical mainstream organisations for concentrating on 'universal' issues such as wildlife and natural resource protection, whilst ignoring those environmental hazards that hit poorer (often non-white) communities hardest (see Box 6.4).[13] The environmental justice movement brings the issues of class, poverty, race and gender to the forefront of environmentalism. It holds that, because environmental hazards are inextricably linked to inequality, solutions will not be found in the middle-class issues of conservation and preservation, but in transforming entrenched economic and political structures. Environmental justice is thus a practical political expression of both the social justice principle of ecologism and the socialist critique of environmentalists as middle-class elitists (see Chapter 3). The environmental justice movement clearly offers a tough challenge to the whiteness of the environmental movement (Gottlieb 1993), although it is too early to judge its wider impact. The absence of an equivalent working-class or non-white grassroots environmental justice movement in Europe may reflect different political opportunity structures, notably the more pluralistic nature of the American polity, and the greater possibility in Europe of expressing social justice issues in partisan terms through left-wing or green parties.[14]

One of the most significant recent coalitions in Europe, the UK anti-roads protests, did develop a social justice agenda, but it had a more overtly 'green' character than the American environmental justice movement. The anti-roads movement involved a series of linked struggles against the building of new roads as part of the Conservative government's massive construction programme, starting in 1992 with opposition to the M3 motorway extension at Twyford Down, and moving on to similar campaigns throughout the country, notably at

> ### 6.4 The environmental justice movement
>
> Environmental justice is broader than just preserving the environment. When we fight for environmental justice we fight for our homes and families and struggle to end economic, social and political domination by the strong and the greedy.
>
> (Lois Gibbs, quoted in Schlosberg 1999a: 127)
>
> The environmental justice movement emerged in the USA during the 1980s with the mushrooming of networks of grassroots groups, such as the Clearing House for Hazardous Waste and the Southwest Network for Environmental and Economic Justice. It is a bottom-up movement that is rooted in the struggles of local communities against environmental hazards: people get involved through personal experience and local networks, not because they happen to be on a mailing list.
>
> The key idea underpinning the environmental justice movement is the recognition that environmental hazards are closely linked to race and poverty. It is poor people who live in the poorest environments, and in the USA the poorest people tend to be non-whites. Disproportionately large numbers of African-Americans and Hispanics live close to hazardous and toxic waste sites (Bullard 1990). In short, ecosystem destruction is often connected to racism. Hence the second principle of the environmental justice movement states that: '*Environmental justice* demands that public policy be based on mutual respect and justice for all peoples, free from any form of discrimination or bias'.

Bath, Glasgow, Wanstead, Newbury and Fairmile. The loose coalition of some 250–300 anti-road groups was co-ordinated by two volunteer umbrella groups, Road Alert and Alarm UK. An interesting feature of the anti-roads protests was that each individual campaign involved a coalition of two kinds of grassroots group (Doherty 1999: 276). There was always one group of local residents who had opposed the specific scheme for many years, primarily from NIMBY motivations, and had exhausted all legal avenues of opposition. They were then joined by a second group of activists from the green counter-culture, popularly known as 'eco-warriors' or eco-protesters. Thus the public was treated to graphic images of middle aged, middle-class residents bringing food and drink to the eco-warriors in their treehouses and tunnels.

The radical eco-protester wing of the anti-roads movement, like the environmental justice movement, was born out of disillusionment with the perceived ineffectiveness of the mainstream, professional environmental groups, especially FoE and Greenpeace.[15] An important symbol of their impotence was the decision by FoE to withdraw from Twyford Down soon after construction began, when it was landed with a series of injunctions that threatened the sequestration of its assets. Into this political void stepped the eco-warriors, who were prepared to take those forms of direct action that frightened off the mainstream groups. The emergence of Earth First! (UK) in 1991 was critical: by 1997 there were around 60 active groups and its annual gathering was attended by about 400 activists (Doherty 1998: 68).[16] Not all eco-protesters identified with Earth First!, but common practices characterised the whole anti-roads movement. Organisationally, it was informal, decentralised and non-hierarchical. The activists were deeply alienated from the political parties, groups and institutions. Eco-protest appealed to a particular kind of person:

> Mostly young, in their twenties or late teens, in education or choosing to live on a low income and most are in effect full-time political activists. Becoming an eco-protester means making a commitment to a lifestyle based mainly in protest camps or communal houses, in which many possessions are shared, income is minimal, and codes of conduct that minimise impact on the environment are observed. [They] have little concern with formal ideology, even of a green kind, but share a belief that 'do-it-yourself political action' is the only viable means of improving democracy and overcoming the ecological crisis.

(Doherty 1999: 276–7)

Although the road-building programme was their main focus, their concerns embraced broader questions about the centralised power of the British state, land ownership and the curtailments of civil liberties. The eco-protesters also campaigned against a second runway at Manchester Airport, open-cast mining and quarrying. As the anti-roads movement began to wind down in 1997, many individuals became involved in groups like Reclaim the Streets and The Land is Ours that developed a more positive agenda linking existing patterns of car use and land ownership to environmental problems. From 1999, many joined the direct action protests against GM crop experiments. Doherty's (1999) description of the eco-protesters as 'the first full expression of the new social movement type in British environmental politics' (p. 290) seems apt.[17]

CRITICAL QUESTION 3

Is a vibrant grassroots sector a sign of an effective environmental movement?

A NEW CIVIC POLITICS?

The two preceding sections have shown that the environmental movement encompasses a rich mix of organisational forms, strategies and tactics (see Box 6.5). The typology (Table 6.3) reveals a dynamic movement in

6.5 The repertoire of environmental protest

Environmental protests can involve a wide range of unconventional and indirect actions to influence policy-makers:

1. The *logic of numbers*: to demonstrate the sheer size of support to the government and the wider public – around 20 million Americans celebrated the first Earth Day in 1970, a critical event in persuading policy elites that the public wanted legislation to protect the environment.

2. The *logic of material damage*: to inflict material losses on business or government. Includes:

    (i)   economic sanctions – the Greenpeace-orchestrated consumer boycott of Shell petrol stations during the Brent Spar campaign (Box 6.3);

    (ii) economic disruption – the anti-road protests hoped the huge security costs of policing road-building sites would dissuade construction companies and the government from future developments;

    (iii) violence against property – Earth First! 'ecotage'; computer hacking offers a new means of inflicting huge material damage on corporations and government.

3. The *logic of bearing witness*: to 'demonstrate a strong commitment to an objective deemed vital for humanity's future' (della Porta and Diani 1999: 178). It reinforces the moral message by showing that activists are willing to take personal risks because of the strength of their convictions:

    ❑ In 1995 Greenpeace vessels sailed into the exclusion zone around Mururoa in the Pacific where the French were about to carry out nuclear tests.

    ❑ Ecological activists take up residence in treehouses or a maze of tunnels.

Source: della Porta and Diani (1999).

which the convergence amongst the major environmental groups towards the 'public interest' model should be set against the resurgent grassroots sector made up of both 'participatory pressure' groups of local citizens opposing specific LULUs and 'participatory protest' ecological social movements. Yet, contrary to the doubts of writers like Bosso (1999), there does seem to be sufficient common ground to talk in terms of one broad environmental movement. Apart from the obvious points of similarity, such as a shared concern about environmental destruction, two particular manifestations of this unity are significant.

First, there seems to be a creative tension between the different wings of the movement. Certainly, the vitality of the grassroots sector is partly a result of the widespread negative perceptions of the mainstream movement amongst concerned citizens, with many grassroots groups springing directly from a deep-seated frustration at the perceived impotence of the environmental lobby, notably for their neglect of local campaigning. For their part, established groups, particularly those with radical roots, have tried to respond to the challenge from below. FoE (UK), for example, stung by criticisms that it has neglected its participatory principles, has encouraged its often moribund local groups to become more active (Rawcliffe 1998: 231) and has even trained some local groups in techniques of non-violent direct action. Even Greenpeace has been sensitive to criticisms of its authoritarian, undemocratic structure. In 1995, for example, Greenpeace

UK relaxed its prohibition on local support groups engaging in activities beyond fund-raising and publicity in support of national and international campaigns (Rootes 1999c: 302). Greenpeace USA has also worked closely with grassroots groups and made a concerted effort to recruit more staff from ethnic minorities (Dowie 1995: 147). One factor contributing to this change of heart was that, in common with other major groups, FoE and Greenpeace experienced a fall-off in support and a decline in income during the mid-1990s – a direct threat to the 'protest business' strategy. This stagnation may also be a function of the grassroots challenge. In the USA, the Sierra Club and National Audubon Society have faced internal criticism from members demanding that they should become more radical and less Washington-focused (Dowie 1995: 214–19). One manifestation of this discontent was the election of both David Brower (who originally founded FoE) and Dave Foreman (ex-Earth First!) to the Sierra Club Board of Directors (Bosso 1997: 64–5).[18] Thus there seems to be a symbiotic relationship between the main-stream and grassroots sectors that will probably regularly reproduce similar cycles of activity and stagnation across the 'green rainbow'.

Secondly, environmental groups have shown an increasing willingness to form coalitions and networks to pursue their aims more effectively. The established groups are now regularly involved in coalition activity at both national and international levels, reflecting (and contributing to) the growing convergence between them. The big conservationist and environmental groups have built up years of experience working together in the lobby, on government committees and developing joint responses to consultative documents. Many of their staff have even swapped organisations as a career structure for professional environmentalists has developed. So it is hardly surprising that they have increasingly chosen to pool their resources. The emergence of loose-knit coalitions of grassroots groups, such as the anti-roads protesters and the environmental justice movement, suggests that the differences within the much more eclectic grassroots sector are also not necessarily irreconcilable, or, at least, there may be sufficient common ground to work together on key issues. Indeed, McNeish (2000: 190) found that many British anti-roads protesters were also members of mainstream groups such as Greenpeace and FoE. There have been some attempts to bridge the gap between the different wings of the movement. The successful conventional campaign against the proposal to build a Thames river-crossing through Oxleas Wood in London involved an alliance of FoE, WWF, Alarm UK and Earth First! (Doherty 1998: 284). Although the anti-roads campaigns initially saw considerable hostility between FoE and the eco-warriors, particularly at Twyford Down, subsequently improved relations saw them work alongside each other in later campaigns (Seel and Plows 2000: 118). Elsewhere, Gould et al. (1996: 195–6) concluded from their study of local environmental mobilisation in the USA that groups are most effective when they build alliances with regional or national organisations. The massive international mobilisation of NGOs protesting against the World Trade Organisation (WTO) convention in Seattle in November 1999 reflected a significant degree of co-ordination between mainstream and grassroots networks.

The Seattle events also identify the internationalisation of environmental politics as a key challenge for the contemporary environmental movement. In an interdependent global economic system the actions of non-democratic international capitalist institutions such as the WTO, International Monetary Fund and World Bank have a profound effect on the environment. International environmental diplomacy between nation states has also expanded. With critical decisions increasingly taken beyond the level of the nation state by international organisations, transnational corporations and national governments, how can environmental NGOs hope to compete against such powerful players?

Yet the international arena offers opportunities too. In recent years the environmental movement has shown its capacity to construct transnational alliances of NGOs which have scored some notable successes, helping make possible international agreements banning ozone-depleting CFCs (see Chapter 9), preventing mineral exploitation of the Antarctic (Wapner 1996) and protecting biodiversity (the Cartagena Biosafety Protocol was signed in January 2000). Major groups like Greenpeace and FoE have often shown their old dynamism at this international level, perhaps because global campaigns are often quite glamorous, attract wide publicity and offer different challenges to groups such as FoE that are increasingly shackled by domestic institutionalisation. Indeed, environmental NGOs are now so active at the international level that some writers see the emergence of a new *global civic society*, which is 'that slice of associational life that exists above the individual and below the state, but also across national boundaries' (Wapner 1996: 4; also Lipschutz 1996). They argue that, instead of identifying with the nation state, people are increasingly seeing themselves as part of a broader global community where they can be represented by environmental social movements: an international 'new politics'. While this inspiring vision may currently appear a little fanciful, it does nevertheless identify an important arena in contemporary environmental politics. We may already be seeing similar processes in the international arena as have occurred at the domestic level. Environmental NGOs are now participating in a wide range of international institutions, notably the *Agenda 21* process of sustainable development round-tables (see Chapter 8) and similar UN initiatives. However, real power still lies elsewhere – in the non-democratic global financial institutions and corporations (Williams and Ford 1999). Just like the domestic level, the institutionalisation of environmental groups in the international arena is likely to achieve only limited influence and may bring a further backlash from the grassroots sector. Thus, at Seattle, while the mainstream NGOs were lobbying national government representatives, thousands of eco-protesters were demonstrating on the streets (and grassroots networks co-ordinated direct action protests all around the world).

CRITICAL QUESTION 4
How realistic is the global civic society thesis?

THE IMPACT OF THE ENVIRONMENTAL MOVEMENT

The environmental movement has clearly become an important political actor in all western liberal democracies, but it is very difficult to measure its overall impact, or to draw any firm conclusions about the relative effectiveness of conventional and unconventional strategies. It may be possible to assess the impact of an action in specific cases, such as the Greenpeace Brent Spar campaign, but how can the influence of the wide-ranging Greenpeace campaign for climate change prevention be measured? At best, we may only be able to make broad, unquantifiable assessments. Nevertheless, this section makes a step in this direction by applying a framework which distinguishes five kinds of impact: individual identity, sensitising, procedural, structural and substantive (see Table 6.4).

One direct political aim of collective action is to raise the ecological consciousness of activists (who might then convert others to the cause). One yardstick is thus whether involvement in environmental groups affects individual political *identity*. This kind of politicisation is most likely in activist grassroots groups where individuals engage personally in a collective struggle. Involvement in those ecological social movements located in the counter-cultural milieu, such as Earth First!, is likely to provide a particularly powerful political experience, as illustrated by the anti-roads

---

Table 6.4 Types of impact of environmental pressure groups

Internal

Impact on identity
Politicisation of membership/supporters of group

External

Sensitising impacts
Changes in the political agenda and public attitudes

Procedural impacts
Access to decision-making bodies

Structural impacts
Changes in institutional or alliance structures, such as the creation of an environment agency or shift in attitude of parties

Substantive impacts
Material results: closure of a nuclear plant or new pollution legislation

Modelled on Kriesi et al. (1995: 209–12) and van der Heijden (1999: 202–3).

eco-protesters. There is also evidence from both the UK (Rootes 1999c: 298) and the USA (Szasz 1994) that even NIMBY activity can be a politically educative experience. Here, the key question, as Freudenberg and Steinsapir (1992) put it, is whether a NIMBY reaction can become a Not in Anyone's Back Yard (NIABY) belief. Does involvement in a struggle against a LULU encourage individuals to ask broader questions, such as 'If I don't want this incinerator or by-pass in my neighbourhood, why should anyone else have to put up with it?' People might then start to ask wider questions about the nature of energy production and consumption, or our dependency on cars. In short, they may begin to develop a wider ecological consciousness. The involvement of local groups in coalitions such as the National Toxics Campaign in the USA, by encouraging people to link their struggles with those of other communities, can play a vital role in this educative process. By contrast, 'couch' members of major environmental organisations may salve their environmental consciences through the limited act of paying a regular donation to a major group, whilst continuing their consumerist lifestyle.[19] If an annual payment is the limit of an individual's activity, then involvement clearly has little additional politicising effect. Yet 'couch' membership should not be dismissed lightly. The very act of joining is a political statement. The access to magazines and campaigning literature may prove educative, encouraging people to reflect on their own and others' lifestyles. Membership may also be the first step towards a wider involvement, particularly if individuals become frustrated that their membership seems to be making little 'difference'.

The environmental movement has exerted a significant, and continuing, *sensitising* impact by helping place the environment on the political agenda and stimulating public support for environmental protection. Indeed, perhaps its main achievement has been to create a climate in which governments are expected to pay greater attention to environmental protection, even if it is not yet on a par with traditional material issues. Both insider and outsider strategies have played their part in this process of ecological sensibility. Whereas the environmental lobby provides a constant educative and persuasive pressure on policy elites to consider the environment, confrontational actions that capture media attention have repeatedly succeeded in pushing environmental issues into the public gaze (Freudenberg and Steinsapir 1992: 35).

One consequence has been a tranche of *structural* changes in the way governments treat environmental problems. In particular, environmental pressure was largely responsible for the creation of environmental ministries in most governments (see Chapter 10).

The insider strategy has achieved some notable *procedural* successes. Everywhere the environmental lobby is listened to more closely and across much of Northern Europe, North America and Australasia it is now regularly consulted on many subjects. The international environmental lobby has achieved similar access to several international consultation networks and agencies, and within the EU. A key question is whether procedural gains translate into influence. As Chapter 7 shows, environmental groups have achieved only limited access to the policy networks that shape core economic decisions – in finance, industry, trade, energy and agriculture – which are still dominated by corporate and producer interests. Where regular access is gained, there is a price to being an insider group which involves compromise, obedience to the rules of the game and doing business with interests whose values and actions may be anathema to most environmentalists. The incorporationary pressures of the Washington lobby, for example, were apparent in the negotiation of the North American Free Trade Agreement (NAFTA) in the early 1990s. Having opposed NAFTA when it was proposed by Bush, most environmental groups eventually supported it in order to maintain their access to the Clinton White House and because they had been 'purchased' by large corporate donations, upon which they depend so heavily (Bosso 1997: 66). Insider status can also prove fragile. In both the USA and the UK, the environmental lobby found that the improved access to government that it achieved in the 1970s was dramatically reduced under the anti-environmentalist leadership of Reagan and Thatcher respectively (Dowie 1995; McCormick 1991), although the doors began to reopen from the late 1980s onwards.

The acid test of the environmental movement – its *substantive* impact – is particularly difficult to evaluate. Grassroots groups have certainly scored many individual local successes (although the prevention of a LULU in one location often results in its being built elsewhere). They have also endured many defeats: for example, most of the British roads that were the subject of an extensive anti-roads direct action campaign during the 1990s were eventually built.[20] Grassroots campaigns have rarely proved decisive in the wider policy arena. The strongest claim for the British anti-roads protests is that their campaigns succeeded in pushing the road-building issue high up the political agenda and created the climate in which the Conservative government made dramatic cuts in the road-building programme, but it was not the decisive factor (Robinson 2000). In the USA, some commentators argue that grassroots campaigns have helped change legislation on pollution control and right-to-know provisions, and encouraged business and government to take a more preventive approach to environmental contamination (Freudenberg and Steinsapir 1992: 33–5), although other writers are more circumspect about the influence of grassroots groups (Gould et al. 1996). The impact of the mainstream environmental movement has also been primarily negative; a powerful, united green lobby can frequently repulse undesirable policy initiatives and block environmentally damaging development projects. It has had less success in building support for its own reforms or changing the policy discourse. In this respect it will be interesting to see whether the recent entry of green parties into government will bring the environmental lobby better access or greater influence over policy in those countries. More generally, the influence of the environmental lobby seemed to stagnate during the 1990s along with the fall-off in membership. The shift towards a constructive dialogue with the business sector, illustrated by the growing interest in ecological modernisation (see Chapter 8) and Greenpeace's 'solutions-led' strategy, suggests that the major groups themselves recognise that they may be at a crossroads and are casting around for new channels of influence.

CONCLUSION

Two main trends have characterised the contemporary environmental movement. The extensive convergence of most major environmental organisations towards an institutionalised, professional public interest model has seen even once radical groups, such as FoE and Greenpeace, drawn increasingly into the establishment fold. Yet this trend contrasts sharply with the revitalisation of the grassroots sector, which has reaffirmed the importance of local activism and questioned the effectiveness of the moderate insider strategy of the big groups. Thus there is evidence of a new politics in the emergence of the environmental groups as a significant political force, in the innovative repertoires of protest and in the radical organisational forms and ideologies of ecological new social movements. However, the institutionalisation of the mainstream movement also suggests the continuing stability of established patterns of political behaviour. The overall impact of the environmental movement, although hard to measure, has been profound; yet the continued marginalisation of environmental considerations by policy elites fuels the rumblings of discontent and disappointment within the movement. If the environmental movement does stand at a crossroads, much will depend on its response to the enormous challenge posed by the internationalisation of environmental politics. At this level, as at national and subnational levels, environmental groups are just one actor in the policy process, and therefore cannot be judged in isolation. A complete assessment of the impact of the environmental movement, therefore, requires an understanding of their role within the policy process, which is the subject of Part III.

Further reading and websites

The special issue of *Environmental Politics* (1999, 8, no. 1) provides coverage of current debates on the environmental movement, and includes interesting country studies (Germany, Spain, the USA) and several comparative European studies. Also see van der Heijden (1997) and Rootes (1999b) for a comparative European perspective. Dowie (1995) provides a good broad coverage of the US environmental movement, and Bosso (1999) brings it more up to date. Schlosberg (1999b) offers a detailed coverage of the environmental justice movement. Rawcliffe (1998) is good on the UK environmental movement. See Wall (1999) for a study of Earth First! (UK) and Seel et al. (2000) for an examination of recent direct action in Britain. Wapner (1996) offers an interesting analysis of international environmental NGOs.

International websites

Friends of the Earth International (*http://www.foei.org/*)
Greenpeace International (*http://www.greenpeace.org/*)
World Wildlife Fund (*http://www.panda.org/*)

UK websites

Council for the Protection of Rural England (*http://www.cpre.org.uk/*)
The Land is Ours (*http://www.enviroweb.org/tlio/*)
National Trust (*http://www.nationaltrust.org.uk/*)
Reclaim the Streets (*http://www.gn.apc.org/rts/*)
Royal Society for Nature Conservation (*http://www.rsnc.org/*)
Royal Society for the Protection of Birds (*http://www.rspb.org.uk/*)

USA websites

Defenders of Wildlife (*http://www.defenders.org/*)
Earth First! (*http://www.enviroweb.org/ef/primer/*)
Izaac Walton League of America (*http://www.iwla.org/*)
National Audubon Society (*http://www.audubon.org/*)
National Parks and Conservation Association (*http://www.npca.org/*)
National Wildlife Federation (*http://www.nwf.org/*)
Natural Resources Defense Council (*http://www.nrdc.org/*)
Nature Conservancy (*http://www.tnc.org/*)
Rainforest Action Network (*http://www.ran.org/*)
Sierra Club (*http://www.sierraclub.org/*)
The Wilderness Society (*http://www.wilderness.org/*)

Notes

1. Grassroots here refers to groups that are more bottom-up, decentralised, have fewer members and less financial resources than large mainstream organisations (it excludes the network of local groups of a large organisation such as Friends of the Earth and the Sierra Club).
2. Although some writers (notably Lowe and Goyder 1983, and Dunlap and Mertig 1999a) distinguish different trends or phases within these broad waves.
3. For example, in the late 1980s around 20,000 people were joining British environmental groups each week, with Greenpeace growing by 68 per cent in 1988/89 alone (Rawcliffe 1998: 73).

4. Examples of the resource mobilisation approach to social movements include Zald and McCarthy (1987) and Tilly (1978).

5. See Pearce (1991) for an early history of Greenpeace.

6. Although, ironically, FoE has stagnated in the USA where it originated.

7. Many publications report larger membership figures but Greenpeace has changed the way it records its supporters, resulting in a scaling down of numbers as it now counts regular donors only, whereas it used to include all merchandise purchasers.

8. The FoE website reported 'around 219' local groups in England and Wales in March 2001 (*www.foe.ac.uk*).

9. The significance of this threat was illustrated in August 1997 when BP obtained a legal injunction, backed by a freeze on Greenpeace assets, preventing a Greenpeace direct action campaign that was obstructing BP oil exploration in the North Atlantic.

10. Monkey wrenching was stimulated by the Edward Abbey novel, *The Monkey Wrench Gang*. See also Foreman and Haywood (1985).

11. The use of the NIMBY acronym is not intended to imply that such groups are motivated solely by selfish or materialistic considerations.

12. Since renamed the Center for Health, Environment, and Justice.

13. For an analysis of the environmental justice movement, see Cable and Cable (1995), Szasz (1994), Dowie (1995), Pulido (1996) and Schlosberg (1999b).

14. The Real World coalition of thirty-two pressure groups, ranging from FoE and WWF to Christian Aid and Oxfam, has tried to push environmental and social justice issues up the British political agenda (Jacobs 1996a), but it is a top-down initiative which has had little impact to date.

15. See Seel (1997: 121–2) and Wall (1999) for eco-protester perceptions of Greenpeace and Friends of the Earth.

16. See Wall (1999) for an account of Earth First! (UK).

17. See Seel et al. (2000) for coverage of the direct action campaigns in Britain.

18. However, the Sierra Club subsequently appointed a Republican as its new leader (Bosso 1999: 68).

19. The classic rational choice explanation (Olson 1965) for group membership assumes that individuals will only join (and remain in) groups if they are offered selective incentives, such as the protection provided by a trade union. Environmental organisations are public interest groups that seek collective benefits, i.e. environmental protection, not selective benefits. However, Jordan and Maloney (1997) argue that a broad range of incentives persuades people to join environmental groups, notably psychological factors (self-esteem, status) and a belief that membership of a group will contribute in some small way to blocking collective bads or achieving collective goods.

20. One exception was the government's pre-emptive abandonment of the Oxleas Wood river-crossing in July 1993 to avoid a politically damaging direct action campaign.

PART III ENVIRONMENTAL POLICY: ACHIEVING A SUSTAINABLE SOCIETY

The discussion of environmental policy in Part III is in many respects a long way away from some of the abstract debates covered in Part I, or even the ambitious aspirations of some forms of environmental activism examined in Part II. It focuses on the practical challenges facing governments today. The interdependence of environmental issues poses a distinctive set of problems for policy-makers. Few other policy areas can match it for sheer complexity. Nor are failures in most other policy areas likely to be as catastrophic or irredeemable as those affecting the environment, especially if the more pessimistic harbingers of environmental doom are correct.

The belief that economic growth must be given priority over environmental protection continues to govern the way many policy-makers approach environmental issues. This traditional policy paradigm has proved inadequate for resolving the intractable problems posed by contemporary environmental issues. Consequently, since the late 1980s, the alternative policy paradigm of sustainable development has gradually come to dominate thinking about environmental policy. The central premise of sustainable development is that there need not be a trade-off between economic growth and environment; no longer need policy-makers think in terms of the environment *versus* the economy. This message has made sustainable development politically appealing, with most governments, international institutions, political parties, business organisations and environmental NGOs now keen to proclaim their commitment to sustainable development. The broad aim of Part III is to examine the difficulties facing governments seeking to make the transition to sustainable development.

The two opening chapters analyse the competing policy paradigms that shape the way governments are responding to contemporary environmental problems. It is argued in Chapter 7 that the traditional policy paradigm which emerged in the 1970s to deal with environmental problems, and which is still deeply entrenched amongst most policy elites, reflects the way power is distributed and exercised in all capitalist liberal democracies. Chapter 8 identifies the key features of the alternative policy paradigm of sustainable development, and of its close relation, ecological modernisation, and provides a broad analysis of their respective strengths and weaknesses. The remaining chapters assess progress towards sustainable development and ecological modernisation by evaluating how far their key principles have been implemented. Chapter 9 examines the development of international co-operation to protect the global environment, with case studies of climate change and ozone depletion. The final two chapters shift down to the national level where most environmental policy-making, including the implementation of international agreements, takes place. Chapter 10 looks at a range of efforts to integrate environmental considerations into the policy-making process, while Chapter 11 focuses on implementation by assessing the relative merits of different policy instruments, with a particular focus on climate change strategies in the transport and energy sectors.

Throughout Part III many of the recurring themes arising from the relationship between politics and the environment reappear. Familiar issues in environmental politics, such as equity, social justice and democracy, lie at the very heart of environmental policy. Moreover, Part III shows that an understanding of environmental policy requires us to look beyond government to the central role played by industrial and producer interests, and by the wider public, as both citizens and consumers. Put differently, Part III highlights how difficult it is for governments to develop radical responses to environmental problems in a liberal democratic polity and a capitalist economic system.

7

The environment as a policy problem

Contents

- What are the core characteristics of environmental problems?
- What theories and models explain environmental policy-making?
- Where does power lie in environmental policy-making?
- What are the structural and institutional barriers to policy change?
- Why does policy change?

KEY ISSUES

Policy-makers have been slow to recognise or acknowledge that environmental problems might require special treatment. When new environmental imperatives emerged during the 1960s, forcing policy-makers to confront the environment as a broad policy issue for the first time, all governments adopted a technocentric perspective which regarded environmental problems as the unfortunate side-effects of economic growth (see Box 3.8). It was assumed that most environmental problems had solutions and that there was no need to question the underlying commitment to economic growth or to the political-institutional structures of the modern liberal-democratic state. The standard approach to environmental problems – here called the 'traditional policy paradigm' – was reactive, tactical, piecemeal and end-of-pipe. This traditional paradigm has been found wanting, unable to stem long-standing problems of pollution and resource depletion or to deal with the new tranche of global problems that have emerged in recent years. Consequently, during the 1980s the traditional paradigm was increasingly challenged by the alternative paradigm of sustainable development. However, despite the mounting environmental crisis and the rhetorical commitment of policy elites to sustainable development, many elements of the traditional model remain firmly entrenched, even in those countries that have pioneered progressive environmental policies (Andersen and Liefferink 1997a). Why has this traditional paradigm proved so resilient? What does its persistence tell us about the obstacles impeding the adoption of more progressive environmental policies?

The first section of this chapter identifies the core characteristics that distinguish the environment as a policy problem and make it such a difficult problem for policy-makers. The next part of the chapter examines the process of environmental policy-making by drawing on a range of theories of the policy process. It is argued that the resilience of the traditional paradigm is reinforced by the structural power of producer interests in capitalist society and the institutional segmentation of the policy process. However, policy change can and does occur, and in the second half of the chapter several models are used to assess the potential for policy change, ending with a detailed study of the nuclear power industry.

CORE CHARACTERISTICS OF THE ENVIRONMENT AS A POLICY PROBLEM

This section identifies seven core characteristics that distinguish the environment as a policy problem.[1]

Public goods

Many environmental resources can be described as 'public goods'. By this we mean that 'each individual's consumption leads to no subtraction from any other individual's consumption of that good'.[2] Public goods are both 'non-rival' and 'non-excludable'. They are 'non-rival' because one individual's consumption does not limit the consumption of others; someone breathing clean air (normally) does not stop another individual also enjoying clean air. Public goods are 'non-excludable' in that, if one individual refrains from a polluting activity (e.g. driving a car), others cannot be excluded from the resulting benefits (cleaner air). By contrast, with private goods (a washing machine or a handbag), rivals can be excluded by the law of property (Weale 1992: 5).

The public nature of environmental problems has important consequences for policy-makers because efforts to protect the environment may encounter significant collective action problems. The benefits to be gained from using a public good are often concentrated among a handful of producers while the costs may be spread widely: for example, a power station releasing sulphur dioxide which will eventually fall as acid rain far away, or a factory dumping chemicals into a river that pollutes it for miles downstream. If a government wishes to prevent this pollution, the cost of dealing with the problem may fall largely on the polluter, which in these examples would be the electricity generator or the factory owner. Consequently, a small number of spatially concentrated polluters who may have to pay for clean-up measures have an incentive to act collectively to protect their interests (perhaps by dissuading the government from taxing the pollution), whereas the individual citizens who suffer from the pollution are generally ill-informed, geographically dispersed and insufficiently motivated to mobilise as a group in defence of their interests (Olson 1965).

Furthermore, if individuals cannot be excluded from the benefits that others provide, then each has the incentive to *free-ride* on the joint efforts of others to solve the problem (ibid.). So, if a government exhorts citizens to save water by refraining from 'unnecessary' activities such as washing cars or watering lawns, or it seeks to prevent air pollution by asking people to use their cars less, there will be a strong temptation for individuals to ignore these instructions in the expectation that others will be more dutiful. Free-riding will therefore result in a less than optimal provision of the collective benefit, which in these examples would be a constant water supply or clean air.

It is also useful to distinguish between *common-pool resources* (Ostrom 1990: 30) and *common-sink resources* (Weale 1992: 192–5). Common-pool resource systems are sufficiently large for it to be costly, though not impossible, to exclude potential beneficiaries from using them; they include fauna, forests and fish stocks. People benefit from these stocks by depleting the common pool, so the challenge for policy-makers is to ensure that, say, the fishing fleets of different nations do not catch more fish than is prudent for the maintenance of the overall stocks. As common-pool resources can be individually appropriated – elephants can be shot, trees chopped down, fish can be caught – they are not pure public goods,

7.1 The Tragedy of the Commons

The idea of the 'Tragedy of the Commons' was popularised by Garrett Hardin. He invites us to picture a medieval village pasture that is open to all and to assume that each peasant will try to keep as many cattle as possible on this land. Eventually, the carrying capacity of the land will be reached. However, when confronted with a decision about whether or not to put an extra cow on the common land, the rational self-interested peasant will recognise that, whilst all the benefits of the extra cow accrue to her or him alone, the costs – the effects of overgrazing – will be shared with the other villagers. Thus each villager will keep adding more cows until the common land is destroyed:

> Therein is the tragedy. Each man is locked into a
> system that compels him to increase his herd without
> limit – in a world that is limited. Ruin is the
> destination toward which all men rush, each pursuing
> his own best interest in a
> society that believes in the freedom of the commons.
> Freedom in a commons brings ruin to all.

(Hardin 1968: 1244)

Hardin uses the common land of a medieval village as a metaphor for contemporary environmental problems to show how private benefit and public interest seem to point in opposite directions.

This metaphor can be used to analyse contemporary problems such as over-fishing and deforestation. Ostrom et al. (1999) make a persuasive argument demonstrating that tragedies of the commons 'are real, but not inevitable'(p. 281). See Ostrom (1990) for a critical discussion of common property issues.

although they share many attributes.[3] However, common-sink resources, such as fresh air, are pure public goods. The problem here is not about the consumption of air, but how individuals use this resource to dispose of waste materials such as sulphur dioxide or carbon dioxide. The collective challenge posed by common-sink resources is to control their level of pollution (Weale 1992: 192–3). Failure to protect either pools or sinks can lead to a 'tragedy of the commons' (Box 7.1) in which a resource is either completely exhausted or damaged beyond use.

Transboundary problems

Problems of the global commons are frequently transboundary: for example, climate change, ozone depletion and marine pollution do not respect national borders. Global problems represent a major threat to the environment and can only be solved through concerted action by the international community. However, if one nation takes action to reduce ozone depletion or prevent global warming, it cannot exclude other nations from the benefits. Whereas an individual government can use the law of the land to require citizens or companies to change their behaviour, the doctrine of national sovereignty means that there is no equivalent international authority – no world government – that can force every country to conform. Consequently, as Chapter 9 shows, efforts by the international community to address transboundary problems have required unprecedented levels of co-operation between states and the building of new international institutions to help and persuade reluctant nations to support joint action.

Complexity and uncertainty

Policy-making may be hampered by the complexity and uncertainty that characterise many environmental problems. It is often difficult to identify the complex and interdependent relationships between natural and human-made phenomena. The interconnectedness of ecosystems means that many problems are non-reducible: they cannot be resolved by addressing individual parts in isolation. Indeed, policies that deal with one discrete problem may have unintended and damaging consequences elsewhere. For example, in the 1950s local air pollution in Britain's industrial towns was reduced by building taller factory chimneys, only for it to be discovered many years later that this 'solution' had simply exported the pollution to fall as acid rain in Scandinavia. Similarly, cars can be fitted with catalytic converters to reduce the nitrogen oxide emissions that cause acid rain, but the resulting reduction in engine efficiency increases fuel consumption and, therefore, carbon dioxide emissions which contribute to global warming.

Political constraints also contribute to the non-reducibility of problems. Thus solutions to the many environmental problems associated with modern farming practices (including soil erosion, river pollution, destruction of habitats) need to take account of broader public policies, such as national food production strategies, the rules governing international trade or, in EU member states, the price supports provided by the Common Agricultural Policy. Similarly, a government wishing to ban **genetically modified** crops may be stopped by World Trade Organisation rules that encourage free trade.

Genetically modified organism: New organisms created by human manipulation of genetic information and material.

Uncertainty surrounds many environmental problems. For example, is the climate changing? If it is, is this due to natural phenomena or to human activity? If the latter, what will be its impact and how quickly will its effects be noticed? Climate change may be an extreme case, but it is not exceptional. Are localised leukaemia clusters linked to emissions from nuclear power stations or caused by a virus? Are GMOs dangerous to human health or natural habitats? (see Box 7.2).

Complexity and uncertainty underline the importance of science, scientists and professional expertise in environmental policy-making. Problems such as climate change and ozone depletion cannot even be identified without science. Some environmental degradation is reasonably visible, such as fumes from road traffic, or relatively easy to detect, such as falling fish stocks, but scientific knowledge is needed to make an accurate assessment of the nature of either problem. What is a safe level of lead in the atmosphere? What is a sustainable fish catch? Yet science frequently struggles to fulfil its role as objective arbiter between policy options. The scientific knowledge informing our understanding of environmental problems is often based on a theory which is contestable and evidence that can be interpreted in several different ways, so scientific judgements will always be provisional and open to revision (Yearley 1991). The fluidity that characterises science can make it difficult for policy-makers to make adequate responses to 'new' problems such as climate change, ozone depletion and GMOs. These issues may be subject to resistance or even denial by affected interests, such as industrialists or farmers, who may discourage or oppose fuller scientific inquiry into the environmental impact of such

7.2 Genetically modified food crops and scientific uncertainty

A GMO is 'any organism that has had its genetic material modified in a way that could not occur through natural processes' (Food Ethics Council 1999:6).

GM food crops have many *potential* benefits, notably:

1. *Better for the environment* because their resistance to pesticides simplifies and reduces the spraying regime; i.e. lower use of ecologically damaging pesticides (and reduces costs);
2. *Increased crop productivity* because their resistance to disease, pests and weeds, and to extreme weather conditions, increases crop yields.
3. *Improved human health* from 'functional foods' that can lower cholesterol or provide vital vitamins to supplement diets of poor people.

Thus advocates of GM food crops suggest they may help combat world hunger and poverty.

However, if cross-pollination from GM plants results in the spread of pesticide-resistant genes in the wild population, then weeds and pests could spread uncontrollably and the species composition of wildlife communities could be altered, with devastating consequences for biodiversity.

We are not *certain* whether this cross-pollination will happen, or what the exact effects would be if it did. More broadly, there are other *political* solutions, such as land redistribution and debt relief, to problems of poverty and hunger.

Policy problem: How strictly should we regulate the development and commercial release of GM crops as a precaution against the worst-case scenario (see Box 7.6)?

issues. There is also considerable disagreement within the scientific community concerning many long-established problems. For example, there are sharply contrasting views about whether bathing-water pollution should be prevented by building longer pipes to take sewage further out to sea, or by stopping all marine sewage disposal. Nor are scientists immune from twisting their findings to suit vested interests, such as their corporate funders, or even to promote their own chances of securing future research funding.

Uncertainty and complexity complicate policy-making. If policy-makers understand the causes of a problem then it is obviously easier to design effective solutions, but frequently they have to act with incomplete information. Faced with uncertainty, should they adopt a precautionary approach to a problem, or continue depleting an environmental resource until scientific evidence proves that action must be taken? How policy-makers respond will be shaped by their position on the ecocentric–technocentric divide (see Box 3.8), with ecocentrics opting for caution while technocentrics are more likely to assume optimistically that things will pan out satisfactorily. Moreover, in liberal democracies such dilemmas open up decisions to political conflict by providing ammunition for both proponents and opponents of remedial action, which further complicates and politicises the decision-making process.

Irreversibility

The problem of uncertainty is exacerbated by the irreversibility of many environmental problems. Once the Earth's carrying capacity is exceeded, then environmental assets may be damaged beyond repair. Scarce resources may be exhausted and species may become extinct. Some environmental assets are substitutable, although rarely is the process straightforward or costless. Technological advances may eventually enable solar energy and wind power to replace depleted fossil fuels as generators of energy, but probably only if there is also an overall reduction in energy consumption. Irreversibility places even greater pressure on policy-makers to get it right, for unlike fiscal or welfare policy, where a poorly judged tax rate or benefit payment can be corrected in the following year's budget, it may not be possible to correct an earlier mistake.

Temporal and spatial variability

Many environmental issues are complicated by the fact that their impact will be long-term, probably affecting future rather than present generations, whereas remedial policies need to be adopted before the full negative effects of a problem are felt. Indeed, there are serious pragmatic constraints on policy-makers wishing to respond to the ethical concerns for future generations discussed in Part I. Although action to protect future generations may be needed now, politicians tend to have short-term concerns – tomorrow's papers, forthcoming opinion polls or the next election – and they know how difficult it is to persuade people to accept self-sacrifice today in order to protect those who are not yet born. In short, it is easier to make policy that responds to today's political pressures than policy which addresses tomorrow's environmental problems.

Similarly, there are huge variations in the spatial impact of environmental problems. Rising sea-levels caused by global warming will cause most damage to low-lying lands such as Bangladesh and Egypt. The closure of unstable East German nuclear power stations after German unification may have reduced the risk of accident but it caused significant local job losses. The construction of a high-speed railtrack may help shift passengers from planes to trains and so reduce carbon emissions, but it will reduce the quality of life of those people living along its route.

Spatial and temporal variability mean that the costs of environmental problems, and their solutions, are unevenly distributed. Inevitably, environmental policies will produce winners and losers. The challenge for governments is to balance competing interests, but this raises important issues of equity and social justice between both current and future generations.

Administrative fragmentation

The administrative structure of government is usually divided into distinct policy sectors with specific responsibilities such as education, defence or health care. A core group of economic ministries – typically, finance, industry, employment, energy, agriculture and transport – make policy decisions affecting production, consumption, mobility and lifestyles that will frequently have negative consequences for the environment. Yet these individual ministries often engage in a blinkered pursuit of narrow sectoral objectives with little consideration for their environmental impact. A transport ministry might implement a massive road-building programme, or the agriculture ministry might encourage intensive farming methods, while responsibility for protecting the environment is typically given to a separate ministry. The instinct of bureaucrats is to break problems down into separate units, but the interdependence of economic and ecological systems does not respect these artificial administrative or institutional boundaries. Many environmental problems are cross-sectoral and require co-ordinated responses that transcend sectoral boundaries. An effective climate change strategy, for example, will need the involvement of all the ministries responsible for transport, energy, industrial emissions, livestock, forestry as well as overall economic policy.

Regulatory intervention

Environmental damage is frequently a by-product of otherwise legitimate activities; consequently, governments may have to intervene in the economy and society to regulate these damaging activities (Weale 1992: 6). Regulatory intervention can involve a mix of policy instruments, not just legal instruments: for example, setting factory emission standards or encouraging the recycling of waste paper. The regulatory character of much environmental policy contrasts with many other policy areas, notably welfare policy, where taxes and public spending are used to alter the distribution of resources. Although public spending is rarely the primary instrument of environmental policy, regulatory interventions will usually impose some kind of cost on key interests in society and may have significant distributive consequences. Consequently, regulatory proposals are likely to provoke howls of outrage from businesses and trade unions about the dangers of reduced competitiveness or jobs lost, or from consumers who have to pay higher prices for cleaner or safer goods. Thus the effectiveness of regulatory interventions may be limited by this historical tension between economic growth and environmental protection.

   This section has identified seven core characteristics of environmental problems. The first five are intrinsic to the environment as a policy issue; the remaining two characteristics reflect the institutional structures and policy-making processes of modern government.

CRITICAL QUESTION 1

How unique is the environment as a policy problem?

THE TRADITIONAL POLICY PARADIGM

A policy paradigm provides policy-makers with the terminology and a set of taken-for-granted assumptions about the way they communicate and think about a policy area. While none of the seven core characteristics identified in the previous section is unique to the environment, taken together they pose a range of problems that are particularly challenging to policy-makers. Yet the traditional paradigm that emerged during the 1970s treated the environment like any other new policy area, rather than recognising the interdependency of the relationships between ecosystems and political, economic, social and cultural systems. The traditional paradigm has been characterised by Weale (1992: 10–23) in the following way.[4] Government policies were reactive, piecemeal and tactical: few countries possessed a comprehensive national plan setting out an anticipatory, comprehensive and strategic approach to the environment. Instead, a specialist branch of government – an environment ministry – and various new agencies were formed to deal with environmental issues. Environmental policy was treated as a discrete policy area. Agencies had few powers over decisions taken in other policy sectors and there was little policy co-ordination and considerable scope for problem displacement. Pollution control, for example, typically involved the use of single-medium regulations to control industrial releases, whilst separate agencies dealt with discharges to air, water and land. End-of-pipe solutions were usually seen as adequate; policy-makers preferred to deal with symptoms rather than causes. Administrative regulation was the preferred policy instrument. Many policies were prone to 'implementation deficit' involving a shortfall between policy intent and outcome. For example, although major legislative programmes such as the US Clean Air Act 1970 and the UK Control of Pollution Act 1974 introduced stringent controls on pollutants and toxic substances, many deadlines and targets were missed and key provisions remained unimplemented many years later (Lundqvist 1980: 131–58; Ward 1998: 245–6). Above all, a balance had always to be struck between environmental protection and economic growth, with the latter frequently taking priority. The traditional paradigm was not reproduced identically in all countries, but something akin to it could be identified everywhere.

This traditional paradigm was fundamentally flawed in design and practice. Most indicators and trends showed that the 'objective' state of the environment in advanced industrialised nations worsened through the 1970s (OECD 1991),[5] whilst the appearance of new problems such as acid rain and climate change posed novel challenges to policy-makers. During the 1980s the weaknesses in the traditional paradigm became increasingly apparent to policy elites. Yet, despite the emergence of the alternative paradigm of sustainable development, the traditional paradigm has proved very resistant to change.

POLITICAL OBSTACLES TO CHANGE

The traditional paradigm is bolstered by two core characteristics of the policy process: first, the privileged position of business and producer groups; secondly, sectoral divisions within the institutional structure of government both reflect and reinforce a special-interest approach to public policy in which each ministry tends to act as a sponsor for the key groups of producers or professionals within its policy sphere. This section uses theories of state–group relations and policy network analysis to show how the power of producers and the fragmented nature of government have reinforced the traditional paradigm.

The power of producers

In political science, it is common to explain policy outcomes in terms of the power exercised by competing interests. This section uses some central theories of state–group relations (pluralist, neo-pluralist, Marxist)[6] and the theory of three-dimensional power (Lukes 1974) to explain the continuing strength of the traditional paradigm in shaping environmental policy outcomes.

The *pluralist* model regards public policy as the outcome of competition between different groups. For every environmental issue there will be a wide range of institutions, organisations and interest groups seeking to influence the formation and implementation of public policy. Each interest group will use the resources at its disposal – expertise, finance, membership, public opinion – to influence policy outcomes. It is assumed that power is diffuse: no single group or set of interests dominates the decision process, many groups can gain access to government and, if sufficiently determined, most groups can achieve at least some of their objectives. The government will obviously have its own preferences on many subjects, but it will consult widely and respond to powerful outside demands (Dahl 1961).

Of course, not every group has equal influence. In particular, a primary aim of any government is to manage the economy, so in core economic sectors it regularly consults and seeks the co-operation of business groups (Truman 1951). Environmental policy often has a direct impact on businesses, so they will mobilise against proposed (or existing) regulations or eco-taxes, or to win approval for a new development such as a motorway or a dam. As insider groups, businesses will usually remain within the law: lobbying politicians and civil servants, financing publicity campaigns or funding sympathetic pressure groups. Sometimes producers may threaten to flout legislation or even take direct action to make their case; French farmers have an unrivalled record in achieving their aims by blocking roads and ports.

Pluralist accounts therefore concede that producers have both the motivation and the means to play an active role in the policy process, but they do not regard business as a privileged participant. Businesses may exercise disproportionate influence compared to environmental groups because they have more resources at their disposal. The pluralist would anticipate that when environmental groups are able to mobilise sufficient resources (members, income, professional staff) to counter the strength of business, they too should win better access to government and a matching influence over policy outcomes (unless, like Greenpeace, they deliberately resist entry for fear of being 'captured'). Yet, in practice, in many key areas affecting the environment, those 'insider' pressure groups operating closest to government typically consist of a handful of powerful producer interests.[7] Governments regard the views of key producer groups as legitimate and important, so they benefit from good access to ministers and civil servants to discuss matters affecting their interests and they are regularly consulted by government officials. Conversely, environmental and consumer groups are often 'outsider' groups excluded from the corridors of power; they are less routinely consulted and they may struggle to get their voice heard by government. Consequently, more often than not, policy outcomes show the interests of producer groups trumping those of environmentalists.

One weakness of pluralism is its use of an incomplete, one-dimensional model of power which underestimates the influence of business interests (Lukes 1974) (see Box 7.3). Pluralists focus on *observable* influence, examining each individual decision to assess whether the preferences of business groups hold sway. However, Bachrach and Baratz (1962) argue that observable power measures only one aspect of power. They identify a second dimension of power – 'non-decision-making' – which refers to the ability of powerful groups to keep issues off the agenda. Producer groups can manage conflict before it even starts by using political routines to produce or reinforce dominant values and interests, suppress dissenting demands or co-opt challenging groups, a process that Schattschneider (1960) called the 'mobilisation of bias'. In practice, observable 'pluralist' decision-making is frequently confined to safe issues that do not threaten the fundamental interests of the dominant (producer) groups, while the grievances of those interests excluded from the policy process, such as environmental groups, are marginalised. Indeed, opposition groups may not even raise their dissenting views in

---

7.3 The three dimensions of power

First dimension

A has power over B to the extent that she can get B to do something that B would not otherwise do. A defeats B by mobilising superior bargaining resources in open conflict over clearly defined issues.

Second dimension

A constructs a barrier against the participation of B in decision-making – A engages in 'non-decisions' and uses the 'mobilisation of bias' to suppress or thwart challenges to its values or interests by B.

Third dimension

A influences or shapes the consciousness of B to accept inequalities (through myths, information control, ideology) and to induce a sense of powerlessness and acceptance in B. Very difficult to detect.

Based on Lukes (1974). See discussion of Crenson (1971) for examples of each dimension.

the formal policy process because of a fatalistic assumption that they will be rejected by the dominant producer interests.

A classic environmental illustration of non-decision-making is provided in Crenson's (1971) study of air pollution in two neighbouring American steel towns: East Chicago and Gary. Whereas East Chicago introduced legislation controlling air pollution in 1949, Gary delayed acting until 1963, even though the pollution problem was identical in the two towns. A key difference between the towns was that, whilst many steel companies were located in East Chicago, just one big corporation, US Steel, dominated Gary. US Steel did not lobby overtly against regulation, but it was able to exercise enormous indirect influence because local political leaders feared that the company might leave the town if anti-pollution laws were introduced. Environmental groups saw little point in even seeking to raise the issue of air pollution because they anticipated the negative reaction of US Steel were they to do so. Yet no observable decision opposing anti-pollution legislation was ever taken; it was a 'non-decision'. By contrast, the fragmentation of the steel industry in East Chicago made the negative employment impact of legislation less risky and allowed proponents of legislation to get pollution control on the agenda much earlier.

This broader two-dimensional model of power underpins the *neo-pluralist* theory of state–group relations which, like pluralism, sees businesses as exercising power through their ability to mobilise resources in the political arena but, in contrast to pluralism, claims that they also possess structural power. Lindblom (1977) provides a forceful elaboration of the view that business holds a privileged interest within the political system owing to its structural importance in the capitalist economy.[8] Any government in a liberal democracy will routinely take account of producer interests in its decision-making because the overall performance of the economy is likely to influence its popularity, and hence its chances of re-election. Governments therefore assume responsibility for creating the conditions under which business can make high profits. In anticipating the needs of business, a government will take decisions that reflect business interests without businesses having to take any observable action, not even to organise as a lobby. Lindblom does not see business as uniformly privileged across all policy areas: he distinguishes 'grand majority' issues affecting significant economic interests over which the public can exercise only limited influence, from secondary issues that do not impinge directly on powerful business interests and where the policy process is more competitive, or pluralistic (for example, land-use planning). The contribution of neo-pluralism is to point to the privileged position of business in many core economic policy sectors affecting the environment, without claiming that business will always determine policy outcomes, or keep all 'undesirable' issues off the agenda.

Nevertheless, from a more radical perspective, the two-dimensional model still does not capture all aspects of the concept of power. Structuralist explanations, notably *neo-Marxism*, emphasise the significance of the underlying economic structure in determining the distribution of political power in favour of a ruling elite, or class. A key contribution made by structuralists is to identify an ideological dimension to power in which the role of the state is to support and promote the process of capitalist accumulation. Offe (1974) argues that within capitalist societies there are various mechanisms, or exclusion rules, which identify those issues that merit attention and filter out issues that threaten the values and rules of capitalist societies. Broad principles, such as the right to private property, provide the legitimacy to screen out undesirable challenges to the status quo, including some of those posed by environmentalism. Within individual policy sectors, non-decision-making mechanisms keep certain issues off the agenda and ideological mechanisms will define issues and problems in ways that produce a systematic bias in favour of capitalist interests. This ideological role of the state reflects what Lukes (1974) calls 'third-dimension' power whereby the 'very wants' of individuals are shaped to accept the preferences of the ruling elite, or class (even when they run counter to their own 'objective' interests), so that conflicts remain latent. Thus, returning to the Crenson study, the selective perception within the local community in Gary that jobs and economic development were the only real concerns – even though air pollution might be damaging public health – may indicate that political institutions had managed to mould citizen preferences to reflect the interests of capital.[9]

Structuralist and neo-pluralist theories of the state help explain how business interests have retained a privileged position within the policy process despite the increasingly large, vocal and professional environmental lobby. Business can exercise the second and third dimensions of power to reinforce the traditional paradigm and to resist more strategic and holistic approaches to environmental policy. Of course, this structural power is not deterministic. Sometimes environmental interests will prevail and governments do overrule producer objections, as illustrated by the raft of environmental regulations introduced over the past thirty years. Nor should it be assumed that producers will always oppose measures to protect the environment, as will be shown in the discussion of ecological modernisation in Chapter 8. However, on balance, it seems that business power has been used to reinforce the traditional paradigm.

CRITICAL QUESTION 2

Is industry the main villain in environmental policy?

Administrative fragmentation

Another factor giving some groups and interests disproportionate access to the policy process is the institutional structure of the state. The fragmentation of government into sectoral divisions produces a special-interest approach to public policy in which each ministry tends to act as a sponsor for the key groups of producers or professionals within its policy sphere. Agriculture ministers, for example, will typically see themselves as speaking on behalf of farmers, rather than acting to protect consumer interests or the environment. Similarly, energy ministers see their role as protecting the commercial interests of the major energy producers in the coal, oil, gas and nuclear industries, and consequently they may ignore or downplay the environmental damage associated with the energy sector. Each policy sector is characterised by administrative arrangements that reflect the different groups whose interests are built into that sector and the underlying power relations between those interests. This section uses an institutional model of the policy process – *policy network analysis* – to argue that the sectoral fragmentation of government further entrenches the structural power of producer groups over many areas of environmental decision-making.

In many countries, pluralistic patterns of environmental policy-making seem to be the exception rather than the rule. Even in the USA, one of the most pluralistic political systems, the widely used 'iron triangle' metaphor acknowledges the enormous influence of producer groups in key policy areas where decision-making is dominated by three powerful actors: congressional committee, administrative agency and producer group (Cater 1965). The congressional subcommittee provides money and monitors regulations, the bureau hands over the money or enforces the regulation, and the producer group is the benefiting special interest. Each actor needs the others, so this cosy relationship would break down without the participation of the others; conversely, it is in their mutual interest to limit the access of other actors to the policy process. Thus it is an 'iron' triangle because it is largely impenetrable to outsiders.[10] In those countries where **corporatist** structures prevail, notably Austria, Finland and Sweden, policy-making is dominated by representatives of government, capital and labour which may exclude environmental groups from the corridors of power.[11] The main corporatist actors share the common policy goal of unchallenged economic expansion which may suggest that environmental considerations will struggle to make the agenda (Hukkinen 1995).[12] A third model is policy network analysis which examines the relationship between actors involved in the public policy process (Rhodes 1988; Marsh and Rhodes 1992; Smith 1993). There is evidence that policy networks exist in most countries, including the USA (Heclo 1978), Canada (Pross 1992), several European countries (Kickert et al. 1997; Marsh 1998) and within the EU policy process (Peterson and Bomberg 1999). This section uses the influential policy network approach to illustrate how the *structural* power of producer groups discussed above is frequently institutionalised within the segmented policy process (although a similar argument might also be applied to iron triangle or corporatist institutional arrangements).

Corporatism: A system in which major organised interests (traditionally, capital and labour) work closely together within the formal structures of government to formulate and implement public policies.

Policy networks are clusters of public and private actors connected to each other by resource dependencies, such as information, expertise, money and legitimacy, and separated from other clusters by breaks in the structure of resource dependencies. Marsh and Rhodes (1992) distinguish two ideal types of policy network at opposite ends of a continuum: policy communities and issue networks. The *policy community* has a closed and stable membership, usually involving a government ministry or agency and a handful of privileged producer groups, who regularly interact and share a consensus of values and predispositions, almost a shared ideology, about that policy sector that sets the community apart from outsider groups. The cement that joins the members of the policy community together is their mutual resource dependency: each has resources that can be exchanged or bargained with so that a balance of power prevails, allowing every member to benefit from a positive-sum game. Through their ability to control the agenda, the members produce continuity and stability in policy outcomes that transcend changes in the political complexion of government and are largely immune from the gaze and control of either Parliament or the public. According to Smith (1993: 66–74), policy communities provide the state with four advantages: a consultative policy-making environment; a consensual, depoliticised policy arena; predictable, stable surroundings; and a reinforcement of policy segmentation by the building of barriers against encroachment by other ministries.

In contrast, the more open *issue network* has many competing groups with fluctuating membership and less regular interaction. The government tends to consult rather than bargain with members of this more pluralistic network. As a result, policy outcomes are far less stable and predictable. It is important to note that the policy community and issue network are at the two extreme ends of a continuum, and various hybrid networks exist between these two poles.[13]

The significance of policy network analysis in explaining the strength of the traditional paradigm lies in the prevalence of policy communities in those policy sectors where environmental issues impinge on major economic interests and the government is dependent on producer groups for implementation. Here the power and interests of producers and the fragmented administrative structure become mutually reinforcing; neither producers nor the state want anything to disrupt this cosy situation. So, how common are policy communities and, where they exist, how do they influence environmental policy outcomes?

The empirical evidence supporting the widespread existence of closed policy communities is strongest in Britain, where it reflects central features of the political system such as the strong executive and the culture of secrecy (Marsh and Rhodes 1992; Smith 1993). For example, for much of the post-war period transport policy has emerged from a policy community consisting of officials from the Department of Transport and representatives from the motor industry, road construction industry, oil industry and various road haulage and motoring organisations (Dudley and Richardson 1996; Rawcliffe 1998: 121–3). Consequently, British transport policy has been heavily biased towards road-building and encouraging car use, with little interest in alternative, less environmentally damaging, forms of transport such as railways or cycling. Similarly, for many years a policy community dominated by the Atomic Energy Authority and its scientific experts underpinned the strong commitment of successive governments to the development of the nuclear power industry as a clean, cheap source of electricity (Saward 1992; Greenaway et al. 1992: 233–4). Tight policy communities have also been identified in other areas affecting the environment, including the energy and water industries (Ward and Samways 1992; Maloney and Richardson 1994). A growing number of studies suggest that policy communities are also to be found in environmental policy-making elsewhere in Europe, including the water (Bressers et al. 1994) and energy (Kasa 2000) sectors.

The *agriculture sector* provides the classic illustration of how policy communities have hampered the development of sustainable environmental policies in a range of European countries, including Denmark (Daugbjerg 1998), Finland (Jokinen 1997), the Netherlands (Glasbergen 1992) and Britain (Cox et al. 1986; Smith 1990). In each case the policy community normally consists of officials from the agriculture ministry and leading farmers' groups. The British policy community, for example, primarily involves the Ministry of Agriculture, Fisheries and Food and the National Farmers' Union (NFU). It first emerged in the late 1930s and was formalised in the Agriculture Act 1947 when farmers were given a statutory right to be consulted over policy. The members were bound together by the shared belief that farmers should maximise the output and efficiency of their land. Smith (1990) shows that the state deliberately created the policy community to ensure a secure war-time food supply and, to do so, it was prepared to guarantee prices to farmers. It suited both the farming ministry and the farmers' union to plan a mutually beneficial expansionist agricultural policy and to maintain this arrangement after the war. The policy community was, therefore, a result of a structural feature – a political context that demanded a secure food supply – that has subsequently institutionalised the power of the National Farmers' Union.

In most EU states, but particularly in Britain, Denmark and the Netherlands, the objective of agricultural policy has been to stimulate the competitive position of the agrarian sector by adopting increasingly intensive farming methods. Livestock production, wherever possible, has maximised the use of factory farming methods. The specialisation of arable production has seen the appropriation of every possible piece of land and the lavish use of chemical fertilisers and pesticides. The benefits are obvious: a stable farming sector, readily available and affordable farm produce for the consumer and a food surplus that has contributed to exports; but the environmental damage has also been immense. The British countryside, for example, has been transformed since the war by the massive destruction of hedgerows, ancient woodlands, wetlands and lowland heaths, which have harmed many species of animals, birds and insects (Lowe et al. 1986). Intensive farming gradually erodes soil quality, consumes vast amounts of water and run-off from slurry pollutes rivers and underlying water tables. Yet the efforts of environmental and consumer groups to get new issues onto the agricultural agenda were, for many years, effectively rebuffed by policy communities across Europe (Cox et al. 1986; Smith 1990; Glasbergen 1992). Until recently, any group questioning the underlying expansionist ideology of agricultural policy would be marginalised. Typically, when a new environmental issue emerges, the agricultural policy community will initially seek to deny the existence of the problem or to play down the danger. As concern grows, delaying tactics are employed, such as a call for further research or to set up a commission of inquiry (Glasbergen 1992). When action can no longer be avoided, problems are dealt with in ways that suit the interests of the policy community. Some issues, such as the Dutch problem of surplus manure, are depoliticised by defining them as 'technical' problems – i.e. uncontroversial – which can be solved by expert insiders. Alternatively, the EU set-aside scheme, which encourages conservation by farmers through financial compensation, also created a new justification for high public support for the agrarian sector. British farmers' groups have tried to deflect criticism from environmentalists for their destructive methods by using the concept of set-aside to recast their role to become 'stewards of the countryside'. Thus agricultural policy communities, by institutionalising the power of farmers, have managed to keep new issues off the policy agenda or, where this is impossible, impeded or diluted policies intended to reduce the environmental damage from agri-industry – although agricultural policy communities have become increasingly unstable in recent years (see below, pp. 184–5).

The example of the agricultural sector shows how the state, by facilitating the formation of a closed policy community, has helped institutionalise the structural power of producer groups within individual policy sectors. Producer groups derive structural power from the policy network because 'rules, procedures and beliefs support the interests of the powerful without the powerful having to decide on every occasion what should be allowed on that agenda' (Smith 1990: 39). Hence the values underpinning sectoral policy communities frequently produce policy outcomes that are explicitly expansionist and likely to damage the environment.[14] If a policy community is forced to address an environmental issue, the major actors will seek solutions that require no questioning of the principles shared by the policy community, such as the commitment to agricultural price support. When environmental issues grew in importance after the 1970s, policy networks were already well established in many traditional sectors such as agriculture, energy and industry (Daugbjerg 1998), so that environmental groups confronted entrenched institutional frameworks that were resistant to the penetration of new ideas and issues, and sought to prevent access to environmental groups (Rawcliffe 1998). Policy communities also reinforce a sectoral approach to environmental policy-making. Individual ministries, such as agriculture or energy, are wary of co-ordinated strategies to address cross-sectoral problems such as climate change, fearing disruption of established sectoral patterns of policy-making. Overall, it would seem that the institutional structure of the state has reinforced the traditional environmental policy paradigm.

However, policy communities are neither ubiquitous nor static. Even in Britain some policy areas, usually those concerned with 'secondary issues' (Lindblom 1977) such as nature conservation and countryside recreation, where there is no major threat to the interests of economic or professional groups, are characterised by more pluralistic issue networks. Elsewhere, particularly in North America, pluralistic relations are more common. Moreover, where policy communities do exist, these institutional arrangements are not set in stone and environmental policy change can occur. The next section examines the dynamics of policy change.

CRITICAL QUESTION 3

Does the capitalist state present insuperable barriers to a co-ordinated environmental policy?

ACHIEVING POLICY CHANGE

Despite the powerful structural and institutional factors reinforcing the traditional environmental policy paradigm, policy change is not impossible. In recent years, all governments have introduced new measures to improve environmental protection, although evidence of *radical* change is scarce (see Box 7.4). This section draws selectively from the wide literature on policy-making by highlighting the agenda-setting, advocacy coalition and network approaches as useful frameworks for exploring the potential for policy change and, in particular, to indicate how the traditional paradigm might be superseded by an alternative framework.

Agenda-setting

Issue attention cycle: The idea that there is a cycle in which issues attract public attention and move up and down the political agenda.

The agenda-setting stage of the policy process is a critical point at which policy change can be initiated. Amongst several models that seek to explain how issues can get onto and ascend agendas, a crude but influential model, specifically designed to account for the rise and fall of environmentalism in America in the early 1970s, was the **Issue Attention Cycle** (Downs 1972) (see Box 7.5). The notion that environmental issues go through cycles of attention is attractive because it resembles the way that public and media interest latches onto an issue before lurching off in pursuit of another. Moreover, evidence from the USA suggests that peak periods of relevant organisational activity (new institutions, programmes and policies) often coincide with peak periods in the attention cycle, implying that governments do respond to public concern (Peters and Hogwood 1985). More cynically, it could be suggested that policy-makers are simply making sure they are seen to be 'doing something', even if their action has minimal impact on the problem (Parsons 1995: 119). Indeed, Downs presents an essentially pessimistic view of the importance of agenda-setting as a process which generates a temporary public fascination with the topic of concern, but has little long-lasting importance. This pessimism is particularly appropriate where policy communities exist because, even if an issue attracts widespread public attention, a policy community may be strong enough to resist pressure for substantial change, confident that public attention will not sustain an issue long enough to define a new agenda (Smith 1993: 90).

However, other theorists have argued more optimistically that these brief moments of public interest are occasions when structural changes can be forced through which may permanently alter the rules of access and participation. Kingdon (1995) outlines a sophisticated model of agenda-setting based on a dynamic picture of the policy process. Agenda change occurs when problems, policy solutions and political receptivity combine in a 'window of opportunity': a compelling problem is recognised, a technically viable solution exists and the political circumstances are right for change. Similarly, Baumgartner and Jones (1993) outline a model of 'punctuated equilibrium' in which the policy process is characterised as having long periods of stability in which only incremental changes occur, interspersed with short periods of instability when major policy change occurs. Disruption to the equilibrium may allow access by new groups seeking to challenge the dominant policy paradigm. Sometimes that challenge is sufficiently powerful and persuasive to overthrow the dominant policy consensus and to replace it with new

7.4 Defining policy change

Hall (1993) outlines a three-level taxonomy of policy change:
First-order changes affect the levels or settings of basic policy instruments, such as adjustments to an emissions standard or a tax rate.
Second-order changes also see no change in the overall policy goals, but involve alterations in the instruments used to achieve them, perhaps the replacement of an emissions standard by an eco-tax.
First- and second-level changes can be seen as 'normal policy-making', in which policy is adjusted without challenging the existing policy paradigm.
Third-order change is marked by a radical shift in the overall goals of policy that reflect a fundamental paradigm shift (such as the transition from Keynesianism to monetarism in economic policy). Such radical changes are rare and usually follow a wide-ranging process of societal debate and reflection on past experience, or 'social learning'.
Although incremental changes in environmental policy are possible within the traditional paradigm, an accumulation of first- and second-order changes will not automatically lead to third-order changes because genuinely radical change requires the replacement of the traditional paradigm with an alternative.

7.5 Downs's Issue Attention Cycle

Stage 1   *Pre-Problem* – knowledge exists about a problem, experts and interest groups may be worried, but public interest is negligible.

Stage 2   *Alarmed discovery and euphoric enthusiasm* – a dramatic event or discovery makes the public aware of and alarmed by the problem. People demand action and the government promises solutions.

Stage 3   *Counting the cost of progress* – both politicians and the public become aware of what 'solving' the problem will cost in terms of financial cost and personal sacrifices.

Stage 4   *Gradual decline of intense public interest* – people have second thoughts. Attention is distracted by new issues.

Stage 5   *Post-problem* – public interest wanes but the institutions, policies and programmes set up to solve the problem remain in place.

Source: Downs (1972).

perspectives, institutions and policies. A key role during these moments of instability is played by the media, which can direct public attention to new issues or developments, or offer a new perspective on familiar issues. Suddenly issues that are normally confined to policy subsystems are thrown open to wider scrutiny. New participants from other subsystems may become interested in the debates so that previously low-profile policy arrangements are permanently disrupted (see Box 7.6).

Baumgartner and Jones (1993: 93–102) use developments in the American pesticides industry as one illustration of their argument. Pesticides attracted enormous public attention immediately after the Second World War because of the claims that new synthetic organics such as DDT could achieve amazing results, including the eradication of malaria and increased food production to the point of ending world hunger. The popular wave of enthusiasm for pesticides saw the emergence of an iron triangle of the Department of Agriculture, farm and chemical interests, and congressional agriculture and appropriations committees, which controlled the regulation of these chemicals and set up an institutional structure that promoted the industry for decades to come, long after public interest had waned. However, during the 1960s, growing awareness of the dangers of some of these pesticides, stimulated by a series of food scares and by Rachel Carson's (1962) bestseller *Silent Spring*, produced a new, negative wave of interest, that eventually peaked with the banning of DDT in 1969 and several new pieces of legislation regulating pesticide use. Thus positive issue attention in the late 1940s provided a window of opportunity to create a producer-dominated iron triangle promoting the pesticide industry, whilst negative issue attention during the 1960s provided a second window of opportunity that contributed to the collapse of this cosy network and ushered in policy change.

This example of punctuated equilibrium suggests that the Downs model overlooked the longer-term institutional legacies of agenda-setting which can produce change through an unfolding historical process. As the 'euphoria' surrounding an issue fades away and public attention turns elsewhere, the organisations created during that period of heightened interest remain (Baumgartner and Jones 1993). Another example arose from the huge public interest provoked by the *Exxon Valdez* oil-tanker disaster in

7.6 GM crops and agenda-setting

During the 1980s and 1990s the rapid commercialisation of GM crops, led by large multinational corporations such as Monsanto, resulted in their widespread use throughout the USA. The EU had been gradually developing a system for the regulation of the release of GM crops, so it seemed that it was just a matter of time before European farmers followed suit. Early in 1999 Tony Blair enthusiastically declared: 'There is no scientific evidence on which to justify a ban on GM foods and crops . . . we should resist the tyranny of pressure groups.' Just one year later a chastened prime minister conceded that there was 'legitimate public concern' about their 'potential for harm' to health and the environment (*Guardian*, 28 March 2000).

During 1998–9 a 'window of opportunity' opened, allowing the GM issue to be catapulted dramatically on to the political agenda and prompting a huge increase in public concern:

1. *A compelling problem was identified*
   A series of well-publicised scientific findings alerted the public to a problem:
   (i) Professor Arpad Pusztai claimed that the immune systems of rats had been damaged by eating GM potatoes;
   (ii) American scientists reported that GM crops harmed the Monarch butterfly;
   (iii) a series of reports – from English Nature, the British Medical Association and Christian Aid – highlighted the environmental and food safety risks posed by GM crops.
2. *The right political circumstances*
   (i) a decision by Monsanto to mix GM and non-GM grain;
   (ii) the imminent approval by the EU of a range of GM crops;
   (iii) high public sensitivity and distrust of science and politicians regarding food safety issues following the BSE crisis;

(iv) an obvious 'bad guy' – the American multinational Monsanto;
(v) high-profile pressure group campaigning, especially by Greenpeace, and repeated direct action by eco-protesters that destroyed many of the British government's GM crop trials.

3. *Viable short-term solutions existed*
   (i) Although eighteen GM products had been approved up to April 1998, several EU states announced their refusal to approve further releases of GM crops until a tougher regulatory regime, governing labelling and tracing of products through the food chain, was approved and further crop trials had been carried out. Eventually, in February 2001 the European Parliament agreed a new set of regulations, but this decision was immediately met by six EU states (including France and Italy) reaffirming their *de facto* moratorium on GM crops.
   (ii) The British government agreed a voluntary three-year moratorium on the commercial planting of GM crops with the biotechnology industry, pending further crop trials testing their safety (although these trials continued to be disrupted by protesters).

The agenda-setting framework shows how significant policy change can occur. However, although European consumers are still locked in a period of alarmed discovery about GM crops, growing pressure from the WTO, USA, Japan, as well as those European nations with strong biotechnology industries, notably the UK, makes it uncertain how long the moratorium will stay in place.

Alaska Sound in 1989 which disrupted a previously complacent policy network responsible for marine safety in the Sound and led to the creation of new institutions. After the public interest died away, the institutional legacy remained, notably a regulatory framework introduced to oversee the implementation of improved safeguards in Alaska Sound and a new regional citizens' advisory council that has acted as an effective 'sentinel' by promoting further policy change to improve safety (Busenberg 1999).

The advocacy coalition framework

Sabatier (1988) argues that it is unrealistic to distinguish agenda-setting so sharply from the wider policy process as a major source of policy change. His Advocacy Coalition Framework (ACF) is a comprehensive model of the policy process emphasising the role of ideas, information and analysis as factors contributing to policy change at all 'stages' of the policy process.[15] A central claim of the ACF is that an understanding of policy change requires a focus on elite opinion and the factors that encourage shifts in elite belief systems over long periods of time.

The ACF, like network theory, focuses on the policy subsystem which is composed of all the actors – politicians, bureaucrats, interest groups, academics, journalists, professionals – who are actively concerned with a particular policy issue such as air pollution control, and who regularly seek to influence public policy on that issue. Within each subsystem these actors may form several (usually between one and four) 'advocacy coalitions' drawing together people who share the same normative and causal beliefs about how policy objectives should be achieved. The belief systems of each coalition are organised into a three-level hierarchy: (1) *deep core beliefs* are the broad philosophical values that apply to all policy subsystems (e.g. left–right); (2) *policy core beliefs* are the fundamental values and strategies across that specific policy subsystem (e.g. the seriousness of the problem and the best policy instruments to deal with it); (3) *secondary aspects* are the narrower beliefs about specific aspects of the problem and policy implementation. Typically, a policy subsystem will be dominated by one powerful coalition, with several competing minority coalitions each seeking to impose its approach on the policy process. Sabatier, like Hall (see Box 7.4), argues that change will normally be incremental because it is secondary beliefs that are most prone to change, usually as a result of 'policy-oriented learning' by coalitions as they acquire new information and reflect on the best methods of achieving their policy objectives. Changes to policy core beliefs are less frequent and will normally only occur when non-cognitive factors are disrupted by exogenous shocks from outside the subsystem, such as macro-economic developments or a change in government. At these infrequent moments, the opportunity exists for a minority coalition to impose its belief system on the policy process.

The ACF provides considerable insight into the way policy changes. By emphasising the importance of belief systems, it complements the policy network focus on interests and power. The ACF is particularly relevant to issues where there is some technical complexity and open political conflict: it has been widely applied to environmental and energy policy issues in North America, such as air and water pollution, where there is plenty of scope for policy oriented learning through the analysis of quantitative data and its application to natural systems (Sabatier and Jenkins-Smith 1999).

The ACF (and the agenda-setting model) is underpinned by pluralistic assumptions, no doubt reflecting its American origins. Consequently, it may be less applicable in countries where conflict is less open, as in the étatist French system, or where closed policy communities prevail, as in Britain.[16] Nevertheless, where policy processes are pluralistic, the ACF can be a useful tool for explaining policy outcomes. Within EU institutions, for instance, much policy-making affecting the environment is made within open issue networks which offer interest groups better access to policy elites than is normally available at the national level (Bomberg 1998b). Coalitions made up of lobbyists and politicians have frequently emerged around divisive issues such as the biotechnology, waste packaging (see Box 7.7) and auto-emissions directives, with each coalition seeking to control the policy networks in order to shape policy outcomes.

Finally, what the agenda-setting and ACF models suggest, unsurprisingly, is that change in environmental policy is probably easier to achieve where policy-making is relatively pluralistic than where it is dominated by closed policy networks. Moreover, there are many areas of environmental policy, particularly in the USA, which do fall into this category. However, *radical* change is rare, even in pluralistic policy processes. Without major exogenous changes there are few genuine windows of opportunity that provide access to different interests and advocacy coalitions to push new issues and ideas onto

---

7.7 The EU packaging waste directive

The European Commission, after months of consultation, published a formal proposal for a Council directive on Packaging and Packaging Waste in October 1992. It contained ambitious targets such as 90 per cent of packaging to be recovered within ten years, of which 60 per cent was to be recycled. However, the final directive approved in December 1994 was much toned down: for example, it stipulated that within five years not less than 50 per cent and not more than 65 per cent of packaging waste should be recovered with a minimum 25 per cent recycled, and within ten years a new set of targets should be agreed.

The policy network shaping the legislation was characterised by an open and fluid membership. No less than sixteen different EU directorates (or ministries) were involved at some stage, scientific experts were needed to advise on the most effective means of treating waste, lobbyists from over fifty Euro-level interest groups, dozens of environmental NGOs, and trade and industry associations were all active. Access to policy-makers was loose and open, but uneven. Whereas the Commission was heavily influenced during the early stages of consultation by the environmental advocacy coalition (notably Friends of the Earth), after the draft directive was published the industry coalition was able to gain the upper hand. Manufacturers and industry interests had a huge superiority of resources which they used very effectively, employing sophisticated lobbying techniques, excellent access to scientific and technical data and sheer intensity of activity, 'they had consultants, scientists and lobbyists in every corridor . . . and that is where decisions are made'.

The loose issue network allowed extensive bargaining between opposing advocacy coalitions, but the clear resource advantage was critical in enabling the industry coalition to win the day by exercising first-dimensional power.

Based on Peterson and Bomberg (1999: 196–7).

the policy agenda. It is also worth noting that, where policy change does emerge from a pluralistic process, there is no guarantee that the policy outcomes will be better for the environment. As Box 7.7 illustrates, industry coalitions will often prevail over environmental coalitions simply because they can mobilise far more resources in an exercise of one-dimensional power. Incremental policy changes can occur within the traditional paradigm, but they are unlikely to accumulate into radical change without the replacement of the traditional paradigm by a new policy paradigm.

Policy communities and exogenous change

The strength of policy network analysis lies in its capacity to explain continuity and stability, but it has been widely criticised for offering a static model that is poor at explaining policy change (Dowding 1995; Dudley and Richardson 1996). After all, if a policy community is stable, why should it ever introduce changes that are not directly in the interests of its members? Yet no subsystem is immune from external developments. Just as Sabatier recognises that radical change requires the belief systems of policy elites to be shaken up by exogenous non-cognitive factors, similarly network analysts have identified a number of structural factors that may destabilise a strongly institutionalised policy community and so make policy change more likely (Smith 1993: 93–7). In short, exogenous factors can play a catalytic role in changing power relations. Five external factors seem particularly significant in shaping environmental policy.

1. A *sudden crisis* may throw a policy community into disarray. The discovery of a link between bovine spongiform encephalopathy (BSE) and the human disease new variant Creutzfeld–Jakob disease in 1996 provoked a food scare so profound that the EU introduced a complete ban on the export of British beef, profoundly weakening the powerful agricultural policy community. During 2000–1, the discovery of BSE elsewhere in Europe and an outbreak of foot-and-mouth disease provoked a public debate about the nature of intensive agriculture that may destabilise agricultural policy communities right across Europe. The 1989 *Exxon Valdez* oil spill in Alaska Sound produced immediate local improvements in the safeguards against marine oil pollution (Busenberg 1999).

2. A policy community may also be disturbed when a government is confronted by a *new problem*, such as climate change or food safety, for which the dominant interests in the policy community have no immediate solution. In such circumstances governments seeking answers to policy puzzles may turn to alternative interests outside the established network. The need to reduce carbon emissions from road traffic has prompted policy-makers to look beyond powerful road lobbies in their search for alternative transport policies. The development of new technologies such as GMOs may similarly

disrupt established methods of consultation in the agricultural sector, forcing governments to listen to a wider range of interests, including consumers and environmentalists.

3. Changes in *external relations* can disrupt the structural conditions underpinning a policy community. International agreements such as the ban on chlorofluorocarbons (CFCs) or commitments to reduce greenhouse gas emissions impose new external obligations that may require a national government to override the resistance of powerful producer interests. The extensive privatisation of public assets since the 1980s has also undermined some established policy communities, particularly in Britain where, for example, greater competition transformed the energy market (resulting in a major shift from coal to gas as the source of electricity generation) and therefore disrupted the established energy policy community. EU environmental directives, particularly in areas where policy has been most stringent, such as drinking- and bathing-water quality, have helped destabilise some policy networks (Maloney and Richardson 1994). In the British water industry, the combination of regulatory restructuring arising from privatisation and tough European directives destabilised a previously cohesive policy community (consisting of engineers and water scientists) to provide a window of opportunity for environmental groups to politicise water quality issues. This flux eventually forced the government to make several significant policy changes, including a shift away from the established policy of low-cost, long-pipe sewage disposal at sea that was blamed by many for the low quality of bathing water in many tourist resorts (Jordan 1998a).

4. The emergence of *new social movements and pressure groups* has contributed to the growing importance of environmental issues on the political agenda. It has become harder for politicians, civil servants and even producer groups to ignore these issues and many environmental groups are now routinely consulted by most governments across a wide range of issues (see Chapter 6).

5. Political actors, notably ministers, have the capacity to use their *despotic power* to break up a policy community and to allow access to new groups. Mainstream political leaders may come to accept that certain powerful environmental groups can no longer be excluded from the policy process, so they force a change upon a subsystem. A change of government can have the same outcome. It will be interesting to see whether the entry of green parties into government (see Chapter 5) will disrupt the consensus underpinning established policy networks, leading to more routine consultation of the environmental lobby.

Nuclear power provides an interesting example of policy change because, on the one hand, opposition to nuclear power is a key plank of green party political programmes but, on the other hand, nuclear power contributes a significant *carbon-free* share of electricity generation in many industrialised nations. The following case study shows how, in recent years, a combination of exogenous factors has profoundly disrupted established patterns of policy-making to produce a radical reversal of the previous pro-nuclear consensus.

CRITICAL QUESTION 4

Under what conditions is radical reform of environmental policy possible?

The rise and fall of nuclear power

The potential threats to human safety and the environment posed by the use of nuclear power highlight many of the core characteristics of environmental policy identified in the introduction to Part III. There can certainly be few issues that pose such a *potentially* irreversible, transnational and long-term threat to the environment (although the actual risk of damage is statistically extremely low). Despite these concerns, from the late 1950s to the 1980s, as strong pro-nuclear policy communities developed, most industrialised nations invested heavily in the expansion of nuclear energy. Yet, remarkably, since the 1980s, an extraordinary coincidence of exogenous factors has profoundly weakened these entrenched policy communities, resulting in a dramatic reversal of the enthusiastic pro-nuclear consensus amongst policy elites. By the late 1990s, most North American and Western European nations had abandoned all plans to build new nuclear reactors.

Historically, decisions about nuclear power generally emerged from tight-knit, closed policy communities or corporatist institutional arrangements. In Britain, for example, the policy process was dominated by the Atomic Energy Authority (UKAEA) – a government-funded, largely unaccountable, cross-breed between a ministry and a nationalised industry – and its scientific experts – with the Department of Energy only a secondary actor in the policy community (Greenaway et al. 1992: ch. 6; Saward 1992). The government gave the policy community its full support and ensured that it was subject to minimal democratic control via Parliament.

In the 1950s and 1960s, two key factors explained government support for nuclear power. First, for nuclear powers such as Britain, France and the USA, the military objective to develop nuclear weapons generated a demand for plutonium (for weapons) which was only to be extracted from reprocessing spent uranium (from nuclear power stations). This military–industrial link was critical in the decision to push ahead with what was, even to its most enthusiastic supporters in the 1950s, still an uncommercial technology. Secondly, the belief that nuclear power offered a modern, technological solution to future energy requirements was widespread. All governments, including many with no pretensions to develop nuclear weapons, were persuaded that nuclear power had the potential to provide an abundant supply of cheap energy to underpin future economic growth. Other factors contributed to this growing love affair with nuclear energy. Concern about pollution from coal-fired plants was a major stimulus to the US nuclear programme in the 1960s. The Middle East oil crisis of 1973–4 prompted several European countries, notably West Germany and France, to launch huge construction programmes in order to reduce their dependency on oil supplies from volatile overseas markets. In the early 1980s, the Thatcher government in Britain saw the expansion of nuclear power as a means of reducing the power of the National Union of Mineworkers. The development of the global nuclear industry meant that the 435 nuclear reactors in operation across the world in January 2001 were generating around one-sixth of world and one-third of European energy (Uranium Institute 2001).

Yet the nuclear industry is now in deep crisis. There were no reactors under construction anywhere in Western Europe or North America in 2001, with a moratorium on the construction of new reactors in five out of eight European nations with nuclear power. Britain had no plans for further expansion and the US nuclear industry had come to a complete standstill. Sweden launched its policy of abandoning nuclear power – the source of half its electricity – by closing the Barsebäck-1 reactor in November 1999. Germany and Belgium are also committed to a gradual phase-out of nuclear power. It amounts to a truly dramatic policy reversal. Significantly, all five exogenous factors identified in the previous section have contributed to the destabilisation of pro-nuclear policy communities.

First, the nuclear industry has been hit by a series of crises. The partial meltdown of a reactor at the Three Mile Island plant in 1979 prompted a major global debate about nuclear safety and destroyed the industry in America: no new nuclear power stations have been ordered there since 1978 and 108 proposals have been cancelled (Smith 1995: 132). The 1986 accident at Chernobyl had a similar impact on the nuclear consensus in Europe: Italy held three referenda on nuclear power in 1987, the German SPD declared its commitment to a phase-out of nuclear power and opposition in Scandinavia strengthened.[17]

Secondly, new problems have undermined the political case for nuclear energy; in particular, it has failed to deliver on its promise to be safe and reliable. Nuclear plants have been beset by malfunctions that have put them out of action for long periods of time. Public fears have been repeatedly rekindled by the frequency of accidental releases of low-level radioactive materials and heated debates about the potential dangers (e.g. links with cancers) of living in close proximity to nuclear plants. There is wide concern about the safety of leaking East European power stations, illustrated by the German government's decision to close all the plants in the former East Germany immediately after German unification. Perhaps most important is the still largely unresolved problem of how the growing stockpile of spent fuel and waste – some of which will be active for 1,000 years – should be safely stored (Kemp 1992).

Thirdly, external changes have opened up pro-nuclear political communities and led to serious challenges to the economic case for nuclear energy. The policy communities managed to conceal the true costs of nuclear power behind the veil of state ownership and regulatory structures for many years, but privatisation and liberalisation of European electricity markets have made this more difficult. For example, proposals to privatise the British nuclear power industry in the late 1980s helped break up the policy community because the exposure to financial scrutiny required for market flotation revealed the true (i.e. enormous and previously unquantified) costs of the industry (Greenaway et al. 1992). Although uranium fuel is cheap and plentiful, the capital cost of building a nuclear plant – which takes at least ten years to complete – is enormous compared to, say, a gas-fired power station. Moreover, the massive costs of decommissioning reactors were never properly included in the cost–benefit analysis of nuclear energy. In short, cheap nuclear energy proved to be a myth.

Fourthly, the anti-nuclear movements in the 1970s and 1980s were amongst the most popular, persistent and successful new social movements, especially in Germany (Flam 1994); indeed, nuclear power is often defined as a classic postmaterial issue (see Chapter 4). They have played an important part in turning the public against nuclear power and persuading many mainstream parties to alter or moderate their former pro-nuclear stances. At the local level, combined opposition from environmental groups and local citizen action groups has made it almost impossible for most western governments to secure support for a new nuclear plant.

Lastly, as green parties have entered government, their anti-nuclear roots have prompted them to lead a direct assault on the nuclear industry. The German red–green coalition government in 1998 promised a complete phase-out of nuclear energy. The appointment of a Green environment minister in France, Dominique Voynet, also produced the first crack in the powerful bipartisan French pro-nuclear consensus when she announced the closure of the Creys-Malville Super Phenix nuclear generator in 1997, although this was later delayed. A commitment to a 'progressive withdrawal from nuclear energy' starting with the decommissioning of reactors more than forty years old was one of the conditions set by the Belgian green parties when they formed a coalition government with the Liberals in July 1999 (Hooghe and Rihoux 2000: 134).

To summarise, exogenous factors have disrupted established patterns of policy-making, leading many western countries to call a halt to their nuclear expansion programmes. Certainly the decline of the nuclear lobby provides clear evidence that even the strongest of policy communities can be destabilised and broken down, although it took a remarkable combination of exogenous events to produce this transnational decline. For Baumgartner and Jones (1993: ch. 4), the rise and fall of the US nuclear industry is a classic example of punctuated equilibrium: popular enthusiasm about the promise of nuclear technology, followed by years of policy stability and industry growth under the control of a powerful policy community (or, as they call it, a 'policy monopoly'), to be replaced by growing questioning of the nuclear industry that peaked with the Three Mile Island accident in 1979 and the subsequent disintegration of the policy community.

However, the death certificate of the nuclear industry should not be signed prematurely, not least because several industrialising nations, notably South Korea and China, are still investing heavily in nuclear power. Elsewhere, governments have certainly found it much easier to stop building new plants than to close existing ones. Nuclear reactors have high capital costs but, once built, they are relatively cheap to operate. Closure will harm the nuclear industry and make many people unemployed. The combination of international and domestic obstacles encountered by the German government in trying to agree a decommissioning programme illustrates the continuing strength of the pro-nuclear advocacy coalition (see Box 7.8) The longer the nuclear industry in each country can delay the implementation of a serious closure programme, the more chance it has that new exogenous factors may swing back in its favour. Ironically, global warming may provide a boost for the industry because many countries will be unable to meet their carbon emissions reduction commitments if they close their nuclear plants. After all, a short-term cost of closing nuclear reactors is certain to be an increased dependency on electricity generated by fossil fuels. Rather than import power from Danish coal-burning power stations, Sweden has delayed further closures of reactors until they can be replaced by renewable energy sources. There is growing evidence of a shift back towards nuclear power amongst policy elites. The EU adopted a green paper on energy supply in November 2000 which suggests that carbon emission reduction targets may only be met by building new nuclear reactors to replace declining stock. In the same month, Western European governments agreed to provide financial support for the construction of two new nuclear power stations in the Ukraine to replace the Chernobyl plant. In Finland, the TVO energy utility applied to the government for permission to build a fifth reactor. Most significantly, following a series of power cuts in California, President Bush unveiled an energy policy in May 2001 that specifically promoted the construction of new nuclear plants. Soon after, Tony Blair launched a fundamental review of UK energy policy chaired by a pro-nuclear minister.

7.8 German nuclear shutdown?

The phasing out of nuclear power has always been an article of faith for the German Greens, so they made it a condition of the October 1998 SPD–Green coalition agreement that the government would launch a decommissioning programme for Germany's nineteen nuclear power stations. Jürgen Trittin, the Green environment minister, wanted a rapid decommissioning programme: all reactors to be closed within twenty years, with seven shut by the next election, and an end to the export of nuclear waste by January 2000. However, his proposals met strong resistance from the energy industry:

1. German nuclear energy companies had firm contracts, guaranteed by the government, to export nuclear waste to Britain and France for reprocessing. To renege on these contracts would be diplomatically damaging and make the government liable for damage claims possibly running to more than DM3 billion/year.

2. The nuclear energy companies responded with a strong campaign calling for a longer lifespan for their reactors. By focusing their efforts on the SPD, they were able to exploit the weakness of the red–green coalition during 1999–2000 as it stumbled from one crisis to another and suffered a series of setbacks in *Länder* elections.

3. Nuclear power contributes around 36 per cent of German energy capacity. If reactors were to be closed, the lost generating capacity, at least in the short term, would be replaced by fossil fuel sources which would raise carbon emissions.

The arguments dragged on for over eighteen months, causing serious tensions between the SPD and the Greens, until a decommissioning package was eventually agreed with the energy producers, approved by 2:1 vote at a Green Party conference in June 2000 and formally agreed in 2001.

❑ Each nuclear plant will be set an operating life on the basis of an average overall lifespan of thirty-two years from the start of commercial production (but productive capacity can be switched between plants so the early closure of one plant might allow another to stay open longer than thirty-two years).

❑ Recycling of waste to be halted 'as soon as possible' and certainly by 1 July 2005.

This diluted package bears witness to the capacity of a united and powerful industry sector to influence policy. Indeed, the German nuclear industry should not be written off yet, for much could change in thirty years, both politically and environmentally, which could yet see this agreement torn up.

What does the nuclear case study tell us about the potential for radical policy change? The reversal of the commitment to nuclear expansion undoubtedly represents a radical policy change; in Hall's taxonomy, it resembles third order change. Nevertheless, the pro-nuclear paradigm has not yet been replaced by a new, alternative paradigm, such as a commitment to a sustainable energy policy. Significantly, although frequently defined as a postmaterial issue, the radical change in nuclear policy has been driven primarily by two *materialist* arguments: the risk it poses to human safety and the collapse of the economic case for nuclear power. Moreover, there has been no process of social learning in which policy elites have questioned the sustainability of the core assumptions underpinning energy policy. Drawing on Sabatier, the changes have affected the *policy core* beliefs within one subsystem, resulting in expectations about the contribution of nuclear energy to overall energy production to be scaled down. However, the *deep core* beliefs about the wider role of energy production and consumption in the economy remain largely intact. In a consumerist society in which energy conservation remains a low priority and where profit-seeking energy utilities encourage increased energy consumption, it is not surprising that few countries have made any serious attempt to develop an alternative energy strategy (See Chapter 11).

CRITICAL QUESTION 5

Will climate change save the nuclear industry?

CONCLUSION

This chapter has identified a major problem: why has the traditional paradigm proved so resilient, despite its patent inadequacy in dealing with the complex challenges thrown up by contemporary environmental problems? Familiar concepts in political science – interests, ideas, institutions and power – and the relationship between them have been used to explain this resilience.

It has been argued that the traditional paradigm is underpinned by the structural power of producer interests, the segmentation of the policy process and the belief systems of policy elites. Policy-makers are informed by a technocentric commitment to economic expansion which encourages them to define the interests of the state as largely synonomous with those of producers and, therefore, to 'recognise some social interests as more legitimate than others and privilege some lines of policy over others' (Hall 1993: 292). More often than not, the interests of producer groups trump those of environmental groups, and economic growth takes priority over environmental protection. The expansionist paradigm and the institutional structure of government are mutually reinforcing: organisational structures, administrative procedures and policy networks are designed to implement the dominant ideas and, in turn, sustain and support them (Jordan 1998a: 34). Even where policy processes are more pluralistic, producer groups are often able to dominate policy-making by mobilising sufficient resources to exercise effective first-dimensional power. The need to overcome powerful structural and institutional obstacles makes the replacement of the traditional paradigm no easy task, and probably dependent on the capacity for significant exogenous changes to disrupt the power of established interests. Even then, as the nuclear case study reveals, a radical policy reversal in one sector may not be matched by the adoption of a more strategic approach to energy policy. The nuclear industry may be wounded, perhaps fatally, but fossil fuel suppliers remain in the ascendancy everywhere. It would seem therefore that policy-makers will be best equipped to overcome the various structural and institutional obstacles to change when 'armed with a coherent policy paradigm' (Hall 1993: 290) such as sustainable development. In identifying the importance of belief systems, both Sabatier and Hall show that paradigm change is also dependent on a process of social learning by government and business policy elites (and wider society). The success of the alternative paradigms of sustainable development and ecological modernisation will depend on their capacity to win the hearts and minds of policy elites and to persuade them that their interests are compatible with a sustainable society.

Further reading

Weale's (1992) study of pollution policies includes an insightful critique of the traditional environmental paradigm. Crenson (1971) is a classic treatment of power and environmental policy-making. Parsons (1995) and Ham and Hill (1993) provide good general introductions to the policy-making literature, while the innovative contributions by Kingdon (1995), Baumgartner and Jones (1993) and Sabatier and Jenkins-Smith (1993, 1999) all contain interesting case studies relevant to the environment.

Notes

1. This list echoes similar categorisations found in Weale (1992) and Jordan and O'Riordan (1999).
2. Samuelson, quoted in Mueller (1989: 10).
3. See Ostrom (1990: 32–3) for a discussion of the distinction between common-pool resources and public goods.
4. Weale (1992: ch. 1) refers to the traditional paradigm as 'old politics'.
5. During the 1970s there was a general deterioration across a range of key pollution indicators, including sulphur oxide, nitrogen oxide, particulates, carbon monoxide and carbon dioxide. Some of these trends were reversed in the 1980s (notably sulphur oxide, which declined rapidly), others stabilised, but others, notably carbon dioxide, worsened (European Environment Agency *http://www.eea.eu.int*). Of course, whether or not any improvements in environmental quality are linked to government policy, as opposed, say, to fluctuations in the economic cycle is a quite separate 'cause and effect' issue (Ringquist 1995).
6. See Dunleavy and O'Leary (1987), Ham and Hill (1993: ch. 2) and Marsh and Stoker (1995: chs. 11–14) for reviews of state theory.
7. See Grant (1995) for a discussion of insider and outsider groups.
8. See Vogel (1987) for a critique of Lindblom's thesis.
9. Other 'environmental' applications of the three-dimensional model include two British case studies of pollution from a brickworks (Blowers 1984) and of agricultural pollution (Hill et al. 1989). The three-dimensional model of power is not without its critics (see Polsby 1980). See Ham and Hill (1993: ch. 4) and Parsons (1995: 134–45) for a general discussion of the model.
10. Heclo (1978) argued that the 'iron triangle' metaphor has been overplayed; it was probably only ever relevant to certain policy areas and, even there, it is now less applicable. However, Peters (1998a: 29) warns against the complete rejection of the iron triangle and notes the persistence of elite dominance in many sectors.
11. Corporatism is used here to describe the institutions that govern relations between national interest groups and the state, rather than as a theory of state–group relations. See Williamson (1989) for a review of the corporatist literature.
12. However, see Crepaz (1995) and Scruggs (1999) for the opposite view that the consensual politics of corporatism produces better environmental outcomes than does pluralism. This issue is discussed further in Chapter 8.

13. For a critical discussion of the policy network approach see Dowding (1995), and a rejoinder by Marsh and Smith (2000).

14. Policy communities can be made up of either public or private producer groups. Water and energy utilities are often public sector organisations, but this is unlikely to make the policy community any more sympathetic to environmental concerns. For example, the British government's resistance to acid emission controls during the 1970s and 1980s reflected the views of a policy community in which the nationalised Central Electricity Generating Board and British Coal were leading members (Boehmer-Christiansen and Skea 1991).

15. Sabatier and his collaborators have developed and applied his Advocacy Coalition Framework in a series of publications including Sabatier (1988) and Sabatier and Jenkins-Smith (1993, 1999).

16. Sabatier (1998), however, makes a robust case for the applicability of the ACF to the European context.

17. Only in France did the powerful pro-nuclear elite consensus produce a complacent response to Chernobyl (Liberatore 1995).

8

Sustainable development and ecological modernisation

Contents

- What is sustainable development?
- Why is it such a complex and contestable concept?
- What are its core principles?
- What is ecological modernisation?
- What are its strengths and weaknesses?

KEY ISSUES

The tension between economic growth and environmental protection lies at the heart of environmental politics. The concept of sustainable development is a direct attempt to resolve this dichotomy by sending the message that it is possible to have economic development whilst also protecting the environment. Not surprisingly, policy-makers the world over, told that they can have their cake and eat it, have seized on the idea. Almost every country is now committed, at least on paper, to the principles of sustainable development. Yet sustainable development is an ambiguous concept, with a meaning that is contested and complex. This elusiveness is both a strength and a weakness: it allows a multitude of political and economic interests to unite under one banner, while attracting the criticism that it is an empty slogan with little substance. Policy-makers have also found it difficult to turn this loose set of ideas into practical policies. Indeed, in those industrialised countries that boast the most progressive environmental policies, the narrower concept of ecological modernisation has acquired increasing resonance.

Sustainable development and its half-sister, ecological modernisation, offer an alternative policy paradigm to the traditional model of environmental policy. The first part of this chapter examines the various meanings attributed to sustainable development and identifies five core principles underpinning most definitions of the concept. The second half outlines the key features of ecological modernisation before analysing its strengths and limitations.

SUSTAINABLE DEVELOPMENT

Spreading the word

Sustainable development has rapidly become the dominant idea, or discourse (Dryzek 1997), shaping international policy towards the environment. The concept was first endorsed in the World Conservation Strategy (IUCN/UNEP/WWF 1980) produced by three international NGOs. This document was primarily concerned with ecological sustainability, or the conservation of living resources, and directed little attention to wider political, economic or social issues. Sustainable development was given a broader social meaning in *Our Common Future*, published by the World Commission on Environment and Development (WCED 1987), and commonly known as the Brundtland Report (see Box 8.1). The Brundtland Report popularised sustainable development so successfully that it has since been taken up by almost every international institution, agency and NGO. The principles of sustainable development underpinned the Rio Earth Summit agenda where approval was given to the *Agenda 21* document outlining a 'global partnership for sustainable development' (see Box 8.2). This massive document addresses a wide range of environmental and developmental issues

8.1 The Brundtland Commission

The United Nations General Assembly established the World Commission on Environment and Development in 1983 in response to growing concerns about both environmental degradation and the economic crisis. The Commission, chaired by Gro Harlem Brundtland, the Norwegian prime minister, consulted widely for four years, soliciting reports from expert bodies and holding public meetings in several countries. In 1987 it produced its final report, *Our Common Future*, popularly known as the Brundtland Report (WCED 1987), which popularised the concept of sustainable development worldwide.

To understand the Commission's approach to sustainable development, it is important to be aware of the political context in which it operated. Since the 1972 Stockholm Conference there had been growing awareness of the severity of environmental problems, accentuated by new worries about the global problems of climate change, ozone depletion and biodiversity loss. However, the environmental agenda had been largely hijacked by the affluent North. Meanwhile, poorer countries in the South were experiencing major economic problems with the collapse in commodity prices, the debt crisis and economic stagnation all contributing to worsening poverty (and environmental degradation). Against this background the continuing East–West tensions associated with the Cold War raised serious security concerns.

This political context explains why the Commission deliberately designed sustainable development as a *bridging* concept that could unite apparently diverse and conflicting interests and policy concerns (Meadowcroft 2000). Specifically, it sought to bring together the environmental agenda of the North with the developmental agenda of the South; hence the title of the final report, *Our Common Future.*

and is intended to provide a strategy for implementing sustainable development throughout the world.[1] The UN Commission on Sustainable Development (CSD) was created to monitor and promote the implementation of *Agenda 21* in each country (see Box 8.3). By the mid-1990s most industrialised countries had published national sustainable development strategies (Jänicke and Jörgens 1998; Lafferty and Meadowcroft 2000a) and many local authorities have launched Local Agenda 21 strategies (O'Riordan and Voisey 1997; Lafferty and Eckerberg 1998).

The reach of sustainable development has extended far beyond government into the world of business and civil society. The World Bank has sought to throw off its poor reputation with environmentalists by publishing environmental reports, holding regular seminars and sponsoring research on a wide range of environmental issues.[2] The World Bank is host to the Global Environmental Facility, which is the institution responsible for channelling financial assistance for sustainable development from Northern to Southern

8.2 *Agenda 21*

Agenda 21 (UNCED 1992) provides the blueprint for implementing sustainable development agreed at the 1992 Earth Summit (and approved by over 170 nations). This substantial document covers an enormous number of environment and development issues, with forty chapters ranging from 'Changing Consumption Patterns' and 'Combating Deforestation' to 'Children and Youth in Sustainable Development' and 'Strengthening the Role of Farmers'. Indeed, a key feature of *Agenda 21* is that it does not confine itself to the traditional agenda of environmental degradation and conservation, but devotes considerable attention to the political, economic and financial aspects of sustainable development. Thus twenty-five of the forty chapters focus on non-ecological issues.

Agenda 21 website: *http://www.un.org/esa/sustdev/agenda21.htm.*

8.3 Commission on Sustainable Development (CSD)

The CSD was created in December 1992 and charged with the responsibility for following up and implementing *Agenda 21*, from the activities of the various inter-governmental bodies to the implementation of Local Agenda 21s at community level. It has a small secretariat and an assembly of representatives from fifty-three countries, but it has no legal powers to hold states to account.

The CSD has proved an important forum for keeping key issues in sustainable development on the international agenda, including forestry, freshwater and energy conservation, and has launched several important initiatives, such as a programme to draw up indicators of sustainable development. It also enables a wide range of NGOs to get involved in UN processes.

At the follow-up Earth Summit in New York in 1997, the CSD was given a new five-year agenda based around the primary aims of poverty alleviation and over-consumption, and speeding up the implementation of *Agenda 21*. However, the rejection of a proposal to allow the CSD to peer review the national *Agenda 21* reports submitted by each country underlines the problems it faces: it can require a state to produce a report, but it cannot insist that these reports are adequate, let alone implemented.

CSD website: *http://www.un.org/esa/sustdev/ csd.htm.*

nations (see Box 9.3). The World Business Council for Sustainable Development, formed in 1995, is a coalition of 125 international companies from 30 countries and over 20 industrial sectors, with the broad aim of developing 'closer cooperation between business, government and all other organisations concerned with the environment and sustainable development . . . [and] to encourage high standards of environmental management in business' (*www.wbcsd.ch/whatis.htm*). Many trade associations have also declared their support for sustainable development; for example, the insurance industry (which potentially has much to lose if climate change leads to rising sea-levels, floods and storms) issued a *Statement of Environmental Commitment* in March 1995 signed by over 50 leading insurance companies. These international efforts have been widely replicated at the national level, where state-sponsored round-tables have brought together representatives from all sections of society – politicians, business, trade unions, churches, environmental groups, consumer groups – to discuss how sustainable development can be implemented. Despite this widespread enthusiasm, the precise meaning of sustainable development remains elusive.

A complex and contested concept

The sheer proliferation of definitions of sustainable development is evidence of its contestability; for example, Pearce et al. (1989: 173–85) provide a 'gallery' of over forty definitions. The most widely used definition, taken from the Brundtland Report, is that 'sustainable development is development that meets the needs of the present without compromising the ability of future generations to meet their own needs' (WCED 1987: 43). This definition sets out the two fundamental principles of intragenerational and intergenerational equity, and contains the two 'key concepts' of needs and limits (ibid.: 43). The concept of *needs* demands that 'overriding priority' should be given to the essential needs of the world's poor, both North and South. Poverty and the unequal distribution of resources are identified as major causes of environmental degradation: 'Sustainable development requires meeting the basic needs of all and extending to all the opportunity to satisfy their aspirations for a better life' (ibid.: 44). Crucially, the Brundtland Report stresses that these goals can only be achieved if consumption patterns in the richer countries are readjusted. Secondly, the concept of *limits* recognises that the current state of technology and social organisation imposes limits on the ability of the environment to meet present and future needs, so we must moderate our demands on the natural environment. Yet Brundtland rejects the crude anti-growth arguments of the 1970s, asserting that 'Growth has no set limits in terms of population or resource use beyond which lies ecological disaster' (ibid.: 45). Indeed, Brundtland demands a revival of growth in developing countries to help alleviate poverty and provide basic needs, although it seeks a more 'eco-friendly' type of growth that is 'less material- and energy-intensive and more equitable in its impact' (ibid.: 52).

A central, distinguishing feature of sustainable development as a policy paradigm is that it shifts the terms of debate from traditional environmentalism, with its primary focus on environmental protection, to the notion of sustainability which requires a much more complex process of trading off social, economic and environmental priorities. Box 8.4 shows that the Brundtland definition is as much concerned with economic and social development as it is with environmental protection. *Development* is a process of transformation which, by combining economic growth with broader social and cultural changes, enables individuals to realise their full potential. The dimension of *sustainability* brings the recognition that development must also adhere to the physical constraints imposed by ecosystems, so that environmental considerations have to be embedded in all sectors and policy areas. Brundtland's unapologetic anthropocentrism, displayed in its concern for human welfare and the exploitation of nature, in preference to an ecocentric interest in protecting nature for its own sake, has opened up environmental politics to a wider audience.[3] The promise of sustainable development is that it seems to offer a way out of the economy versus environment impasse; no longer need there be a trade-off

---

8.4 Core elements of sustainable development

Sustainable development is a normative concept used to prescribe and evaluate changes in living conditions. Such changes are to be guided by four Brundtland aspirations:

1. To satisfy basic human needs and reasonable standards of welfare for all living beings. (**Development**)
2. To achieve more equitable standards of living both within and among global populations. (**Development**)
3. To be pursued with great caution as to their actual or potential disruption of biodiversity and the regenerative capacity of nature, both locally and globally. (**Sustainability**)
4. To be achieved without undermining the possibility for future generations to attain similar standards of living and similar or improved standards of equity. (**Sustainability**)

From Lafferty (1996: 189).

between growth and environmental protection. Far from it: growth is seen as a 'good thing' because it enables less developed countries to develop and so improve the standard of living of their impoverished citizens, while the material quality of life in the affluent North can be maintained. All these benefits . . . and environmental protection too!

Sustainable development, like beauty, is in the eye of the beholder; it therefore promises something for everyone. As Lele has put it, with just a hint of irony, 'Sustainable development is a "metafix" that will unite everybody from the profit-minded industrialist and risk-minimising subsistence farmer to the equity-seeking social worker, the pollution-concerned or wildlife-loving First Worlder, the growth-maximising policy maker, the goal-oriented bureaucrat, and, therefore, the vote-counting politician' (Lele 1991: 613). This universal appeal is enhanced by the apparent ideological neutrality of sustainable development. It offers no clear vision of an ideal endstate, whether green utopia or otherwise, and no set of political or economic arrangements is specifically excluded. Instead, sustainable development involves a *process of change* in which core components of society – resource use, investment, technologies, institutions, consumption patterns – come to operate in greater harmony with ecosystems.

These chameleon characteristics attract a wide array of supporters, but they also make sustainable development a highly contestable concept. Some aims appear radical: the elimination of poverty, the pursuit of global equity, reductions in military expenditure, wider use of appropriate technologies, democratisation of institutions and a shift away from consumerist lifestyles. Other themes, such as the acceptance of the capitalist economic system and the need for continued economic growth, seem to accept the status quo. The core principles also beg many hoary but unresolved political questions. For example, what are basic needs? Should they reflect the needs of citizens in the USA or Bangladesh? How far will the living standards of rich industrialised nations have to be readjusted to achieve sustainable consumption patterns? Different answers to these questions produce conflicting interpretations of sustainable development. These ambiguities have not been helped by the absence of a detailed framework in the Brundtland Report to help individual countries turn these broad principles into practical policy measures. Consequently, policy-makers have been able to pick and choose from the pot-pourri of often contradictory ideas in the *Agenda 21* document while the endless stream of reports and books seeking to give flesh to this concept seems to have fuelled disagreement as much as it has brought consensus.

The proliferation of meanings is not just an exercise in academic or practical clarification but a highly political process of 'different interests with different substantive concerns trying to stake their claims in the sustainable development territory' (Dryzek 1997: 124). As it has become more important, key interests have tried to define sustainable development to suit their own purposes. Thus an African government might emphasise the need for global redistribution of wealth from North to South in order to eliminate poverty, while a transnational corporation might insist that sustainability is impossible without vibrant economic growth to conquer poverty, stabilise population levels, provide for human welfare and, of course, maintain profit levels.

With so much ambiguity surrounding the meaning of sustainable development, there have been several attempts to construct typologies distinguishing different 'versions' of sustainable development (Pearce et al. 1993; O'Riordan 1996; Baker et al. 1997a, *inter alia*). Most typologies identify 'weak' and 'strong' forms of sustainable development, with some normatively outlining a transition from weaker to stronger versions. O'Riordan (1996) provides an illustrative typology which distinguishes between levels of sustainability according to the way human and environmental resources are valued ranging, broadly speaking, along a continuum from technocentrism to ecocentrism. In *very weak sustainability* the overall stock of human capital and natural capital (i.e. natural resources and ecological processes) remains constant over time, but it allows for infinite substitution between the various kinds of capital so that the natural resources might dwindle providing they are compensated for by the extension of human capital. *Weak sustainability* accepts that certain critical natural processes which are essential to life, such as ozone, tropical forests and coral reefs, need protection, but allows for substitution between other types of natural capital. *Strong sustainability* extends the definition of critical natural resources much further through the wider use of the precautionary principle (see below, pp. 207–8). It anticipates that, as far as possible, the use of any natural resources should be compensated for through processes such as reafforestation and recycling of products, or by social improvements such as community betterment or reduced inequality. Finally, *very strong sustainability* equates with radical forms of ecologism such as bioregionalism and deep ecology, and is characterised by a steady-state economy, local social, political and economic self-reliance and a redistribution of property rights through burden-sharing. In Table 8.1 the columns represent the degree of attainment in categories corresponding to different levels of sustainable development. Of course, these categories often overlap and there are many grey areas. Currently, most countries are only starting to move into the mode of 'very weak sustainability' and, at present, 'the modest aim must be to avoid obvious cases of non-sustainability' (O'Riordan 1996: 147).

This typology of sustainability begs a question about the compatibility of sustainable development with ecologism. Many deep greens are understandably suspicious of a strategy that seems incompatible with the radical changes they demand. Thus, at a philosophical level, Richardson (1997: 43) condemns sustainable development for being a 'political fudge' that 'seeks to bridge the unbridgeable divide between the anthropocentric and

Table 8.1 A possible map of the sustainable transition

	Policy	Economy	Society	Discourse
Stage 1 Very weak sustainability	Lip service to policy integration	Minor tinkering with economic instruments	Dim awareness and little media coverage	Corporatist discussion groups; consultation exercises
Stage 2 Weak sustainability	Formal policy integration and deliverable targets	Substantial restructuring of microeconomic incentives	Wider public education for future visions	Round-tables; stakeholder groups; parliamentary surveillance
Stage 3 Strong sustainability	Binding policy integration and strong international agreements	Full valuations of the cost of living; 'green' accounts alongside national accounts	Curriculum integration; local initiatives as part of community growth	Community involvement; twinning of initiatives in the developed and developing world
Stage 4 Very strong sustainability	Strong international conventions; national duties of care; statutory and cultural support	Formal shift to sustainable economic accounting both nationally and internationally	Comprehensive cultural shift coupled to technological innovation and new community structures	Community-led initiatives become the norm

Source: O'Riordan (1996).

biocentric approaches to politics'. From a political perspective, radical greens may regard sustainable development as compromised by its acceptance of capitalism. They argue that sustainable development is a contradiction in terms because much economic growth cannot be ecologically sustainable, so it is impossible to achieve sustainable development without replacing capitalism with a more decentralised, self-sustaining social and economic system. Uneasy about the compromises involved in sustainable development, some radicals, such as deep ecologists, prefer an oppositional strategy that stands aloof from any dealings with established political and economic institutions. However, this isolationism represents a minority position within contemporary green politics. Most green parties are firmly committed to the principles of sustainable development. The four pillars of the German Greens (see Box 3.4), for example, emphasise the centrality of development issues such as social justice, equality and democracy. It therefore seems reasonable to regard very strong sustainability, which clearly differs sharply from the other categories, as fitting within ecologism, with strong sustainability representing the boundary distinguishing ecologism from other doctrines.

Does it matter that so many versions of sustainable development exist and that there is so much disagreement about its meaning? Is contestability damaging? It could be argued that without a clear meaning almost anything could be said to be sustainable, leaving it as little more than an empty political slogan. A universally acceptable definition is needed, with a list of measurable criteria against which it would be possible to judge progress towards sustainability. Better to have clarity and risk losing a few unwanted adherents, than retain a vacuous 'anything goes' approach. Policy-makers would also benefit from a clear technical definition to help them implement sustainable development. Yet this perspective may undervalue one of the great strengths of sustainable development which is that the fluidity of the concept should be celebrated rather than condemned. Rather like other political concepts such as democracy or justice, sustainable development is widely seen as a 'good thing' and has a generally accepted common-sense meaning within broad boundaries, but within those parameters there is deeper contestation around its constituent ideas (Baker et al. 1997a: 7; Dryzek 1997: 125). On this view the contestability of sustainable development has several virtues. Its 'all things to all people' quality has helped the message to resonate around the world and attract followers to the flag. Hajer (1995) suggests that the 'coalition for sustainable development can only be kept together by virtue of its rather vague story-lines at the same time as it asks for radical social change' (p. 14), whereas insistence on a precise formulation of the term is more likely to deter potential supporters. Thus the 'motherhood' idea of sustainable development can win broader acceptance for radical ideas such as equity and democratisation.

These debates can be a dynamic and positive feature of the incremental process of change. At the international level the sustainable development discourse has provoked fierce political struggles – particularly between North and South – which have pushed many environmental and development issues up the diplomatic agenda. International institutions such as the CSD have helped drive the debate down to national and sub-national levels. The proliferation of sustainable development round-tables and Local Agenda 21 strategies has helped diffuse the idea throughout society and generated many practical initiatives. Even when governments pay lip-service to international commitments, they may indirectly initiate change simply by creating new institutions and promulgating different ideas which can disrupt established patterns of policy-making and alter the belief systems of policy elites. For example, when an unenthusiastic British government was obliged by its commitment to *Agenda 21* to produce a sustainable development strategy (HM Government 1994), the process provided a window of opportunity for the Department of the Environment to bring environmental issues to the attention of other ministries, and may have contributed to the British government's decision to scale back its road-building programme.

So the ambiguity and contestability that make sustainable development such a complex and elusive concept may also be a political strength. Its optimistic message offers something for everyone and allows all actors to speak the same language (even if it means different things to different people). However, can such a wide-ranging set of ideas be turned into practical policy proposals? Although the wide-ranging *Agenda 21* document contains many practical suggestions, there is no compact toolkit setting out the policies and instruments needed for sustainable development. The next section identifies five fundamental principles which, nevertheless, seem to underpin all versions of sustainable development.

CRITICAL QUESTION 1

Is sustainable development too vague to be helpful to policy-makers?

Core principles of sustainable development

Equity

> Our inability to promote the common interest in sustainable development is often a product of the relative neglect of economic and social justice within and amongst nations.

(WCED 1987: 49)

Equity is a central feature of environmental policy. Governments always consider the distributional implications of any measure to prevent or alleviate environmental degradation. Will a tax on petrol consumption fall disproportionately on the poor, or on people dependent on cars such as rural dwellers? Will tough emission standards requiring companies to invest heavily in cleaner technology reduce their competitiveness and lead to job losses? Most environmental issues generate winners and losers; few are immune from some form of equity consideration.

The significance of sustainable development is that, by showing how environmental problems are inextricably linked to economic and social inequalities, it has brought development issues to the forefront of the environmental debate. The Brundtland Report deflected some of the criticisms of 1970s environmentalism – epitomised by the 1972 Stockholm Conference – that it was an elitist doctrine which placed the concerns of nature and the environment above the immediate basic needs of the world's poorest people. Instead, Brundtland emphasised two key features of the poverty–environment nexus. First, environmental damage from global consumption falls most severely on the poorest countries and the poorest people who are least able to protect themselves. Secondly, the growing number of poor and landless people in the South generates a struggle to survive that places huge pressure on the natural resource base. The resulting resource depletion – desertification, deforestation, overfishing, water scarcity, loss of biodiversity – continues the downward spiral of impoverishment by forcing more people onto marginal, ecologically fragile, lands. By underlining the interdependence between environmental and developmental issues, the Brundtland Report drew attention to the

8.5 Sustainable consumption

Sustainable consumption is the use of goods and services that respond to basic needs and bring a better quality of life, while minimising the use of natural resources, toxic materials and emissions of waste and pollutants over the life cycle, so as not to jeopardise the needs of future generations.

According to the Human Development Report 1998, consumption must be:

shared	– ensuring basic needs for all.
strengthening	– building human capabilities.
socially responsible	– so the consumption of some does not compromise the well-being of others.
sustainable	– without mortgaging the choices of future generations.

United Nations Development Programme (UNDP 1998: 1).

environmental impact of key North–South issues such as trade relations, aid, debt and industrialisation. It concluded that sustainable development is impossible while poverty and massive social injustices persist; hence the importance attributed to intragenerational equity alongside the more straightforwardly environmental principle of intergenerational equity.

However, putting intragenerational equity into practice can generate enormous political conflict, particularly along North–South lines. A key issue in international environmental diplomacy is the extent to which the rich North is willing to accept the political and financial responsibility for addressing global problems such as climate change and ozone depletion (see Chapter 9). The concept of *sustainable consumption* is even more contentious[4] (see Box 8.5). The Brundtland Report was rather quiet on the need to change consumption patterns in the North; no doubt because its authors recognised that the issue was political dynamite. Subsequently, growing interest in sustainable consumption has helped direct attention onto the disparities between mass consumption in affluent countries and the billion or more poorest people in the South whose basic consumption needs are not being met (UNDP 1998).

Numerous initiatives have been launched with the twin aims of reducing the direct impact of Northern consumption on scarce resources and improving the social and economic lot of the communities who supply those resources. A sustainable development treaty between the Netherlands and Costa Rica aims to make the total coffee chain, from production to consumption, more supportive of sustainable development. The programme, which involves Costa Rican farming cooperatives, coffee-processing plants, Dutch coffee roasters and sales organisations, seeks to increase the market for sustainable coffee, protect the environment and improve social conditions in coffee-producing areas, and strengthen information and accounting systems (UNDESA 1999). Café Direct is a British scheme in which a group of 'alternative' trading organisations (Equal Exchange, Oxfam Trading, Traidcraft, Twintrading) buy directly from farming organisations in less developed countries such as Nicaragua, with a fixed minimum price, prepayment of orders and a commitment to a long-term trading partnership. Many of the producer cooperatives then invest their profits directly in community development projects, such as new schools (UNDP 1998: 90).

Of course, equity is not an exclusively North–South concern. According to the UNDP human poverty index,[5] some 7–17 per cent of the population in industrial countries is poor (UNDP 1998: 2). Homelessness, unemployment and social exclusion are common in rich nations too. Poor, socially deprived households are the least likely to pursue sustainable consumption. The pressures of competitive spending and conspicuous consumption in affluent societies exacerbate disparities between rich and poor, encouraging poorer households to go deeper into debt in their unsuccessful attempt to meet rising consumption standards, thereby crowding out spending on food, education and health. Achieving sustainable consumption will therefore involve both an overall readjustment in the levels and patterns of consumption in rich countries and the provision of basic needs to the socially excluded poor.

Thus the sustainable development paradigm, by emphasising the complex links between social, economic, political and environmental factors, introduces a new layer of dilemmas to the issue of equity and environment (as illustrated by the controversial debate over trade in ivory outlined in Box 8.6). In so doing, it underlines how 1970s environmentalism misdiagnosed the problem by its narrow and inaccurate focus on economic growth, over-population and nature protection.

Democracy

> Sustainable development requires: a political system that secures effective citizen participation in decision making . . .
>
> (WCED 1987: 65)

Sustainable development emphasises the importance of democracy in solving environmental problems. The traditional paradigm saw no direct link between democracy and environmental problems, whereas sustainable development holds that the achievement of intragenerational equity will require measures to help poor and disadvantaged groups, and that these groups should have the opportunity to define their own basic needs. Although this democratic message was particularly aimed at developing countries, the encouragement of community participation through consultative processes, citizen initiatives and strengthening the institutions of local democracy is equally applicable in developed countries. It is vital that all local interests, whether poor inner-city or isolated rural communities, can participate in policy and planning decisions, such as urban development and transport planning, that have a direct effect on their lifestyles.

Democracy can also play an important legitimation role, particularly in richer countries, where it is necessary to win public support for environmental initiatives that may have a detrimental effect on lifestyles, such as new eco-taxes or the regulation of car use. If information is widely available and people can participate in decision-making, they may see the need for action and be more willing to accept sacrifices in their material quality of life.

8.6 Equity and the elephant

During the 1980s the African elephant was officially defined as an endangered species: one estimate reported the elephant population crashing from 1.3 million in 1979 to 609,000 in 1989, especially in East Africa. The primary cause was the thriving international trade in ivory, concentrated in Japan, which encouraged widespread poaching. The plight of the elephant became a *cause célèbre* for environmental organisations such as WWF and western governments, including Britain, France and the USA. In 1989 the Convention on International Trade in Endangered Species (CITES) voted to ban the ivory trade by placing elephants on its Appendix I list of sacrosanct creatures. The ban had an immediate impact on western demand for ivory, slashing its price and reducing poaching, and the elephant population began to recover during the 1990s.

However, several southern African states lobbied hard for a partial relaxation of the ban on the following grounds:

1. Rather than being under threat, the elephant population in their countries is too large. Zimbabwe claimed that its elephant population had grown from 30,000 to 70,000 in recent years, which is about 25,000 more than its scrubland can support, causing the government to cull elephants and build up a huge stockpile of ivory.
2. Is it right that western governments, by banning the ivory trade, should deny poor African countries the opportunity to make money from one of their few natural resources? Nor is the ban costless; elephant herds often trample precious crops and damage property.

In 1997 a CITES meeting agreed to a partial relaxation of the ban in ivory trade so that Zimbabwe, Botswana and Namibia could sell stockpiled ivory to Japan, under a strictly controlled international monitoring and reporting system. The first sales took place in February 1999.

The case for a ban (preservation)
1. Any trade in ivory legitimates it and makes it difficult to regulate: it is hard to tell whether ivory has been legally or illegally traded.
2. Many westerners adopt the preservationist position that it is simply wrong to kill any elephant.

Conclusion: the relaxation of the ban will stimulate a massive increase in poaching and an illegal ivory trade, sending the elephant population back into decline.

The case for trade (sustainable utilisation)
1. A strictly regulated, limited trade in ivory from culls will bring much-needed revenue to impoverished indigenous communities. In Zimbabwe, the Campfire community-based programme permits local communities to sell lucrative hunting licences so that rich western tourists shoot elephants as trophies, with the revenues being ploughed back into conservation. However, critics claim that most revenue goes to the safari companies and very little trickles down to local people.
2. Sustainable utilisation provides an incentive for local communities to protect their elephant population in return for a share of the revenues.

Conclusion: the partial lifting of the ban represents a shift from preservation to sustainable development because (in theory) the environment is protected whilst social injustices are reduced.

In the event, the decision to resume sales led to a significant increase in poaching, especially in Kenya, so a CITES meeting in April 2000 reinstated the ban for a two-year period, pending the implementation of an effective system to prevent widespread poaching.

See Barbier et al. (1990). CITES website: *http://www.cites.org*.

The precautionary principle

> In order to protect the environment, the precautionary approach shall be widely applied by States according to their capabilities. Where there are threats of serious or irreversible damage, lack of full scientific certainty shall not be used as a reason for postponing cost-effective measures to prevent environmental degradation.

(*Agenda 21*, Principle 15)

The sustainable development paradigm deals with the complexity and uncertainty that surrounds so much environmental policy-making, particularly where technical and scientific issues are involved, by insisting on the widespread application of the precautionary principle. This principle states that the lack of scientific certainty shall not be used as a reason for postponing measures to prevent environmental degradation.

The precautionary principle is consistent with the notion of ecological sustainability in that it is about relieving pressure on the environment and giving it more 'space'. It is also a practical expression of intergenerational equity because to protect the world for our descendants we need to be sure that our actions will not cause irreparable harm to the environment. The debate around genetically modified organisms provides a good illustration of this issue. The great promise of GM crops, for example, is that by increasing agricultural productivity they can make a real contribution to preventing hunger and starvation in the poorest countries of Africa, Asia and Latin America. Yet GMOs are also characterised by chronic uncertainties about the possible threat they pose to ecosystems (see Box 7.2). Should companies be given free rein to develop these products, as has largely been the case in North America, or should governments invoke the precautionary principle to justify a step-by-step approach employing strict safeguards on trials and the use of moratoriums on production, as has occurred in Europe? The Cartagena Protocol on Biosafety agreed in January 2000 explicitly invokes the precautionary principle by giving countries the right to refuse to accept the import of GM agricultural products (Depledge 2000). The principle of intragenerational equity also drives the precautionary principle when industrial countries accept the burden of helping poorer countries prevent damage, such as climate change, that might arise from their future economic development (O'Riordan and Cameron 1994).

It is important to note two qualifications within the above UNCED definition. First, the qualification 'according to their capabilities' implies that less developed countries might not have to apply the approach so rigorously – this idea has informed the use of the precautionary principle in the ozone and climate change treaties (see Chapter 9). Secondly, it is not clear what kind of cost–benefit analysis should determine whether measures are 'cost-effective'. Are these internal or external costs? How should future costs be discounted and, given the uncertainties involved, at what stage of decision-making should they be applied? Not surprisingly, there is plenty of disagreement about precisely what the precautionary

8.7 Six rules for a precautionary world

Tim O'Riordan has identified the following guidelines to help policy-makers put the precautionary principle into practice:

1. Where unambiguous scientific proof of cause and effect is not available, it is necessary to act with a duty of care.
2. Where the benefits of early action are judged to be greater than the likely costs of delay, it is appropriate to take a lead and to inform society why such action is being taken.
3. Where there is the possibility of irreversible damage to natural life-support functions, precautionary action should be taken irrespective of the forgone benefits.
4. Always listen to calls for a change of course, incorporate representatives of such calls into deliberative forums, and maintain transparency throughout.
5. Never shy away from publicity and never try to suppress information, however unpalatable. In the age of the internet, someone is bound to find out if information is being distorted or hidden.
6. Where there is public unease, act decisively to respond to that unease by introducing extensive discussions and deliberative techniques.

From Economic and Social Research Council (1999: 17).

principle involves. A strong interpretation would effectively reverse the burden of proof so that the responsibility is vested with the polluter (the factory that wants to release toxic chemicals into the atmosphere or the water company wishing to dump sewage in a river) to prove that an activity is safe before it is allowed. Similarly, if damage has already occurred, the relevant industry would have to prove it was not responsible: guilty until proven innocent! The advantage of this tough approach should be that industries would be less inclined to risk releasing a pollutant if the onus rested with them to prove that they had not done so. A weaker version may simply encourage policy-makers to act cautiously in accordance with the old adage that 'it is better to be safe than sorry', although it is less clear what this might mean in practice.[6] It is significant that O'Riordan's suggested rules for applying the precautionary principle (see Box 8.7), no doubt influenced by recent difficulties encountered by the British government in dealing with both BSE and GMOs, are underpinned by strong democratic principles of openness and participation.

Policy integration

> The objective of sustainable development and the integrated nature of the global environment/development challenges pose problems for institutions . . . that were established on the basis of narrow preoccupations and compartmentalised concerns.
>
> (WCED 1987: 9)

The problems for the environment posed by the segmentation of the policy process into distinct sectors such as industry, agriculture, transport and energy were discussed in Chapter 7. Individual ministries pursue narrow sectoral objectives with little consideration for their overall environmental impact. This fragmentation of responsibility is a major obstacle to sustainable development because environmental considerations need to be integrated into the formulation and implementation of policies in every sector. Individual ministries must broaden their horizons and discard their narrow compartmentalised concerns. Integration involves the creation of new structures, the reform of existing institutions and the transformation of established policy-making processes. In short, it requires an administrative revolution. However, as the previous chapter showed, there are many structural and political barriers impeding integration.

Planning

Sustainable development must be planned. Only free-market environmentalists believe that the unfettered market can, of its own volition, produce sustainable development. There are too many complex interdependencies between political, social and economic factors to leave it to chance; equally, those same complexities set limits as to what can be achieved by planning. What is at issue is not 'whether' but 'how much' planning should take place – and which policy instruments should be used.

Governments have to work with a wide range of non-state actors to achieve sustainable development. As *Agenda 21* makes clear, every level of government – supranational, national, regional and local – has to plan sustainable development strategies. Yet this exhortation is not a recipe for a state-planned economy. An active planning role does not mean that the government has to shoulder the responsibility for implementing sustainable development alone. On the contrary, the sustainable development discourse is enthusiastic about partnerships of all shapes and forms. However, it is interesting to speculate whether those political systems with a strong planning tradition, such as France and Japan, will be able to adopt this principle more easily than those where the planning tradition is weaker, such as the USA or the UK.

Government intervention in the market and society can take many forms. Policy-makers can select from a range of instruments to tackle environmental problems – regulations, market mechanisms, voluntary mechanisms and government expenditure – which may all involve some form of intervention in the market (see Chapter 11). The sustainable development discourse is agnostic about these instruments, displaying no *a priori* preference for one type of measure. It is recognised that all policy instruments have a role to play and that the precise balance between them will vary according to the particular problems faced and the political, administrative and judicial traditions of each country. However, whatever the mix of policy instruments, they need to be part of a strategic plan that is designed, co-ordinated and supervised by the government.

Sustainable development: reform or revolution?

Probably no proponent of sustainable development would dissent from any of the five principles identified above (although some might suggest additional principles), but the nature and degree of support will vary. Different actors will attribute different meanings to each principle; for example, as Chapter 9 shows, several fundamentally different definitions of the principle of equity have been applied to climate change negotiations. The relative importance attributed to each principle will also differ. The five principles are central to the discourse initiated by Brundtland, which is driven by a firm commitment to the development ethos, but this message has not been taken up with equal enthusiasm by all supporters of sustainable development. A Northern government may be more concerned about addressing domestic environmental problems than alleviating global poverty and social injustices, so it might emphasise planning, integration and the precautionary principle rather than equity. How far each principle is turned from rhetoric into reality will also depend on which version of sustainable development is in play. Consequently, assertions such as 'sustainable development requires X, Y or Z' need to be carefully considered because a weaker version may not require the same degree of change as a stronger version. For example, stronger forms of sustainable development demand that citizen involvement be encouraged wherever possible by the extension of participatory democracy, whereas weaker versions might be content with formal structures of representative democracy and greater consultation.

Nor should the enormity of the barriers confronting the successful implementation of sustainable development be underestimated. The structural and institutional factors underpinning the traditional paradigm that were identified in the previous chapter pose problems for all five principles. Not least, the demand for greater equity goes to the very heart of the capitalist system which underpins the structural power of business interests. The clarion call for greater democracy focuses on the first dimension of power by seeking more democracy where decisions are observable, yet the wider use of democratic mechanisms alone may have little impact if business is still able to exercise structural second-dimension power. Attempts to apply the precautionary principle more extensively are likely to encounter strong commercial and developmental pressures to allow new products such as GM crops, or to proceed with a project such as a new dam. The quest for greater integration and strategic planning will be obstructed by the institutional segmentation of the administrative system.

Yet the potential radicalism of the sustainable development discourse also should not be underestimated. Sustainable development may accept the underlying capitalist system, but if the five principles were implemented as part of a strategy of very strong, or even strong, sustainability then the outcome would be a very different form of capitalism from that which exists today. Even an incremental process of weak sustainability might eventually gather sufficient momentum to generate extensive change. The great strength of sustainable development is that the compromises it makes with the current political and economic system may produce a more feasible programme of change than that outlined by deep ecologists. Sustainable development is driven by practical politics. It is regarded as the antidote to the romantic visions of a green utopia popular among ecocentrics, and it is preferable to 1970s-style pessimistic survivalist predictions that the catalyst for change will be a planetary eco-crisis. The proponents of sustainable development recognise that a wide and diverse range of interests need to be won over for lasting change to take place. By looking to reconcile the environment versus development dichotomy, sustainable development confronts the practical issues of agency that ecocentric ideologies tend to avoid or ignore. Sustainable development may be incrementalist, accommodationist and reformist, but (in the right hands) it can still be radical.

CRITICAL QUESTION 2

How radical is sustainable development?

ECOLOGICAL MODERNISATION: THE PRACTICAL SOLUTION?

It is clear that the implementation of sustainable development is likely to confront many deep-seated obstacles, particularly associated with North–South issues and the development agenda. At best progress is likely to be slow, and radical changes difficult to achieve. Partly as a result of these difficulties, interest is growing in ecological modernisation, a variation of sustainable development that has emerged in a handful of the most industrialised countries which, significantly, have the best records of environmental protection. Ecological modernisation has its roots in the work of the German social scientist Joseph Huber, who observed that from the late 1970s some policy-makers in a few countries such as Germany and the Netherlands had begun to adopt a more strategic and preventive approach to environmental problems.[7]

The concept

Ecological modernisation concedes that environmental problems are a structural outcome of capitalist society, but it rejects the radical green demand for a fundamental restructuring of the market economy and the liberal democratic state. The political message of ecological modernisation is that capitalism can be made more 'environmentally friendly' by the reform (rather than the overthrow) of existing economic, social and political institutions.[8] Ecological modernisation seems to offer a weak version of sustainability in which the 'opposing' goals of economic growth and environmental protection can be reconciled by further, albeit 'greener', industrialisation.

Ecological modernisation differs from the sustainable development discourse in the way that this argument is turned into a more forceful and positive utilitarian claim that *pollution prevention pays* (Hajer 1995: 26); in short, business can profit by protecting the environment. Consequently, ecological criteria must be built into the production process. On the supply side, costs can be reduced by improving productive efficiency in ways that have environmental benefits. Savings can be made by straightforward technological fixes to reduce waste, and hence pollution, but also through a more fundamental rethinking of manufacturing processes so that large-scale production systems such as 'smoke-stack' industries, that can never be made ecologically sound, are gradually phased out. On the demand side, there are growing markets in green technologies such as pollution abatement equipment and alternative forms of energy. The rise of 'green consumerism' has stimulated demand for goods that minimise environmental damage both in the way they are made (by using recycled materials or minimising packaging) and in their impact when used (by containing less harmful chemicals such as phosphate-free washing powders).

Several kinds of social and institutional transformations flow from these core ideas (Jansen et al. 1998; Mol and Spaargaren 2000). First, science and technology, although contributing to many environmental problems, are also regarded as central to their resolution. Ecological modernisation rejects standard technocentric end-of-pipe solutions in favour of a holistic 'pollution in the round' approach that recognises the complex and interdependent nature of environmental problems which often renders them capable of solution only at source (Weale 1992). Through concepts such as integrated product policies, environmental considerations should be built into the design, production and final disposal of all products and technologies. Secondly, the market will play a central role in the transmission of ecological ideas and practices, with producers, financial institutions and consumers all playing their parts. A key requirement is that the costs of environmental damage must be made calculable through the internalisation of external costs (Hajer 1995: 26). This message is directed especially at businesses and governments. Businesses can take account of environmental factors through techniques such as environmental audits, but they may need some encouragement to drop their focus on short-term profits. The government can provide such an incentive by applying the polluter pays principle, notably through the use of market-based instruments such as eco-taxes and tradeable permits which penalise environmentally damaging activities (see Chapter 11). Thirdly, the role of government therefore changes under ecological modernisation from the traditional centralised, regulatory nation state towards a more flexible, decentralised state that employs a range of instruments to 'steer' production and consumption in more efficient, environmentally benign directions. The emphasis will be on partnership and co-operation between government, industry, scientists and those moderate environmental groups that are willing to be co-opted into the system.

Ecological modernisation as a positive-sum game?

Ecological modernisation clearly has much to offer. A country that seizes the commercial opportunities it offers – lower costs, niche markets, new advanced products – will prosper in terms of jobs, wealth and a better environment; truly a positive-sum game (Hajer 1995: 26). Ecological modernisation also discards much of the political baggage of sustainable development, notably the 'development' agenda of North–South issues, inequalities, social justice and democracy which can prove controversial and costly to implement.[9] Moreover, while sustainable development struggles to provide a clear, precise blueprint for policy-makers, ecological modernisation seems to offer a practical set of principles and techniques for dealing with the problems facing advanced industrialised countries. Its model of a flexible and enabling state reflects recent developments in the idea of 'governance' as involving 'steering' rather than 'rowing', whereby governmental organisations set strategic objectives but leave day-to-day implementation to other actors (Rhodes 1997).

Perhaps the most distinctive feature of ecological modernisation is that it directly addresses the business sector, whose support, as shown in Chapter 7, is vital for any transition towards a more sustainable society. Although the critical role of industry in contributing to environmental degradation is certainly recognised in the sustainable development literature, the Brundtland Report offers little beyond some mild words of exhortation, such as '[industry] should accept a broad sense of social responsibility and ensure an awareness of environmental considerations at all levels' (WCED 1987: 222), to persuade producers of the virtues of sustainable development. By contrast, ecological modernisation appeals to business in a language it understands – profit – which makes it more likely that business will be won over. Consequently, ecological modernisation may offer a way of diminishing the barriers to environmental protection posed by existing producer-dominated policy processes. For if business and political elites were to accept the principles of ecological modernisation then the goals, values, institutions and decision-making processes affecting environmental policy might be reformed in a co-operative way.

Ecological modernisation theory also reflects contemporary developments in several industrialised countries where policy-making elites have adopted a more holistic, strategic approach to environmental issues. With its roots in countries such as Germany, the Netherlands, Sweden, Norway, Austria and Denmark, which are consistently picked out as having the best records of environmental performance in the world, ecological modernisation offers a practical lesson in 'best practice' environmental policy-making. The Dutch National Environmental Policy Plan, which is discussed in Chapter 10, is presented as a classic example of the way environmental criteria can be integrated into every aspect of government; other success stories include the rapid expansion of the environmental technology sector in the German economy (Weale 1992). All these countries have adopted elements of ecological modernisation – policy integration, the precautionary principle, the polluter pays principle, integrated pollution control – in several policy sectors, although nowhere has it been universally implemented. The fifth EU Environmental Action Plan (1993–2000) was also explicitly couched in the language of ecological modernisation.

Limitations of ecological modernisation

Ecological modernisation is not, however, immune from criticism. In the first place, although it is a narrower, less ambitious and therefore more cogent concept than sustainable development, ecological modernisation does not escape definitional problems. Whilst there is a reasonable consensus about the core characteristics of ecological modernisation, there are sufficient differences between writers to distinguish between 'weak' and 'strong' versions along a continuum (Christoff 1996b). In its weaker 'techno-corporatist' form, ecological modernisation focuses on the development of technical solutions to environmental problems through the partnership of economic, political and scientific elites in corporatist policy-making structures (Hajer 1995). It is a narrow understanding of the concept, 'a discourse for engineers and accountants' (Dryzek 1997: 147), that largely excludes consideration of development and democratic issues. The stronger 'reflexive' version of ecological modernisation adopts a much broader approach to the integration of environmental concerns across institutions and wider society which envisages extensive democratisation and concern for the international dimensions of environmental issues (Hajer 1995). Seen in this light it is not clear how far the stronger version differs from sustainable development; indeed, Hajer (1995) identifies the Brundtland Report as 'one of the paradigm statements of ecological modernisation' (p. 26). This strong version of ecological modernisation is perhaps best regarded as a particular variant of sustainable development that focuses on the role of business and the problems of industrialised countries. Paradoxically, the weaker version of ecological modernisation is more distinct from sustainable development, although, as 'little more than a rhetorical rescue operation for a capitalist economy confounded by ecological crises' (Dryzek 1997: 148), that vision may be rather less attractive. Mol and Spaargaren (2000) suggest that this simplistic dichotomy reflects a rather dated interpretation of the literature that does not take account of the mushrooming of theoretical and empirical studies since the mid-1990s. In particular, they suggest that the narrow conceptualisation of ecological modernisation as involving little more than the introduction of 'add-on' technologies misrepresents the way the discourse has moved on to consider fundamental structural changes to socio-technical systems.

Secondly, although ecological modernisation is attractive to Northern policy elites precisely because its narrower focus omits the political baggage (i.e. the development agenda) that comes with sustainable development, perhaps the omission of social justice issues is a potential Achilles' heel. For example, techniques such as 'life-cycle assessment' are increasingly used to analyse the environmental impact of a product 'from cradle to grave' to include all the inputs of raw materials and energy and all the outputs of air, water and solid waste emissions generated by the production, use and disposal of a product. Life-cycle assessment offers enormous potential benefits but it largely ignores the issues of equity and social justice raised by the broader sustainable development discourse. Ecological modernisation is predicated on the utilitarian argument that by making pollution prevention pay, all actors – government, business, consumers, environmental groups – can play a positive-sum game in which everyone benefits and everyone participates. The problem is that many people will be unable to participate because their basic needs are not being met. Social justice issues are prominent in the sustainable development literature precisely because, as noted above, most environmental issues involve distributional questions that can rarely be resolved without winners and losers. As Hajer (1995: 35) observes, it may be rather naive to believe that ecological modernisation can avoid addressing basic social contradictions (see Reitan 1998).

Indeed, ecological modernisation is strangely silent on North–South issues. It is not hard to envisage a scenario in which large transnational companies operate along 'ecomodernist' lines in the North, with efficient clean technologies and products, while locating their more polluting activities in developing countries where environmental regulations are weaker (Christoff 1996b; Dryzek 1997). Perhaps ecological modernisation requires a large periphery of poor countries to act as a waste tip for the polluting activities of a rich core of nations.

Thirdly, in its attentiveness to production and the message that pollution prevention pays, ecological modernisation generally understates the importance of consumption, especially the overall *level* of consumption. The implicit assumption seems to be that greening the production process allows consumption to be infinite. Despite its name, ecological modernisation is only superficially *ecological* because it largely ignores the integrity of ecosystems and the cumulative impact of industrialisation on them (Christoff 1996b: 486). Its technocentric view of nature recognises no limits to growth and assumes that all problems are open to solutions. Yet even if businesses do adopt every available environmentally sound technique, the benefits are likely to be offset by overall growth in the economy. If, for example, ecological modernisation leads to the replacement of 8 million fuel-inefficient cars with 10 million more fuel-efficient cars, the overall impact on the environment may be little different. Many environmental problems can only be solved if individual citizens accept their share of the responsibility by changing both the nature and the level of consumption.

The rise of 'green consumerism' since the late 1980s has encouraged some manufacturers and retailers to advertise the 'greenness' of products, such as 'chlorine-free' toilet cleaners, 'forest friendly' wood products and cosmetics that have not been tested on animals. They hope to win the custom of a more discerning and usually affluent shopper. Companies like the Body Shop grew exponentially in the 1990s by selling its franchises worldwide on the back of the cosmetics market for 'beauty without cruelty'. As more people have begun to invest directly in the stock market, ethical investment has also become big business. In the USA, between 1995 and 1997 the total volume of 'responsibly invested assets' rose from $639 billion to $1,185 trillion – an increase of 85 per cent, and in the UK, between 1994 and 1998, ethical funds rose from £0.7 billion to £2.2 billion – a 214 per cent increase (Holden Meehan 1998) – reaching over £3 billion by 2001.

It is easy to decry green consumerism. Consumers are frequently subjected to false or misleading claims about products: washing powders that never contained phosphates are suddenly marketed as 'phosphate-free'; refrigerators described as 'ozone-friendly' when, although CFC-free, they may contain HFCs; and cosmetics described as 'not tested on animals' without the qualification that this claim refers only to 'within the last five years'. Stricter advertising codes of practice and tough eco-labelling standards could remedy some of these flaws. A bigger problem is that green consumerism remains a minority activity; too few people engage in it on too few occasions. An important equity issue here is that most poor people simply cannot afford the higher prices of most 'green' products. Yet many middle-income consumers are also only intermittent green consumers, either because they are selective about which high prices they will pay, or because there are numerous lifestyle compromises, such as giving up the second car (let alone dispensing altogether with a car) or dishwasher, that they are not prepared to make.

More fundamentally, green consumerism appears to be a contradiction in terms, for how can we *consume* our way out of the environmental crisis? By encouraging consumers to alter the type, rather than the level, of consumption, green consumerism does nothing to address the core problem of the rising volume of consumption. Indeed, there is a danger that individuals will think they have done their bit by buying a few green products, while carrying on with a high-consumption lifestyle. Consumers need to undergo a much deeper process of social learning. However, Press and Mazmanian's (1999) observation that in the USA 'There is simply no visible governmental or corporate leadership devoted to reducing extreme consumption and the perceived need for high-volume, high-polluting, high-obsolescence products' (p. 277) is universally true. In short, ecological modernisation theory has given insufficient attention to the consumption side of the sustainability equation.[10]

CRITICAL QUESTION 3

Is ecological modernisation only suitable for a handful of affluent industrialised nations?

Ecological modernisation in practice

This section offers some broad empirical observations about the role of two key actors in the ecological modernisation discourse: the state and industry.

The state

Despite the plaudits it receives, there are still only a few policy developments that clearly fit within the ecological modernisation framework, most of which are concentrated in a handful of 'pioneer' nations (Andersen and Liefferink 1997a). Some political systems appear more open to ecological modernisation than others; in particular, it has taken root most firmly in countries with policy styles containing significant corporatist traits (Dryzek 1997: 141). Where there is a corporatist tradition of seeking cooperative relations with powerful non-state interests, there may also be a willingness to deal with emerging environmental and consumer groups. Thus the Norwegian government 'has expanded Norway's traditional consensus-corporatist style of policy-making into the environment field' (Jansen and Mydske 1998: 188) by gradually including environmental groups in most phases of the routine policy process. Sweden, Denmark and Austria, where the corporatist culture has also traditionally sought consensus, have intermittently included environmental groups in planning and decision-making (Kronsell 1997; Andersen et al. 1998; Lauber 1997). It is perhaps ironic that corporatist arrangements which were originally intended to maximise economic growth by giving privileged access to business and trade union groups, have produced a consultative policy style that is relatively open to environmental interests and ideas that may challenge some of those expansionist assumptions.[11] Yet in these pioneering nations the state has traditionally played a key developmental role by engaging in extensive planning and intervention. The emergence of ecological modernisation, which also requires a close working relationship between the state and industry, has allowed policy elites in these countries to reinterpret the development role of the state, broadening the progrowth agenda to include a greater awareness of environmental protection. In a comparative study of pollution control policy, Weale (1992) showed how German policy-makers were more receptive to elements of ecological modernisation during the 1980s than their counterparts in Britain. German policy elites were able to make the link between economic interventionism and the growth potential of the emerging pollution control industry. Consequently, by investing heavily in the green technology sector and applying the concept of 'best available technology' (BAT), which makes the award of an operating licence conditional on a business installing the most modern, cleanest equipment, the German state provided a massive stimulus to the green technology sector. By contrast, British policy elites failed to make this connection. The absence of close links with peak economic associations, combined with the Thatcher government's ideological objection to interventionism, rendered it both unable and unwilling to consider a proactive developmental role for the state. The consensual, interventionist policy style required by ecological modernisation may make it less suitable for English-speaking countries such as the USA, Britain, Australia and New Zealand, where environmental groups generally remain outsiders in the policy process and market liberal ideologies have exercised most influence since the 1980s (Dryzek 1997: 151).

Yet the pioneer states are not paragons of ecological virtue; the empirical basis of ecological modernisation is actually very limited. The ecological modernisation paradigm has not yet colonised the belief systems of all policy elites. One authoritative study of the Dutch response to the acid rain problem found that a discourse of ecological modernisation coexisted with traditional, sectoral policy responses (Hajer 1995). Consequently, 'anticipatory story-lines were combined with end-of-pipe solutions', so that rather than reducing sulphur and nitrate emissions by attacking the source of the problem – discouraging road traffic, cutting cattle stocks or conserving energy – the Dutch fell back on the remedial solutions associated with the traditional paradigm, such as requiring catalysts in cars, building slurry-processing plants and fitting FGD equipment to power stations (Hajer 1995: 267). Similarly, German pollution policies focus on symptoms rather than causes, so they too mainly employ end-of-pipe solutions rather than attempting to change behaviour by, for example, reducing speed limits on the autobahn (Weale 1992: 84–5). A study of Norwegian climate change policy found little evidence that the state was promoting ecological restructuring; indeed, several key state institutions such as the Ministry of Industry and Energy actively impeded attempts to reconcile economic and environmental objectives by levying a carbon tax (Reitan 1998: 22). Whilst there have been genuine attempts to institutionalise environmental values across a range of Norwegian public policy issues, these have usually broken down whenever 'significant economic interests have been at stake' (Jansen and Mydske 1998: 203), usually resulting in defeat for the environment ministry. In the pioneer states, as elsewhere, governments still provide many perverse subsidies that encourage pollution and environmental damage. An obvious example is the price support system underpinning the EU Common Agricultural Policy which promotes the use of environmentally damaging intensive farming methods. Lastly, although they are the favoured policy instrument of the ecological modernisation discourse, market-based instruments, such as eco-taxes, are still used sparingly (see Chapter 11).

Industry

If state structures show tardiness in adapting to ecological modernisation, evidence of genuine conversion in the business world is also scarce. Admittedly there are many entrepreneurs, industrial executives and trade associations who will proclaim the virtues of greening industry, but the rhetoric is not always matched by behavioural changes. For every company that has made a serious attempt to build ecological criteria into its operations, there are dozens more that have done little or nothing. The slow progress of ecological modernisation within European industry can be illustrated by the limited impact of initiatives to promote environmental improvement at the enterprise level. The voluntary EU Eco-Management and Audit Scheme (EMAS) involves firms publishing an externally verified environmental statement of their operations.[12] EMAS is a very weak scheme. Firms can select the sites they wish to enter and set their own objectives and targets (which do not even have to match the industry best environmental practice), so the external audit does little more than check that the documentation is in order (Neale 1997). Even so, take-up is low. EMAS was available to companies from April 1995 yet, by 1998, just 1,538 sites were registered throughout the EU and Norway, of which 1,127 were in Germany, where external verification requirements are lower than elsewhere (ENDs 1998a). Many European firms have chosen to register with the international standard ISO14001 which, as it involves no independently verified statement, is even less demanding than EMAS.[13] Recognising these weaknesses, the EU adopted a new EMAS regulation in February 2001 that extends the scheme to all areas of economic activity including local authorities, encourages greater employee participation and transparency, and incorporates ISO14001 as part of a tougher environmental statement. Of course, many firms do undertake their own environmental audits without bothering to register with official programmes, but the general indifference to schemes that would publicly advertise their green credentials does suggest the limited penetration of ecological modernisation in the industrial sector (see Box 8.8).

One factor in the general reluctance to embrace ecological modernisation may be ignorance. Many industrialists, particularly in smaller and medium-sized firms, may not have the opportunities or resources to gain access to the ecological modernisation discourse. However, even when the 'pollution prevention pays' message has been absorbed, individual firms may still make the economic calculation that the costs of greening outweigh

8.8 Eco-labelling: the limited appeal of ecological modernisation?

Eco-labelling is a voluntary system that seeks to harness market forces by helping consumers identify products that are less harmful to the environment. Manufacturers pay for the right to display a logo demonstrating the 'greenness' of their products. If this logo proves attractive to consumers, then other manufacturers have a market incentive to make their products greener – a clear example of the 'pollution prevention pays' principle. The widespread use of eco-labelling would be an indicator that industry was absorbing the message of ecological modernisation.

Some eco-labelling schemes, notably the German Blue Angel and the Scandinavian Nordic Swan programmes, have proved successful, but most have not. The EU scheme launched in 1992 has had limited impact. Between 1992 and 1996 just nine firms were awarded an EU eco-label. By February 2001 still only 61 licences had been granted to use the eco-label logo on about 250 products in the EU (none in Germany).

Problems

1. Eco-labelling depends on the willingness of industry to compete for the logo, but trade associations dislike schemes that pit their members against each other or might impose new costs on them. Consequently, many industry trade associations have lobbied against the introduction of eco-labelling schemes or persuaded their members to boycott them once in place (Harrison 1999).

2. Opponents of eco-labelling, such as the Coalition for Truth in Environmental Marketing Information which represents 2,900 US companies, argue that it contravenes World Trade Organisation (WTO) rules because the criteria used to award eco-labels are biased in favour of domestically produced goods; i.e. they are a barrier to free trade.

EU eco-label website: *http://europa.eu.int/comm/ environment/ecolabel/index.htm.*

the benefits. Certainly, the transaction costs of green innovations may be significant: investments in new cleaner technologies are likely to be 'lumpy', requiring a major short-term expenditure in anticipation of long-term benefits. Firms may be reluctant or even unable to make such a commitment, especially if it involves compromising short-term competitive advantage.

Consequently, several writers have argued that progress in greening industry is most likely to occur at the sectoral level (Porter 1990; Press and Mazmanian 1999). Here the transaction costs of change can be reduced by sharing the financial burden and integrating technical expertise so that industry-wide networks of companies can gain sectoral, as opposed to single-firm, advantages in the global market. Moreover, if an entire sector acts in unison then the problems of collective action are reduced; individual firms are more likely to innovate if they believe their direct competitors will too. In the USA, one sector where such voluntary initiatives have achieved notable advances in recent years is the pulp and paper industry, where major changes include reducing emission levels and energy intensity, phasing out the use of chlorine and other toxic chemicals, and increasing the volume of recycled waste (Press and Mazmanian 1999: 275–6). The lesson here is that governments might be wise to adopt a strategy of ecological modernisation that targets particular (highly polluting) sectors by working with the relevant trade associations and encouraging voluntary industry self-regulation.

Overall, the evidence presented here suggests that the greening of industry remains an aspiration. Many companies are increasingly aware of the environmental impact of their activities, but business elites have not yet absorbed the ideology of ecological modernisation and there is limited evidence of ecological criteria being built into production processes. Even in 'pioneer' countries, industry has been selective about which ideas are adopted, with huge variations between sectors. The business community has shown little interest in state-sponsored schemes to encourage ecological modernisation and effective state–industry collaboration remains the exception rather than the rule. Indeed, as the following chapters show, many industries are actively hostile to ecological modernisation initiatives, opposing the use of innovative policy instruments such as eco-taxes that are specifically designed to implement the 'pollution prevention pays' principle.

CRITICAL QUESTION 4

Why has ecological modernisation struggled to win the hearts and minds of industrialists?

CONCLUSION

The significant contribution of sustainable development has been to question the long-standing assumption that there is an inevitable trade-off between environmental and economic objectives. By setting environmental considerations in a broader social, economic and political context, it has also produced a development agenda that can marry the often conflicting aims of rich and poor countries. Although there are many different meanings attributed to sustainable development, it is undoubtedly the dominant paradigm driving the discourse about contemporary environmental policy. While all governments claim to be committed to the principles of sustainable development, some Northern policy elites have been drawn to the narrower concept of ecological modernisation. It is best regarded as a 'half-sister' to sustainable development, for they share many principles, aims and policies, but ecological modernisation may represent a more practical and effective means of transforming the traditional paradigm because it directly addresses the issue of producer power. By offering a utilitarian incentive to industry to build environmental considerations into the profit calculus, ecological modernisation anticipates that the belief systems of business elites will change so that they see the instrumental advantages of better environmental protection. It also provides an incentive for the state to transform itself by identifying a key role for it in facilitating industrial change. The 'discourse of reassurance' (Dryzek 1997: 146) offered by ecological modernisation is particularly attractive to policy-makers and residents of prosperous industrialised countries, who are confronted with fewer hard choices than are posed by stronger versions of sustainable development. Nevertheless, the jury is still out on whether or not ecological modernisation offers a practical programme for achieving sustainability.

One lesson to take from this chapter is that the widespread agreement that sustainable development is a good thing belies deep conflict over its meaning and, therefore, its implementation. The following chapters explore how far there has been a shift from the traditional paradigm towards sustainable development or ecological modernisation. One measure of change will be evidence that the core principles identified here are shaping policy practice. In the next chapter, particular attention will be given to the significance of equity, democracy and the precautionary principle in international environmental politics.

Further reading

There is a huge literature on sustainable development. A good place to start is with the Brundtland Report itself (WCED 1987) and *Agenda 21* (UNCED 1992). For an academic analysis see Redclift (1993), Carley and Christie (2000), Lafferty (1996), Baker et al. (1997a) and Meadowcroft (2000). Pearce et al. (1989) offer a perspective from economics. Dryzek (1997) provides a perceptive comparison of the discourses of sustainable development and ecological modernisation. Christoff (1996b) and Blowers (1997) are also good surveys of the ecological modernisation literature. Weale (1992) and Hajer (1995) provide excellent empirical studies of ecological modernisation in a comparative context. The journal *Environmental Politics* has acted as a forum for conceptual and empirical studies of both sustainable development and ecological modernisation; see, in particular, the special issues on *Agenda 21* (O'Riordan and Voisey 1997) and on ecological modernisation (Mol and Sonnenfeld 2000).

Notes

1. Several other agenda-setting documents were produced in the run-up to the 1992 Earth Summit by global networks of NGOs, grassroots organisations, scientific and academic communities, business and indigenous peoples in the hope of pushing their particular ideas about sustainable development onto political agendas. MacDonald (1998) provides a survey of eleven major documents and assesses progress in implementing them.
2. See World Bank (1999) and its website: *www.worldbank.org.*
3. The Brundtland Report contains a few isolated non-anthropocentric observations (Achterberg 1993: 86), but the overall tone is anthropocentric.
4. A wider discussion of sustainable consumption can be found in Lafferty (1996), UN Development Programme (UNDP 1998) and UN Department of Economic and Social Affairs (UNDESA 1999).

5. Based on the UNDP Human Poverty Index HPI-2 index which is a multi-dimensional measure designed specifically for industrial countries based on human longevity, knowledge, standard of living and social exclusion (UNDP 1998: 15).
6. See Wildavsky (1995, conclusion) for a robust critique of the precautionary principle.
7. Key ecological modernisation studies include Jänicke (1991), Weale (1992) and Hajer (1995).
8. It is possible to distinguish two broad approaches within the ecological modernisation discourse (Mol 1996): first, those writers who regard (and promulgate) ecological modernisation as a political programme for contemporary environmental politics; secondly, environmental sociologists who have constructed a social theory labelled ecological modernisation. The discussion here focuses on the former; for the latter, see Spaargaren and Mol (1992).
9. There are exceptions, notable Hajer (1995), who stresses the importance of democracy.
10. Spaargaren and van Vliet (2000) try to rectify this imbalance.
11. These observations are consistent with comparative research findings which suggest that corporatism produces better environmental outcomes than pluralist systems (Crepaz 1995; Scruggs 1999).
12. Indeed, an initial proposal to make certain external audits mandatory was dropped after strong industry resistance.
13. Around 5,400 companies were certified to ISO14001 worldwide in 1998 (ENDs 1998b).

9

International environmental politics

Contents

- What is environmental diplomacy?
- How can the growth of international environmental co-operation be explained?
- What are the obstacles to international environmental co-operation?
- Are environmental treaties effective?
- Has international environmental co-operation contributed to sustainable development?

KEY ISSUES

International environmental problems pose major challenges to the achievement of sustainable development. The distinguishing feature of an *international* environmental problem is that it does not respect national boundaries. Some transboundary issues, such as the conservation of endangered wildlife, natural habitats and marine life, have been around for many years. Other problems which were once predominantly regional or local in cause and effect, such as deforestation, desertification and water scarcity, now have international dimensions. A 'new' range of issues, including climate change, ozone depletion and biodiversity loss, are truly *global* in that they affect everyone. All states contribute to problems of the global commons and all suffer the consequences, although the extent to which each country is culpable for causing a particular problem and vulnerable to its effects varies enormously. Thus industrialised countries have made the largest contribution to climate change, while low-lying countries, such as Bangladesh and Egypt, face the greatest risk from rising sea-levels caused by global warming.

International environmental problems require international solutions; they cannot be solved by nation states acting alone. Only if individual nation states cooperate with each other can environmental problems be resolved. As governments have grown increasingly aware of their mutual vulnerability, environmental issues have become firmly established on the international policy agenda. The UN conferences at Stockholm in 1972 and Rio de Janeiro in 1992 were important milestones in this transition. Multilateral environmental agreements did exist before 1972, covering issues such as wildlife conservation and maritime pollution, but the Stockholm Conference marked the start of a wide-ranging debate about the environment in international politics. Twenty years later the Rio Earth Summit pushed the environment centre-stage: it was the largest ever gathering of world leaders and was attended by a host of non-governmental organisations (NGOs) and interest groups. Two conventions on climate change and biodiversity were agreed and *Agenda 21* was launched, committing the international community to the principles of sustainable development. By the end of the century the rising tide of international co-operation had produced almost 200 multilateral environmental agreements and spawned a plethora of institutional structures to monitor, enforce and strengthen them (see Table 9.1).

Yet the mere existence of these agreements, which are undoubtedly a real achievement of environmental diplomacy, is something of a puzzle because they represent a degree of international co-operation that seems to fly in the face of traditional assumptions about the way states behave in a system of international relations where, historically, conflict and mistrust have been the norm. This chapter starts with a short conceptual discussion of this paradox, drawing principally on neo-realist and institutionalist theories of international relations. The next section outlines the emergence of two of the most important recent international treaties

Table 9.1 Some major multilateral environmental treaties

1946	International Convention for the Regulation of Whaling
1959	Antarctic Treaty
1972	Convention for the Protection of the World Cultural and Natural Heritage
1973	Convention on International Trade in Endangered Species of Wild Fauna and Flora (CITES) Convention on the Prevention of Pollution from Ships (MARPOL)
1979	Geneva Convention on Long-Range Transboundary Air Pollution (LRTAP)
1982	UN Convention on the Law of the Sea
1985	Vienna Convention for the Protection of the Ozone Layer
1989	Basel Convention on the Control of Transboundary Movements of Hazardous Wastes and Their Disposal
1992	UN Framework Convention on Climate Change UN Convention on Biological Diversity
1994	UN Convention to Combat Desertifiation

dealing with ozone depletion and climate change, and the following section provides a wide-ranging discussion of the factors determining whether or not nation states choose to cooperate to protect the global commons. Although an international environmental agreement may represent a diplomatic triumph, it does not guarantee that the problem addressed will be resolved, and the next section assesses some of the difficulties confronting the implementation of international environmental treaties, emphasising how the capacity of states to enforce environmental agreements is inextricably linked to wider issues of international political economy. The chapter concludes with an assessment of the relationship between international environmental politics and sustainable development.

THE PARADOX OF INTERNATIONAL CO-OPERATION

International environmental co-operation may be desirable, but severe collective action problems make it difficult to achieve. As Hurrell and Kingsbury (1992a) ask: 'Can a fragmented and often highly conflictual political system made up of over 170 sovereign states and numerous other actors achieve the high (and historically unprecedented) levels of cooperation and policy coordination needed to manage environmental problems on a global scale?' (p. 4). Unlike a domestic political system where a national government can regulate behaviour and levy taxes, there is no central sovereign authority in the international arena to co-ordinate policy responses to global commons' problems or to ensure that sovereign states comply with agreements. According to the neo-realist perspectives that dominate academic international relations, individual sovereign states operate in an anarchic system in which their behaviour is almost exclusively shaped by considerations of power politics (Morgenthau 1978).

The primary aim of each nation state is to survive by accumulating more power relative to other countries. As no nation can fully trust the intentions of others, individual countries are unlikely to cooperate to protect the global commons. If individual states cannot solve global environmental problems by acting alone, there is little point in one state changing its behaviour without the assurance that others will too. On the contrary, game theory can be used to show that it is rational for states *not* to cooperate (i.e. to free-ride) if some other states are cooperating because the benefits of co-operation, such as pollution prevention, will be secured anyway (Weale 1992: 191).[1]

Realists, therefore, often regard the environment primarily as a security issue in so far as global commons problems could be a source of conflict between states. Modern military conflict obviously wreaks massive environmental destruction, as illustrated by the use of the Agent Orange defoliant in Vietnam, the burning Kuwaiti oilfields during the Gulf War and the pollution of the River Danube following the NATO bombing of Serbia in 1999, but fortunately there have been few examples of military conflict arising directly from environmental conflicts. Water shortage is often cited as a potential cause of conflict, having contributed to tensions in the politically volatile Middle East where several countries compete for the limited waters supplied by a few major rivers (Bulloch and Darwish 1993). As Table 9.2 shows, the growing flood of environmental refugees fleeing from drought, famine, deforestation and degraded land – 25 million in 1998 – is an issue of increasing international importance, especially when refugees seek safety by crossing national borders. As the effects of climate change begin to bite, these 'natural disasters' are likely to increase in number and intensity, and may become a future source of inter-state disagreement.[2]

The rising tide of international environmental co-operation therefore poses a problem for the Realist view that in international politics 'Anarchy

Table 9.2 Environmental disasters and environmental refugees, 1998

Country	Disaster	No. affected	No. killed
1. China	Floods	180m	4,150
2. North India/Nepal	Heavy monsoon	36m	3,250
3. Bangladesh	Monsoon/cyclones	31m	1,300
4. Central America	Hurricane Mitch	6.7m	10,000
5. Philippines	Nine typhoons	5m	500
6. Vietnam	Tropical storms	2.4m	50
7. Indonesia	Drought	1.5m	unknown
8. Caribbean	Hurricane Georges	600,000	4,000
9. Argentina	Floods	360,000	20
10. Sudan	Floods	338,000	1,400

Source: World Disasters Report 1999 (see *http://www.ifrc.org/*).

and conflict are the rule, order and co-operation the exception' (Hurrell and Kingsbury 1992a: 5). One explanation is that it may be rational for actors to cooperate when they are assured that others will cooperate too.[3] If individual states have common interests, such as to prevent pollution, then the mutual recognition that each state will have to interact repeatedly with others over the long term might build the trust necessary to provide the assurance that co-operation will be forthcoming and that other states will not free-ride (see Paterson 1996: 101–8). Realists may be also inaccurate in characterising all international relations as concerned with power politics; for example, the claim that states seek to maximise *relative* gains can be replaced with the (reasonable) assumption that they pursue *absolute* gains. So, if each state is seeking to improve its absolute position rather than always seeking to 'win' each play of the game (i.e. to accept an absolute gain even if it is lower than the gains accruing to another country), then co-operation is more likely because everyone can end up a winner. Such assumptions underpin institutionalist perspectives which regard environmental co-operation as perfectly rational whenever self-interested states judge that the benefits of co-operation will outweigh the costs (Keohane 1989).[4]

The apparent paradox of international co-operation may, therefore, not be so 'irrational' as Realists suggest. Of course, Realist reservations should not be dismissed lightly. Collective action problems, not least the incentive to free-ride on the efforts of others to cooperate, ensure that each international agreement will represent a hard-won diplomatic triumph. Nevertheless, the existence of so many concrete examples of co-operation suggests that the obstacles are not insuperable. Instead, following the lead of institutionalist writers, and also drawing on constructivist approaches (e.g. Haas 1999), it may be more productive to focus on the factors that influence the emergence of international treaties addressing global commons problems.

ENVIRONMENTAL REGIMES: THE OZONE AND CLIMATE CHANGE TREATIES

Regime: The principles, norms, rules and decision-making procedures which form the basis of co-operation on a particular issue in international relations.

Regimes are 'sets of implicit or explicit principles, norms, rules, and decision-making procedures around which actors' expectations converge in a given area of international relations' (Krasner 1983: 2) (see Box 9.1). Part of the significance of a regime is that, by agreeing to it, a government voluntarily accepts external interference in the way it exploits resources within its own sovereign territory. The growth of multilateral agreements since the early 1970s is clear evidence of growing international co-operation to deal with global commons problem. This section describes the processes leading to the signing of the ozone depletion and climate change treaties. These treaties are interesting not only because they address two of the most serious contemporary global atmospheric problems but also because they offer a contrast between one apparently successful regime (ozone) and one that has had only limited success (climate change).

Ozone protection[5]

The stratospheric ozone layer plays a critical part in protecting life on Earth by absorbing harmful ultraviolet radiation. In 1974 two American-based scientists, Molina and Rowland, suggested that the

9.1 Regime terminology

A *convention*, or treaty, is the main form of multilateral legal instrument, containing binding obligations, rules and regulations.

A *framework convention* is negotiated in anticipation of later texts and may contain only a broad set of principles and aims relating to the issue. Subsequently, maybe over several years, it is strengthened by the negotiation of protocols.

A *protocol* spells out specific, binding obligations, such as specific emission reduction targets.

From Porter and Brown (1996: 16–17).

concentration of ozone in the atmosphere could be extensively damaged by anthropogenic chemicals, notably chlorofluorocarbons (CFCs) – used as propellants in aerosols, refrigerants, solvents, foam products – and halons, used in fire extinguishers. These synthetic chemicals leak into the atmosphere, then rise into the stratosphere where they release chlorine and bromine which destroy ozone. A thinner ozone layer would increase skin cancers and cataracts, harm human and animal immune systems (which will weaken resistance to infectious diseases) and damage ecosystems. The sheer volume of these chemicals in the stratosphere is indicative of their significance in modern industrialised economies, being safe (i.e. non-inflammable and non-toxic), stable and versatile. Consequently, any attempt to limit their use was sure to encounter strong resistance from economic interests, notably the major chemical corporations that manufactured them, such as Dupont (USA) and ICI (UK).

The first steps towards international action were tentative, as scientific fact-finding, consensus-building and policy developments proceeded hand in hand (see Table 9.3). Initially, it was essential to establish the scientific basis of the ozone problem, so in 1975 the UN Environment Programme (UNEP) funded a study by the World Meteorological Society to examine the link between CFCs and ozone depletion. Two years later a UN conference of experts from thirty-two countries drew up a World Plan of Action on the Ozone Layer to co-ordinate future research, but not until the discovery in 1985 of a 'hole' in the ozone layer above the Antarctic – regular springtime decreases of ozone in excess of 40 per cent between 1977 and 1984 – did a scientific consensus about the existence of ozone depletion begin to emerge.[6] This consensus was completed in 1988 when the Ozone Trends Panel, which had a membership of over 100 leading atmospheric scientists from ten countries, concluded that the ozone layer in the northern hemisphere had been reduced by up to 3 per cent between 1969 and 1986: 'ozone layer depletion was no longer a theory; at last it had been substantiated by hard evidence' (Benedick 1991: 110). Crucially, the

Table 9.3 Ozone protection – key developments	
1974	Two US scientists hypothesise that CFCs might cause ozone depletion
1977	UNEP Co-ordinating Committee on the Ozone Layer established to assess ozone depletion
1982	Twenty-four states begin discussions towards an ozone convention
1985	Vienna Convention signed by twenty states and European Community: to co-ordinate reporting and monitoring (entered force 1988) British scientists discover 'hole' in ozone layer over Antarctic
1987	Montreal Protocol signed by twenty-four states and the European Community: to regulate consumption and production of CFCs and halons (entered force 1989)
1988	Ozone Trends Panel report confirms the link between CFCs and the ozone hole
1989	EC and USA agree to phase out all production of CFCs by 2000
1990	London Amendments to Montreal Protocol: all CFC/halon production to be phased out by 2000 (entered force 1992); more substances banned
1992	Interim Multilateral Fund established USA, then EC, announce CFC production to halt by 1996 Copenhagen Amendments – HCFC controls agreed leading to ban by 2030

See UNEP (*http://www.unep.org/ozone*) and International Institute for Sustainable Development (*http://www.iisd.ca*) for recent developments in ozone diplomacy.

panel had also gathered enough evidence to confirm that CFCs and other synthetic chemicals were the primary cause of ozone depletion.

Meanwhile, international negotiations had gradually picked up pace. In 1977, the USA, Canada, Norway, Sweden and Finland (collectively known as the Toronto Group) together urged UNEP to consider remedial action; when this was not forthcoming they took unilateral action to ban non-essential aerosol uses of CFCs. The European Community, which accounted for 45 per cent of world CFC production, strongly resisted such action. In the absence of firm scientific evidence, EC member states were subjected to strong industrial lobbying to protect export markets and avoid the costs of developing substitutes. When multilateral negotiation of a framework convention commenced in 1982, the representatives from twenty-four nations were broadly divided between the Toronto Group, which pushed for a complete ban on non-essential uses of CFCs, and the European Community, which would only consider a cap on production. Unable to resolve this fundamental conflict, the resulting 1985 Vienna Convention for the Protection of the Ozone Layer represented little more than an agreement to cooperate on monitoring, research and information-exchange, for it imposed no targets or controls to reduce CFC production, although the USA was able to win an important commitment to start negotiations for a binding protocol (Benedick 1991: 45–6). Nevertheless, the Vienna Convention was significant because it was signed without firm scientific evidence that ozone depletion was happening, making it the first instance of international environmental law based (implicitly) on the precautionary principle.

During the nine months of negotiations leading up to the signing of the Montreal Protocol in September 1987, the European Community and Japan shifted from resistance to any cut in production into accepting a compromise proposal to reduce CFC production by 50 per cent of 1986 levels by 1999 and to freeze halon production at 1986 levels by 1992. Several factors contributed to this dramatic change of heart. Opponents were subjected to energetic US diplomatic manoeuvring. The negotiations were skilfully handled by the UNEP Executive Director, Mustafa Tolba. European states were increasingly split as West Germany, under strong domestic political pressure to make concessions, disagreed with the other major CFC producers, France, Italy and the UK. Most important, though, was the firming up of scientific evidence following the discovery of the ozone hole, which had a profound impact on national representatives and even influenced industrial interests (Brenton 1994: 140–1). Again, as the Ozone Trends Panel report proving the link between CFCs and ozone depletion only appeared several months *after* the Montreal Protocol was signed, it was significant that politicians had signed an agreement in advance of scientific evidence supporting their action (Seaver 1997: 33–4).

The Ozone Panel's findings that ozone depletion was far worse than expected also prompted Dupont to declare that it would accelerate research into substitutes and stop manufacturing all CFCs and halons by the end of the century – a declaration that was soon followed by other major international chemical producers (Benedick 1991: 111–15). This scientific evidence led to further strengthening of the regime at follow-up meetings of the signatories. The London Amendments (1990) agreed a total phase-out by developed countries of CFCs, halons and carbon tetrachloride by 2000, with intermediate targets of 50 per cent by 1995 and 85 per cent by 1997. Subsequent meetings ratcheted forward reduction and phase-out dates (e.g. to phase out halon by 1994, and CFCs and carbon tetrachloride by 1996) and set targets for new chemicals, including the ozone-damaging substitute hydrochlorofluorocarbon (HCFC).

One major problem unresolved at Montreal was the need to persuade developing countries to participate in the regime. Industrialised nations are responsible for almost 90 per cent of global CFC consumption, with a per capita consumption more than twenty times higher than in less industrialised nations (Benedick 1991: 148–9), so it was obviously incumbent on the former to take the initiative in reducing emissions. However, the long-term success of the regime was in jeopardy without the involvement of developing countries, notably China and India, where the consumption of ozone-depleting substances in refrigeration and air-conditioning systems will grow with further industrialisation. Developing countries complained that it would be unfair if they were expected to incur the costs for a problem that they did not cause, and were therefore insistent that either they be allowed to continue using CFCs or that they receive financial and technological help to develop substitutes. The Montreal Protocol contained no such facility, so only a handful of developing states signed it, with the three largest countries – Brazil, China and India – refusing to do so (Porter and Brown 1996: 74), although Mexico was the first to ratify it.

Industrialised countries were reluctant to make open-ended commitments to pay for a fund, with the USA particularly concerned about the possible precedent for future environmental regimes, notably climate change. It was increasingly apparent that the success of the protocol depended on providing sufficient incentives to persuade developing countries to sign up. Consequently, the London meeting in 1990 established a multilateral fund for financial and technology transfer to help developing countries. The fund was $160 million, rising to $240 million if China and India signed (which they eventually did), to be administered by UNEP, UNDP and the World Bank. By 25 June 2001 the Montreal Protocol and London Amendments had 177 and 148 ratifications respectively (UNEP 2000).

Climate change[7]

The major climate change issue concerns the 'greenhouse effect', a natural phenomenon whereby various atmospheric gases keep the Earth's temperature high enough to sustain life as we know it. These gases, which include carbon dioxide (CO_2), methane, nitrous oxide and halocarbons, allow radiation from the Sun to pass through but then absorb radiation reflected back from the Earth's surface, trapping heat in the atmosphere. Without the natural greenhouse effect it is estimated that the average global temperature would be about 33 degrees centigrade lower. However, it seems that human activities, notably carbon emissions from burning fossil fuels and deforestation, and methane emissions from agricultural activities such as livestock and paddy fields, have strengthened the greenhouse effect by increasing the concentration of these gases in the atmosphere. It is the fear that a human-made process of global warming is taking place with a range of potentially devastating implications for the planet that makes climate change the most important contemporary global environmental issue.

Scientific research has focused on three key questions. Is there evidence of global warming? If so, is it caused by human activities or is it a natural cyclical fluctuation in temperature? What is the likely impact of global warming? There have been huge advances in the science of climate change in recent years, co-ordinated by the work of the Intergovernmental Panel on Climate Change (IPCC), but the direct relationship between rising temperatures, emission levels, higher concentrations of gases and, crucially, their combined impact remains uncertain. Nevertheless, there is now a broad consensus on the answers to the three questions. Climatological evidence shows that the Earth is getting warmer; global mean surface temperature rose between 0.2 and 0.6 degrees centigrade over the last century, and is projected to increase by between 1.4 and 5.8 degrees (relative to 1990) by 2100 (IPCC 2001). Concentrations of the key gases in the atmosphere have increased substantially during the twentieth century. Most scientists now agree that these gases have contributed to temperature increases and that human activities have produced these higher concentrations.

If temperatures continue to rise at a similar rate, the impact of global warming could be devastating.[8] A rise in global average sea-level of between 9 and 88 centimetres by 2100 (ibid. 2001) will flood many low-lying lands while the disruption of global weather systems will alter patterns of land-use, reduce agricultural yields, increase water stress and create millions of environmental refugees. Although it remains in the world of informed speculation precisely which countries and regions will suffer most, how soon and by how much, it is clear that less developed countries will suffer the worst effects, partly because most are located in tropical and sub-tropical zones, but also because their weak infrastructures limit their capability to adapt to these changes.

The scientific consensus emerged slowly during the 1980s and 1990s (see Table 9.4). The World Climate Programme conference at Villach, Austria, in 1985 produced the confident scientific conclusion that increased carbon dioxide concentrations would lead to a significant rise in mean surface temperatures (Paterson 1996: 29). Over the next five years this scientific consensus rapidly strengthened as the quality of the data and the climate models improved. The scientific community also started to reach out to the wider political world. The 1988 Toronto Conference, attended by leading scientists and policy-makers from many countries, recommended a 20 per cent reduction in CO_2 emissions by 2005 (Paterson 1996: 34). Toronto prompted

Table 9.4 Climate change – key developments

1970s	Growing scientific concern about impact of human activities on climate expressed at series of international conferences.
1979	First World Climate Conference – agreed that human activities had increased levels of CO_2 and that more CO_2 may contribute to global warming which could have damaging consequences.
1985	Villach Conference – scientific consensus that increased CO_2 was linked to global warming.
1988	Toronto Conference – recommended 20 per cent cut in CO_2 emissions by 2005. IPCC set up.
1990	Preliminary IPCC report and Second World Climate Conference confirmed scientific consensus and called for policy response.
1992	Framework Convention on Climate Change signed by over 150 nations at Rio Summit.
1995	Berlin Mandate (COP-1) – agreed timetable to negotiate stronger commitments. IPCC Second Report: scientific consensus strengthened.
1997	Kyoto Protocol (COP-3) – agreed legally binding targets and timetables for developed countries.
2000	Collapse of COP-6 talks at The Hague, primarily due to intransigence of a small group of industrialised nations led by USA. Key disagreement over how to treat carbon sinks for the purpose of measuring carbon emissions.
2001	IPCC Third Assessment report presents 'new and stronger evidence that most of the observed warming of the last 50 years is attributable to human activities'. Binding agreement at Bonn on implementing Kyoto targets – excluding USA.

See IPCC (*http://www.ipcc.ch/*), International Institute for Sustainable Development (*http://www.iisd.ca/climate*) and the UN framework convention website (*http://www.unfccc.de*) for recent developments in climate change negotiations.

a host of follow-up intergovernmental conferences and encouraged some countries, including all European Community and European Free Trade Association members, to make unilateral commitments to stabilise carbon emissions. A key role was played by the IPCC, formed by UNEP and the World Meteorological Organisation in 1988; its first report confirmed the scientific consensus that human activities were contributing to climate change, and called for immediate policy action to reduce carbon emissions (Houghton et al. 1990). The combination of growing scientific consensus, intergovernmental conferences and unilateral commitments generated a political momentum that resulted in the international convention on climate change agreed at the 1992 Rio Earth Summit.

The Framework Convention was initially signed by 155 countries and the EU, and entered into force in March 1994. It identified a set of principles – precaution, equity, co-operation and sustainability – and a wide range of measures to enable the international community to stabilise greenhouse gas concentrations at levels that should mitigate climate change. However, no firm targets or deadlines were agreed; developed countries were simply given the 'voluntary goal' of returning greenhouse gas emissions to 1990 levels (Elliott 1998: 69). Developed countries were expected to take the lead in combating climate change and to transfer financial and technological resources to developing countries to help them address the problem, but no one was committed to anything specific, apart from establishing a fund under the auspices of the newly formed Global Environment Facility (see Box 9.2).

9.2 The Global Environment Facility (GEF)

The GEF was established in 1991 as a joint programme between the UNDP, UNEP and the World Bank. The GEF provides funding to help less developed countries implement measures to protect the global environment.

The GEF has four priority areas:
- ❑ protection of biological diversity
- ❑ reduction of greenhouse gases
- ❑ protection of international waters
- ❑ protection of ozone layer

Projects financed by GEF include alternative energy programmes, conservation measures and grassroots/community NGOs.

The main criticism of the GEF is that it was located in the World Bank, which is treated with enormous suspicion by developing nations because it is dominated by industrialised countries, acts as standard-bearer of neo-liberal ideologies and has been historically insensitive to environmental concerns. The GEF has been criticised for the lack of transparency in decision-making, the absence of participation by NGOs and local communities and its pursuit of a Northern agenda (e.g. a small GEF-funded biodiversity project in the Congo provided a green veneer for a much larger World Bank loan for road-building and industrial logging).

However, the South has won some important concessions in the way GEF operates, including some reform of GEF decision-making structures. Although the GEF budget is small in global terms – the initial three-year pilot phase of GEF had total funds of around $1.4 billion and it has since been refinanced with $2 billion in 1994 and $2.75 billion in 1998 – it does represent a significant first step to addressing the issue of intragenerational equity.

See GEF website: (*http://www.gefweb.org/*) and UNEP website: (*http://www.unep.org/gef*).

9.3 The Kyoto Protocol

The 1997 Kyoto Protocol strengthens the UN Framework Convention on Climate Change agreed at Rio in 1992 by committing developed countries to reducing their collective emissions of six key greenhouse gases by at least 5 per cent below 1990 levels throughout the 2008–2012 period (which, in effect, means 10 per cent below 2000 levels and 30 per cent below what would be expected in 2010 without emissions-control measures).

Individual targets

Carbon emissions to *decrease* by:

8 per cent	The EU, Switzerland, most central/east European states
7 per cent	USA
6 per cent	Canada, Hungary, Japan, Poland
0 per cent	Russia, New Zealand, Ukraine

Carbon emissions to *increase* by:

1 per cent	Norway
8 per cent	Australia
10 per cent	Iceland

See *http://www.unfccc.de*

The EU 'bubble' of 8 per cent contains wide variations between member states: some richer states have to make large reductions, e.g. Denmark (−21 per cent), Germany (−21 per cent), UK (−12.5 per cent); others merely need to stabilise emissions, e.g. France and Finland; while less developed members can increase emissions, e.g. Portugal (+27 per cent), Greece (+25 per cent), Spain (+15 per cent) and Ireland (+13 per cent).

❑ An international emissions trading regime will be established allowing industrialised countries to buy and sell emission credits amongst themselves.

❑ A 'clean development mechanism' will enable developed countries to finance emissions-reduction projects in developing countries and receive credit for doing so.

Although the USA subsequently rejected the Protocol, 178 countries eventually reached a binding agreement for its implementation at Bonn in July 2001.

Nevertheless, an elaborate institutional framework was established to continue negotiations aimed at strengthening what everyone acknowledged was just the first step towards an effective climate change regime. The first Conference of the Parties to the framework convention (COP-1) in Berlin in 1995 was unable to agree any new commitments, although the 'Berlin mandate' recognised the need to work towards a protocol that set targets and strengthened commitments to reduce greenhouse emissions (Arts and Rüdig 1995). Eventually, the Kyoto Protocol, hammered out over ten days of intense negotiations in December 1997 (COP-3), agreed legally binding targets for developed countries intended to achieve an overall reduction in carbon emissions of 5.2 per cent of 1990 levels in the period 2008 to 2012 (Newell 1998) (see Box 9.3).

Each stage of the regime strengthening process, in Rio, Berlin and Kyoto, was greeted with both acclamation and criticism. Praise for the environmental diplomacy that brokered each agreement in the face of apparently irresolvable political conflicts was matched by criticism about the weakness of the commitments and sanctions in the treaty. These contrasting responses simply reflected the compromises that had to be made if agreement was to be reached between sharply opposing negotiating positions. However, subsequent efforts to firm up the details agreed at Kyoto floundered at The Hague (COP-6) in 2000. In particular, two fundamental tensions have dogged the bargaining process, neither of which, despite the Bonn agreement in July 2001, has yet been satisfactorily resolved.

First, there have been divisions amongst developed countries concerning their willingness to make firm commitments. Resistance has coalesced around the unwillingness of the USA (plus Australia, Canada and Japan) to agree greenhouse gas reduction targets. As the producer of around one-quarter of global greenhouse gas emissions alone, the inclusion of the USA in any regime is vital to its success. Yet, while the EU and other industrialised nations pressed for quantified targets throughout the negotiations, the US government was initially reluctant to sign the Framework Convention at Rio and later blocked agreement on targets or timetables at Berlin. Before eventually agreeing to a 7 per cent reduction target at Kyoto, the USA won significant concessions, including the introduction of a tradeable permit system (see Chapter 11) that would allow rich polluting nations (i.e. the USA) effectively to buy the right to maintain high emission levels from countries emitting less than their target. The main sticking point at the unsuccessful Hague Conference in 2000 was the insistence of the USA that it be allowed to set off its emissions against its carbon sinks (i.e. its vast forests). Subsequently, in 2001, President Bush renounced the Kyoto Protocol. Disagreements between developed countries can be attributed primarily to differences in energy resources and the structure of the energy industry (Paterson 1996). Countries that rely on fossil fuels for export income, such as Middle Eastern oil-producing states, and those with large energy resources, such as the USA have been most resistant to cuts. The USA has an abundance of fossil fuel energy: it is the world's second largest oil and natural gas producer, and the largest coal producer. America has developed a 'gas-guzzler' culture of cheap, available energy, which generates strong resistance to improving energy efficiency. The economic and political costs of implementing emission cuts are therefore seen as higher in the USA than elsewhere and the costs of adapting to climate change are regarded as affordable (whereas most European governments see the potential costs of rising sea-levels as very high). The US government has been subjected to strong pressure from a powerful domestic industrial lobby, particularly energy and motor interests, to obstruct the regime building process (Newell and Paterson 1998). Indeed, it has played the role of veto state with some aplomb. In the face of growing scientific consensus about climate change, the US government has exploited remaining uncertainties – such as the heavy dependence on scientific modelling – to justify its procrastination and opposition to agreement.[9] By contrast, EU countries are heavily dependent on imported energy and do not have the same gas-guzzling energy culture as the USA, while governments have a stronger balance-of-payments incentive to cut carbon emissions because of the knock-on effect of reducing imports of fossil fuels. Consequently, although domestic energy industries are strong, they do not wield the same power as the US energy corporations (which bankrolled Bush's presidential campaign).

A second fundamental tension dogging negotiations has been the North–South divide. Of course, this simple dichotomy does not capture the complexity of climate change politics; just as there are strong differences of opinion between the USA and other developed countries, there are also opposing interests among developing countries. For example, the Alliance of Small Island States has lobbied for firm targets and commitments, whereas oil-producing and exporting states have opposed them. The major developing countries, such as China and India, have ensured that the issues of development, sovereignty and equity have had a prominent place on the agenda. Many disputes boil down to conflict over the transfer of financial and technological resources from North to South. There has been little disagreement with the principle that developed countries should transfer resources to help developing countries invest in energy-efficient technology, but putting it into practice has thrown up many knotty problems. Developed countries have been unwilling to put their hands in their pockets, and big private corporations are reluctant to give up control of technologies without economic or financial compensation (e.g. access to markets) – hence the paucity of firm obligations in the Framework Convention and the Kyoto Protocol.

Underlying both these key tensions lies the familiar trade-off between economic and environmental interests. Short-term concerns about economic growth and development have outweighed the longer-term need to mitigate climate change. With little visible evidence of global warming that might whip up public concern, it is all too easy for governments to bow to producer and consumer opposition to costly remedial measures such as carbon taxes. Certainly international efforts to mitigate climate change have been far less successful than action on ozone depletion.

CRITICAL QUESTION 1

Why has it been easier to obtain international co-operation to prevent ozone depletion than climate change?

ACCOUNTING FOR REGIMES

This section analyses environmental regimes, drawing in particular on the ozone and climate change treaties, to identify the key factors determining the success of regime bargaining.

Regime formation is aided by the willingness of a powerful nation, or group of nations, to take a leadership role by cajoling or bullying weaker states into supporting a treaty. A *lead state* will be committed to achieving effective international action on an issue; it will accelerate the bargaining process and it will seek to win the support of other states for a regime (Porter and Brown 1996: 32). The USA, as the most powerful country in the world, is the most obvious candidate for playing a hegemonic role similar to the way it imposed the Bretton Woods system of trade liberalisation and stable currencies on the international community in the aftermath of the Second World War (Gilpin 1987). However, although the USA played a leading role in ozone diplomacy, its record on the Antarctic, acid rain, biodiversity and climate change shows that it has more often obstructed international co-operation. Consequently, it has fallen to other economically powerful states to take a lead role. Australia and France were instrumental in pushing for the 1991 Madrid Protocol banning mineral extraction in the Antarctic (Elliott 1994). On acid rain, Sweden and Norway were lead states in bringing about the Geneva Convention on Long Range Transboundary Air Pollution (LRTAP) in 1979, while Germany later took the lead in reaching agreement on the Helsinki Protocol (Levy 1993). During the Vienna Convention ozone negotiations, Finland and Sweden submitted the initial draft agreement before the USA adopted a lead role in proposing the 95 per cent reduction in CFCs, and eventually a coalition of OECD states led the pressure for a phase-out before 2000. Groups of states can also make a significant contribution, as illustrated by the Toronto Group in ozone diplomacy (see above, pp. 230–1) and the EU in pushing for firm emission reduction commitments at the Kyoto Summit (Newell 1998). Indeed, the EU, representing a rich and powerful bloc of industrialised nations, is an increasingly important player in environmental diplomacy.

Conversely, a *veto state* will impede negotiations or stall implementation of an agreement. Veto states are most significant where the involvement of a particular country, or group of countries, is essential for the negotiation of an effective regime. Thus the US government, knowing that any climate change agreement would be ineffective without its involvement, was able to wring important concessions at Kyoto. The LRTAP regime was weakened without British support as the major source of acid precipitation in Northern Europe. A ban on the ivory trade is meaningless without the support of Japan as the largest market for ivory. Key veto states are usually OECD countries, but the largest developing states, notably China and India, have played an astute veto role in extracting important concessions, as in the ozone negotiations. Lead states need to persuade veto states of the error of their ways, a task that will usually involve offering them some form of compromise or incentive to drop their opposition, such as the payments to China and India that persuaded them to sign the London Amendments on ozone depletion, or acceptance of the American proposal at Kyoto to set up a tradeable permit scheme.

The resistance of veto states is usually motivated by a desire to protect vital economic interests. EU members initially resisted attempts to freeze CFC production because their chemical industries had not yet developed substitutes. Japan, Iceland and Norway have championed their coastal communities by resisting bans on commercial whaling (Stoett 1997). British opposition to an acid rain agreement reflected a wish to protect its energy industries from the enormous costs of compliance (Boehmer-Christiansen and Skea 1991). In each case, governments have been subjected to strong lobbying from powerful domestic economic interests opposing the regime. One of the most effective lobby groups has been the Global Climate Coalition, which was instrumental in President Bush's refusal to sign the Climate Convention at Rio in 1992 and later in persuading the Clinton Presidency to take a tough negotiating stance at Berlin and Kyoto. It should be noted that economic interests will not always oppose international environmental co-operation. The insurance industry, for example, is relatively sympathetic towards action on climate change because damage to property from rising sea-levels and the disruption of weather patterns is likely to generate massive insurance claims (Salt 1998). Moreover, where it is clear that a changing political climate makes environmental regulations inevitable, then government and industry may unite to win the deal that best suits their national self-interest. The US government was encouraged to maintain its lead role in ozone diplomacy after 1988 by the American chemical conglomerate Dupont, which hoped to snatch a competitive advantage over rival European CFC manufacturers in the development of alternatives such as HFCs (Benedick 1991: 30–4). Whilst it is therefore clear that industry will not always obstruct environmental agreements, nevertheless, on balance, economic interests do push governments towards a veto rather than a lead role.

Conversely, domestic political pressure from environmental groups, the media or public opinion may persuade a government to become a lead state. When the West German government swung from veto state to lead state on acid rain in the early 1980s, it was responding directly to the rising importance of environmental issues and the emergence of the Green Party as an electoral force. The decision of the Australian Labor Party to reject an Antarctic minerals treaty and push for a moratorium on minerals extraction on the continent was a result of its pro-green stance at the 1987 election aimed at winning the support of environmentally concerned voters (Elliott 1994). The 'ideal' lead state position would probably involve a government responding to a concerned public in the absence of any national economic interests, as illustrated by American and British support for bans on the ivory trade, where domestic popularity can be achieved at little economic cost.

Another consideration is the availability of salient solutions (Young 1994: 110–11). Some problems have identifiable and feasible solutions, such as the bans on whale hunting, the ivory trade and the exploitation of Antarctic mineral resources. Technological progress can make political co-operation more likely: the availability of substitutes certainly hastened agreement to phase out CFC production, and agreement to reduce acid precipitation was eased by the development of catalytic converters and flue-gas desulphurisation equipment that cut emissions from cars and coal-fired power stations. By contrast, one of the continuing obstacles to progress on climate change has been the absence of viable and affordable alternatives to fossil fuels in energy production and road transport.[10]

Regime formation may be hastened by exogenous shocks such as ecological disasters. Within six months of the accident at the Chernobyl nuclear power station in 1986 an international agreement on dealing with nuclear accidents was signed. The discovery of the hole in the ozone layer gave a massive boost to negotiations that led to the Montreal Protocol. In contrast, the absence of any similar disaster or dramatic discovery has probably hampered the progress of climate change diplomacy. Not surprisingly, scientists may play a vital part in regime formation. Because of the uncertainty surrounding each new environmental issue, governments are inevitably dependent upon expert scientific and professional advice throughout the policy process. Scientists are central in identifying problems, evaluating their significance, developing solutions and monitoring the effectiveness of remedial action. Consensus within the scientific community about a particular problem is likely to be a catalyst for international co-operation, as occurred in ozone diplomacy after the discovery of the hole in the ozone layer and the subsequent hardening of scientific knowledge. Conversely, where scientific uncertainty remains, co-operation may prove elusive. During the 1970s and 1980s, the British government cited the inconclusiveness of scientific findings to justify its refusal to reduce acid emissions (Boehmer-Christiansen and Skea 1991; Weale 1992). However, science is not always of paramount importance in regime formation, for it played only a limited role in reaching agreements on whaling, the ivory trade, hazardous waste, tropical deforestation and Antarctic minerals (Porter and Brown 1996: 105).

Furthermore, scientists are not just passive reporters of 'neutral' scientific knowledge and advice; they may also adopt a highly pro-active role in the policy process (Andresen et al. 2000). Peter Haas has analysed the influence of scientists through the idea of 'epistemic communities' which he defines as 'knowledge-based groups of experts and specialists who share common beliefs about cause-and-effect relationships in the world and some political values concerning the ends to which policies should be addressed' (Haas 1990: xviii). Having identified an environmental problem, groups of scientists (usually from several countries) are sufficiently moved to intervene in the political process to encourage international action. Their capacity to influence the political process rests on their ability to persuade others that their knowledge is valid and sufficiently important to require a policy response. Haas (1990) showed how epistemic communities helped spur the international co-operation that produced the Mediterranean Action Plan (1975) dealing with sea pollution. Having been asked to investigate the problem of pollution in the Mediterranean, scientists were able to broaden the focus of policy concern beyond the narrow issue of oil pollution from tanker traffic to encompass a wider range of sources, including agricultural run-off, river flows and atmospheric deposition (Haas 1990; Weale 1992). By showing that land-based sources were the most important cause of pollution, epistemic communities helped persuade doubting nations, such as Algeria, of the benefits of co-operation. The Ozone Trends Panel and the IPCC have played a similar role promoting international action against ozone depletion and global warming.

The political activities of scientific organisations also offer a broader lesson about the importance of non-state actors in environmental diplomacy, particularly in informing, educating and shaping cognitions. International institutions can provide astute political leadership, as illustrated by the skill of Mustafa Tolba, UNEP's executive director, in facilitating and guiding the negotiations that led to the ozone protection regime. These 'institutions for the earth' (Haas et al. 1993) can encourage co-operation by setting agendas, winning over doubters and co-ordinating policy responses.

International environmental NGOs, such as Greenpeace, WWF and FoE, have acquired a growing role in international environmental politics, although it is difficult to evaluate their influence (see Chapter 6). There is certainly scope for NGOs to play a part at all stages of environmental diplomacy. By whipping up public concern about a wide range of global issues, communicating the findings of scientists and co-ordinating campaigns against governments and companies, they have contributed to domestic pressure on governments to act (Litfin 1998a; Haas 1999; Young 1999). They have also gained increasing access to international conferences, notably at Rio where there were over 20,000 representatives from some 1,500 NGOs, although their influence was limited (Chatterjee and Finger 1994; Arts 1998). Greenpeace and other NGOs were a powerful voice in the rejection of an Antarctic minerals treaty in favour of a further moratorium on mineral extraction (Elliott 1994) and in persuading sufficient non-whaling nations to join the International Whaling Commission (IWC) to enable a moratorium on whaling to be passed in 1985 (Stoett 1997). Benedick (1991) credits NGOs with a significant role in bringing about the Montreal Protocol by proposing key policy alternatives to negotiators. Overall, NGOs have exerted a growing, but rarely decisive, influence in environmental diplomacy.

Another factor in regime formation may be the nature of the problem itself, perhaps by influencing the strength of the opposition to co-operation or shaping the choice of solutions. Weale (1992) argues that the history of regime formation suggests that some global commons problems lend themselves to co-operation more easily than others. Specifically, he points out that regimes for the protection of common-pool resources such as fisheries stocks and endangered species emerged much earlier than those protecting common-sink resources such as clean air. Weale then moves from this empirical observation to construct a theoretical argument that agreement 'ought' (p. 194) to be easier to reach for common-pool problems than for common-sink problems.[11] One mild objection to Weale's argument is that he probably exaggerates the significance of the historical record in so far as several global common-sink problems are relatively new, or have only recently been identified; for example, an ozone or climate change regime would have been inconceivable before the 1980s. More significantly, as wider empirical evidence does not convincingly support his argument, it is worth examining his case in some detail.

Weale identifies three clear differences between common-pool and common-sink problems that underpin his argument. In the first place, he suggests that because the benefits of common-pool resources can be individually appropriated,[12] it should be easier to monitor compliance with a common agreement; for example, to ensure that fishing fleets do not catch more than their quota of a particular fish. In contrast, the benefits of common-sink resources are difficult to allocate individually, which makes them prone to collective action problems, particularly where there are multiple sources of a problem. Thus agreement on climate change has been obstructed by the difficulty of establishing adequate monitoring mechanisms, especially for carbon sinks such as forests, where the science is still primitive. Nevertheless, not all sink problems pose significant monitoring difficulties; after all, it was the relative ease of monitoring the manufacture of CFCs by the handful of major producers that hastened the agreement of an ozone regime.

Secondly, this problem of non-appropriability has led to the practice of inventing proxy measures and negotiating proportionate reductions from that baseline figure. Unfortunately, the baseline figure may be a poor proxy for the value of that sink to individual countries, so proportionate reductions in emissions may have different marginal costs in each economy. The selection of the base year for emission reduction targets (e.g. to cut sulphur emissions to 30 per cent of 1980 levels by 1993) places some countries at a comparative disadvantage because the marginal costs of reducing emissions in economies that were in recession in the base year (i.e. already relatively low) will be higher than where the economy was booming (and emission levels were relatively high). Although Weale is right to draw attention to this issue, the proxy problem is just one aspect of the broader issue of equitable burden-sharing which characterises all regime bargaining, rather than being exclusive to common-sink problems (see below, pp. 249–51). International fishing agreements that allocate catch quotas to countries on the basis of historical catches, such as the European Common Fisheries Policy (Gray 1997), are no more immune from fierce disputes over what counts as an equitable baseline. The need to agree burden-sharing arrangements that are regarded as equitable by all the signatories of a regime – whether these arrangements involve the use of proxies, quotas, prohibitions or tradeable permits – confronts both common-pool and sink problems.

Thirdly, Weale argues that, whilst the exhaustion of common-pool resources hurts those who benefit from them most, the over-exploitation of common-sink resources may not fall on those who cause the problem. Thus, the fishing communities that will suffer from a depletion of fishing stocks have an incentive to cooperate for it is their own livelihoods that are endangered, unlike the UK power-generating companies responsible for acid emissions that damage Swedish lakes and trees. Put differently, as Oran Young (1994: 107) has pointed out, some problems lend themselves more readily to contractarian solutions than others. Yet several common-sink issues fall fully or partly into this category. The regime dealing with the control of radioactive fallout resulting from nuclear accidents was speedily and easily negotiated following the Chernobyl accident in 1986 because, as no individual person or state could be certain that they could avoid harm from such an accident, it was in everyone's interest to produce a common solution (ibid.: 108). Similarly, all countries will suffer from the damaging effects of ozone depletion. It was the recognition by West Germany that it was both a producer and a victim of acid rain that turned it into a lead state pushing for a tough regime and, eventually, it was a similar realisation that eventually brought about a change of heart by the British government (Boehmer Christiansen and Skea 1991).

Weale certainly identifies some important factors influencing regime formation, but they do not provide unambiguous support for his claim that it will usually be easier to reach agreement on common-pool problems than on common-sink problems. Instead, they join the wide range of factors that might influence regime formation. No one factor stands out as being decisive. The attempt to secure international co-operation to solve an environmental problem will be shaped by a complex mix of scientific, economic, political and social factors. More specifically, to return to the ozone and climate change examples, it is clear that climate change is one of the most complex and perplexing issues confronting policy-makers today. Compared to ozone diplomacy, international co-operation over climate change has been harder to achieve because the various obstacles – powerful veto states, strongly opposed economic interests, scientific uncertainty, a multitude of distributional and equity issues, non-appropriability and the general unwillingness of citizens to make the necessary lifestyle sacrifices – have proved much harder to resolve. Perhaps the key differences lie in the cost and availability of solutions. In ozone diplomacy, CFCs were not critical to the entire well-being of the economy and substitutes exist for most uses. Solutions to ozone depletion are largely technological and can be dealt with by co-operation between the state and industrial sectors with little observable impact (or cost) on citizens. In contrast, energy production and consumption is of central economic importance. Affordable and practicable solutions, such as **renewable** sources of energy (wind, solar, waves) or cleaner technologies (electric cars), may not be readily available or acceptable. Effective measures to combat climate change will inevitably involve fundamental socio-economic changes affecting economic growth, energy production, transport and individual lifestyles. There are few votes to be won and many to be lost on these issues. Not surprisingly, no country has yet committed itself to such radical solutions (see Chapter 11).

> **Renewable energy:** Energy sources, such as wind, geothermal and hydroelectric, that never run out.

CRITICAL QUESTION 2

Is the role of environmental NGOs in securing international environmental co-operation undervalued?

IMPLEMENTATION

How effective are environmental regimes in solving the problems they address? Hurrell (1995) has observed that 'the weakest link in the chain of international environmental cooperation may well not lie in the difficulties of negotiating formal agreements but, rather, in ensuring that those arrangements are effectively implemented' (p. 141). Yet implementation issues have been relatively neglected in the literature compared to the extensive coverage of the formation and strengthening of environmental regimes (but see Jordan 1998b; Young 1999). One reason is that most environmental regimes have been concluded since the 1972 Stockholm Conference, and those dealing with major global issues have only been agreed since the late 1980s, making it rather early to evaluate implementation. Another factor may be that researchers regard the study of implementation as less interesting than the high politics of international diplomacy (Jordan 1998b). Either way, this gap in the literature makes it difficult to draw overall conclusions about the effectiveness of environmental regimes.

It is also important to be clear about the meaning of 'effectiveness' (Young 1994: ch. 6; Kütting 2000). One approach is to regard a regime as successful if the institutional arrangements it creates are able to change the behaviour of states, for example by overcoming the objections of veto states or persuading countries to sign up to new or tougher targets. This definition is only really a proxy measure of effectiveness, for it works on the assumption that commitments made on paper will be implemented. In practice, not least because the responsibility for monitoring and verification of domestic implementation of international agreements largely resides with the states themselves, there are countless examples of non-implementation.

Even if commitments are implemented, a comprehensive assessment of effectiveness must also determine whether a regime contributes to the improvement of the environmental problem it is intended to remedy: have the objectives of an agreement been achieved? If so, can this success be put down to the regime? Sometimes it is very difficult to evaluate regime effectiveness, as illustrated by the 1979 LRTAP Convention and subsequent protocols on sulphur and nitrogen emissions and depositions. There is certainly no doubt that overall emissions of both gases have fallen. The Helsinki Protocol target of a 30 per cent reduction on the 1980 levels of sulphur emissions by 1993 was achieved by most parties, although further targets, particularly for nitrogen, are unlikely to be reached (EEA 1997a). However, it is less clear whether reduced emissions are a direct result of the measures introduced by the various agreements, or are due to the unintentional consequences of developments such as economic restructuring in Eastern Europe (which closed many old polluting factories and power stations) and the privatisation of the UK energy utilities (which prompted a rapid switch to gas-fired power stations) (see also Kütting 2000: ch. 6).

Nevertheless, the Antarctic Treaty banning the mining of minerals on the continent is one clear example of a regime where the objective has been achieved and this success can be directly attributed to the regime. The Montreal Protocol is also widely regarded as one of the most successful international environmental regimes. Total consumption of CFCs worldwide fell from 1.2 million tonnes in 1986 to 164,000 tonnes in 1997, with consumption in developed countries falling from 1 million tonnes to just 24,000 tonnes. It has been estimated that, without the Montreal Protocol, global consumption would have reached about 3 million tonnes in 2010 and 8 million tonnes in 2060, resulting in a 50 per cent depletion of the ozone layer by 2035 (UNEP 2000). Of course, the success of a regime is often much less clear-cut than these examples suggest. For many years after its formation in 1946 the International Whaling Commission (IWC) was hopelessly ineffective in preventing the overfishing of whales; indeed, more whales were killed under the new regime than before regulation was introduced. It was only after anti-whaling nations seized control of the IWC and forced the implementation of a moratorium from 1986, leading to a dramatic reduction in the number of whales killed, that the institutions created by the regime began to achieve their objectives. Although the IWC itself has no sanctions, the reluctance of whaling nations, notably

Japan and Norway, to incur the wrath of the anti-whaling nations and of international NGOs such as Greenpeace, has ensured their broad, if uneven, compliance with the ban (Stoett 1997).[13]

All regimes face serious implementation difficulties. Even the Montreal Protocol on ozone depletion will have to overcome serious obstacles if it is to achieve long-term success. Several countries, notably those in the Russian Federation and China, have admitted that they will be unable to comply with the phase-out timetable for CFCs. The efforts of developing countries have not been helped by the failure of some richer countries to make the required payments to the multilateral fund. Another serious problem is the flourishing illegal trade in CFCs. It is estimated that since CFC production ceased in developed countries, up to 20,000 tonnes of CFCs have been illegally imported each year into industrialised countries, especially the USA (Stirpe 1997; UNEP 2000). The major source of smuggling seems to be Russia, which is still manufacturing CFCs, from where virgin products are either smuggled as unlicensed imports or, more commonly, falsely substituted for recycled CFCs, which can still legally be traded.

Sometimes the problem lies with a weak regime agreement. A framework convention may be a triumph of diplomacy, but its substance is initially usually rather thin, as illustrated by the ineffective voluntary emission carbon targets agreed at Rio which few developed states met. For example, only three EU member states (Britain, Germany, Luxembourg) reduced carbon emissions between 1990 and 1998 (EEA 2000a). States generally prefer non-binding targets and schedules, but without meaningful sanctions and effective monitoring systems it is difficult to hold countries to their commitments; for example, compliance with reporting requirements for acid emissions has been uneven (Levy 1993). Much may depend on the effectiveness of the institutional structures that oversee implementation. Sustained political commitment is also critical. The good intentions of a government during regime negotiations, spurred on perhaps by an enthusiastic public and environmental lobby, may have diminished by the time it comes to act on its promises. Where the solutions are very expensive, such as fitting expensive scrubbers to power stations, or politically unpopular, such as a carbon tax, governments may give priority to short-term domestic considerations rather than longer-term international commitments. Consequently, environmental pressure groups can play a vital part in implementation by constantly pressing governments to fulfil their commitments, monitoring compliance and lobbying for the regime to be strengthened. Thus the International Institute for Environment and Development, WWF and Greenpeace played a critical role in the implementation of the conservation features of the International Tropical Trade Agreement (Princen and Finger 1994: 5). A more proactive example was the successful Greenpeace 'greenfreeze' refrigerator campaign (see Box 6.2) which forced leading manufacturers to produce CFC/HFC-free refrigerators much sooner than they had initially planned (Jordan 1998b).

More fundamentally, a government may be simply unable to implement an agreement. Environmental regimes are agreed between nation states, but governments often have only limited control over the behaviour of actors (notably corporations or citizens) and the activities (road transport) they have promised to change. Even implementing the ozone regime, which involves a relatively simple relationship between state and a limited number of industries, poses difficulties. In Japan, although all CFC production halted by 1993, the government had not implemented an effective CFC recovery programme by the late 1990s. While CFCs were recovered from 57 per cent of home use refrigerators entrusted to the local government for disposal, the figure fell to just 18 per cent for commercial refrigerators and air conditioners, 8.6 per cent for old refrigerators taken back by retailers and 7.2 per cent for car air conditioners (*Financial Times*, 3 December 1997). Despite the close state–industry relations in Japan, private industry had clearly failed to change its behaviour. There are plenty of potential solutions to this shortfall, such as improving the infrastructure for collection and disposal (or reuse) of CFCs, providing incentives to companies to dispose of them safely, and introducing legislation requiring it, but these all require greater political commitment and public investment. Thus even developed countries with strong political structures and a culture of compliance with the law have problems in implementing global agreements.

Elsewhere, many governments simply lack the state capacity to meet their regime obligations, as illustrated by the following three points. First, many countries do not possess the political and social infrastructure that enables a government to enforce its policy decisions. It is hardly surprising that Russia, where the government is crippled by its chronic inability to collect its tax revenues and corruption is endemic, has no effective recovery and recycling system for CFCs and cannot prevent them from being smuggled abroad. In developing countries that are wracked by political conflicts and civil unrest, or where deep-set poverty and inequalities are widespread government pronouncements about global warming, ozone depletion or loss of biodiversity will receive low priority.

Secondly, many governments have insufficient resources to implement the costly changes needed to meet many environmental commitments. Developing economies are frequently heavily dependent on the export of one or two commodities or cash crops, rendering them highly vulnerable to market fluctuations and changes in the terms of trade. Many were badly weakened by the debt crisis of the 1980s and 1990s and have been subjected to stringent structural adjustment programmes imposed by the International Monetary Fund (IMF) and the World Bank – measures that have further reduced the capacity of state structures to implement environmental policies. In short, without financial and technical aid, it is unlikely that investment in energy efficiency measures or the recovery of CFCs will be possible, let alone given priority.

Thirdly, some Northern transnational corporations (TNCs) are so powerful that they are almost autonomous from national governments and can ride roughshod over the law. Many developing countries not only have weaker environmental regulations and laxer enforcement than in the North, but their governments, desperate for the input of wealth and jobs generated by factories and industrial plants, are often prepared to turn a blind eye to the environmentally damaging activities of TNCs. While environmental costs alone may usually be insufficient to warrant widespread 'industrial flight' to 'pollution havens', because many other factors influence decisions about industrial location, Clapp (1998) shows that some of the most hazardous industrial processes have been relocated to the South in recent years.

These examples of state incapacity underline both the important role of domestic factors in the implementation of environmental regimes and, in turn, how the analysis of implementation cannot be separated from the broader international political economy that is largely responsible for that state incapacity. Indeed, one conclusion is that some implementation problems do not have institutional solutions, even though many institutionalists imply that they do (Young 1994). While institutions do have a major role to play, the perennial nature of certain implementation problems suggests that they have deep-seated causes that lie beyond the reach of institutional solutions. Institutional structures may help bring opposing parties to the negotiating table, facilitate co-operation and, especially by administering financial and technical transfers, enhance the political and administrative capacity of individual governments to implement regime commitments. However, environmental regimes can do little to transform the system of capitalist development which underpins the increasingly globalised world economy in which power is shifting from the nation state to transnational actors, financial institutions and international economic institutions such as the IMF and World Bank. The resulting 'quasi-sovereignty' is at its sharpest in the poorest developing countries where the key features of global economic interdependence, such as the international trading system, aid programmes and the structures of debt relief, exacerbate the interlinked problems of poverty, inequality and environmental degradation (Jackson 1990). National governments are unable to resolve these problems because they lack the autonomy to choose their own economic path or the capacity to deliver the radical policies that might benefit the environment. Thus many forms of environmental degradation are no accidental outcome of development but are inextricably tied up with the working of the global capitalist economy: not only are they beyond the reach of institutional solutions but state institutions are structurally enmeshed in the causes of environmental degradation.[14]

CRITICAL QUESTION 3

Does the successful implementation of environmental treaties depend on the greening of global financial institutions such as the World Bank?

INTERNATIONAL ENVIRONMENTAL POLITICS AND SUSTAINABLE DEVELOPMENT

International environmental politics has implications for all five core principles of sustainable development identified in Chapter 8. This section focuses on the *precautionary principle*, *equity* and *democracy* which lie directly at the heart of international politics. By contrast, the relationship between international co-operation and the principles of *planning* and *integration* involves a more indirect impact on national policy-making; for example, the Kyoto emission reduction targets will require individual states to plan national climate change programmes and improve the integration of government activities across sectors (see Chapter 10).

First, recent environmental diplomacy has undoubtedly strengthened the importance of the *precautionary principle*. Both the ozone and climate change conventions and the Cartagena Biosafety Protocol agreed in January 2000 (Depledge 2000) have either implicitly or explicitly applied the precautionary principle to a problem still characterised by scientific uncertainty. While earlier regimes addressed problems that were already apparent and requiring urgent action, such as declining whale populations or polluted seas, in promising to ban CFCs, reduce greenhouse gas emissions or limit the trade of genetically modified products, states have agreed to act before there is conclusive proof of a problem. However, while states may more readily accept the precautionary principle at an international level, national governments find that political short-termism makes it difficult to turn this principle into practical policy measures.

Secondly, *equity* considerations have dominated environmental diplomacy, particularly the climate change and ozone depletion negotiations. Developed states effectively conceded that they have a historic responsibility for causing the problems and they continue to be the major contributors to it. By setting up mechanisms such as the Global Environmental Facility (see Box 9.2) and the Interim Multilateral Fund, they also accepted the principle that developing countries will need help in implementing environmental agreements. Conversely, less developed countries have (more or less) conceded that Northern concern about the environment does not represent a simple 'eco-colonial' attempt to prevent them from benefiting from the fruits of economic growth. They accept that these global environmental problems will harm everyone – North and South, rich and poor, big and small – and require some kind of preventive action. Indeed, it may be that environmental diplomacy can offer new bargaining opportunities for the South. Although the interests of developed countries have generally prevailed in regime bargaining, it is the mutual vulnerability of all states to global problems that has persuaded developed states to concede limited resource transfers and even to address some of the underlying causes of environmental degradation in the South, for example through 'debt-for-nature' swaps.[15]

However, turning the principle of equity into something concrete has posed many problems and generated considerable conflict. The success of regime bargaining will depend on all participants accepting that the proposed arrangements are not only effective but seen to be equitable and fair. However, the concept of equity is highly contestable. Climate change politics have thrown up several competing interpretations of what constitutes a 'fair' allocation of carbon emission reductions between different countries (Grubb et al. 1992; Rose 1992; Rowlands 1997). Grubb et al. (1992: 312–14), for example, identify seven possible equity rationales applicable to greenhouse gas burden-sharing, ranging from the idea that all humans should be entitled to an equal share in the atmospheric commons, through the 'polluter pays' principle that countries should pay for the pollution that they generate or have generated, to a 'status quo' position that accepts a state's current rate of emissions almost as a 'squatter's right'. The different perspectives are informed by a wide variety of philosophical concepts of justice, including egalitarian rights, utilitarianism, Rawlsian and basic needs approaches (Grubb 1995). These concepts, in turn, raise other tricky issues, such as whether a 'right to pollute' exists and how responsibility should be allocated, which have implications for the way history is treated. For example, does historical usage create a kind of common law right to continue producing at a particular level, or should countries pay for their historical responsibility in using up a disproportionate share of a global resource (Rowlands 1997: 5–6)? The concept of 'common but differentiated responsibilities' has been widely adopted in recent regimes 'in an attempt to meet Northern concerns that all countries have obligations and Southern concerns that those obligations are not the same' (Elliott 1998: 176). However, this concept has done little to resolve equity conflicts because it allows the South to argue for reductions based on historical responsibility (i.e. placing the burden on the North), while the North can argue that future emission levels must be built into the equation (i.e. the South must make commitments too).

Each approach to equity will affect countries very differently (Rowlands 1997). Within Europe, those states with the biggest populations – Germany,

France, Italy, the UK – are responsible for the largest *volume* of greenhouse gas emissions. By contrast, per caput emissions vary by a factor of three, between the lowest, France, which has a large nuclear industry, and the highest, Luxembourg, because of its important metallurgical industry (EEA 1997a). Not surprisingly, countries tend to lobby for the equity principle that best matches their national self-interest. At Kyoto, the EU tried to resolve such conflicts through a Community-wide 'bubble' strategy that set an overall reduction target for Community emissions but incorporated different targets for individual states so that increased emissions in poorer states such as Greece and Portugal would be offset by larger cuts in richer states such as Germany and Britain. The bubble approach attracted criticism from non-EU states which wanted all industrialised countries to make the same percentage cut in emissions, and from some, such as the USA, who believed this collective strategy conferred unfair advantages on the EU (Newell 1998). The bubble strategy allowed the EU to take a lead role in pushing for tougher targets at Kyoto, but it also resulted in its being allocated a larger share of the burden for making emissions reductions (see Box 9.3). Thus equity is a source of conflict between developed countries as well as between North and South.

Lastly, it is less clear how far international environmental co-operation has enhanced *democracy*. The growth of environmental diplomacy raises many interesting questions about the role of the state in delivering sustainable development; in particular, environmental problems threaten national sovereignty in several ways (Litfin 1998b). Obviously, the transboundary nature of an international environmental problem by definition puts it beyond the competence of an individual state to defend itself unilaterally from damage. Consequently, the creation of a complex structure of international treaties, institutions and laws has required nation states to concede some authority and control to these higher bodies – what Hurrell (1995) calls 'the erosion of sovereignty from above' (p. 136). Many NGOs note that this growing network of international institutions has taken power even further away from the local communities and indigenous peoples who, they argue, should be at the centre of sustainable development initiatives. Conversely, as we have seen in the case of less developed countries, sovereignty is also threatened from below by the incapacity of many states to implement environmental commitments. Yet, while state sovereignty is apparently ebbing away, the willingness of governments to defend this principle at all costs has been a major bone of contention in environmental diplomacy. Few countries have been prepared to sacrifice even small areas of sovereignty, hence regimes rarely carry meaningful sanctions that have any force over the sovereign territory of nation states. Developing countries have been particularly suspicious of Northern attempts to control their economic development, as illustrated by the initial refusal of countries such as Malaysia at Rio to agree to a convention to protect forests which would

9.4 Why no global forestry convention?

Deforestation is bad for the environment – it contributes to soil erosion, flooding, droughts and climate change. Yet deforestation is proceeding rapidly – over the last thirty years about 40 per cent of rainforests have disappeared and around 2 per cent of tropical forest cover disappears annually.

Deforestation has many causes – mining, conversion to agricultural land, colonisation for settlements, fuelwood demand, commercial logging and industrial pollution – which are often linked to broader development factors such as poverty, unemployment, debt repayments and the need for foreign income from logging.

Everyone agrees we need to manage our forests sustainably, so why did the international community fail to agree a Forestry Convention at Rio, at the follow-up UNGASS convention or at the subsequent Intergovernmental Forum on Forests (IFF) negotiations between 1997 and 2000?

1. At Rio in 1992 there was a sharp and acrimonious North–South polarisation: the North wanted a convention; the South (led by Malaysia and India) was strongly opposed. The key stumbling-block was that the South demanded important concessions from the North, such as technology transfer, financial assistance and debt relief, in exchange for any erosion of sovereignty over their forestry resources.

2. At UNGASS in 1997 the North–South divide was much less clear-cut. Some Southern nations, notably Malaysia and Indonesia, now supported a convention as the best way of getting formal commitments on finance and technology from the North. Conversely, the US government, influenced by strong corporate lobbying against further environmental regulations, now opposed a convention. Later, during the IFF discussions, the common EU position in favour of a convention splintered as the UK came out against and Germany and the Netherlands grew increasingly lukewarm.

3. Leading environmental NGOs have also switched position. At Rio, they supported a convention with commitments to conservation and protecting the rights of indigenous peoples. At UNGASS, they opposed a convention because NGOs are increasingly disillusioned by global governance structures that give authority to states whilst excluding wider civic society, notably local and indigenous communities, from a say in forestry policy.

Although the IFF agreed in 2000 to begin negotiations for a convention within five years, significant progress is unlikely until the North promises substantial financial assistance and technology transfer to aid sustainable forest management in the South.

See Humphreys (1998).

have imposed external constraints on the way they exploited their own resources (see Box 9.4). Developed countries have been equally resistant to the notion that sustainable development might involve any changes in their production or consumption patterns. Consequently, conflicts over environmental burden-sharing are played out in debates about state sovereignty.

However, it could be argued that whatever sovereignty a state surrenders by participating in a regime is partly compensated by the benefits it gains from collective action, and by the resulting influence it is able to exercise over the activities of other states. The importance of the EU as an actor in environmental diplomacy is partly linked to the strength it derives from the willingness of each member state to transfer a range of environmental competencies to this supranational body.[16] Institutionalist writers claim that regimes can also enhance the capacity of weaker states by transferring finance and technologies to them (as illustrated by the Global Environment Facility and the Multilateral Ozone Fund), or by providing the support and resources to resist TNC power, so that their sovereignty is effectively enhanced (Haas et al. 1993; Conca 1994). If developed countries press for tougher, more effective regimes, as occurred in ozone diplomacy, they effectively strengthen the bargaining position of less developed nations, particularly bigger players such as China, India, Brazil, and enable them to extract better concessions, such as the Multilateral Ozone Fund.

CRITICAL QUESTION 4

For poor nations in the South, is 'sovereignty lost, influence gained'?

CONCLUSION

The growth of environmental diplomacy, with its accompanying baggage of international treaties, institutional arrangements and policy initiatives, is evidence of the substantial progress made by the international community (national governments, international NGOs, epistemic communities) in addressing global commons problems. International co-operation can be a perfectly rational strategy for states to pursue. Although collective action problems ensure that the agreement of each new regime represents a considerable diplomatic achievement, with each success the international community becomes more adept at brokering agreement and the obstacles seem a little less intractable.

However, caution is necessary. Much of the momentum engendered by the Rio process has dissipated. The follow-up UN General Assembly Special Session (UNGASS) Earth Summit in New York in 1997 was widely regarded as a failure, and progress on climate change since Kyoto has been tardy. The enthusiasm for environmental issues expressed by many Northern governments expressed in the late 1980s/early 1990s has waned. Although recent treaties have applied the precautionary principle and made genuine efforts to grapple with equity issues, many aspects of environmental diplomacy are still permeated by the traditional paradigm. Most international problems are treated in isolation and, where possible, end-of-pipe technical solutions are found. There has been little concrete or integrated action addressing the bigger questions raised by sustainable development, such as poverty, the debt crisis and the international trading system. Not surprisingly, institutional responses have had only limited success. Many regimes, notably the climate change treaty, still represent an inadequate response to the problem; considerable regime strengthening is required and greater effort made to 'green' the key institutions of global political economy such as the World Bank and the IMF. Serious implementation gaps impair the effectiveness of even the most successful regimes such as the ozone treaty. These difficulties demonstrate how the narrow institutionalist focus on issues of regime formation and strengthening needs to be supplemented by the recognition that many sources of environmental degradation reside in broader structural factors such as the functioning of the capitalist economic system and globalisation, and that they are therefore often beyond the reach of environmental diplomacy.

Further reading and websites

Elliott (1998) and Porter and Brown (1996) provide a good introduction to international environmental issues, regimes and institutions, as do the more dated Hurrell and Kingsbury (1992b) and Brenton (1994). For a more conceptual discussion of regime formation, see Young (1994), Vogler (1995) and Vogler and Imber (1996). Andresen et al. (2000) discuss the role of science in regime formation. Weiss and Jacobson (1998) assess regime strengthening and Young (1999) and Kütting (2000) evaluate regime effectiveness. Miller (1995) presents a Third World perspective on regime formation. Litfin (1994) and Rowlands (1995) provide detailed accounts of ozone diplomacy, while Paterson (1996) and Rowlands (1995) do a similar job for climate change. Newell (2000) examines the role of non-state actors in climate politics. Litfin (1998b) contains some interesting essays on sovereignty and Haas (1999) provides a critique of institutionalist approaches. See the journals *Global Environmental Change*, *International Environmental Affairs*, *Environmental Politics*, and *International Affairs* for developments in international environmental politics.

For details and updates on recent developments in environmental diplomacy, see the *Earth Negotiations Bulletin* published by the International Institute for Sustainable Development (*http://www.iisd.ca*). Useful websites for other key conventions include biodiversity (*http://www.biodiv.org/*), combating desertification (*http://www.unccd.de/*), CITES (*http://www.cites.org/*) and hazardous wastes (*http://www.basel.int/*). See also the International Whaling Commission (*http://www.wcmc.org.uk/cms/*) and for information about the Antarctic Treaty (*http://www.antarctic.com.au/encyclopaedia/hist/AntTreSys.html*).

Notes

1. See Axelrod (1984) and Oye (1986) for an analysis of game-theoretic approaches to international relations.
2. Environmental security issues are discussed more fully in Deudney (1997), Mathews (1989) and Myers (1989).
3. Put in game-theoretic language, repetitive, or iterated, playing of games like the 'prisoner's dilemma' can come to resemble an 'assurance game' where 'cooperation is an individually rational strategy provided that the actor contemplating cooperation can be assured that others will cooperate' (Weale 1992: 191; see also Axelrod 1984; Oye 1986).

4. The term 'institutionalist' is used here to refer to a wide range of approaches, notably neo-liberal institutionalism, but also those from alternative epistemological perspectives which focus on the role of international regimes and institutions in managing conflict and solving collective action problems and have dominated the study of international environmental politics (e.g. Vogler 1992; Young 1994). For a critique of this perspective, see Paterson (1996: ch. 6), Saurin (1996), Haas (1999) and Kütting (2000).

5. Detailed accounts of ozone diplomacy include Benedick (1991), Litfin (1994) and Rowlands (1995). See Seaver (1997) for an interesting analysis of ozone diplomacy using a range of IR theories.

6. During the 1990s, the land area under the ozone-depleted atmosphere over Antarctica varied between 20 and 26 million square kilometres – over twice the size of Europe (UNEP 2000).

7. Detailed accounts of the politics of climate change include Brenton (1994), Rowlands (1995), O'Riordan and Jäger (1996), Paterson (1996) and Newell (2000).

8. See special issue of the journal *Global Environmental Change*, 'A New Assessment of the Global Effects of Climate Change' (vol. 9, 2000), for a synthesis of predicted outcomes of climate change. IPCC (2001) provides the fullest, most recent analysis.

9. There is a thriving industry in producing ideologically driven assaults on the scientific consensus. See Balling (1995), Morris et al. (1997), Bate (1998). One of the main charges is that the work of the IPCC cannot be trusted because it is in scientists' own interests to play up the dangers posed by climate change in order to get funding for continued research. Whatever the validity of this claim, it is rather undermined by the murky sources of funding supporting this backlash – see Gelbspan (1997) on the backlash in the USA and its corporate funding. For a more objective critique, see Wildavsky (1995).

10. Where the technology is available, such as electric-powered cars, the oil and motor industries have often been unwilling to invest sufficient resources to make alternatives commercially viable.

11. Young (1994: ch. 1) develops a similar argument, but identifies more categories of commons' problems.

12. In game-theoretic terminology: to turn a 'prisoner's dilemma' into an 'assurance game'.

13. Several loopholes in the convention have been exploited so that, for example, the Japanese still kill around 500 whales annually for so-called 'scientific purposes'. Norway announced in 2001 that it would start exporting whale meat and blubber, which will provide greater incentive for pirate whaling and step up pressure for the IWC ban to be lifted. In addition, aboriginal whaling for non-commercial purposes continues in Russia, Greenland, Alaska and elsewhere.

14. This argument is developed within the international political economy approach which provides a radical alternative perspective to neo-liberal institutionalism (see Williams 1996; Saurin 1996; Paterson 1996).

15. 'Debt for nature' swaps involve the purchase of a part of a country's debt by an NGO or government in exchange for taking over an environmental or conservation programme such as a national park. Although not without their critics, most commentators accept that they can make a positive contribution (Klinger 1994; Elliott 1998: 205–7).

16. However, the EU is also plagued by conflict between member states over the erosion of sovereignty which has prevented the introduction of more radical policies such as a Community-wide carbon tax.

Greening government

- How would the principles of sustainable development change the way governments work?
- How might administrative methods improve the integration of environmental considerations throughout government?
- What is green planning?
- How democratic is environmental policy-making?
- Can institutional reforms overcome the political and economic obstacles to greener government?

KEY ISSUES

Governments' general response to the speed and scale of global changes has been a reluctance to recognize sufficiently the need to change themselves . . . Those responsible for managing natural resources and protecting the environment are institutionally separated from those responsible for managing the economy. The real world of interlocking economic and ecological systems will not change; the policies and institutions concerned must.

[The Brundtland Report] (WCED 1987: 9)

In the final two chapters the focus moves down to the national and subnational levels of government where most environmental policy is made and implemented: Chapter 10 is concerned with the way governments build environmental considerations into the policy-making process and Chapter 11 examines the policy instruments that governments use to implement policy.

Sustainable development, even in its weaker forms, has major implications for the way government works. Environmental governance means that institutions, administrative procedures and decision-making processes all need to be overhauled. Policy elites have to re-think the way they perceive the world so that environmental considerations are integrated across government and penetrate routine policy-making processes within every sector. In short, to achieve the environmental policy integration necessary for sustainable development, government must first transform itself.

This chapter assesses the shift towards greener government by examining progress towards the implementation of three core principles of sustainable development: integration, planning and democracy. The opening section distinguishes two broad mechanisms for achieving greater *integration*: first, through organisational reform such as the creation of new environment ministries and the formation of new government committees; secondly, through the use of administrative techniques, notably **environmental impact assessment**, **risk assessment** and cost–benefit analysis. The next section evaluates efforts to improve policy co-ordination through better strategic *planning* of sustainable development at European Union, national and local levels of government. Following the discussion of democracy in terms of the independence of the sovereign state in Chapter 9, the final section analyses the role of *democracy* in environmental decision-making within the nation state by assessing the contribution of public inquiries and other democratic or participatory mechanisms to advancing sustainable development.

Environmental impact assessment: A systematic non-technical evaluation, based on extensive consultation with affected interests, of the anticipated environmental impact of a proposed development such as a dam or road.

Risk assessment: An evaluation of the potential harm to human health and the environment from exposure to a particular hazard such as nitrates in drinking water.

INTEGRATION

Two notions of integration can be distinguished (see Box 10.1). Broadly speaking, reforms of the machinery of government, such as the creation of new organisations and committees, are primarily, but not exclusively, intended to improve inter-sectoral integration, while the use of administrative techniques

10.1 Forms of integration

Two different notions of integration can be distinguished:
The *inter*-sectoral approach pursues a co-ordinated and coherent strategy of environmental protection across different sectors and media,
> e.g. a climate change strategy aimed at reducing carbon emissions must encompass different sectors (notably transport, energy and economic policy) and media (land, water, air).

The *intra*-sectoral approach focuses on the integrated management of a single natural resource,
> e.g. a sustainable water management strategy has to reconcile conflicting demands on water for drinking, irrigation, fishing, leisure uses and waste disposal.

The two forms of integration often overlap, sometimes complementing, sometimes conflicting, but each is an essential ingredient of sustainable development.

such as environmental impact assessment can enhance intra-sectoral integration by encouraging policy-makers in each sector to consider the environmental consequences of their actions more routinely.

Integration through organisational reform

In many countries, initial attempts to improve inter-sectoral integration saw the creation of a new ministry of the environment (ME). The first MEs were formed in the early 1970s in Denmark, the Netherlands, Norway, Austria and Britain, although Germany, Sweden and Finland delayed until the mid-1980s and Spain waited until 1996.[1] Every EU member state now has a ME, as do most other OECD countries (but not the USA). Typically, the decision to create a ME was symbolic of the traditional paradigm: a visible token of a government's concern with environmental protection, whilst neatly categorising it as a separate policy area. However, in practice, separation usually meant marginalisation.

MEs have only partially resolved horizontal co-ordination problems. Although they bring together a range of functions that had previously been carried out by other departments and agencies, many environmental competencies remain outside the ambit of MEs. For example, after the formation of the UK Department of Environment in 1970, many core environmental issues such as marine pollution control, vehicle emissions, farm waste management, pesticide control, energy policy, industrial hazards and nuclear safety were still the responsibility of other ministries, notably agriculture and energy, or of non-departmental agencies. The extent of fragmentation found in Britain may be unusual, but it persists everywhere to some degree. Since the mid-1980s, the emergence of global issues such as climate change which require greater co-ordination of strategies encompassing energy and transport policies has increased pressure towards amalgamating some economic and environmental functions. Thus a joint Swedish Environment and Energy Ministry was established in 1987, although the energy functions were transferred to the Industrial Ministry in 1990 after a conflict over the phasing out of nuclear energy. A similar merger in Denmark in 1994 seems to have been more successful. The British government created a new 'super-department' of Environment, Transport and the Regions (DETR) in 1997, but this unwieldy and internally divided ministry was broken up again in 2001. The limited number of examples suggests that attempts to extend the jurisdiction and power of a ME are likely to be met with resistance from established 'economic' ministries anxious not to relinquish further functions to it (Jansen et al. 1998: 302).

Two models of environment ministry can be identified. One has an exclusively environmental remit which produces a clear but narrow policy focus. A danger here is that the ME might be politically isolated. A small, unimportant department, often with a correspondingly weak minister, may be a lone, ineffective voice for the environment within government. The French Ministry of the Environment, for example, has a clear mission, but it possesses few independent policy-making powers and can only get things done by working with other departments. Although it bangs the drum of environmental protection loudly, the ministry has been marginalised, frequently behaving more like 'an internal government pressure group than the central focus of a major sectoral policy domain' (Buller 1998: 77). Similarly, even the more powerful German Ministry for the Environment is excluded from the decision-making processes affecting many core 'environmental issues' that fall within the competency of other ministries, such as transport and agricultural policy (Pehle 1997: 176).

A second, generalist, ME model has seen the merger of several environmental and non-environmental functions within one department. The UK Department of Environment was given important non-environmental responsibilities, notably local government and housing; indeed, in 1980 only about 3.2 per cent of its staff dealt directly with environmental issues, rising to about 10 per cent in the early 1990s. Not surprisingly, environmental issues often struggled to reach the top of the department's agenda; for example, in the late 1980s public discontent with Mrs Thatcher's poll tax meant that the attention of Department of Environment ministers was directed towards their local government responsibilities rather than the burgeoning concern with the environment. Despite being a major department of state whose voice carries considerable weight, the Department of Environment has frequently failed to make a persuasive case for environmental protection. Similar titles elsewhere, including the Ministry of Environment, Physical Planning and Public Works (Greece), Ministry of Environment, Youth and Family (Austria), Department of Environment, Sports and Territories (Australia) and even the Ministry of Housing, Physical Planning and the Environment (the Netherlands), indicate that this is not just British exceptionalism.

The power of a ME is influenced by various factors. An important exogenous variable is the political context, notably the level of public support for environmental protection and the salience of environmental issues which together will largely determine the degree of leadership support. Critical internal factors include the size of the budget and a healthy staff complement, particularly if, as in Norway, the ME has its own field organisation of inspectors, scientists and other professionals (Jansen et al. 1998: 303). If a ME is to act as an effective advocate for the environment, its staff may need to be drawn from a wide variety of backgrounds, so that hard-nosed technocrats, such as engineers, agronomists and economists, are balanced by biologists and environmental managers who by instinct and training are more likely to be 'environmentalists'.

The concentration of environmental responsibilities in a single ministry has undoubtedly given greater prominence to environmental matters within government and gone some way to improving policy co-ordination. The restructuring of functional responsibilities arising from the formation of a ME may disrupt established policy networks or advocacy coalitions, perhaps bringing policy areas traditionally dominated by producer groups within the remit of a ME more willing to listen to the environmental lobby. Where MEs are relatively strong, notably in Denmark, Finland, Norway, Sweden and the Netherlands (Andersen and Liefferink 1997b: 32), they have sufficient autonomy to provide the focus for more powerful coalitions of environmental and consumer interests. Territorial wars may result from attempts by a ME, particularly as it becomes more established, to contest responsibility for a particular policy area. Thus land-use and food safety issues have traditionally been the responsibility of agriculture ministries, but MEs have increasingly demanded control over these activities because they have a major impact on the environment. Nevertheless, neither the small, focused French model nor the large, wide-ranging British model has overcome the entrenched sectoral divisions of government. Everywhere conflict between MEs and the economic ministries remains endemic. Politically weak and often faced by an alliance of opposing ministers, the ME is frequently outgunned in inter-ministry disputes. This is a major problem because in most countries the ME has responsibility for implementing sustainable development across government.

The ME is usually the sponsor for a range of regulatory agencies responsible for the implementation of environmental legislation and policy. In most countries, the administrative history of environmental regulation follows a similar pattern to that of the development of MEs, with an increasing concentration of responsibilities that were previously fragmented across many different departments and levels of government. The pioneering model of a powerful cross-sectoral agency was the US Environmental Protection Agency, a federal agency formed in 1970 with legislative and judicial backing to enforce environmental laws and regulations across states and sectors (see Box 10.2). The Swedish EPA, formed in 1967, has similarly wide-ranging responsibilities and has also become an influential actor in Swedish environmental policy (Lundqvist 1998). Other countries have opted for a weaker model: in Britain the wide range of agencies dealing with air, water, solid and radioactive waste were

10.2 The US Environmental Protection Agency

The EPA has responsibility for implementing all or part of twelve major pieces of federal environmental legislation dealing with clean air, solid waste disposal, safe drinking water, pesticides, toxic substances and radiation. It is the federal government's largest and costliest regulatory agency, with 18,000 employees and an annual budget of $7.3 billion in 1998. The EPA can boast some important regulatory achievements, notably in the areas of air quality, pesticide control and toxic waste, but it has had a troubled history and experienced a major onslaught from the Reagan administration and the Republican-controlled Congress after 1994.

Major criticisms of the EPA include:

- many missed programme deadlines
- failure to achieve numerous key regulatory objectives
- spiralling costs of administration and litigation
- strong congressional dissatisfaction (especially from Republicans)
- the lack of flexibility to set their own policy priorities and the financial burden of regulation, which are resented by the states.

However, many of these problems are caused by inadequacies in the environmental legislation that the EPA has to implement: the heavy dependency on 'command and control' regulation, unrealistic programme objectives, little cross-media pollution control and, crucially, the lack of guidance about how the EPA should allocate priorities between different pieces of legislation and the seventy congressional committees it has to serve.

Reinventing EPA

The pressures for change led to the launch of a major programme in 1995, supervised by Vice-President Al Gore, to 'reinvent' the entire system of regulatory control through greater use of community-based environmental protection, collaborative decision-making, public–private partnerships, enhanced flexibility in rule-making and enforcement, and major cuts in red tape and paperwork.

Early evaluation of these reforms is mixed and inconclusive. Ultimately, much will depend on the political acumen of the EPA leadership in rallying the support of its stakeholders (e.g. environmental pressure groups), and on the attitude to environmental issues of the Bush administration that took office in January 2001.

Sources: Rosenbaum (1999) and EPA website: (*http://www.epa.gov/*).

gradually rationalised until a unified, but relatively weak, Environment Agency was set up in 1996 (Carter and Lowe 1995).

As the principles of sustainable development have gained wider currency, many governments have launched various 'managerial' initiatives to improve policy co-ordination, including new 'in-house' cabinet committees, inter-departmental working groups and departmental 'green' ministers, as well as the formation of specialist advisory groups operating alongside the formal administrative structure. Some of the more promising reforms are to be found in those countries, such as Norway, Sweden and Canada, which have taken a 'whole of government' approach that aims to integrate the responsibility for sustainable development across the public sector (Lafferty and Meadowcroft 2000b: 350). Norway established a State Secretary Committee for Environmental Matters in 1989 to co-ordinate its sustainable development strategy. More recently, the creation within the Swedish Cabinet of a 'Delegation for Ecologically Sustainable Development' consisting of the ministers of environment, agriculture, taxation, schools and labour, suggested an important step towards more integrated political leadership (Lundqvist 1998: 249). It produced a new strategy document, *A Sustainable Sweden*, in 1997 and procured significant government resources for a range of ecological and integrative initiatives.[2] In Canada, the office of Commissioner of Environment and Sustainable Development, an independent officer of Parliament, was created in 1995, with a remit that includes making an independent, public assessment of each departmental sustainable development strategy (Toner 2000: 54). In each case the aim is to co-ordinate and institutionalise environmental considerations into the routine decision-making of every department. Admittedly, evaluations of these reforms in Sweden (Backstrand et al. 1996), Norway (Sverdrup 1997) and the UK (Jordan 2001) suggest that most have had only a limited impact to date. In the UK, for example, an official parliamentary report found that the Cabinet environment committee was 'not driving the Government's pursuit of sustainable development nor acting in a positive way to unearth and deal with related policy conflicts' (Environmental Audit Committee 1998–9: para. 12). Even in Norway, a leading environmental nation which has introduced numerous integrative initiatives, an OECD review of environmental performance concluded that the transport, agriculture, manufacturing and energy sectors 'do not always seem to work as closely with the Ministry of Environment as might have been expected in view of their role in environmental protection and degradation' (quoted in Reitan 1997: 301).

The *Agenda 21* process has also spawned numerous specialist advisory groups and round-tables that sit alongside the formal administrative structure. The Ecologically Sustainable Development process in Australia set up nine working groups consisting of representatives from government, universities, industry, trade unions, environmental and consumer groups, which were given the responsibility for producing strategic recommendations in a core policy area such as agriculture, manufacturing and transport (Australian Government 1991; Doyle and McEachern: 1998: 35–6). In the USA, President Clinton in 1993 created a Council on Sustainable Development, comprising twenty-nine leaders from business, government and non-profit organisations, and later an Interagency Working Group to oversee implementation of the Council's recommendations (Vig 1999: 115; Bryner 2000). Similarly, the British government formed a Panel for Sustainable Development made up of five eminent experts reporting directly to the prime minister and a Round Table on Sustainable Development with representatives drawn from business, local government, environmental groups and other organisations (HM Government 1994), later subsumed into a new Sustainable Development Commission in 2000. The Finnish government set up a National Commission on Sustainable Development in 1993 whose members included the prime minister, senior ministers and representatives from local government, churches, trade unions and the media. While none of these groups has exercised great influence, they mostly persevere, drip-feeding ideas and reports into the policy process and trickling down to sub-national government. Some, notably the Swedish National Committee for Agenda 21, have engaged in extensive consultation and education throughout civil society. However, at best it seems that such bodies have done little to encourage policy-makers to think more holistically about sustainable development.

Although there is evidence that in some of the more 'enthusiastic' countries, such as Sweden and Norway, these reforms have exerted a creeping impact on the way government thinks about environmental issues, overall they have brought only limited improvements in inter-sectoral integration of environmental policy, with departments showing minimal engagement with the sustainable development agenda (Lafferty and Meadowcroft 2000b). Perhaps this is not surprising, as the wider history of administrative reform shows that the perennial quest for better horizontal co-ordination in government has repeatedly confronted insurmountable barriers (Peters 1998b). Indeed, Rhodes (1997) argues that the increasing complexity of policy-making and the 'hollowing out' of the modern state now make co-ordination of all policies – not just environmental – even more difficult. Nevertheless, the prospects for better environmental integration have not been helped by government initiatives that frequently appear timid in design and half-hearted in execution. In particular, it seems that the rhetoric of sustainability has not yet penetrated the hearts and minds of policy-makers in economic sectors where the traditional paradigm still generally holds sway.

CRITICAL QUESTION 1

Should the environment ministry be responsible for co-ordinating sustainable strategies across government?

Integration through administrative techniques

One alternative means by which governments might improve integration is through the use of administrative techniques that bring environmental issues into the decision-making process in a 'rational' way, so that decisions are based on full scientific and technical knowledge and expertise rather than short-term political motivations. The three techniques discussed in this section – environmental impact assessment (EIA), risk analysis and cost–benefit analysis (CBA) – offer the promise of bringing environmental considerations into decision-making in individual policy sectors in a more routine way. All are used quite widely, if sporadically and inconsistently, in policy sectors where actions frequently have significant environmental implications.

Environmental impact assessment (EIA) is the only one of the three techniques that was designed specifically to resolve environmental problems.

It provides a systematic process for the evaluation of the anticipated environmental impacts, including social, political and cultural factors, from a proposed development such as a dam, road, power station or out-of-town shopping complex.[3] An environmental impact statement (EIS) is a non-technical report based on extensive consultation with a wide range of affected government agencies, professional experts, interest groups and the public. The explicit aim of EIA is to encourage the developer, whether government department or private company, to incorporate environmental considerations into its decision-making processes. The USA led the way in the use of EIA when its National Environmental Policy Act 1969 required that an EIS accompany all major legislative proposals or federal actions that might affect the human environment. After an initial burst of some 2,000 EIA reports in 1971, the annual figure settled down to around 500 in the mid-1980s (Rosenbaum 1995: 213). EIA has become increasingly popular in Europe, particularly since a 1985 EC Directive required all member states to undertake an EIA of major public and private projects. Approximately 8,000–9,000 EIAs are carried out each year within the EU, although around 6,000 of these are in France (European Commission 1997: 15).

Risk assessment evaluates the potential harm to human health and the environment from exposure to a particular hazard such as nitrates in drinking water, lead in the air or toxic waste on a derelict industrial site.[4] Risk is often expressed as a dose-response assessment which measures quantitatively the relationship between the amount of exposure to a substance and the degree of toxic effect from it, or as an overall risk characterisation which assesses the health risk from exposure to a hazard, for example the additional risk of developing cancer from exposure to a particular chemical over an average lifetime might be estimated at one in a million people. Risk assessment is now used extensively to evaluate environmental risk, especially by the USA where, by the late 1980s, it had become 'the dominant language for discussing environmental policy in the EPA' (Andrews 1999: 210). It is potentially a key tool in the application of the precautionary principle.

Cost–benefit analysis (CBA) is a long-established economic technique that can be applied to almost any decision. The costs and benefits of an intervention, such as a plan to build a new road or regulate the use of a harmful pesticide, are weighed up to determine 'objectively' whether the proposal will increase or decrease total social welfare. To ensure that like is compared with like, CBA places a monetary value, or shadow price, on every potential cost and benefit. Historically, CBA tended to ignore or undervalue environmental costs, allowing many environmentally damaging projects to proceed. Yet many environmental economists argue that, as most decisions are made on financial grounds, an extended CBA that properly values environmental harms can be an excellent way of protecting the environment. By valuing the environment in the same 'currency' as other costs and benefits, policy-makers are forced to look beyond the narrow economic benefits of a proposal to give proper consideration to its environmental impact (Pearce et al. 1989).[5] CBA is used worldwide across all areas of public policy, although it is applied to environmental regulation much more extensively in the USA than in Europe. Pearce (1998: 4–5) offers two explanations for its relative popularity in the USA. First, CBA has been regarded, especially by Republicans, as an instrument to improve the 'efficiency' of government. Secondly, the widespread use of liability legislation in the USA and a greater proclivity to use the courts than in Europe have seen the extensive employment of CBA to determine court settlements.

To summarise, the environmental case for all three techniques is twofold: they offer a 'rational' means of building environmental considerations, particularly those characterised by scientific uncertainty, into formal decision-making processes and, therefore, they should also encourage policy-makers to anticipate and address the environmental implications of their actions more routinely. Yet the techniques generate widespread criticism, particularly (but not exclusively) from environmentalists; indeed, many experts suggest that these techniques may *harm* environmental interests rather than advance them. The debate about their strengths and weaknesses focuses around five key issues.

First, each technique claims to be a 'rational' tool of analysis, yet none is an exact science. Risk assessment, for example, is usually empirically based on either animal studies or epidemiology, but often neither is reliable or accurate enough to support conclusive risk assessments (Wildavsky 1995; Armour 1997). The scientific claims of risk assessment are based on a supposedly rigorous methodology that, in practice, usually relies on 'a multitude of assumptions and subjective judgements as much as it depends upon empirical observation or testing' (Rosenbaum 1997a: 42). Consequently, many risk estimates are very tentative, making them vulnerable to challenge from further scientific research, which can have embarrassing and expensive consequences for policy-makers. Thus, in 1974, when studies revealed that dioxins contained in waste oil sprayed on roads in Times Beach, Missouri, might be highly carcinogenic and have contributed to ill-health in children and horses, government officials ordered all residents to evacuate the city at a cost of $139 million. A few years later the senior official responsible testified that subsequent studies suggested that the evacuation, although based on the best available scientific evidence, had been unnecessary (Rosenbaum 1997a: 43). When the science underpinning risk assessment is rapidly advancing into new territory, as is currently the case with GMOs, definitive risk assessment is almost impossible. The bottom line for risk assessment, as the respected Royal Commission on Environmental Pollution (1998) in Britain put it, is that 'No satisfactory way has been devised of measuring risk to the natural environment, even in principle, let alone defining what scale of risk should be regarded as tolerable' (para. 9.49).

Similarly, a serious methodological problem with CBA is the difficulty of putting a price on environmental harms, such as the loss of scarce habitats or damage from acid rain. Techniques do exist that attempt to overcome this problem, such as contingent valuation, which asks people how much they would pay to protect a threatened habitat (Pearce et al. 1989: 69–71). There are also several techniques for calculating the value of human life. However, they cannot disguise the imprecision and subjectivity that lie at the heart of CBA (ironically, many policy-makers like the way CBA produces a single, definitive figure for each proposal that allows them to announce a decision apparently based on incontrovertible objective criteria). Conversely, whilst an EIA can also be undermined by unreliable or incomplete data, it is the qualitative methodology and the openness of its conclusions that may reduce its authority. The terms of reference for an individual EIA may also produce biased outcomes, particularly where, as in Australia, it is the responsibility of the private developer, rather than an independent body, to carry out the EIA. Overall, although promulgated as objective tools of rational analysis, each of the three techniques contains fundamental conceptual and technical weaknesses that render it vulnerable to charges of bias, unreliability and imprecision.

Secondly, these methodological weaknesses contribute to the uneasy interface between science and politics that characterises many environmental problems. Even risk assessment practitioners are unable to reach a consensus about what constitutes an 'acceptable' level of risk; instead, they hand the problem over to the policy-maker, who may be guided by public opinion when deciding how to manage a particular risk. Yet public perceptions of risk are socially constructed and depend on a wide range of factors, including the position of an individual in society, and whether the possible consequences of an action are delayed or immediate (Adams 1995; Liberatore 1995). Thus 'NIMBYism' is often fuelled by a gross exaggeration of the real risk to health from a proposed development such as an incinerator or landfill site, but fierce public opposition may persuade the politician to override a 'scientific' risk assessment that judges the proposal to be 'safe'. By contrast, people are more tolerant of risks they bear voluntarily, such as smoking, or where, as with car ownership, halting an activity might have high personal costs.

From a radical ecocentric standpoint, CBA is morally unacceptable because it places a monetary value on wildlife or wilderness, although from a more moderate 'environmentalist' position it could be countered that the practice of valuing human life is common in healthcare provision, where similar difficult trade-offs between priorities need to be made when scarce resources are being allocated, so why not extend this practice to nature too? A more persuasive, non-ethical objection to CBA is that, while monetary valuation may be meaningful for some small-scale, localised air or noise pollution issues, many important environmental goods are simply not commensurable in this way (Jacobs 1991). How can a value be placed on endangered species, irreplaceable rainforest or a permanently damaged ozone layer? A CBA may provide useful information for policy-makers but, like risk assessment, its claims to objectivity often leave them no better equipped to arbitrate between different interests. Ultimately, this 'weakness' may be no bad thing, for political decisions cannot – and should not – be reduced to a mathematical exercise: 'such choices must be a matter of judgement, not computation' (ibid.: 219). In this respect, whereas CBA reduces the flexibility for political judgement by a cut-and-dried calculation about whether or not the benefits of a proposal exceed costs (Pearce 1998), an advantage of EIA is that underpinning its longer checklist of potential impacts and lack of a definitive conclusion is the recognition that broader social, cultural and political considerations must be taken into account.

Thirdly, once in the political arena, all three techniques are open to contestation and manipulation. The uncertainties inherent in risk assessment make it a weapon to be used in the conflicts between regulators and regulated, or between the developers and the public (Armour 1997). Some of the methodologies commonly used in risk assessment, such as 'worst case scenarios' and the inclusion of an 'extra margin of safety', are often accused of over-estimating risk (Armour 1997; Rosenbaum 1997a; Andrews 1999). While neo-liberal critics believe that this conservative bias may unnecessarily alarm the public and encourage the government to regulate more than is necessary, environmentalists applaud the 'better to be safe than sorry' approach to human and environmental safety (which also chimes well with the precautionary principle). In practice, a risk assessment is open to wide and contrasting interpretations. The fact that a particular insecticide or herbicide may be legal in one country but not in another partly reflects the particular constellation of political interests – industrial, farming, consumer and environmental – lined up for and against a ban in each country. Similarly, Liberatore (1995) shows how after the 1986 accident at the Chernobyl nuclear plant there were widely contrasting responses to the possible risk posed by low doses of radiation from the fallout. In Germany and Italy, key actors in politics and the media emphasised the risks, defined it as a public health problem and advocated a range of precautionary measures. Yet in France, where the large indigenous nuclear industry was strongly supported by all the major political parties, the same uncertainties were downplayed and there was almost no political or public response to the problem.

These administrative techniques are also open to manipulation. Policy-makers may use them to justify decisions they have already taken. Or, faced by public opposition to a controversial project such as a new road or incinerator, civil servants might employ an EIA not because it makes the decision more rational but because 'it enhances the *appearance* of rationality and thus serves to undermine environmental opposition to development projects' (Amy 1990: 63). Not surprisingly, opinion is therefore divided about the impact of EIAs on specific agency decisions. In the USA, few projects are stopped directly as a result of an EIA; rather, the 'politics of accommodation' will delay a project, usually by requiring another EIA, rather than stop it. Similarly, a survey of EU member states found that very few projects have been discarded as a result of an EIA, although limited modifications to the design are quite common (European Commission 1997: 79–80). Thus in Sweden, major infrastructure developments during the 1990s, notably the ring-road round Stockholm and the Öresund bridge linking Sweden and Denmark, were approved after an EIA had produced no conclusive evidence regarding their environmental acceptability. In short, they proceeded because powerful economic interests supported them (Lundqvist 1998: 246–7).

CBA is also vulnerable to political manipulation, notably to 'institutional capture' by government and public agencies. In particular, it is relatively easy to use the discount rate, which calculates future costs and benefits, to justify decisions made on other (political) grounds. By choosing a low discount rate, public agencies have been able to justify many projects, notably dam and irrigation works in the USA, in the face of strong environmental objections (Amy 1990; Hanley and Spash 1993: 161). Indeed, owing to its focus on monetary cost, CBA has found support amongst right-wing opponents of 'excessive' environmental regulation who believe that the wider use of CBA would reduce the regulatory burden on industry and help inculcate bureaucrats with a greater sensitivity to costs. Both the Reagan administration in the early 1980s and the Republican Congress in 1995 extended the range of issues for which federal agencies were required to use CBA before introducing any significant new regulation (Rosenbaum 1997a: 36–7). In the UK, the Conservative government ensured that legislation setting up a new Environment Agency requires it to carry out CBA before making any significant intervention, a requirement that environmentalists claimed would undermine its capacity to protect the environment (Carter and Lowe 1995: 55). With such friends, it is not surprising that many environmentalists are suspicious of CBA.

Fourthly, there is a strong anti-democratic element inherent in all three techniques because their 'administrative rationalism' legitimates 'government by the experts' (Dryzek 1997) and denies citizens the opportunity to voice their views. By allocating a primary role to professional experts such as economists, scientists or lawyers, these techniques privilege certain elite stakeholders, particularly when the detailed analysis is not made public. CBA limits conflict about a decision to those parties with something at stake for which they are willing to pay, and who know about or are immediately affected by the conflict. Indeed, CBA effectively tries to prevent a conflict from breaking into the public realm, where it might come to the attention of democratic institutions such as legislatures, political parties, courts and the press (Sagoff 1988: 96–7). Proponents of

CBA defend it as democratic on the economic argument that its values are those of the public expressed through their private choices in the market place (Amy 1990: 68), but Sagoff (1988) argues persuasively that our choices as consumers may be quite different from our choices as citizens. As consumers we may prefer the convenience of plastic disposable bottles, but as citizens we might vote to ban them as ecologically damaging. From the point of view of sustainable development, it might be better if policy-makers put their trust in the citizen's long-term concern to protect the environment rather than the consumer's short-term individual preference – although there may not be many votes in it! By contrast, EIA has more democratic potential because it involves a formal process of consultation with a wide range of stakeholders including public agencies, private organisations and groups representing environmental, consumer and citizen interests. Consequently, EIA provides an opportunity for environmental and citizen groups to engage in the decision process by giving them access to information, the right to comment on draft reports and to apply for judicial review of the EIA preparation. In Australia, governments have used EIA as a means of gauging public opinion on a project and as a means of deferring difficult decisions (Papadakis 1993: 112).

Finally, these techniques, if insensitively applied, ignore distributional and equity considerations. Risk assessment often glosses over any unequal distribution of risk between different groups. Yet such information raises important political questions, such as whether a risk that is concentrated on certain groups is more or less acceptable than one that is evenly distributed. There are also deeper ethical issues concerning the extent to which socially and economically disadvantaged groups are exposed to higher levels of risk. In the USA the frequency with which heavily polluting factories, incinerators and waste disposal units are located in neighbourhoods populated by minority ethnic groups underlines the importance of this issue (Bullard 1990). Similarly, few CBAs identify variations in the incidence of costs and benefits on different groups (Pearce 1998). EIA, in theory, is more likely to pick up these distributional issues, provided the terms of reference are drawn sufficiently wide to cover the full range of distributional impacts.

To assess whether these administrative techniques improve integration, we can return to the twofold case that they bring a more rational approach to environmental decision-making and, in so doing, encourage policy-makers to consider environmental factors more routinely. We are clearly a long way away from a situation in which, say, EIA is a routinised part of day-to-day government decision-making, rather than an add-on extra; that when considering a proposal bureaucrats will automatically consider environmental factors just as automatically as they check the financial cost. Indeed, as 'rational' instruments, the three techniques are still treated with ambivalence or hostility by many environmentalists: they promise a more systematic and rigorous treatment of environmental factors, but they are frequently used (or mis-used) to the detriment of the environment. Yet they are only administrative *tools* which provide information to improve the policy-making process. Once certain methodological improvements are made, particularly to CBA, these techniques are not necessarily inherently biased against the environment. Instead, it is the way that powerful actors, particularly government agencies representing economic interests, use and manipulate these tools to serve their own political ends that can unfairly prejudice environmental interests. Despite their flaws, the techniques, particularly EIA, can help introduce environmental considerations into the bureaucratic mind-set and contribute to social learning by policy elites. Some positive environmental outcomes will probably rub off on agency policies simply as a result of their routinised engagement in the preparation of EIAs, as several American studies confirm. There may be a creative tension between EIA specialists and other bureaucrats that contributes to greater environmental awareness amongst all staff. Policy-makers may learn to anticipate certain environmental objections and pre-empt an EIA by amending proposals accordingly (Rosenbaum 1995: 212–15). At the very least, the techniques force policy-makers to think about the environment – even if they are only looking for ways to defeat environmentalist objections to a project.

One wider problem is that all three techniques still tend to be used within the traditional paradigm in that they are applied to specific decisions rather than the underlying policy. Thus, although several of the individual road schemes that provoked anti-road protests in Britain during the 1990s were the subject of an EIA, the environmental impact of the Conservative government's underlying massive road-building programme was never assessed. There is evidence of a gradual shift from this 'tactical' EIA focus on individual projects towards strategic environmental assessment. The European Commission (1997), in particular, regards the extension of environmental assessment to plans, programmes and overall policies as a vital step towards the full integration of sustainable development across core economic sectors. One of the most innovative examples of this strategic shift is the New Zealand Resource Management Act 1991, which made it mandatory for all regional policies, regional and district plans, and resource consent applications to be accompanied by an EIA, and for the authorities to monitor the impact of their activities on the environment (Bartlett 1997). This kind of strategic framework is more likely to emerge where governments have begun to plan their national approach to sustainable development.

CRITICAL QUESTION 2

Are these administrative techniques friends or foes of the environment?

PLANNING

Sustainable development needs to be planned at several different levels of government. Traditionally, central government has usually taken responsibility for controversial or dangerous issues such as nuclear power, hazardous waste or air pollution legislation, leaving sub-national government to deal with a wide range of environmental issues, including land-use planning, where flexibility and local knowledge may produce better policy. In federal systems, such as Germany, Australia and the USA, the states have retained extensive environmental competencies. In recent years, twin-pronged pressures seem to have shifted the locus of policy-making towards central government. From the supranational level, national governments have encountered increasing pressure to introduce new legislation and policy in order to fulfil international commitments such as carbon emission reductions or, in the EU, to implement environmental directives. Conversely, from within the nation state, the worsening condition of the environment and the growing political salience of the issue have encouraged most national governments to rein in responsibilities that traditionally resided at the sub-national level.[6] Overall, there is probably no one universal 'best' level of environmental government. Instead, government should adopt a multi-level approach based on the principle of subsidiarity, so that responsibilities should lie at the lowest appropriate level of government. Thus, to return to the centralisation–decentralisation dilemma discussed in Chapter 3, subsidiarity contains a primary principle of administrative effectiveness underpinned by a secondary principle of decentralisation. With this multi-level approach in mind, this section examines efforts to improve planning at three levels of government: supra-national, national and local.

EU Environmental Action Plans

The environmental programmes of the EU are a unique attempt to co-ordinate and integrate environmental policy across national boundaries. The original Treaty of Rome that set up the Common Market in 1957 was committed to the promotion of 'continuous expansion' and made no mention of environmental protection, let alone sustainable development (see Box 10.3). Ironically, it was the need to ensure that common standards existed across member states – the so-called 'level playing field' – that led to European Community environmental regulations designed to prevent some countries gaining a competitive advantage from having lower environmental standards (and therefore lower industrial costs) than others. Consequently, the first Environmental Action Plan (EAP) was launched in 1973. EU environmental policy can claim some major regulatory achievements in certain policy areas, notably bathing and drinking water quality, air pollution and waste policy.[7] Although the first EAP established several

10.3 The European Union: from traditional paradigm to sustainable development?

Treaty of Rome (came into effect) 1957
Article 2 stated that the Community should promote 'a harmonious development of economic activities, a continuous and balanced expansion'. No mention of environmental protection.

Single European Act 1987
For the first time provided a formal, legal underpinning for EU environment policy. Article 130r(2) established a new principle of integration: 'environmental protection requirements shall be a component of the Community's other policies'.

Maastricht Treaty 1993
Introduced the word 'sustainable' (not sustainable development) to the formal aims of the EU. Hence Article 2 was amended so that 'continuous expansion' was replaced by 'sustainable and non-inflationary growth respecting the environment' while Article B stated that a Community objective was 'to promote economic and social progress which is balanced and sustainable'.

Treaty of Amsterdam 1999
Introduced the term 'sustainable development' so that Article 2 seeks 'to promote throughout the Community a harmonious, balanced and sustainable development of economic activities' and a new Article 6 strengthens the integration principle: 'Environmental protection requirements must be integrated into the definition and implementation of the Community policies and activities referred to in Article 3 [i.e. the full range of EU policies] in particular with a view to promoting sustainable development.'

See European Commission Environment Directorate (*http://europa.eu.int/comm/environment/*).

important and progressive principles, notably the need for preventive action, in practice the first three EAPs pursued a regulatory, end-of-pipe approach that lay firmly within the traditional paradigm. After an integration clause was included in the 1987 Single European Act, the fourth EAP (1987–92) brought a small shift towards greater sustainability and took tentative steps towards integrating environmental considerations into other EU policies.

The fifth EAP (1992–2000), *Towards Sustainability* (European Commission 1992), outlined a bold strategy to improve integration focused on five key sectors – tourism, industry, energy, transport and agriculture – using a wide range of policy initiatives and instruments, including sustainable tourism, industrial eco-audits and eco-labels, energy conservation schemes, carbon taxes and set-aside schemes protecting environmentally sensitive areas (Liberatore 1997; Wilkinson 1997). However, although several of these initiatives have been implemented, an official evaluation of the fifth EAP acknowledged that 'practical progress towards sustainable development has been rather limited' (European Communities 2000: 9). It has proved especially difficult to persuade other Directorate-Generals inside the Commission to place environmental issues above their own sectoral priorities. There has been little significant progress towards inter-sectoral integration, particularly in the agricultural and tourism sectors where the initiatives were relatively new, but also in energy and transport (European Communities 2000). A mid-term review specifically picked out the absence of 'the attitude changes and the will to make the quantum leap to make the necessary progress to move towards sustainability' (European Commission 1996: 3) and a later evaluation bemoaned the absence of 'clear recognition of commitment from member states and stakeholders' (European Communities 2000: 9). Thus the failure of member states to agree the necessary fundamental reform of the Common Agricultural Policy, which provides the huge financial incentives, such as guaranteed farm prices and export subsidies, that underpin the intensification of European agriculture, completely outweighs any marginal benefits from set-aside schemes. It seems that the EU mirrors many national governments in struggling to bring about the kind of deep-seated social learning by policy elites that might usher in greater integration of environmental considerations. An effort to kick-start the integration process at the Cardiff Summit of EU leaders in June 1998 by generating stronger political commitment to integration and identifying key strategies and tools needed to bring it to fruition had little effect (European Communities 2000: 22–4). Currently, there is little to suggest that the sixth EAP, *Environment 2010: Our Future, Our Choice* (2001–10), adopted by the European Commission in January 2001 (the first stage in the long process of approval by the EU legislative process), might succeed where its predecessor failed.

National green plans

Since the late 1980s most OECD countries have published 'green plans' setting out the long-term goals, policies and targets of national strategies for sustainable development and which are also intended to improve both inter-sectoral and intra-sectoral integration (Jänicke and Jörgens 1998; Lafferty and Meadowcroft 2000a). The most comprehensive initiatives have come from countries such as Norway, Sweden and the Netherlands where the traditional assumption that there must be a trade-off between environmental and economic goals had been challenged long before the *Agenda 21* process pushed the idea of green plans onto the international stage (see Andersen and Liefferink 1997a). Australia was also ahead of the pack, launching an 'ecologically sustainable development' process in 1990 to produce its National Strategy document. However, many documents were produced simply to satisfy the *Agenda 21* requirement that all governments produce a national plan and made few commitments regarding implementation. In the USA and Canada, *Agenda 21* has virtually no domestic political salience (Lafferty and Meadowcroft 2000a) while the German document was not translated into German or even published there (Beuermann and Burdick 1997: 90). While these plans are a step towards a more strategic and comprehensive approach to environmental policy, one comparative study of sixteen green plans concluded that they are little more than 'pilot strategies . . . a first step towards intersectoral communication' (Jänicke and Jörgens 1998: 47). The goals are generally inadequate, there are few new policy initiatives, the commitments are vague and only a handful of (mostly qualitative) targets are identified. The timidity of these plans usually reflects the compromises that governments had to make with powerful economic sectors and producer interests. However, another comparative study, whilst acknowledging the limitations and instability of many of these plans, identifies two positive trends. First, a tendency for goals, especially in Sweden, Britain and Canada, to become more carefully defined over time, with measurable targets to judge success. Second, a strengthening of collaborative and participatory dimensions within the strategic planning process in several countries, notably the Netherlands, as governments recognise the need to consult more widely to find and legitimate solutions to complex environmental challenges (Lafferty and Meadowcroft 2000b: 356–72).

The pioneering model of a green plan is the Dutch National Environmental Policy Plan (NEPP), a wide-ranging and ambitious strategy that, since its launch in 1989, has been widely praised as a genuine 'success' (Weale 1992; Jänicke and Jörgens 1998). The aim of NEPP is to improve both inter-sectoral co-ordination of policy and intra-sectoral integration of environmental considerations into the day-to-day policy processes in core ministries such as transport, energy and agriculture. NEPP explicitly rejects the reorganisation of the *structure* of government in favour of an approach based on inventing *processes* of policy planning that establish co-ordination and integration (Weale 1992: 148). At its core is a set of 50 strategic objectives, with over 200 specific quantitative targets to be achieved by various dates up to 2010. The objective of reducing acidification, for example, is accompanied by costed targets setting out percentage reductions in the level of emissions of critical chemicals such as sulphur dioxide and nitrogen oxide, which in turn are broken down into individual targets for different activities such as traffic, energy supply, industry and households (Weale 1992: 125–6). This process of target-setting is repeated for other environmental problems including climate change, eutrophication and waste disposal. Having been agreed by the four key ministries of environment, economics (industry), transport and agriculture, the NEPP provided the ME with the tools to co-ordinate a national environmental strategy – NEPP has had a legal basis since 1993 – and a significant degree of political clout to enforce it. The cooperative process of agreeing and implementing the plan has also helped to integrate environmental considerations more effectively across a full range of public policies. Weale (1992) argues that by making its theoretical assumptions explicit[8] and showing how environmental problems such as acidification simply cannot be dealt with by traditional political and administrative compartmentalisation, NEPP provides the framework for 'social learning' by policy-makers towards a more synoptic approach in which they 'think environment' all the time.

A central feature in the implementation of NEPP is the 'target group policy' based on structured consultation and negotiation of the targets in the form of voluntary agreements (covenants) between government representatives and key industrial interest groups. The intention is to persuade these target groups to accept a greater share of the responsibility for environmental protection by encouraging them to develop a sense of ownership of the targets, whilst allowing them the flexibility to achieve them in their own way.

NEPP remains firmly in place, and updated plans were published in 1994, 1998 and 2001. One study showed that around half the targets set for 1995 were met and that, even where targets were not attained, nearly every trend showed an improvement on the pre-NEPP period (Jänicke and Jörgens 1998: 45–6). Hanf and van de Gronden (1998) report that with regard to key pollutants such as sulphur dioxide, nitrogen oxide and phosphate, 'evaluation studies indicate that environmental policy in the Netherlands has, in recent years, indeed achieved a marked reduction of pressures on and threats to the environment' (p.178).

There is no one factor explaining the relative success of NEPP, but a critical feature is that NEPP reflects a fortunate congruence of two phenomena: one, the consensual style of Dutch politics which places a high premium on avoiding conflict and seeking negotiated solutions; two, the redefinition of environmental problems, encouraged by the discourse of ecological modernisation, as one that requires the self-responsible participation of economic actors (notably industry) who were once seen as the cause of environmental problems, but are now regarded as an essential part of their solution (ibid.: 153). This situation was able to flourish through the 1990s, partly because successive Dutch governments provided sustained political support for the NEPP (backed by sympathetic public opinion), but also because fundamental clashes between economic and environmental interests were largely avoided. Put differently, because of its innovative efforts the Dutch government has been able to extract maximum benefits from its policy of planned industry self-regulation. One concern is that industry may have reached the limits of its willingness to act voluntarily out of self-interest, particularly in the context of the fundamental changes required to meet future climate change targets. With declining public enthusiasm for environmental issues, the government has increasingly struggled to follow through on the challenge of implementing the ambitious NEPP goals (van Muijen 2000: 172). Nevertheless, the NEPP remains a powerful model for the design of green plans elsewhere.

Local Agenda 21

There is also enormous potential for effective planning and integration at the local level, where there are many examples of individual municipalities implementing innovative and radical sustainability programmes. An important catalyst has been the Local Agenda 21 (LA21) process which has gained a firm footing in several countries. Chapter 28 of *Agenda 21* focuses on the role of the local authority in the implementation of sustainable development because it is the level of government closest to the people. It called on all local authorities to engage in a process of consultation and consensus-building with their citizens, local organisations and businesses to produce, by 1996, a LA21 action plan for sustainable development. LA21 does not provide a single blueprint to follow, but it does make two important assumptions: first, that the local authority will take a leading role in planning and facilitating change; secondly, that sustainable development requires on-going consultation and partnership with a wide range of actors in the local community.

Although there are huge variations in the take-up of LA21 both between and within countries, overall progress seems rather limited (see O'Riordan and Voisey 1997; Lafferty and Meadowcroft 2000a). Nevertheless, there are some exceptions, mainly in Northern Europe, particularly in Britain and Sweden (see Box 10.4). The reasons for the relative success of LA21 in these two countries seem, in some respects, to be quite different. In Britain, where the Thatcher era had seen a significant reduction in the autonomy, functions and power of local authorities, many local authorities saw LA21 as providing an opportunity to carve out a new role for themselves, building on their traditional responsibilities for implementing environmental regulations. In particular, authorities were attracted by the potential of LA21 to restore their legitimacy by improving public participation and

---

10.4 Local Agenda 21 in Sweden: a qualified success?

By 1996 all 288 Swedish municipalities reported to UNGASS that they had launched a LA21 process and, by late 1998, 56 per cent had adopted an action plan – (one of) the highest anywhere. Key features:
* almost 90 per cent of authorities had given co-ordination of LA21 to the overall council rather than the environment department, i.e. LA21 is not regarded as just about the environment.
* over 70 per cent have a full or part-time *Agenda 21* co-ordinator. 78 per cent have allocated (limited) special funding to LA21 activities.
* the focus of activities has gradually shifted from waste and water management and 'green purchasing' to a wider range of issues including renewable energy, biological diversity and auditing systems.

* 52 per cent have decided to include LA21 within the structure planning process, which reflects a common view among local authorities that LA21 is a strategy for local economic development as well as sustainability.
* innovative policy instruments include: 69 per cent of municipalities use differentiated refuse collection tariffs to encourage recycling and composting; 60 per cent have a green purchasing policy; 12 per cent have differentiated tariffs on water and sewage, and 20 per cent use environmental auditing.
* there is a growing gap between the 40–60 'pioneer' authorities which have implemented quite radical changes to infrastructure, resource use and individual lifestyles, and the remaining 'lingering' authorities.

Based on Eckerberg and Brundin (1999).

contributing to local economic development (Voisey and O'Riordan 1997: 46; Mason 1999: ch. 6). In short, LA21 took off despite a lack of support from central government. By contrast, the baseline for many Swedish local authorities was that they already possessed sufficient autonomy and powers to develop innovative and far-reaching programmes for sustainable development, including the use of various eco-taxes (Eckerberg and Brundin 1999). Moreover, the Swedish national government has provided much more support for LA21 both in terms of publicity and support networks and with the provision of financial resources specifically for LA21 projects. However, there are factors that are common to the two countries; in particular, the presence of individual politicians and bureaucrats – firebrands (ibid. 1998) – who are dedicated to bringing sustainability onto the local political agenda.

Overall, the spate of green plans produced since the early 1990s reflects the growing recognition that government at all levels must adopt a more integrated, strategic approach to sustainable development. To date, green plans have generally proved unimpressive in both design and execution; in particular, despite tentative efforts to plan better integration, governments have found it difficult to generate sectoral environmental responsibility in core polluting sectors such as transport, energy and agriculture. Nevertheless, drawing on those green national plans, such as the NEPP, that have had some success, it is possible to identify some key characteristics of 'successful' plans (see also Jänicke and Jörgens 1998: 48–9). In particular, it is important to have effective monitoring and measurement systems in place; without them it is difficult to include meaningful targets in plans or to evaluate progress in achieving sustainable development. To this end, many international organisations and governments have put considerable effort into developing robust and comprehensive sustainability indicators.[9] Apart from the NEPP sectoral target system, Germany has also outlined an 'environmental barometer' setting out indicators and targets for air quality, soil, nature protection, water, energy and raw materials (Meadowcroft 2000) and the British government has published a set of fifteen 'headline indicators' backed up by a supporting tier of over 150 core indicators that provide a more detailed picture of progress (DETR 1999) (see Box 10.5). Ultimately, the most important lesson is that effective planning requires strong, sustained political

---

10.5 Headline indicators of sustainability

1. Total output of the economy (GDP)
2. Investment in public, business and private assets
3. Proportion of people of working age who are in work
4. Qualifications at age 19
5. Expected years of healthy life
6. Homes judged unfit to live in
7. Level of crime
8. Emissions of greenhouse gases
9. Days when pollution is moderate or high
10. Road traffic
11. Rivers of good or fair quality
12. Populations of wild birds
13. New homes built on previously developed land
14. Volume of waste
15. Satisfaction with quality of life (to be developed)

DETR (1999).

leadership that can be institutionalised through legislation, institutional reform, target-setting and monitoring of progress. One way of institutionalising and sustaining this political momentum might be to extend the use of democratic and participatory mechanisms throughout government.

CRITICAL QUESTION 3

Is the Dutch NEPP a model that can be transferred elsewhere?

DEMOCRACY AND PARTICIPATION

The central argument for extending democracy and participation in decision-making is that ordinary citizens will play a key role in the achievement of sustainable development. As the Brundtland Report put it: 'The law alone cannot enforce the common interest. It principally needs community knowledge and support, which entails greater public participation in the decisions that affect the environment' (WCED 1987: 63). A complementary argument holds that greater democracy will improve the quality of decision-making about complex environmental problems. By listening to a full range of voices, including environmental, consumer and citizen viewpoints, the government is more likely to anticipate environmental impacts and build these considerations into the policy process. These claims echo the green case for democracy discussed in Chapter 3. This section briefly assesses the role of democracy in environmental decision-making.

Most liberal democracies have long recognised that where major environmental decisions mobilise deeply held competing interests, then democratic mechanisms may be the best form of conflict resolution. The public inquiry, in particular, is often used when controversial projects provoke considerable conflict. In Britain, for example, there have been several big public inquiries into proposed nuclear installations, notably the THORP reprocessing plant at Windscale (now Sellafield), a fast-breeder reactor/reprocessing plant at Dounreay, Scotland, and a pressurised water reactor at Sizewell B, Suffolk; airport developments including a third London airport and new terminals at Heathrow and Manchester airports; and numerous major road schemes including the M16 in the Aire Valley, the Winchester bypass and the M3 extension at Twyford Down, Hampshire. Public inquiries into major wilderness developments, such as uranium mining in the Kakadu National Park, have been commonplace in Australia too, especially since the creation of the Resource Assessment Commission in 1989, which one commentator describes as 'a permanent public inquiry mechanism to arbitrate on land-use conflicts' (Papadakis 1993: 124).

A public inquiry into a specific proposal is chaired by an individual who will receive a range of depositions and listen to many witnesses representing a wide range of interests before producing an assessment based on that evidence. The inquiry report is then considered by the relevant government authority in making its final decision on the proposal. In theory, this participatory process allows all information to be heard and every interest to have its say, before a 'rational' planning decision is made. However, although public inquiries may appear to provide an open, pluralistic forum where all views can be expressed, much depends on the terms of reference given to the inquiry, the independence of the presiding 'judge' and the resources available to the various interests giving evidence.[10] These variables are often biased in favour of the developers; most obviously, a well-researched case will require a huge financial outlay for research, expert witnesses and legal fees. Large corporations can usually mobilise far more resources – the UK Central Electricity Generating Board spent £20 million on the Sizewell B inquiry (O'Riordan et al. 1988) – than are available to environmental groups. The formal proceedings, dominated by legalistic jargon and techniques of cross-examination, intimidate community groups and individuals and so impede genuine public participation (Rydin 1998: 258–9). Mason reports that a study of the British, French and German public inquiry processes concluded that everywhere the public held an ambiguous attitude towards them: while people strongly demand participation, there is a widespread perception that they are no more than a 'mock consultation' intended to give legitimacy to decisions that have effectively already been made (in Mason 1999: 78).

Nevertheless, even when a government uses a public inquiry to legitimise a decision it wants to make, or when developers lavish vast resources in presenting their side of the argument, the openness of the forum can still provide a window of opportunity to be exploited by environmentalists (Kingdon 1995). At the very least, opponents can gain publicity, and perhaps cause delays or even win modifications to the project. Sometimes proposals are abandoned, as were plans to sand-mine on Fraser Island on the Australian barrier reef. In Britain during the 1970s, a leading campaigner, John Tyme, by astute political tactics and clever use of the mass media, was able to cause such disruption to a series of inquiries into individual road schemes that the government was forced to reappraise its entire road-building programme (Tyme 1978; Dudley and Richardson 1996: 74–5). Other democratic mechanisms can also act as 'focusing events' (Kingdon 1995) around which environmental groups can mobilise and use to push new issues onto public agendas. Referenda, for example, which are frequently used for specific decisions in Switzerland and California, and for local planning decisions in many countries, allow groups to campaign and may raise public awareness about environmental issues. Indeed, one outcome of the 1980 Swedish referendum on its nuclear power programme was that activists involved in the 'No' campaign went on to form the Green Party.

One drawback of big public inquiries and referenda, as with EIA, is that they are unique events that are designed to resolve a particular conflict; they do not turn democratic involvement in decision-making into a regular routine. Even where, as in Britain, the public inquiry is widely used within the land-use planning process, each decision is unique and discrete. Alternative dispute resolution, increasingly employed in the USA, takes a step further by drawing a range of affected interests into a mediation process. Again, this practice usually addresses a specific environmental issue, but by absorbing political conflict into the administrative process it allows the possibility for mutual learning and compromise solutions that result in neither complete victory nor defeat for either 'side' of a dispute (Lee 1993; Dryzek 1997: 87–8). The sustainable development discourse envisages this kind of learning through deliberation and dialogue becoming an on-going, routine part of the administrative process, 'by promoting citizens' initiatives, empowering people's organisations and strengthening local democracy' (WCED 1987: 63). Thus many of the round-table and advisory initiatives associated with *Agenda 21* were designed to encourage such dialogue by providing a forum in which representatives from a wide range of interest groups discuss a particular environmental problem in order to agree recommendations for action (see above, pp. 262–3). Other innovative plans to extend deliberative democracy include citizen juries (Ward 1999) and participatory models of planning (Dryzek 1997), although most are still in the early days of development. There is probably most scope for extending democracy in the policy process at the local level. LA21 is built explicitly on the assumption that local authorities must consult widely with local interests, including community and minority groups. As the previous section showed, progress is slow, but the institutional and political obstacles may be less troublesome at grass roots level, precisely because the stakes are lower.

Overall, governments have shown only limited enthusiasm for extending the range of democratic mechanisms to facilitate the implementation of sustainable development. Democratic procedures tend to be used exceptionally – the big public inquiry, the referendum – rather than routinely, although the *Agenda 21* process, particularly at the local level, has generated some innovation in this area.

However, democratic mechanisms, as we saw in Chapter 2, do not guarantee environmentally benevolent outcomes. They may open up policy-making but pluralistic processes are frequently hijacked by powerful interests, especially as producer interests can exercise first-dimensional power by mobilising more resources in their cause. Alternatively, radical voices may be co-opted into the policy process and tamed. Even if the 'democratic will' (whatever that may be) does prevail over power politics, it may not

10.6 Opposition to wind power: democracy or NIMBYism?

Renewable sources contributed just 3 per cent of UK electricity generation in 1999. The British government, as part of its climate change strategy, has set the rather tentative target of 'working towards' increasing this share to 10 per cent 'hopefully by 2010' (DETR 2000). Wind power must contribute a significant share of that amount. It is a safe, clean technology, producing no carbon emissions, which uses an unlimited natural resource, and Britain has the largest potential for wind power in Europe. Who could be against it?

Yet, despite significant government subsidies, the wind energy sector remains tiny. The amount of installed wind power is less than a quarter of Danish capacity and an eighth of German capacity. This shortfall can be explained partly by local planning decisions, often involving a planning inquiry: between 1994 and 1998, of eighteen wind developments that went before planning inquiries, just two small schemes won approval (RCEP 2000: 216).

A key event was the 1994 decision of the local council to reject an application to build a 44-turbine windfarm on Flaight Hill in Yorkshire. The proposal provoked a huge outcry because the site would be in the heart of 'Bronte Country', the setting for the novels of the famous literary sisters.

A broad opposition coalition formed which included local residents, businesses and several environmental groups (WWF, CPRE, RSPB, the Ramblers Association). At Flaight Hill and elsewhere, the main objections to wind farms focus on the:

- *visual impact* – they scar the countryside and may damage tourism
- *noise* – from the blades
- *inefficiency* – the industry is heavily dependent on government subsidy

Of these, the main reason for most planning refusals is their *visual impact.* Unfortunately, the windiest areas of Britain which are most suitable for the turbines are also areas of outstanding beauty – and countryside protection is a major environmental concern in Britain.

The slow development of the UK wind power sector illustrates the complex relationship between democracy and sustainable development. The national climate change strategy is being undermined by the opposition of local communities. Is this an example of self-interested 'NIMBYism', or does it underline the importance of strong grassroots democracy in protecting local environmental and economic interests?

See Department of Trade and Industry report: *http://www.dti.gov.uk/renew/condoc/* and the RCEP report *Energy – the Changing Climate* (*http://www.rcep.org.uk/energy.html*).

represent a victory for sustainable development. As the example of UK wind energy illustrates, local planning decisions may produce conflict between the democratically expressed preferences of a local community and the sustainable development strategy of the national government (see Box 10.6). More broadly, as the next chapter shows, elected governments frequently desist from implementing radical environmental initiatives such as regulating car use or imposing eco-taxes, for fear of upsetting the will of the majority at the next election.

Such dilemmas are in the nature of democracy, and they underpin a difference in emphasis between sustainable development and ecological modernisation. Sustainable development accepts the imperfections in democracy because it believes firmly in its potential to educate citizens to behave with more consideration towards the environment and to improve the quality of environmental policy-making. By contrast, ecological modernisation places greater trust in the capacity of technological innovation and the market place, rather than the wilfulness of democratic mechanisms, to bring about a sustainable society.

CRITICAL QUESTION 4
Does increased democracy and participation improve the quality of environmental governance?

CONCLUSION

Since the early 1990s, spurred on by the *Agenda 21* programme, governments have begun to change the way they approach environmental issues. Most have adopted a more strategic approach that at least genuflects in the direction of (very weak) sustainable development. The plethora of institutional and administrative reforms intended to improve integration and planning, and to encourage a wider democratic dialogue around the concept of sustainable development, have undoubtedly led some policy-makers to consider environmental issues more routinely. In short, there is evidence of a gradual shift away from the traditional paradigm. However, progress towards environmental governance is slow: most reforms are still in their infancy and have exerted only a limited impact on the way government actually operates. In particular, the weakness of environmental ministries, agencies and green plans has hampered efforts to improve the co-ordination of cross-sectoral environmental initiatives across government. It seems that, as Chapter 7 showed, there are many deep-seated obstacles to the successful implementation of sustainable development. Not least, with the political salience of environmental issues remaining low, few governments have been willing to provide strong, sustained leadership. Without such political leadership, sustainable development may promise to end the economy/environment trade-off but, in practice, policy continues to emerge from a sectoral administrative structure where economic growth is the priority, producer interests prevail and environmental considerations remain an afterthought.

Further reading and websites

There are surprisingly few good discussions of environmental governance. One place to start is the Brundtland Report (WCED 1987). Conceptual discussions can be found in Dryzek (1987, 1997), Paehlke and Torgerson (1990) and Jansen et al. (1998). Lafferty and Meadowcroft (2000a) provide a comparative assessment of progress in nine OECD countries towards implementing *Agenda 21*. Jordan (2001) analyses British efforts to achieve 'joined-up government', while European Communities (2000), Sbragia (2000) and Zito (2000) examine EU integration. Rosenbaum (1999) assesses recent reforms to the EPA. Mason (1999) is an interesting analysis of different attempts to democratise environmental decision-making.

Information about all aspects of EU environmental policy can be found on Environment Directorate website (*http://europa.eu.int/comm/environment/*). The European Environmental Agency website (*http://www.eea.eu. int/*) and the European Environment Information and Observation Network (EIONET) (*http://eionet.eea.eu.int/*) provide excellent links to national environmental ministries, agencies and institutions in most European nations and detailed information about the state of the environment in Europe. See also the US EPA (*http://www.epa.gov*), and Environment Canada (*http://www.ec.gc.ca/envhome.html*).

Notes

1. Detailed accounts of the institutional and administrative arrangements for environmental policy in most West and North European countries can be found in Andersen and Liefferink (1997a) and Hanf and Jansen (1998). For the USA, see Vig and Kraft (1999a).
2. This body was replaced after the September 1998 election by a new Commission for Ecologically Adjusted Economic Growth.
3. See Wood (1995) for an account of environmental impact assessment methodology.
4. See Andrews (1999) for an outline of risk assessment methods. Adams (1995) explores the concept of risk.
5. See Hanley and Spash (1993) for a balanced assessment of the use of CBA in environmental decision-making.
6. The decentralised Danish system is an exception (Andersen et al. 1998).
7. See Peterson and Bomberg (1999: ch. 7) and Sbragia (2000) for good introductory overviews of EU environmental policy, while Baker et al. (1997b), Zito (2000) and the special issue of the journal *Environment and Planning C: Government and Policy* 17(1) include more extensive, in-depth analyses.
8. Underpinning NEPP is a systems theory showing how closely the human and natural worlds are interlinked, and directing policy-makers to the source of problems, rather than the effects; i.e. traditional end-of-pipe solutions are to be replaced by preventive policies.
9. For example, World Bank (1997), OECD (1998) and DETR (1999). See also Bell and Morse (1999).
10. The openness of the inquiry process differs between countries: for example, it is open to a much wider range of interests in France than in Germany (Mason 1999: 77).

11

Policy instruments and implementation

Contents

KEY ISSUES

- What are the main environmental policy instruments?
- What are the strengths and weaknesses of regulatory and market-based instruments?
- How do national regulatory styles differ?
- Why are there so few market-based instruments?
- What policy instruments can be used to prevent climate change?

Chapter 10 assessed progress towards sustainable development by examining various ways in which governments have tried to build environmental considerations into the policy-making process. Another way of judging progress towards sustainable development is to examine the policy outputs that emerge from that process. A key element in the policy-making and implementation processes concerns the choice of policy instrument, or levers, by which a government tries to achieve its policy objectives. Policy instruments should be enforceable, effective and educative: they should change the behaviour of target groups, achieve the stated policy objectives and help spread environmental values throughout society. It is conventional to distinguish four broad types of policy instrument available for a government to use in pursuing its environmental objectives: regulation, voluntary action, government expenditure and market-based instruments (MBIs).[1] Trends in the use of different policy instruments provide some clues about progress towards sustainable development and ecological modernisation. A distinguishing characteristic of the traditional environmental policy paradigm was its reliance on regulatory, or 'command and control', instruments. During the 1970s and 1980s, new environmental legislation created an extensive regulatory framework in most countries, but as many environmental problems continued to worsen despite this growing regulatory 'burden', the use of regulation was increasingly criticised, particularly by economists, industrialists and right-wing politicians. Consequently, there has been growing support for MBIs, which are widely regarded as more efficient and effective than regulations. Ecological modernisation in particular is underpinned by an explicit assumption that the market is the best means of delivering sustainability. Hence a growing interest in MBIs may be one indicator of a general shift away from the traditional paradigm and, possibly, a shift towards ecological modernisation.

A central argument of this chapter is that the choice of policy instrument is only partly a 'technical' matter of selecting the instrument that offers the most efficient or effective means of delivering policy objectives. It is also a highly *political* process in which decisions are shaped by competing interests. Policy instruments are intended to alter the behaviour of producers and/or consumers, so it is hardly surprising that affected interests will mobilise resources to influence those choices. Indeed, political considerations have informed the way the 'command and control versus MBI' debate is often stylised as a choice between two sharply contrasting approaches when, in practice, the differences are not so clear-cut.

The first part of this chapter analyses the strengths and weaknesses of different policy instruments, concentrating on the central debate between regulation and MBIs. It also identifies some important contextual features which influence their implementation, such as variations in national regulatory styles. The second part provides a broad overview of climate change strategies in the energy and transport sectors – probably the most pressing and perplexing policy arena for contemporary policy-makers – to illustrate some of the issues raised in the first part of the chapter.

REGULATION AND REGULATORY STYLES

The case for regulation

Regulation is the most widely used instrument of environmental policy. Broadly defined, regulation involves any attempt by the government to influence the behaviour of businesses or citizens, but it is used here to refer to what many observers, rather pejoratively, call 'command and control' or 'coercive' regulation. It involves the government specifying the standards of pollution control that a process or product has to meet, and then using state officials, backed up by the legal system, to enforce its rules. Regulatory standards usually take one of three forms. *Ambient* standards place limits on the total concentration of pollutants permitted in a particular area, such as a street, river or bathing water. *Emission* standards limit what an individual source can emit, so the gases released from factories, exhaust emissions from vehicles and discharges of agricultural silage into rivers are all typically regulated in this way. *Design* standards require the use of a specific type of pollution-control technology or production process, such as a scrubber on a power station or a catalytic converter in a car, or the use of particular materials or products such as unleaded petrol. In addition, stringent controls limit the dumping of hazardous waste. Many chemicals such as DDT, which was once widely used as a pesticide, are completely banned or else their use is tightly controlled. Some regulations are aimed directly at the behaviour of individual citizens. Clean Air Acts have created urban smokeless zones where the burning of coal is banned, traffic-congested cities such as Florence and Athens limit the number of cars entering the city centre, while many local authorities require citizens to separate their household waste for recycling. Regulation is also the main instrument used by international regimes to deal with both common-sink problems (e.g. bans on CFCs and on dumping toxic waste at sea) and common-pool problems (the use of fishing quotas and bans on whaling).

Regulation is the policy instrument most associated with the traditional environmental paradigm. As the political salience of pollution rose during the 1970s, most governments concentrated their initial legislative responses on the large industrial polluters responsible for the bulk of many harmful emissions. As there were relatively few firms compared to consumers, they appeared easy to police; industry had the resources to invest in abatement and factory smoke-stacks and waste-pipes were highly visible symbols of pollution (Braadbaart 1998). The huge extant legislative programmes designed to achieve pollution abatement still make regulation the most widely used environmental policy instrument. In the USA, for example, eight new regulatory programmes, or major amendments to existing ones, were introduced between 1980 and 1994; the 1990 amendments to the Clean Air Act alone required the Environmental Protection Agency to write 55 new regulations (Rosenbaum 1997b: 145). The EU, since the late 1960s, has introduced over 600 regulations directly affecting the environment (Haigh 1998). Environmental policy today is still primarily concerned with the content and implementation of regulations.

Regulation has an obvious appeal to policy-makers. It appears to offer precision, predictability and effectiveness: an exact standard is set, the regulator and regulated both know what is expected of them and enforcement is ensured by a regulatory agency backed up by the force of law. Regulations can be administratively efficient, especially when a substance or an activity is completely banned, as they do not require complete information about a problem. Assuming there is a high level of compliance, they can also be inexpensive as there is no need to investigate each individual case. As the application of uniform standards and rules means that, in theory, all polluters are treated identically, regulations are widely perceived by producers and consumers as equitable. The political, judicial and administrative back-up they receive from the state should make regulations reasonably immune from manipulation and enhance their public legitimacy. There are countless examples of 'successful' regulations, ranging from the world's first comprehensive air pollution control legislation, the Clean Air Act 1956, which dramatically improved air quality in British cities, to the Montreal Protocol banning CFC production in developed countries.

However, the use of regulations has come under increasing attack from many quarters. There has been a widespread neo-liberal backlash against the 'regulatory burden' which informed the efforts by the Reagan and Thatcher governments during the 1980s, and later inspired the Congressional Republican Party's 'Contract with America' in the mid-1990s which attempted to make a bonfire of 'unnecessary' regulations. Most advocates of wholesale deregulation had little sympathy for environmentalism as a political movement. This neo-liberal opposition to environmentalism was strongest in the USA where its populist rhetoric chimed with complaints by industry about an excessive regulatory burden (Rosenbaum 1997b). Vitriolic criticism was heaped upon the many inadequacies of the EPA, the impact on competitiveness of 'unnecessary' regulations and the cost to the taxpayer (see Box 10.2). One rhetorical success of the neo-liberal backlash was to gain wide acceptance of the term 'command and control' in preference to 'regulation'. In practice, as is shown below, regulations are rarely applied in an overtly coercive way, so 'command and control' is a misnomer. Nevertheless, it represents a clever political achievement; after all, how many people will opt for coercion over the 'free' market (Dryzek 1997: 114)?

Not all the criticism of regulation was so partisan. Despite the ever-expanding volume, reach and stringency of environmental regulations in most developed countries, it was clear that the overall environmental record nevertheless remained poor. Research showed that pollution control policies introduced during the 1970s in the USA, UK, Germany and elsewhere had failed to deliver the standards, targets and procedures set out in the legislation (Weale 1992: 17). There were isolated examples of improved environmental performance, and some countries certainly performed better than others, but generally it seemed that the huge resources invested in regulatory programmes had disappointing outcomes. One high-profile example was the US Superfund programme for decontaminating toxic waste sites where costs have multiplied owing to the 'extensive litigation involved in determining responsibility for clean-ups, wasteful spending on elaborate remediation plans, and long delays in implementation' (Vig and Kraft 1999b: 376). In the early 1990s, the estimated cost of clearing up each site was $30 million, with a total cost in excess of $100 billion, or $1,000 per household (Smith 1995: 178). Yet, with clean-up completed on only a small proportion of contaminated sites, Superfund has, arguably, failed to achieve its most basic objective.

Broadly speaking, the criticisms of regulation fall into two categories: that it is inefficient and ineffective. The alleged *inefficiency* of regulation will be discussed in the section on MBIs below (pp. 295–7). The claim that it is *ineffective* is essentially concerned with the implementation deficit – defined here as a failure to achieve policy objectives – that characterises so much environmental regulation. Ineffective regulation can be explained both by the incapacity of the state to monitor and enforce regulations and by variations in national regulatory styles.

CRITICAL QUESTION 1

How persuasive is the political case against 'command and control' regulations?

Implementation deficit and state failure

Regulatory regimes are often weak. The government, or a state agency such as the EPA, is usually responsible for the monitoring, compliance and enforcement of environmental regulation. These activities can be very costly and time-consuming, so implementation problems may arise when inadequate funding prevents regulatory agencies from carrying them out properly. In the USA, there is no doubt that personnel and budgetary shortages have severely affected the ability of many agencies to implement environmental policy (Kraft and Vig 1999: 17–19; Rosenbaum 1999: 169). As one new environmental programme followed another, Congress frequently underestimated the workload generated by new regulations that produced unrealistic deadlines, excessive administrative rules and virtually unattainable programme objectives (Rosenbaum 1999: 172). However, the full explanation for the underfunding was more pernicious: the Reagan administration deliberately sought to reduce the power of the EPA and other natural resource agencies by slashing their operating budgets (Kraft and Vig 1999: 17). Similarly, when the Conservative government set up the new Environment Agency in the UK, there was widespread concern that its budget was too small to enact its wide-ranging responsibilities. Implementation problems can be particularly acute where responsibility for implementation is passed down from one level of government to another. In the USA, the states have complained loudly and bitterly about the financial and administrative burden caused by the implementation of federal environmental regulations, such as the need to issue thousands of industrial permits required by the US Clean Water Act 1990. Rabe (1999: 47) notes that the mayor of Columbus, Ohio, estimated that the cost to his city of complying with fourteen major environmental mandates between 1991 and 2000 would be $1 billion, or $856 per family. In the EU, despite the heavy programme of environmental regulation from the mid-1970s onwards, there was no means of monitoring its impact in individual member states until a European Environment Agency was eventually set up in 1994, and there remains no environmental inspectorate with powers of enforcement.

In less developed countries, infrastructural problems may be even more deep-seated. The southern member states – Greece, Italy, Spain and Portugal – are generally slower at transposing EU environmental directives into national legislation and, more importantly, are rather lax about enforcing them (Lewanski 1998; Font and Morata 1998; Spanou 1998). In part this failure reflects an administrative incapacity to deal with the costly burden of EU directives. Whereas North European states have generally been able to adapt existing management structures to respond to specific directives, in the absence of any tradition of environmental control Southern European states have had to build new institutions and structures. Some observers also refer, rather controversially, to a 'Mediterranean syndrome', meaning a civic culture that sanctions non-cooperative and non-compliant behaviour and impedes the enforcement of regulative policies (La Spina and Sciortino 1993; Ward et al. 1997).

Implementation deficit and national regulatory styles

Most systems of regulatory control face a fundamental administrative dilemma. One of the strengths of regulation is that standards and rules should be applied uniformly across an industry; in practice, there are strong pressures undermining this principle. Pollution control, in particular, is a highly complex process with an informational asymmetry favouring the polluter which may oblige regulatory agencies to build close relationships with those whom they regulate simply to gain an understanding of each situation. Once a relationship is established, officials will often bargain with the polluter over targets, timetables and investment in new technologies. The regulator will make judgements and exercise discretion about whether to enforce rules fully, or whether to negotiate compliance, taking into account individual local circumstances such as culpability, negligence and the likelihood of future compliance (Weale 1992: 17–18). The dilemma is that the benefits of flexibility have to be weighed against the costs of diluting standards so that slippage may occur between policy and implementation. The exact way in which this dilemma is played out may depend on the regulatory style prevailing in each country (Richardson 1982).

One characteristic of a national regulatory style is the extent to which regulation relies on judicial or on administrative procedures. The approach to environmental control pursued in many European countries is primarily formal and legalistic. In France the aim is to establish clear legal frameworks and procedures, backed up by state agencies and the judiciary (Buller 1998: 70). Germany and Austria both have a preference for detailed command-and-control regulations imposing uniform emissions standards and setting clear rules (Lauber 1997; Pehle 1997). In principle, a judicial approach should minimise the opportunity for regulatory officials to exercise discretion in the way they implement policy in individual cases. By contrast, where environmental control is pervaded by administrative procedures, as in Britain, the style is more informal, accommodative and technocratic (Lowe and Flynn 1989). Legislation tends to be broad and discretionary with an avoidance of, indeed, a distaste for, legislatively prescribed standards and quality objectives:

> It has long been traditional to rely upon, where practicable, the characteristics of the local natural environment as a sensible disposal and dispersal route for potential pollutants. This underlying approach in theory requires that agencies should be given complete independence and discretion to determine, in the light of local circumstances, the degree of seriousness of a potential pollutant and the appropriate control measures.

(Macrory 1986: 8)

A second feature of any regulatory style is the way environmental policy is enforced: some systems are confrontational, others more cooperative. Again, the British approach emerges as distinctive. In a comparison of British and American environmental practice, Vogel noted that, despite key similarities in political and cultural traditions, common environmental conflicts and even shared organisational responses, there are sharp differences between environmental controls in the United Kingdom and the United States, 'each nation controls industrial emissions in much the same manner that it regulates everything else . . . Americans rely heavily on formal rules, often enforced in the face of strong opposition from the institutions affected by them, while the British continue to rely on flexible standards and voluntary compliance – including, in many cases, self-regulation'

(Vogel 1986: 77). The British, because they are 'reluctant to adopt rules and regulations with which they cannot guarantee compliance' (ibid.) make regulations in such a way that officials can negotiate arrangements with firms that will not be disallowed by their superiors or the courts. Consequently, government officials seek to 'persuade' industrial and farming interests of the need to modify their behaviour and, when laws are broken, officials usually choose not to prosecute. By contrast, in the USA there is a greater willingness to resort to the courts to prosecute polluters and enforce compliance. However, the USA should not be taken as setting the norm. The existence of a strongly legalistic administrative culture does not necessarily imply that laws will be enforced rigidly with frequent recourse to judicial action. In Austria, for example, producer interests are often accommodated so that criminal courts play a negligible role, allowing most polluters either to go unpunished or to pay insignificant fines (Lauber 1997: 96).

The concept of regulatory style inevitably involves some generalisation and should be applied advisedly. Vogel's characterisation of the USA as formalistic and confrontational was based primarily on a study of just two policy areas, air pollution and land-use; by contrast, US water policy has been far less confrontational (Smith 1995: 111–12). Nevertheless, if the idea of a regulatory style has some resonance, one obvious question arises: which regulatory style produces the best environmental outcomes?

The main criticism of the British style is that its extreme flexibility allows the polluter to escape a tight regulatory embrace. The British preference for administrative discretion over judicial interpretation, combined with the bureaucratic obsession for secrecy, creates the perfect conditions for 'regulatory capture'. The frequent use of voluntary agreements and unquantified standards, and the way secret site-level negotiations between polluter and inspector remain at the heart of industrial pollution control, provide evidence of regulatory capture (Skea and Smith 1998: 268). The notion of the 'best practicable means' (BPM) of controlling pollution, or requirements such as one directing conservation and planning authorities to take into account the needs of agriculture and forestry (under Section 37 of the Countryside Act 1968), have ensured that regulatory authorities are sensitive to the economic and practical constraints that private organisations face. Indeed, the latest principle of pollution control – best available technique not entailing excessive costs (BATNEEC) – enshrines this idea. Perhaps not surprisingly, in the early 1980s Vogel (1986) could not find a single corporate executive in a British-based firm who could recall an occasion when his firm had been required to do anything it regarded as unreasonable. Put differently, regulators accepted too readily the standards and practices of the regulated (Richardson et al. 1983).

So, does a more formalistic regulatory style provide better protection for the environment? Vogel (1986: 23), whilst not claiming that British environmental controls were particularly effective, argued that the emphasis on voluntary compliance had proved no less effective than the more adversarial and legalistic approach adopted by American policy-makers. For although US standards were higher, the level of compliance was much lower. Industries complained that they could not afford to implement strict emission standards. The EPA, constrained by limited resources, frequently took only the most obvious and gross violators to court. This more conflictual style generated bad feeling between the enforcement agencies and industry which, in turn, encouraged further flouting of the law. Higher American air pollution standards encountered greater compliance problems, resulting in a serious implementation deficit, whereas the more cooperative relations between regulator and regulated in Britain ensured that the lower standards were at least implemented effectively. Vogel concluded that different national regulatory styles have little impact on policy outcomes.

An alternative lesson might be that some kind of halfway house is desirable between these two flawed regulatory systems. With this in mind, it is interesting that membership of the EU, with its high volume of environmental regulation, has produced some convergence of national regulatory styles amongst member states. Certainly, since Vogel's research in the early 1980s, Britain has adopted stricter standards, uniform targets, explicit monitoring and review mechanisms and reduced discretion for local officials across a wide range of environmental matters (Jordan 1998c). Conversely, in 1991 the EU modelled its new Integrated Pollution Prevention Control directive closely on the recently adopted British system of integrated pollution control. The directive's concept of best available techniques (BAT) represented a compromise between the German best available technology and the British BATNEEC, although the emphasis on including factors such as the management, maintenance and cost of the technology suggested a particularly strong British imprint (Skea and Smith 1998).

Although contextual factors, such as differing regulatory styles, may influence the effectiveness of regulations, the wide-ranging criticism of command-and-control methods has encouraged policy-makers to cast around for alternative policy instruments to achieve environmental policy goals. The following sections provide brief accounts of voluntary action and government expenditure, and then a more detailed examination of market-based instruments.

CRITICAL QUESTION 2
Does the effectiveness of regulations depend on the national regulatory style?

VOLUNTARY ACTION

Voluntary action involves individuals or organisations doing things to protect the environment that are neither required by law nor encouraged by financial incentive. Voluntary action is probably the main way in which, by changing their lifestyles, most individual citizens can make a contribution to the sustainable society. Individuals can engage in a wide range of voluntary activities, including green consumerism (see Chapter 8), recycling, ethical investment and voluntary conservation work. The government can encourage voluntary action through a range of communicative strategies such as information campaigns setting out the environmental benefits of recycling drink containers or newspapers, extending citizen rights to environmental information and making it easier for individuals and organisations to take polluters to court.

Businesses may also choose to give greater consideration to the environmental impact of their activities, albeit that the incentive is often to increase profits. Governments can actively encourage greater take-up of Environmental Management and Audit Systems (EMAS), standards such as ISO14001 and eco-labelling (see Chapter 8). Probably the most significant instrument is the environmental 'voluntary agreement', which is a commitment undertaken by firms or trade associations in consultation or negotiation with a public authority, and usually recognised by that agency, although normally there will be no sanctions if commitments are not fulfilled. Environmental agreements have become increasingly common since the late 1980s: there are over 2,000 (including site-level agreements) in Japan and growing numbers in Canada, New Zealand and the USA. There were well over 300 voluntary agreements within the EU by 1997, although Germany and the Netherlands accounted for around two-thirds of the total (EEA 1997b). While the Dutch have concluded agreements, or 'covenants', in almost all policy areas as part of the NEPP (see Chapter 10), most countries have just a handful of agreements concentrated in a few core polluting areas, notably the chemical, agriculture, tourism and transport sectors. Some environmental agreements represent a co-ordinated industry response to a legislative development: for example, all EU member states have concluded agreements that implement the European Commission directive on packaging waste (see Box 7.7).

Environmental agreements have several potential advantages. They offer a flexible and cost-effective strategy to achieve policy objectives because they give target groups (i.e. producers) the freedom to decide how best to achieve goals and they require little or no 'policing' by the state. Voluntary agreements may produce constructive co-operation between the state and industry along the lines of ecological modernisation, leading to changes in the environmental values and behaviour of both state officials and producers. Nevertheless, voluntary agreements have their weaknesses too. They are often unambitious, involving commitments at the level of the lowest common denominator acceptable to the least enthusiastic signatories to the agreement. An industry will often only establish a voluntary agreement as a means of forestalling the threat of a tougher regulation or eco-tax, so it is likely to set easier targets and more relaxed deadlines than the government might impose by other means.

Voluntary agreements are also not backed up by mechanisms for enforcing compliance. The absence of sanctions may make implementation very difficult, with free-riding a real possibility. For example, a survey found that the British 'Making a Corporate Commitment' agreement to encourage energy efficiency had over 2,000 signatory firms, but only 67 per cent had even taken the first steps towards drafting an energy policy (ENDS 1997: 7–8). Indeed, it seems that the effectiveness of voluntary agreements is also influenced by regulatory styles. The British voluntarist tradition seems to co-exist with an entrenched bias in favour of corporate interests, nurtured by the continued domination of closed policy communities in key sectors. Nevertheless, while voluntarism inevitably involves some compromise, it does not have to be as sympathetic to corporate interests as it is in Britain. The discussion of the NEPP in Chapter 10 showed how it too has nurtured self-regulation within Dutch industry, but as a means to implement ambitious pollution reduction targets negotiated with particular sectors. The advantage of this approach is that it allows individual sectors to choose the means but not the objectives of policy. Thus the Dutch regulatory style is emblematic of ecological modernisation as it involves close but transparent co-operation between the state and industry, resulting in a framework characterised by a combination of high standards and tough target-setting, but with the flexibility to respond to individual needs and local circumstances. That said, even in the Netherlands it seems unlikely that sustainable development can be achieved through industry voluntary agreements alone.

GOVERNMENT EXPENDITURE

The use of government expenditure to achieve environmental goals may help where the costs of taking remedial action are too great for individual producers or citizens to bear (Jacobs 1991: ch. 13). The classic form of government expenditure is a subsidy which might encourage producers to buy cleaner technologies, farmers to shift to less intensive forms of agriculture, or individuals to insulate their homes. Some forms of voluntary action may also benefit from government investment in basic infrastructure, such as the provision of recycling facilities or public transport, that must exist before people will recycle bottles and newspapers, or reduce car usage. Governments can subsidise nascent green industries such as paper recycling, waste incineration and wind energy. Subsidies are, however, an inefficient means of changing behaviour, notably because they cannot discriminate between people who were going to do something (e.g. fit loft insulation) anyway, and those who were only persuaded to do so by the subsidy. Even so, there is scope for governments to adopt a far more ambitious approach to public expenditure in the cause of sustainable development. For example, in many countries in the northern hemisphere, a massive publicly funded home energy conservation programme could create many jobs, reskill workers, reduce greenhouse gas emissions, slash domestic energy bills and even prove popular with the electorate – truly a win–win strategy. However, even though money can be saved through reduced welfare payments and higher tax revenues from the newly created jobs, the sheer cost of this kind of massive public works programme obviously limits the potential of government expenditure as a policy instrument.

MARKET-BASED INSTRUMENTS

The case for market-based instruments

It will be recalled that, apart from its alleged ineffectiveness, regulation has also been criticised for its *inefficiency* as a means of achieving policy objectives (Turner et al. 1994: 144). Where a regulation imposes a technology or emissions standard on individual factories then the government regulator will need to use up resources to obtain information from the polluter in order to agree, monitor and enforce these rules. Some polluters will also find it easier than others to reduce pollution. Rather than impose a single standard that all polluters have to meet, it might be more efficient to concentrate effort on those who can reduce their pollution most cheaply. In short, regulations provide no incentive for polluters to reduce their pollution any further than that required by law. MBIs are intended to provide that incentive.

Market-based instruments aim to prevent market failure by applying the polluter pays principle (PPP). Market failure occurs when environmental resources are over-exploited because of open access to goods whose market price does not incorporate the external costs of using those environmental resources. The PPP holds that the price of a good or service should fully reflect the total cost of production, including the use of public goods such as air, water or land for emissions. An MBI internalises these external costs into the price of a good (Turner et al. 1994: 145) by means of an explicit government intervention in the market.[2] The MBIs with most potential are eco-taxes and tradeable permits (see Box 11.1), although the refundable deposit, such as the returnable deposit imposed on most Danish drink containers, can also be an effective means of rewarding environmental concern and punishing neglect.

Eco-taxes are levied on pollution or on the goods whose production generates pollution. Direct effluent charges are most appropriate where pollution is concentrated, such as chemical emissions from a power station or factory discharges in a river. Where pollution is widely dispersed, as with farm waste containing fertiliser nitrates or carbon dioxide from vehicle exhausts, it may be easier to tax the source of the emission, namely the fertiliser containing nitrate or the fuel containing carbon

11.1 Market-based instruments

A market-based instrument internalises into the price of a good or product the external costs to the environment of producing and using it.

Eco-taxes

User charges	Fees payable for treatment, collection and disposal costs of wastes or other environmental administration
Emission charges	Charges on the discharge of pollutants into air, water or soil, and on noise generation (i.e. directly linked to quantity and quality of pollutant), e.g. tax on sulphur emissions (France), water effluent charges (Australia, Canada, France, Germany, the Netherlands), tax on aircraft noise (the Netherlands, Switzerland)

Product charges	Charges on harmful products, e.g. fertilisers (Norway, Sweden), pesticides (Denmark, Finland), leaded petrol (widespread), plastic carrier bags (Denmark), batteries (Belgium, Sweden)
Tradeable permits	Environmental quotas or pollution ceilings that are tradeable, e.g. sulphur emissions (USA), fishing quotas (New Zealand)
Deposit-refunds	Deposit paid on a polluting product which is refunded if the product is returned to an authorised point after use (i.e. to avoid/minimise pollution), e.g. beverage containers (widespread)

Sources: Turner et al. (1994); OECD (1997).

(Jacobs 1991: 141). The rationale for eco-taxes is that the government decides the ambient standard of pollution it wants to achieve and sets a tax at a level that will achieve that outcome. In contrast to a regulatory standard, a tax allows the individual polluter the flexibility to decide how (and how far) it will reduce pollution. Those firms which can cut pollution relatively cheaply will pursue abatement further than those for whom it is relatively expensive (who will pay the tax). Thus eco-taxes are more efficient than regulation because the same pollution abatement should be achieved for a lower overall cost to industry. Moreover, whereas regulation offers no incentive for firms to reduce pollution below the ambient standard, eco-taxes provide a constant incentive for polluters to reduce pollution further in order to reduce their tax bill (Pearce et al. 1989; Pearce and Turner 1990).

Whereas an eco-tax is a price-based mechanism, a *tradeable permit* is a rights-based mechanism that combines regulation with a financial incentive. Again, the basic idea is very simple. The government calculates the overall level of emissions for an area and sets a target that either

11.2 Eco-taxes and the double dividend

All governments are currently interested in fiscal reform. One key idea involves shifting the burden of taxation from environmental 'goods', such as enterprise, employment and savings, on to environmental 'bads', such as pollution and inefficient use of energy and resources. Proponents argue that a double dividend is possible: eco-taxes can protect the environment and, by removing inefficient subsidies and tax distortions, they can also stimulate employment, although the existence of the double dividend is hotly debated amongst economists (O'Riordan 1997).

Recent examples of taxes, or tax packages, that apply these principles include the following:

Finland Cuts to income and labour taxes in 1997 were partly compensated by a landfill tax and increased energy taxes.

Germany The first of a three-stage increase in energy taxes was introduced in April 1999, with increases in mineral oil taxes on gas, heating oil, diesel and petrol, and a new electricity tax, together calculated to raise DM 8.4 billion in its first year. The eventual aim is to reduce the social security contributions of employers and employees from 42.3 per cent to below 40 per cent of gross wages.

Britain All revenue from a climate change levy on British industry introduced in 2001 will be recycled to business through a cut in employers' National Insurance contributions and government support for energy efficiency measures. It is estimated that the levy, together with associated voluntary agreements with industry, will reduce carbon emissions by at least 5 million tonnes/year by 2010.

corresponds to that total, or is lower. This target level is divided into individual emission permits, each giving the owner the right to release a specific volume of emissions. These permits are then sold or auctioned to polluters.[3] The government sanctions a market in the permits, which gives firms an incentive to reduce pollution and sell any surplus permits for a profit, while firms that do nothing to reduce pollution will at least pay something towards the cost of environmental damage. Permits offer firms the flexibility to reduce pollution in the most cost-effective way, whilst also giving the government the opportunity to cut the overall level of emissions by withdrawing permits, buying them back or cutting their entitlement.

Apart from the efficiency argument, proponents claim that MBIs have further advantages over other policy instruments. One is that they raise revenues which can be reinvested in environmentally beneficial ways: for example, money from water pollution taxes in France, Germany and the Netherlands is reinvested in water quality improvement (Andersen 1994). Taxes have a potential educative and communicative role by providing a signal to producers and consumers that they should change their behaviour. Many experts also claim that eco-taxation offers a potential 'double dividend', by delivering both environmental protection and additional jobs (see Box 11.2). Amongst several administrative benefits, it is claimed that compliance will be cheaper and more effective because the tax is gathered by the existing revenue collection framework instead of being policed by infrequent on-site inspection. Lastly, MBIs, along with the voluntary agreement, are the preferred tools of ecological modernisation.

Yet MBIs remain the exception rather than a rule in environmental policy. Tradeable permits are particularly rare. The USA has led the way since the mid-1970s with several small-scale experiments arising from various Clean Air Acts. The biggest scheme to date, which underpins a major drive to prevent acid rain, saw the introduction of a permit system in 1995 to control sulphur dioxide emissions. Each source (usually a coal-burning power station) was issued with permits equal to a percentage of its historic emissions level, with permits reduced to the overall emissions target level in 2000. It is anticipated that savings over direct regulations will reach several billion dollars each year (Freeman 1999: 202). Tradeable permits have been used in Australia and New Zealand to regulate fish stocks, but they are almost unknown in Europe. Eco-taxes have been around for a long time: water charges were introduced in France in 1969 and the Netherlands in 1972, and noise fees on aircraft in the mid-1970s in France, Germany, Japan and the UK (Braadbaart 1998). Yet they are still used sparingly. One report found an average of just twelve eco-taxes in each OECD country (OECD 1997). The total tax revenues of EU member states raised from environmental taxes (on energy, transport and pollution) was only 6.7 per cent in 1997 (EEA 2000b: 2). Moreover, many of those taxes were imposed primarily for revenue-raising reasons rather than to shape environmental behaviour. Admittedly the use of eco-taxes did increase steadily through the 1990s, particularly in the Nordic countries, Belgium, Britain and the Netherlands, but they still play a relatively minor role in environmental policy.

Here then is a paradox. There seems to be a convincing economic case that MBIs are more efficient and, possibly, more effective at achieving environmental outcomes than conventional regulatory methods. Influential international organisations such as the OECD (1989, 1997) and the EU in its fifth EAP (European Commission 1992), and national green tax commissions, as in Norway, have strongly recommended wider use of MBIs. Yet, there has still been only limited movement towards green tax reform and tradeable permits are notable mainly by their absence. How can this paradox be explained? The following discussions of the practical and political obstacles to MBIs suggest that the case in favour of them is less persuasive than it first appears.

Weaknesses in the economic case for market-based instruments

One problem with the MBI v. regulation debate is that it often involves a highly stylised and sharply distinguished comparison of perfect 'laboratory' MBIs with flawed real-life regulations. In practice, MBIs encounter implementation difficulties that are either ignored or glossed over in the economics textbooks.

One common claim is that, compared to regulations, MBIs will not encounter the informational asymmetries that force regulators to use resources to acquire vital information from polluters about their behaviour. Yet economic theory places great importance on setting a tax at the correct level; in particular, that it is set sufficiently high to offer a real incentive for firms to reduce pollution and hence to maximise the potential efficiency of the tax. However, to ensure such accuracy the regulator will need detailed technical information which, as with regulations, may only be obtainable from the polluter. Moreover, in theory, the need to monitor performance and update assumptions about pollution levels, demand elasticities and the relative value of goods, might oblige the regulator to make frequent adjustments to the tax level; in practice this would be costly and disruptive to both industry and government planning. Crucially, if a proposed tax is perceived as too onerous, then the government may encounter strong resistance from businesses, trade unions or consumers. Not surprisingly, eco-taxes are therefore often set below the optimum level which will reduce efficiency gains, as with French water pollution charges (Andersen 1994), and limit their effectiveness, as with fertiliser taxes in Sweden and Norway which, at just 10 per cent of the product price, have had little effect on sales (Eckerberg 1997: 31). In practice, the environmental benefits of earmarked taxes may not come from persuading polluting firms or consumers to change behaviour but from investing the revenues raised in environmentally beneficial ways, such as subsidising firms to adopt cleaner technologies (Andersen 1994; Hahn 1996).

Similarly, the case for MBIs seems to have been 'developed in an imaginary world where market solutions are self-enforcing and therefore require little or no policing' (Braadbaart 1998: 143). The flaws of real-world regulations are compared to apparently perfect textbook MBIs, but MBIs encounter implementation problems too. It is unlikely that all polluters will be 'honest' citizens. After all, if polluters are prepared to ignore regulatory standards when they think they can avoid detection, then surely they may also cheat or lie in order to avoid taxes? The introduction of a landfill tax on waste in Britain in 1996, for example, led to a huge increase in illegal fly tipping of waste materials in order to avoid paying duties. Thus eco-taxes still need to be policed. Although the responsibility for this task may fall to the established revenue collection system of a finance ministry rather than a regulatory agency, any savings made are likely to be small. Similarly, a tradeable permit system also needs to be monitored by a regulatory agency to ensure that firms do not exceed their permitted emissions levels.

These technical and practical reservations are given greater credence by the inconclusive empirical evidence about the performance of MBIs, many of which have simply not been subjected to proper evaluation (EEA 1996; Hahn 1996). The evidence supporting the case for emissions trading is thinnest. Hahn (1996) reports that in the USA the limited use of emissions trading has generated considerable cost savings for firms, yet these have been achieved with very little actual trading of permits, so the savings realised fall well short of their full potential. There is little evidence of greater effectiveness as the programmes have had 'little or no net change in the level of emissions relative to the emissions that would have resulted with less flexible regulation' (Hahn 1996: 137). However, a comprehensive assessment of the first three years of the US sulphur emissions trading system suggests that significant cuts in both emissions and costs have been achieved (Ellerman et al. 2000). Nevertheless, compared to regulations, whilst tradeable permits can save firms money, as yet there is only limited evidence that they will be noticeably better at protecting the environment.

There are, however, several examples of successful eco-taxes. Dutch water pollution charges have reduced organic emissions into waterways at low cost and encouraged firms to introduce cleaner technologies, although similar schemes in France and Germany have had mixed results (Andersen 1994). Swedish taxes on sulphur dioxide and nitrogen oxide have produced significant emission reductions (EEA 1996: 31). However, the verdict is not always clear-cut. During the 1990s, many countries introduced tax differentiation between leaded and unleaded petrol to encourage consumers to shift to unleaded petrol but, as the tax coincided with new regulations requiring petrol stations to supply unleaded fuel and new emission standards for motor vehicles requiring catalytic converters, it is difficult to disentangle the precise effect of this tax. On balance, it is likely that the tax differentials hastened a trend that would, eventually, have happened anyway (leaded petrol was eventually banned throughout the EU in 2000). Overall, the efficiency advantages of MBIs over regulation, although real, are probably less significant than many economics textbooks claim (Box 11.3).

11.3　Some successful eco-taxes

Swedish sulphur tax
The introduction of this tax in 1991 resulted in a reduction of the sulphur content of fuel oils by almost 40 per cent beyond the legal standard. The sulphur content of light oils is now below 0.1 per cent on average (below the legal limit of 0.2 per cent) and the tax also stimulated emission abatement measures in combustion plants.
(OECD 1997)

Ozone-depleting chemicals tax in the USA
A tax of $1.37 per pound in 1989 was increased to $5.35 in 1995, and applied to eight, then to twenty ozone-depleting chemicals (excluding those used in feedstuffs or recycled in manufacture). It generated revenues of $1 billion by 1994. The combination of the tax regulations agreed in the Montreal Protocol and government financing of research into substitutes resulted in significant reductions in overall CFC production.
(Gee 1997)

Water pollution charges in the Netherlands
Earmarked water effluent charges have been highly cost-effective because they (a) provided an incentive to polluters to control discharges and (b) generated revenues that were used to subsidise firms investing in pollution control technologies.
(Andersen 1994)

The politics of market-based instruments

Several political obstacles also limit the wider use of MBIs. Policymakers are apprehensive about MBIs. Bureaucracies tend to be conservative institutions which prefer tried and trusted mechanisms such as regulations. They want concrete examples of success before they are prepared to experiment with new techniques, so the inconclusive evidence about MBIs does little to dispel such apprehension. Nevertheless, these reservations are diminishing as the demonstration effect of wider application and successful lesson-drawing is slowly overcoming bureaucratic reservations (Hahn 1996: 153). MBIs also fall foul of the administrative fragmentation identified in Chapter 7. This point can be illustrated by the issue of hypothecation. An environment ministry might wish to raise revenue from a hypothecated, or earmarked, eco-tax which can be reinvested directly in environmental 'goods', perhaps by funding a subsidy to encourage the development of wind power. However, finance ministries usually dislike earmarked taxes because hypothecation undermines the fundamental principle that tax-based programmes of public expenditure never relate directly to tax payments by citizens, as such a system would be unworkable (see O'Riordan 1997). Yet, significantly, even the staunch opposition to hypothecation of the UK Treasury Department has weakened, as illustrated by plans to allow local authorities to retain the revenues from new car-parking and congestion charges for direct investment in public transport improvement schemes.

Some environmental groups offer the ethical objection that, by putting a price on the environment, MBIs effectively allow firms or individuals to buy the right to carry on polluting. Deep green perspectives certainly find this idea repugnant. Yet MBIs are little different from regulations which, by imposing an emissions standard, are effectively granting a right to pollute up to a certain level – free of charge! Indeed, MBIs at least invoke the polluter pays principle by requiring the polluter to pay some of the costs of environmental damage.

A more persuasive ethical objection concerns the potential inequity, or regressive impact, of MBIs. By raising the price of some environmentally sensitive goods such as water or energy, eco-taxes discriminate against lower income groups because a larger share of their disposable income goes on these basic needs than is spent by higher income groups. For example, it has been estimated that a Danish water consumption tax introduced in 1994 would cost an extra 0.38 per cent of the salaries of the lowest income group, but only 0.14 per cent of the highest income group (OECD 1997: 39). An illustration of the political sensitivity surrounding the regressive nature of eco-taxes was a rebellion by British Conservative backbench MPs in the mid-1990s that prevented their own government from raising value added tax on domestic fuel from 8 per cent to 17.5 per cent. Consequently, when eco-taxes are levied on items of basic need, there are strong ethical and pragmatic grounds for taking action to offset their regressive impact. One option is to return the revenue raised by the eco-tax directly to low-income groups, perhaps through cuts in income tax or increased welfare payments. The Dutch small energy users' tax sets a tax-free threshold of energy use which ensures that average energy users will be no worse off under the tax, but that higher and lower energy users in each income bracket will be respectively worse and better off. It seems that this transparent 'fairness' gained public acceptance for the tax, although it helped that it was not set at a very high level (EEA 1996: 37).

Active political support for MBIs is also weak, not least amongst two constituencies – right-wing politicians and businesses – who might appear to have most affinity to the market rhetoric of the environmental economists who advocate MBIs so enthusiastically. Many expressions of support for MBIs from the neo-liberal right are rather half-hearted and even disingenuous. They argue that MBIs are attractive because they represent a counterpoint to regulation and reflect the language of the market, but neo-liberals are driven primarily by their dislike of regulations rather than any support for environmental protection. The British Conservative government declared it would 'make use of economic instruments where possible, rather than regulation' (HM Government 1994), but this pro-market rhetoric was, in practice, a recipe for inaction. While the government's deregulatory zeal led to many 'unnecessary' regulations being removed, the only genuine eco-taxes introduced by the Conservatives between 1992 and 1997 were a discriminatory tax on leaded petrol and a landfill tax. There was little enthusiasm for MBIs in either ministerial or bureaucratic circles. A commitment to MBIs in preference to regulation is worthless if a government has little interest in taking measures of any sort to protect the environment.

Nor do MBIs find much support amongst the business community. Again, this might appear strange as, in theory, industry should benefit from the greater cost efficiency of MBIs. Yet proposals for new eco-taxes are typically met by fierce industrial resistance (Andersen et al. 1998; Kasa 2000). The most common business objection is that eco-taxes increase business costs and reduce international competitiveness. Indeed, some businesses prefer regulation to market incentives, notably where a regulatory agency has been so effectively 'captured' by the industry that it will act in the interests of the producers, perhaps by helping to exclude new entrants into a market. Leading companies might regard the replacement of existing regulations by an eco-tax as a potential threat to their market position by removing a barrier against the entry of new firms (although tradeable permits, when allocated by grandfathering to established firms, act as a barrier to entry because new firms have to purchase pollution permits to enter the market). Moreover, whereas a regulation requires a company to make only those environmental improvements necessary to meet the required standard, a tax or charge is levied on all its discharges, not just those exceeding the standard, making it more onerous (albeit supposedly more efficient) for many firms (Jacobs 1996b: 121).

In practice, the typical response of business is to resist *any* form of imposition on their activities, whether tax or regulation. If change is seen as inevitable, an industry, provided it is sufficiently organised, may offer a voluntary agreement as a means of preventing or delaying a regulation or MBI, in the hope that the government will regard it as quicker and less costly than legislation or taxation. If the path of self-regulation is closed, then industry will lobby for the instrument – whether regulation or MBI – that better suits its self-interest.

To summarise, the relative scarcity of MBIs is less puzzling than at first appears. The theoretical case for MBIs, that they are more efficient and effective at delivering environmental policy objectives than regulations, has several technical and practical weaknesses, and there are significant political obstacles impeding the wider application of MBIs. The next section explores some of the points raised in this general discussion of policy instruments through a brief examination of the use of different policy instruments in the energy and transport sectors to prevent climate change – a policy goal that lies at the heart of contemporary sustainable development strategies everywhere.

CRITICAL QUESTION 3
Will MBIs become the dominant environmental policy instrument?

POLICY INSTRUMENTS AND CLIMATE CHANGE

The energy and transport sectors are the major producers of carbon emissions; for example, they accounted for 32 per cent and 24 per cent of total EU carbon emissions respectively in 1998 (EEA 2000a: 6–7). For most countries to reach, and certainly to maintain, even the relatively unambitious carbon emission reduction commitments promised at Kyoto (see Box 9.3) will require fundamental policy changes in these sectors. Sustainable energy and transport policies will require extensive strategic planning, the use of a mixed package of policy instruments and a willingness to impose genuinely stringent measures on both businesses and consumers. Crucially, for many observers a credible climate change strategy must be underpinned by onerous carbon or energy taxes that create a real financial incentive to change behaviour.

Energy policy

Historically, national energy policies have been designed to guarantee supplies of cheap energy to industry and the home, whilst ensuring sufficient fuel diversity to avoid the kind of dependence on imported fuels that led to economic disruption during the oil crises of the 1970s. Sustainable energy strategies must address both the supply and demand sides of the energy equation. On the supply side there needs to be a shift away from using fossil energy, notably coal and oil, to generate electricity, towards renewable energy sources such as HEP,[4] wind, solar, wave and biomass, which emit low or zero carbon. On the demand side it will be necessary to reduce energy consumption in both industrial and domestic sectors, through improved energy efficiency and conservation measures. To date, few countries have made any significant progress towards sustainability in either the generation or consumption of electricity.

On the supply side, few countries boast a significant renewable energy sector. Renewable energy supplied 14.6 per cent of EU electricity in 1997, but 13 per cent of that was from HEP (EEA 2000a: 29). Although HEP is very important in some countries, including Austria, Norway and Sweden, its growth potential is limited everywhere by the strong political opposition (especially from conservationists) to the damage to habitats and communities arising from the construction of giant dams. The development of other renewable sources has been limited by a wide range of obstacles, including established fossil energy generation, powerful energy producers, competitive liberalised energy markets, discriminatory subsidies and technological problems. Governments still give priority to economic interests over environmental concerns. Where energy supply is based on a large domestic productive industry, such as coal and oil in the USA, governments are likely to be reluctant to take action which might harm that powerful industry. As Jansen et al. (1998) observe, even in Norway, where environmental consciousness is high, 'environmental quality counts, but national economic interests decide' (p. 198). If oil or gas is imported, powerful energy generators will resist any attempt to reduce their market share.[5] Where changes in energy mix have occurred, they owe little to sustainable energy policies; for example, German reunification in 1990 led to major economic restructuring resulting in huge energy efficiency improvements that resulted in significant carbon emission reductions (see Box 11.4).

Nor have renewables faced a level playing field. In many countries, subsidies have historically favoured fossil fuel and nuclear production: one estimate put direct government subsidies for fossil fuel energy sources and technologies worldwide at around $200 billion (Hempel 1999: 297). Given the small scale of operations and lack of investment, it is not surprising that electricity from renewable energy is usually more expensive than from fossil fuels. The balance did start to shift during the 1990s, with many governments seeking to limit further development of coal- and oil-fired generation, whilst introducing subsidies and other forms of protection to stimulate the nascent renewable sector. For example, generous price tariffs have boosted wind energy in Denmark, Germany and Spain, and tax breaks were a catalyst for development in California. Between 2000 and 2005 the price of electricity from wind turbines is expected to drop by 17 per cent, reflecting improvements in technology (Dresdner Kleinwort Wasserstein 2000). Yet the world's total capacity for generating electricity through wind power was about 17.5 GW in 2000, still a minuscule share of the total generating capacity of around 3,500 GW. In the USA,

11.4 The contradictions in UK energy policy

Britain is well on course to exceed its Kyoto target of a 12.5 per cent reduction of 1990 levels in six greenhouse gases by 2010, despite lacking an effective sustainable energy strategy.

British success in cutting greenhouse emissions can be put down almost entirely to one fortuitous factor: a dramatic change in the energy mix from coal to gas. In 1990 coal generated around two-thirds of UK electricity but by 2000 it had fallen to 28 per cent, whereas gas had risen from less than 1 per cent in 1990 to almost 40 per cent in 1998. This 'dash for gas' was made possible by the privatisation of the energy industry during the 1980s and the liberalised, competitive electricity market. Freed of historic state-imposed commitments to purchase expensive coal, the privately owned energy suppliers rapidly built a plethora of modern gas-fired power stations.

Yet British energy policy is currently not sustainable
- Gas is a non-renewable fuel source and will eventually be exhausted; as domestic gas supplies decline, Britain will become a net importer of gas sometime after 2010.
- The nuclear power sector seems to be in terminal decline (it is predicted that just one reactor will remain in 2025).
- The renewable sector is still tiny, with a current market share of about 3 per cent in 1999, with a heavily qualified target of 'working towards 10 per cent . . . hopefully by 2010' (DETR 2000).
- Although domestic energy consumption continues to rise, the Labour government cut

VAT on domestic fuel to 5 per cent in 1997 and is committed to cutting domestic fuel prices in the medium term. Lower prices will stimulate increased consumption.

Major obstacles to a sustainable energy policy
- Privatisation and the liberalised domestic energy market have resulted in a significant decline in energy prices.
- There is a lack of integration in government. The environment ministry (DETR) pursued environmental commitments such as reducing greenhouse and acid emissions, while the industry ministry (DTI) aimed for fuel diversity and lower prices. Thus DETR-sponsored energy efficiency campaigns conflicted with DTI efforts to reduce energy prices to consumers. Indeed, the DTI failed to subject its new energy policy proposals published in June 1998 to an environmental appraisal, in contravention of official guidelines (ENDs 1998a: Report 281)!
- Producer groups have exercised a powerful influence over energy policy whilst environmental groups have been relatively weak, as illustrated by:
  (a) the reluctance of the DTI to invest significant funds in the renewables sector in contrast to its enthusiasm for clean-burn coal technologies;
  (b) the Treasury watering down the new Climate Change Levy in the face of strong industry lobbying.

by far the world's largest producer of carbon emissions, wind power currently contributes only 0.1 per cent of energy. One factor that may encourage a keener interest in renewable energy will be the declining output from the nuclear sector. Thus, when the German government agreed its nuclear power station closure programme (see Box 7.8), it instigated a radical programme, complete with ambitious targets and backed by annual subsidies of 2 billion euros, to expand its renewable energy industry (ibid.). However, it is unlikely that any significant expansion will occur without the imposition of some kind of carbon tax on fossil fuels that is set sufficiently high to make the fledgling renewables sector more competitive and, as in Denmark, tax revenues are reinvested in the renewables sector for research and design, subsidies and preferential agreements (Andersen et al. 1998).

On the demand side, progress in containing, let alone reducing, energy consumption is extremely slow. There are numerous ways of improving domestic and industry energy efficiency. Governments can set high mandatory energy efficiency standards for buildings (Sweden), subsidise home conservation (the Netherlands) and low-energy light bulbs (UK), or agree an energy efficiency classification system for consumer goods such as washing machines and refrigerators (EU). There are many examples of industry voluntarily agreeing to introduce energy-saving measures, notably the detailed energy efficiency targets agreed by Dutch industry covering over 90 per cent of total energy use in industry. The British government, using the threat of a new climate change levy, was able to negotiate agreements with several industrial sectors to reduce carbon emissions. In many countries, increasing numbers of consumers have voluntarily chosen to insulate their homes, use low-energy light bulbs and purchase efficient domestic goods to conserve energy. Nevertheless, existing regulations, subsidies and voluntary actions, although helpful, will not achieve the necessary reductions in energy consumption. Perhaps only more stringent carbon and energy taxes can provide the necessary incentive to change industrial and consumer behaviour.

Carbon and energy tax proposals have encountered fierce opposition from domestic business communities, primarily on the grounds that their international competitiveness would be severely affected. Nevertheless, eight EU member states had introduced carbon taxes by 2001 (EEA 2000b). Sweden imposed a stiff carbon tax on industry in 1991, but the government reduced it a year later, declaring that the resulting competitive advantage to Swedish industry would create over 10,000 jobs (EEA 1996:40). Although subsequently it has been increased for more energy-intensive industries (Lundqvist 1998: 247). The Finnish experience was even more negative, as the carbon tax introduced in 1991 had such a detrimental impact on industry that it was eventually removed. President Clinton, in the face of pressure from the fossil fuel lobby and energy-intensive industries, failed in 1993 to get congressional support for his proposed 'Btu tax', a broad-based tax on the heat content of fuels (Hempel 1999: 298). Business resistance helped persuade the Kohl government to drop plans for a carbon tax in Germany (Pehle and Jansen 1998), although the SPD–Green coalition subsequently introduced a range of energy taxes, while the proposed climate change levy introduced by the Blair government in Britain was watered down by unusually strong and co-ordinated industry lobbying.

Overall, these national carbon and energy taxes have had only a marginal impact on behaviour because, to make them politically acceptable, they have been levied at too low a level. Clearly, climate-change and carbon taxes pose a classic free-rider problem: unless states co-ordinate their actions to impose a uniform carbon tax collectively, then industry in those countries where a tax is levied will be competitively disadvantaged. However, attempts led by the Dutch and German governments to agree a EU carbon tax in the mid-1990s encountered equally fierce industry lobbying of the European institutions and foundered on the opposition of several countries, notably the UK and France (Peterson and Bomberg 1999: 182–3). Without an EU tax no member state is likely to impose carbon taxes at levels that are sufficiently stringent to produce any fundamental improvements in energy efficiency, reductions in energy consumption, or shift to renewable sources of energy. It will be interesting to see whether the Kyoto agreement to set up a tradeable permit system for carbon emissions – if it materialises – will provide sufficient incentive to adopt such measures.

Transport

For the last half century, transport policies in most countries have adopted a 'predict and provide' approach to the expansion of road and air transport: *predict* the anticipated growth in each sector and *provide* the roads and airports necessary to support it. Some governments, notably the Thatcher government, have adopted a pro-roads stance with particular ideological fervour, directly linking road construction to economic growth and freedom of the individual (Department of Transport 1989). Climate change prevention requires a fundamentally different approach to transport policy (see Box 11.5). A sustainable transport policy has to address both sides of the equation: on the supply side, air and road transport need to be made more fuel-efficient; on the demand side, traffic volume must be reduced so that fewer journeys are made by car and plane.[6] All governments now recognise the need to change, but few have made a genuine paradigm shift, for they are reluctant to do anything that might damage the economy or prove unpopular with the public.

Policy-makers have pinned their hopes on the supply side objective of developing 'greener' motor vehicles (Hempel 1995; Whitelegg 1997). In recent years, the impact of individual cars on the environment has

11.5 Transport and climate change

The root of the problem lies in the unremitting growth in road and air vehicles. Without remedial action, the global motor vehicle population is expected to rise from around 500 million in the early 1990s to some 2.3 billion vehicles by 2030 (Whitelegg 1997: 27). Road transport of goods and passengers in the EU increased by 45 per cent and 41 per cent respectively between the early 1980s and the mid-1990s, while rail transport of goods decreased and passenger rail travel increased by just 10 per cent (European Commission 1996: 26). The number of trips per person and the average length of each journey are also continuing to rise as suburban lifestyles result in people living further away from their workplace and friends, and, crucially, making more leisure trips. Global air traffic, measured in terms of passenger kilometres, is also predicted to rise, from 1,834 billion kilometres in 1991 to 4,729 billion kilometres by 2015 – an average of 5 per cent per annum. Fuel consumption is projected to rise from 650 million tonnes in 1995 to 1.3 billion tonnes – the cumulative total consumption of the car fleet alone will be 41.6 billion tonnes out of a world oil reserve figure of 135.7 billion tonnes in 1994 (Whitelegg 1997: 27).

Many countries will only be able to meet their Kyoto commitments by significantly reducing carbon emissions from the transport sector. Together, these external costs of transport represent a major case for sustainable transport policies that would reduce pollution, minimise the use of non-renewable fossil fuels and prevent the current unrelenting destruction of habitats.

been lessened through engine modifications, anti-pollution devices, alternative fuels and new types of vehicle. For example, improvements in engine efficiency reduced fuel consumption per mile of new cars in the USA by almost 50 per cent between 1960 and 1990, although the efficiency of new American cars actually fell by 4 per cent between 1988 and 1992 (Hempel 1995: 67, 71). While there is growing interest amongst the major vehicle manufacturers in converting engines to use biomass products such as ethanol and methanol, liquefied petroleum gas, compressed natural gas and developing electric vehicles, none has yet proved to be a commercial success.

Sometimes technological advances have been helped by voluntary agreements, such as that between vehicle manufacturers and the European Commission to reduce carbon emissions for new cars (ENDs 1998c), which may stimulate the development of innovative solutions. However, regulation has proved to be a stronger pressure for the commercial development of new technologies. Vogel (1995) identifies the significance of the 'California effect': for over thirty years the state of California has boasted the strictest American automotive pollution control standards, obliging motor manufacturers to make technological improvements if they want access to California's large and wealthy car market. The US Clean Air Act 1970 permitted California to set higher vehicle emissions standards than other states, which directly contributed to the development of the catalytic converter. The EU has also imposed numerous emission standards, notably the 1989 small car directive, which have hastened technological improvements. The 1998 EU Auto/Oil programme set new vehicle-emission and fuel-quality standards in an attempt to force manufacturers to develop catalysts for diesels and new low sulphur fuels which are necessary for future CO_2 emission reductions (ENDS 1998a).[7] More radically, a Californian mandate required 2 per cent of the state's new vehicles sold in 1998, rising to 10 per cent in 2003, to be 'zero-emission', such as electric cars (Hempel 1995: 73), although there are serious doubts whether this target will be met because these vehicles are still comparatively very expensive (*Financial Times*, 8 December 2000).

Although regulatory competition has, on balance, made motor vehicles cleaner and more fuel-efficient, there are many limitations to the 'techno-fix' solution. The overall environmental impact is usually complex. For example, while the widespread use of catalytic converters has reduced nitrogen oxide emissions, their lower fuel efficiency has increased carbon emissions. The bottom line is that technological solutions all avoid the core problem of traffic volume; indeed, techno-fixes may even encourage the false belief that driving a 'greener' car will not seriously damage the environment. Yet it is predicted that the damage caused by the inexorable growth in traffic volume (from more vehicles, greater frequency of use and increased average journey length) will rapidly cancel out the benefits from techno-fixes – exacerbated by the current fashion for high fuel-consumption off-road vehicles.

Policy-makers have begun to address the consumption side of the equation. Perhaps the best example of strategic planning is the Netherlands, which has long boasted a well-integrated national inter-modal transport network. Yet in most countries all levels of government are increasingly using transport planning systems both as a stick to discourage car use and as a carrot to encourage alternative forms of travel such as public transport, cycling and walking. Many cities have experimented with a range of sticks, such as restrictions on car access and parking capacity, and carrots, notably schemes to give priority to trams and buses. Cycling and walking are encouraged by the use of speed restrictions, traffic-calming schemes and segregated cycle lanes to make streets safer. Walking is made more attractive by pedestrianised zones, better pavements and safe crossing points.[8] Yet traffic management can exert only a marginal impact without stronger incentives to discourage car use.

Policy-makers have therefore shown growing interest in using MBIs to alter travelling habits. There is a strong economic case for using MBIs to correct market failure as existing taxes on motoring, such as sales, vehicle and fuel taxes, cover only a small proportion of the external costs of motoring. It is estimated that car taxes in Germany cover only 25 per cent of costs, falling to 18 per cent for lorries (in Whitelegg 1997: 187). There are also many subsidies promoting petrol-driven vehicles, particularly in the USA (Hempel 1999: 297), and private road transport generally, such as car parking and company cars. Road transport tax regimes have traditionally focused on raising general tax revenue. Where the aim is to alter behaviour, such as setting lower taxes for unleaded or low sulphur fuels, or linking road taxes to engine size, there has been no impact on traffic volume. A few countries, including Britain, the Netherlands, Norway and Sweden, have increased fuel taxes for explicitly environmental reasons, but with little impact on consumption. For example, a 10 per cent Norwegian carbon tax introduced in 1991 is estimated to have reduced motor vehicle emissions by 2–3 per cent per annum (OECD 1997: 26). The inelasticity of demand for petrol will require a stringent increase, perhaps over 40 per cent, to have any significant impact on consumption, but politicians are understandably resistant to taking such a radical step. There is growing interest in road pricing schemes using microwave technology or satellite positioning equipment which, by charging motorists for every journey, could reduce non-essential trips and hence the overall volume of journeys. Several cities, notably Singapore, have introduced successful schemes. Obviously there are drawbacks. The infant technologies still need more testing. User charges may simply persuade people to visit a different city for shopping or entertainment, rather than avoid a trip (less of a problem in Singapore). Nevertheless, by making the driver aware of the exact cost of each journey, road-pricing systems may represent the most potent incentive to reduce traffic volume.

A package of vehicle, fuel and road taxes would also generate revenue to invest in vital public transport improvements. For example, massive capital investment programmes are needed to expand rail networks, improve rolling stock and increase the frequency and reliability of trains. Modern high-speed rail links, such as the French TGV, have shown that trains can compete successfully for long-distance travellers and freight traffic. Without the carrot of fast, efficient, convenient and affordable public transport, it is unlikely that people will be persuaded to leave their cars at home.

To summarise, progress towards sustainable energy and transport policies remains slow. Significantly, even the Dutch, who have pioneered the use of progressive strategies employing MBIs and voluntary agreements, will struggle to reach their Kyoto reduction targets (EEA 2000a). Although energy and transport sectors are generally in a state of flux, there are few signs of the kind of paradigm shift necessary for even weakly sustainable policies. Governments still rely heavily on the technical solutions that characterise the traditional paradigm, such as tail-pipe emissions control or clean coal technologies, when it seems clear that the reduction of carbon emissions from the transport sector is likely to require a broad mix of policy instruments. The absence of comprehensive stringent carbon taxes, in particular, suggests that policy-makers have not yet accepted that sustainability requires solutions which have a significant impact on the lifestyles of citizens.

CRITICAL QUESTION 4

Does popular opposition to 'excessive' fuel duties demonstrate the limitations of eco-taxes?

CONCLUSION

Rarely does the choice of policy instrument involve a simple exercise of selecting the 'technically' best (i.e. the most efficient or effective) option. There are clearly some environmental problems that can only be resolved satisfactorily by regulation. Where the objective is the *complete* prevention of a damaging activity, such as burning the highly polluting orimulsion for energy generation, or the removal of a dangerous substance, such as lead from petrol, then legal prohibition, provided it is effectively implemented, is the only way to guarantee a successful outcome; an MBI allows the possibility that a polluter may be prepared to pay any price to continue its dangerous behaviour. Regulations are also faster acting than economic instruments; a legal prohibition can take effect immediately, whereas an incentive, such as an emissions tax aimed at persuading firms to invest in cleaner technology, may take longer to influence behaviour. However, most problems can be addressed by a wide range of different policy instruments, and the process of choosing between them will be suffused with political considerations.

The wider political context has contributed to the growing interest in MBIs. The ascendancy of neo-liberal ideas has shifted the terms of debate against the use of regulatory measures by focusing on their negative attributes of inefficiency and inflexibility. The growing influence of the ecological modernisation discourse has also strengthened the support for alternatives. Policy-makers seem more prepared to draw on a wider armoury of measures (Golub 1998). Voluntary agreements are becoming common throughout the EU (EEA 1997b; Jansen et al. 1998; Mol et al. 2000). The number of eco-taxes steadily multiplied in most OECD countries during the 1990s (EEA 1996; OECD 1997). The Kyoto summit agreement on climate change includes a commitment to create an international market in carbon emission permits by 2008 which, if successful, is likely to be a catalyst for the wider use of tradeable permits. Significantly, it seems that these alternatives to regulation are used most widely in 'new' policy areas such as climate change, where the demand for radical solutions is most acute. It is important to note, however, that change is gradual. Currently, ecological modernisation is most apparent as a discourse rather than as an activity. Regulations are, and will continue to be, widely used everywhere, not least because they satisfy administrative convenience, retain public legitimacy and suit industry. One comparative study of European countries concluded that 'the strategy of ecological modernisation has not supplanted the application of traditional regulatory instruments' (Jansen et al. 1998: 311). The knee-jerk resistance in the business community to any new MBI hardly suggests that industry is yet persuaded by ecological modernisation. If it is to change, then the initiative will have to come from those governments that are willing to intervene actively in the market to steer business and consumer behaviour, which again suggests that ecological modernisation is more likely to flourish in some countries than in others (see Chapter 8). The wider use of eco-taxes in Nordic countries reflects public acceptance of a high taxation burden, which is justified in terms of the established institutional logic of the welfare state: that taxes are necessary to improve the common good (Jansen et al. 1998: 312). By contrast, where neo-liberal ideas are predominant, as in Australia, Britain and the USA, there is a stronger anti-tax culture and greater resistance to state intervention which may be less conducive to ecological modernisation.

It is important not to become fixated by the highly stylised regulation v. MBI dichotomy. In practice, rather than choosing between a regulation, a MBI or a voluntary agreement, policy-makers select a mix of instruments to achieve a policy objective. MBIs, in particular, are usually introduced as part of a package of measures, and they are frequently implemented via regulations that remain in place to act as a 'back stop' to ensure that minimum standards are maintained. Although the literature often implies that they are polar opposites, there is actually considerable common ground between regulations and MBIs. Both require active state intervention in the economy; indeed, tradeable permits explicitly involve a combination of regulation and market forces. Perhaps the focus on different types of instrument obfuscates the real issue: whether the package of instruments selected is sufficiently *stringent* to achieve the desired outcomes.

Here, a useful distinction can be made between low- and high-cost environmental policies (Daugbjerg 1998). *Low-cost policies* favour the interests of producers: advice and information are preferred to measures that may impose costs, but where regulations are used, they are couched in broad terms to allow flexible implementation to suit local conditions. Eco-taxes are used rarely but, if imposed, they are set at low levels and producers are often reimbursed through subsidies. *High-cost policies*, by contrast, emphasise more extensive use of eco-taxes and universal regulations setting standards and targets. Put differently, the presence of stringent MBIs at the centre of a broad package of policy instruments may be a good indicator of a serious approach to sustainable development.

As high-cost policies would normally affect key producer, consumer and environmental interests, the distribution of power within the policy process will play a critical role in determining the stringency of policy instruments. For example, where a closed policy community exists, the mix of policy instruments is likely to be more favourable to producer groups than in sectors where an issue network prevails. Daugbjerg (1998) compares agri-environmental policy in Denmark and Sweden to support his claim that in sectors characterised by policy communities, low-cost policies will be introduced, whereas high-cost policies will be associated with issue networks. Danish nitrate policy-making shows that a tight policy community sharing a consensus on policy principles produced a low-cost nitrate policy. By contrast, the open Swedish policy network, with its weaker links between state and farmers and a significant role for environmental interests, has resulted in a high-cost policy consisting of tougher nitrate reduction targets, a higher fertiliser tax, relatively inflexible universal regulations and lower subsidies than in Denmark.

The climate change case study bears the clear imprint of powerful producer interests. Corporate interests were instrumental in dissuading EU member states from introducing a Community-wide carbon tax. Within each country business interests have fiercely, and usually effectively, resisted the imposition of domestic energy and fuel taxation. In Norway, a powerful policy community of employers' organisations, trade unions and the energy and industry ministries successfully blocked repeated proposals during the 1990s to levy the existing carbon tax on a wider range of exempted emission intensive industries, such as metallurgical production (Kasa 2000). Everywhere, resistance to road taxation is typically organised around pro-roads advocacy coalitions consisting of oil companies, vehicle manufacturers, construction companies, trade unions, as well as groups representing car drivers and the road haulage industry. Business resistance is also helped by the administrative fragmentation of the state, which has enabled the energy and roads lobbies to find plenty of allies at the heart of government. The importance of both energy and road transport in the modern economy has ensured that industry and finance ministries have also proved receptive to their interests. Most transport ministries, traditionally enthusiastic advocates of road construction, have only slowly begun to temper their enthusiasm for the motor vehicle and, as in Germany, they may still be avowedly pro-roads (Beuermann and Jäger 1996).

If policy-makers find it difficult to introduce MBIs in the business sector, they are equally reluctant to impose them on consumers. Politicians fear that stringent eco-taxes either on items of basic need, such as domestic energy consumption, or on key lifestyle goods, such as cars, would provoke huge public hostility. Car ownership has become a central part of the culture of the modern consumer society, symbolising individual freedom and personal achievement. Changing consumer behaviour will be no easy task. Moreover, all energy and road taxes are potentially regressive. Fuel taxes, for example, exert a disproportionate impact on low-income groups, who may need extra heating or be dependent on motor vehicles by virtue of ill-health, infirmity, disability or the absence of alternatives. Politicians are understandably nervous about introducing taxes that may be electorally unpopular, particularly since the wave of fuel protests that swept across Western Europe during 2000, forcing concessions from panicky governments. Similarly, the reluctance of successive American presidents to agree to carbon emissions reductions is influenced partly by the powerful energy producers and car manufacturers, but also by the strong gas-guzzling American culture founded on the availability of cheap gasoline.

Arguably, it is precisely this strong resistance that makes the case for eco-taxes so persuasive: by sending the clear financial signal that people should conserve energy or change their travelling patterns, they seem to offer most hope of changing consumer behaviour. The growing enthusiasm for MBIs amongst environmentalists, who were once very wary of them, underlines this point. There has been a strong environmental lobby in favour of landfill, carbon and car engine taxes in Britain. The Environmental Defense Fund in the USA has campaigned actively for the wider use of tradeable permits in air pollution policy (Bailey 1996).[9] Green parties are also converts, with eco-tax packages forming a key plank of coalition agreements in Belgium and Germany. While the use of market mechanisms was once condemned as a reformist blind alley, today many greens have accepted that they have to make compromises with the capitalist system. They may still baulk at the idea of valuing nature, 'buying the right to pollute', or appealing to the profit motive of the very corporations whose activities have caused so much environmental damage. Nevertheless, in supporting the wider use of MBIs, many environmental groups and green parties have indicated a readiness to accept the capitalist economic system, just as the entry of green parties into national parliaments and then into government declared their willingness to work within liberal democracy.

Further reading and websites

Vogel (1986), although dated, still merits reading for an interesting comparison of the US and UK regulatory styles. Dryzek (1997: ch. 6) provides an interesting discussion of the ideas behind market approaches, although it is advisable to dip into the economic textbooks to get a real grasp of the technical arguments for and against different policy instruments: Jacobs (1991) and Turner et al. (1994) both provide an accessible and reasonably non-technical introduction to the subject. A broader political perspective can be found in Eckersley (1996b), Golub (1998) and Freeman (1999). Mol et al. (2000) analyse the development and effectiveness of voluntary agreements in the EU. For coverage of national climate change policies, see Hempel (1999) on the USA, and the comparative Hanf and Jansen (1998) and Lafferty and Meadowcroft (2000a) collections. Whitelegg (1997) provides a passionate analysis of transport issues.

Check out the websites at the end of Chapter 10 for data on national climate change, energy and transport policies, and see the excellent European Environment Agency website (*http://www.eea.eu.int/*).

Notes

1. Some writers use the term 'economic instruments' or 'financial incentives' in preference to MBI.
2. It is this active state intervention that distinguishes the work of environmental economists, such as Pearce et al. (1989), from Free Market Environmentalism (see Chapter 3), which holds that the environment will only be protected by the market regulating itself.
3. The allocation of permits is itself a highly political issue. Permits are usually allocated according to past emissions levels, but this 'grandfathering' method may be inequitable because it effectively grants pollution 'rights' to companies on the basis of their previous record of pollution.
4. See for example the contemporary controversy over the proposed Ilisu dam project in Turkey.
5. The decline of the nuclear industry puts more pressure on governments to find alternatives. Ironically, as Sweden and Germany close down their nuclear reactors, they will probably have to import energy generated from Danish or Polish coal-fired power stations as a substitute (see Chapter 7).
6. For reasons of space the discussion concentrates on road transport.
7. It is a moot point how far the environmental benefits of regulatory competition are outweighed by the environmental degradation from increased traffic movement and trading activity resulting from trade liberalisation within the EU or NAFTA (see Vogel 1995).
8. See the UK government transport white paper (DETR 1998) for details of such schemes.
9. The Sierra Club, National Audubon Society and National Wildlife Federation, however, were all more suspicious of tradeable permits (Bailey 1996).

12

Conclusion

Chapter 11 ended by observing that the environmental movement has become so reconciled to the continuation of capitalism that it is now positively enthusiastic about the role of the market as a tool to protect the environment. This sentiment seems a long way from the anti-industrialism and the anarchistic blueprint of a sustainable world discussed in Part I. Indeed, it reflects the shift in the centre of gravity of environmental politics in recent years from a radical rejection of the existing economic and political system towards a reformist acceptance of capitalism and liberal democracy. This concluding chapter draws together some of the themes discussed in the book by analysing the state of environmental politics some thirty-five years after the emergence of 'modern environmentalism'. More specifically, it examines the significance of ecologism, assesses progress towards sustainable development and speculates about the future path of environmental politics.

A central argument of the book is that ecologism can now be regarded as an ideology in its own right. Ecologism offers a persuasive critique of (capitalist) industrial society and the liberal democratic polity, holding them largely responsible for the current ecological crisis; it outlines a vision of an alternative sustainable society; and it suggests possible strategies of change that might achieve that utopian vision. The most distinctive theoretical contribution of ecologism, as discussed in Part I, resides in its two core ideas: the need to reassess human-nature relations and the belief in ecological limits to growth. These core ideas have been supplemented by a set of principles drawn from other doctrines but reworked to fit green purposes: notably social justice, participatory democracy and decentralisation. These principles are regarded as essential components of a sustainable society and they also inform green theories of agency for getting to that sustainable world.

Ecologism and the environmental movement pose important challenges to established political traditions at the levels of theory, action and policy. First, Part I showed how the distinctive, if contentious, theoretical contribution of ecologism has forced political philosophers to engage with the notion that we might have duties towards nature and to future generations of unborn humans. Greens also make new demands of familiar concepts such as participatory democracy and social justice. Participatory democratic decision-making, for example, in addition to its potential for improving the quality of the democratic polity, is now also expected to raise the ecological consciousness of a community and produce greener policy outcomes. Individualist theories of justice also need to be reworked to address the distribution of collective environmental goods. On the other hand, by invoking familiar political concepts, greens can draw important lessons from mainstream political philosophy; after all, they are not the first to think about participatory democracy or social justice. In particular, green theorists must be aware of the conceptual baggage associated with these concepts. For example, what are the implications of basing an environmental ethical theory on utilitarianism? Would it be better to ground a green theory of justice on equality or on rights? The emergence of green political theory and the flourishing of the environmental movement have also forced other ideologies, especially those on the left, to address environmental issues, such as the possibility that there may be ecological limits to growth. Conversely, green politics has also drawn from other political traditions, notably socialism, for a critique of capitalism and anarchism for its suspicion of the state. The creative tension that exists where ecologism engages with other ideologies is illustrated by the emergence of hybrid doctrines, such as ecosocialism, ecoanarchism and ecofeminism.

Ecologism is theoretically less distinctive in dealing with political action; indeed, it offers a rather incoherent strategy for change. Radical ecologism has thrown up a hotch-potch of approaches which reflect its anarchistic and libertarian roots. Some writers recommend opting out of the existing system by setting up communes or alternative lifestyles; others demand direct action that confronts the existing system. Within the environmental movement there is a strong, albeit diminishing, fundamentalist purity about grassroots democracy which reflects the new social movement origins of many environmental groups and green parties. However, many environmental activists have found these strategies impractical (most people simply do not want to opt out of the system or break the law) and ineffective as a means of engaging in practical political activity. Consequently, as environmental politics has become more mainstream, so environmental activism has become increasingly reconciled to reformist strategies which work within the legislative process and the boundaries of civil society. How should we assess this development? Is it a sensible attempt to bring environmental politics in from the margins or is it a sign of its failure to achieve real change?

Proponents of the reformist strategy point to the undoubted impact of environmental politics on contemporary political behaviour. Chapters 4 and 5 showed how the electoral success of green parties has contributed to a thawing of frozen party cleavages and voter alignments in several European countries and forced all parties to treat environmental issues more seriously, at least by developing a greener rhetoric and strengthening policy programmes. The presence of green parties in red–green and rainbow coalition governments at all levels of government is already having a visible, albeit limited, impact on policy outcomes. Nevertheless, the prospects for the success of green electoral politics are circumscribed by the low electoral salience of the environment: traditional materialist issues continue to dominate electoral politics whilst less than 10 per cent of the electorate regard the environment as a major issue. In short, voters are not yet ready to elect a majority green government. However, environmental groups have become increasingly important actors in the policy process. Chapter 6 showed how the enormous resources and public support that the largest groups can now mobilise have contributed to the institutionalisation of the mainstream movement in recent years. While environmental groups remain less influential than business interests in most critical policy areas, there is no doubting the impact that they have had in changing broad policy agendas and affecting many specific decisions, such as policy towards GM crops in Europe.

By contrast, critics of reformism counter that this limited 'success' of environmental politics actually illustrates the failure of the approach in that it symbolises the incorporation or co-option of green politics by dominant interests. According to this view, the radicalism of green parties will inevitably be compromised by their need to ensure continued electoral success – the *logic of electoral competition* – and to win the support of partners in a coalition government. Similarly, the institutionalisation of the mainstream environmental movement, which has seen international NGOs invited to join UN bodies such as the Commission for Sustainable Development and major domestic groups regularly consulted by national governments, while even Greenpeace now sits down to talk business with Shell and Monsanto, has arguably denuded environmentalism of its radical principles and prevents it from achieving substantive change. It is this suspicion of reformism – of getting into bed with the enemy – that has contributed to the grassroots backlash of eco-protesters who are willing to employ confrontational methods of protest such as the British anti-road movement and the global protests against the WTO. Ultimately, the relative merits of each approach will be judged by the impact of environmental politics on policy outcomes.

Yet ecologism is perhaps at its weakest at dealing with practical policy issues because its utopian vision of a sustainable society offers few concrete suggestions to help policy-makers and activists deal with immediate policy issues. Not surprisingly, since the late 1980s sustainable development has become the dominant policy discourse, not just for governments, international organisations and businesses, but also for the environmental movement itself. In part, this arose from a disenchantment and frustration amongst many environmental activists with the narrow ecological concerns of green politics; or at least with the widespread public perception that green politics is a single-issue movement. By stating that environmental protection does not have to be bought at the expense of economic growth, sustainable development is immediately more appealing to a wider public. More important, though, is its broad development agenda which, by linking poverty, inequality and North–South issues to environmental degradation, offers a more comprehensive analysis of the contemporary ecological crisis than, say, deep ecology. Seen in this light, the emergence of sustainable development has much in common with the left-libertarian programme represented by the four pillars of green politics discussed in Chapter 3. Some radical greens believe sustainable development falls outside the boundaries of ecologism: it is human-centred, denies (or at least doubts) the existence of limits to growth and seeks to reform rather than overthrow capitalism. However, as there is little doubt that the implementation of strong versions of sustainable development would result in a form of capitalism so radically different as to be virtually unrecognisable, it seems wise to adopt an inclusive definition of ecologism that encompasses strong versions of sustainable development which seek to reform, rather than overthrow, capitalism and liberal democracy. Either way, the broad conclusion is that the centre of gravity in environmental politics has undoubtedly shifted from a *radical* rejection of industrialism and a *narrow* concern with ecological issues, to a *reformist* acceptance of capitalism and liberal democracy based on a *broader* (and, in many respects, more radical) social justice agenda.

To date, although sustainable development has been almost universally adopted as the policy paradigm driving strategies to protect the environment, no country has yet got close to achieving even the very weakest forms of sustainability. Despite the deteriorating state of the environment, there is still a wide gap between the rhetoric and reality of sustainable development. Policy-makers are willing to make symbolic gestures but reluctant to approve concrete policy measures. Thus progress towards sustainable development is slow, piecemeal and insubstantial. Certainly there have been many initiatives and some real achievements in the name of sustainable development, but these improvements have only scratched the surface of the problem. Chapter 9 identified many examples of international environmental co-operation. The plethora of new international institutions and projects, including the UNEP, CSD and *Agenda 21*, have been given considerable responsibility for ensuring that international agreements are enforced and the sustainable development message trickles down to national and sub-national governments and throughout civil society. International environmental regimes have generated some genuine success stories: in particular, ozone diplomacy has directly resulted in a massive reduction in the manufacture of ozone-depleting chemicals. However, since the massive Rio jamboree in 1992, the environment has slipped down the agenda of international politics. In part, other issues, notably armed conflicts in Europe and Africa, have pushed it aside; hence the low profile of the UNGASS follow-up conference in 1997 which was attended by relatively few world leaders compared to Rio. Governments have also begun to count the domestic costs of implementing some international agreements, which explains the difficulty in securing agreement on carbon emission reductions. It is clear that many countries will be unable to implement even the minimum targets agreed in the Kyoto Protocol. The breakdown of the Hague talks in November 2000 underlines how the international community has failed to produce a serious strategy to deal with climate change, arguably the most serious environmental problem currently confronting the world.

Similarly, most governments, as outlined in Chapter 10, have taken tentative steps towards environmental governance by introducing a myriad of institutional and administrative reforms with the intention of improving integration, planning and democratisation of the policy process. Moreover, environmental groups have gained better access to policy-making processes, which has allowed them to win isolated victories preventing specific proposals or introducing particular amendments to legislation, but they have rarely been able to seize the policy initiative from industrial interests. Even in those pioneer countries where ecological modernisation has taken root, politicians still tend to 'talk' sustainable development without routinely thinking through the environmental considerations of their actions. Reforms of the machinery of government have done little to resolve the administrative fragmentation that institutionalises the power of sectoral producer interests such as energy companies, the roads lobby or farmers, let alone alter the structural factors that privilege these industrial interests. Consequently, administrative techniques that could build environmental considerations into decision-making processes, such as EIA and risk assessment, rarely disrupt the dominance of industrial interests.

Not surprisingly, therefore, government policies in most areas remain insufficiently stringent, as illustrated in Chapter 11 by the inadequacy of climate change policies in the energy and transport sectors. The share of electricity generated by renewable energy remains tiny and no government has sought to transform the transport sector away from private cars and freight towards a fully integrated public transport infrastructure. Governments do seem increasingly prepared to employ a wider tool-kit of policy instruments, notably market-based instruments and voluntary agreements, thus reducing the traditional dependency on regulatory measures which have been widely criticised for being inefficient and ineffective. Yet the continuing absence of a tranche of stringent market-based instruments reflects the sensitivity of governments to powerful business lobbying and their fear of an electoral backlash against unpopular taxes.

On balance, the benefits from the many environmental protection measures that are in place, such as reductions in certain pollutants and the adoption of cleaner technologies, are far outweighed by the accelerating growth of ecologically unsustainable consumption and resource depletion arising from the apparently inexorable advance of global capitalism and the still rapidly growing world population. Does this provide evidence to support the rejectionist stance of radical greens who question the possibility of achieving sustainable society without transforming the capitalist system? Or is there any evidence suggesting that the reformist approach can be successful? The answers to these questions seem largely to lie in the relationship between three key actors: the state, business, and the individual citizen, and this discussion will close with a few speculative comments about each of these.

Governments at all levels have a key role to play in ensuring that the sustainable development process gains a momentum of its own. There will be further structural reforms as environmental ministries and agencies gradually acquire more powers and wider responsibilities. Green planning will become more extensive, with wider use of sustainability indicators linked to tougher sectoral targets and the development of Green National Accounting measures to complement traditional methods (Ogle 2000). Efforts to extend participation will increase, especially at the local level. Crucially, the growing international pressure to develop more effective responses to climate change is sure to see more experimentation with MBIs, notably the establishment of an international emission trading market. Over time these initiatives may build up to exert a profound transformationary effect. However, politics, as this book shows, is not all about the state. Governments may be held back from taking more stringent measures by the lack of support from two key actors whose active support and participation are essential for the successful implementation of sustainable development: business and citizens.

On balance, business remains probably the major obstacle to sustainable development. As Chapter 7 showed, business retains its privileged position in the policy process, reinforced by the administrative fragmentation of the state, producer-dominated policy networks and pro-industry advocacy coalitions. Not surprisingly, the traditional environmental policy paradigm still prevails in most policy areas. If capitalism is to be reformed, industry must be a willing partner. Hence the attraction of ecological modernisation is that the 'pollution prevention pays' principle demonstrates that business has an economic incentive to care for the environment. Certainly, by working in partnership with industry, the state can play a critical role in facilitating social learning by business elites and providing a framework of regulations and financial incentives to nurture ecological modernisation in specific policy areas. The evidence discussed in Part III suggests an ambivalent view of ecological modernisation. To date, it has colonised only a small minority of business boardrooms in certain sectors in a handful of mostly North European nations, which begs important questions about its applicability elsewhere, particularly in less developed countries. An important problem with the concept of ecological modernisation identified in Chapter 8 is that the literature has focused on the production side of the equation, identifying the possibility of efficiency savings to be gained from adopting less polluting production technologies and practices. By contrast, the consumption side has been relatively ignored. Yet the market can only act as an instrument for change if consumers play their part. Currently, gestures towards green consumerism, such as increased levels of recycling or a switch to organic food products, are swamped by the dominance of consumer capitalism which seems to feed off an apparently insatiable need to consume more and more. While there is some scope for businesses to help shape consumer preferences by, for example, providing information about the energy efficiency of products, there is no incentive for businesses to persuade people to consume *less*. On the contrary, the logic of capitalism – the drive for capital accumulation and profit-maximisation – implies that business must encourage greater consumption.

One of the lessons to be drawn from this book is that the transition to a sustainable society involves more than institutional restructuring by governments and social learning by policy elites. Neither businesses nor governments are likely to change their behaviour until they can be assured that consumers and citizens will support them. The market will continue to provide the goods that consumers demand (although business can of course stimulate and shape those consumer preferences) and, as long as the environment lacks electoral salience, few governments will risk unpopularity by introducing high eco-taxes on, say, domestic fuel or petrol. In short, in a capitalist liberal democracy the individual consumer, or citizen, may be a major obstacle to sustainable development.

It seems that sustainable development also requires a transformation in the beliefs, attitudes and behaviour of individuals along the lines of the 'ecological citizenship' model discussed by some green theorists (Christoff 1996a; Barry 1999a). Although sustainable development does not require the dramatic sacrifices towards frugal living anticipated by deep ecologists, it will nevertheless still involve some significant changes in individual lifestyles if there is to be a shift from a *consumer* society towards a *conserver* society. Such changes will only take root if people accept the underlying ethos and voluntarily make the necessary alterations. The use of MBIs can play a role here. However, ecological citizenship will clearly involve a degree of ecological responsibility towards non-citizens, notably animals and ecosystems, and civic loyalty will stretch beyond the boundaries of the nation state to encompass global considerations, such as poverty in the less developed world. Green citizenship in practice will range from ethical investment to participation in LETS schemes, and from green consumerism to voluntary involvement in community and environmental programmes. If ecological citizenship were to take root, even its weakest forms would act as a potential market stimulus to ecological modernisation.

How might ecological citizenship be nurtured? There are certainly plenty of opportunities for governments to facilitate ecological citizenship through policies that might even prove popular. Not least, policies aimed at the alleviation and removal of poverty and inequality would be critical. Institutional reforms, notably the democratisation and decentralisation of state structures, could encourage greater deliberation and participation by citizens.

Crucially, the state can also invest in education. Many people are mystified or bewildered by the complexity of most global environmental issues. Public understanding of global warming, for example, remains at an alarmingly low level. Things are slowly changing. Today the environment is a familiar feature on the school curriculum from the moment children start formal education. Younger generations are now undoubtedly much better informed about environmental issues than their predecessors. The growing significance of the internet as a source of knowledge, education and communication may enhance this trend (it also offers unknown potential to expand the repertoire of protest, as illustrated by the activist networking behind recent direct action in Seattle and at other 'anti-capitalist' events). Furthermore, there is evidence that higher levels of education enhance public understanding of environmental issues (Rootes 1999c). Here again there is reason for optimism. The proportion of people with higher education is growing in most countries, so public awareness and understanding of environmental issues is likely to grow.

Of great importance, though, is evidence that environmental activism is positively linked to higher education, so a more educated citizenry may also be more willing and more capable of acting on its concerns by changing lifestyles and participating in the political process. One of the most effective forms of political education is through the experience of struggle. Most people who engage in environmental conflict do so at the local level, perhaps resisting a new road or incinerator, but a local struggle frequently involves direct confrontation with a multinational corporation and/or a national government. Such a situation is likely to encourage local groups to look to national and international NGOs for support, which may act as a catalyst for individuals to make links between their local struggle and wider issues, a process of learning and reflection that has the potential to stimulate a wider ecological consciousness. It is the prospect of this reflexivity occurring on a large scale that has led some writers to enthuse about the emergence of a global civil society of international NGOs such as Greenpeace, FoE and WWF linking civil society across national boundaries and providing a new source of identity for individual citizens beyond their own nationality (Lipschutz 1996; Wapner 1996). At present, this kind of ecological citizenship remains, for the most part, at the level of aspiration; whether or not it develops will depend on many factors, notably the interdependent relationship between the state, business and the citizen within the wider structure of global capitalism. Hopefully, if this book helps cast light on these complex relationships, then it might make a small contribution to the development of that ecological citizenship.

References

Aardal, Bernt (1990) 'Green Politics: A Norwegian Experience', *Scandinavian Political Studies*, 13(2): 147–64.

Abbey, Edward (1975) *The Monkey Wrench Gang*, New York: Avon.

Abramson, Paul and Inglehart, Ronald (1995) *Value Change in Global Perspective*, Ann Arbor: University of Michigan Press.

Achterberg, Wouter (1993) 'Can Liberal Democracy Survive the Environmental Crisis?', in Andrew Dobson and Paul Lucardie (eds.), *The Politics of Nature*, London: Routledge, pp. 81–101.

Adams, John (1995) *Risk*, London: UCL Press.

Affigne, Anthony (1990) 'Environmental Crisis, Green Party Power: Chernobyl and the Swedish Greens', in Wolfgang Rüdig (ed.), *Green Politics One*, Edinburgh University Press, pp. 115–52.

Alber, Jens (1989) 'Modernization, Cleavage Structures and the Rise of Green Parties and Lists in Europe', in Müller-Rommel (ed.), pp. 195–210.

Amy, Douglas (1990) 'Decision Techniques for Environmental Policy: A Critique', in Robert Paehlke and Douglas Torgerson (eds.), *Managing Leviathan: Environmental Politics and the Administrative State*, London: Belhaven Press, pp. 59–79.

Andersen, Jorgen Goul (1990) '"Environmentalism", "New Politics" and Industrialism: Some Theoretical Perspectives', *Scandinavian Political Studies*, 13(2): 101–18.

Andersen, Mikael Skou (1994) *Governance by Green Taxes*, Manchester University Press.

Andersen, Mikael Skou, Christiansen, Peter Munk and Winter, Soren (1998) 'Denmark: Consensus Seeking and Decentralisation', in Hanf and Jansen (eds.), pp. 40–59.

Andersen, Mikael Skou and Liefferink, Duncan (eds.) (1997a) *European Environmental Policy: The Pioneers*, Manchester University Press.

(1997b) 'Introduction: The Impact of the Pioneers on EU Environmental Policy', in Andersen and Liefferink (eds.), pp. 1–39.

Anderson, Terry and Leal, Donald (1991) *Free Market Environmentalism*, Boulder: Westview Press.

Andresen, Steinar, Skodvin, Tora, Underdal, Arild and Wettestad, Jørgen (2000) *Science and Politics in International Environmental Regimes*, Manchester University Press.

Andrews, Richard (1999) 'Risk-Based Decision-Making', in Vig and Kraft (eds.), pp. 210–31.

Armour, Audrey (1997) 'Rethinking the Role of Risk Assessment in Environmental Policymaking', in Lynton Caldwell and Robert Bartlett (eds.), *Environmental Policy: Transnational Issues and National Trends*, Westport, CT: Quorum Books, pp. 37–59.

Arrow, Kenneth (and 10 others) (1995) 'Economic Growth, Carrying Capacity and the Environment', *Science*, 268: 520–1.

Arter, David (1995) 'The March 1995 Finnish Election: The Social Democrats Storm Back', *West European Politics*, 18(4): 194–204.

Arts, Bas (1998) *The Political Influence of Global NGOs: Case Studies on the Climate and Biodiversity Conventions*, Utrecht: International Books.

Arts, Bas and Rüdig, Wolfgang (1995) 'Negotiating the "Berlin Mandate": Reflecting on the First "Conference of the Parties" to the UN Framework Convention on Climate Change', *Environmental Politics*, 4(3): 481–7.

Attfield, Robin (1983) *The Ethics of Environmental Concern*, Oxford: Blackwell.

  (1993) 'Sylvan, Fox and Deep Ecology: A View from the Continental Shelf', *Environmental Values*, 2: 21–32.

Australian Government (1991) *Australian National Report to the UN Conference on Environment and Development*, Canberra: Department of Arts, Sport, the Environment and Territories.

Axelrod, Robert (1984) *The Evolution of Cooperation*, New York: Basic Books.

Bachrach, Peter and Baratz, Morton (1962) 'The Two Faces of Power', *American Political Science Review*, 56: 947–52.

Backstrand, Karin, Kronsell, Annica and Soderholm, Peter (1996) 'Organisational Challenges to Sustainable Development', *Environmental Politics*, 5(2): 209–30.

Baggott, Rob (1998) 'Nuclear Power at Druridge Bay', *Parliamentary Affairs*, 51: 384–96.

Bahro, Rudolf (1986) *Building the Green Movement*, London: GMP.

Bailey, Christopher (1996) 'Explaining the Choice of Air Pollution Control Strategies in the United States: Some Evidence of Institutional Bias', *Environmental Politics*, 5(1): 74–92.

Bailey, Ronald (ed.) (1995) *The True State of the Planet*, New York: Free Press.

Baker, Susan, Koussis, Maria, Richardson, Dick and Young, Stephen (1997a) 'Introduction: The Theory and Practice of Sustainable Development in EU Perspective', in Baker et al. (eds.), pp. 1–40.

  (eds.) (1997b) *The Politics of Sustainable Development: Theory, Policy and Practice within the European Union*, London: Routledge.

Balling, Robert (1995) 'Global Warming: Messy Models, Decent Data, and Pointless Policy', in Bailey (ed.), pp. 83–107.

Barber, Benjamin (1984) *Strong Democracy*, Berkeley: University of California Press.

Barbier, Edward, Burgess, Joanne, Swanson, Timothy and Pearce, David (1990) *Elephants, Economics and Ivory*, London: Earthscan.

Barrow, C. J. (1995) *Developing the Environment*, Harlow: Longman.

Barry, Brian (1991) *Liberty and Justice: Essays in Political Theory*, Oxford: Clarendon Press.

Barry, John (1994) 'Beyond the Shallow and the Deep: Green Politics, Philosophy and Praxis', *Environmental Politics*, 3(3): 369–94.

  (1996) 'Sustainability, Political Judgement and Citizenship: Connecting Green Politics and Democracy', in Doherty and de Geus (eds.), pp. 115–31.

  (1998) 'Marxism and Ecology', in Andrew Gamble, David Marsh and Tony Tant (eds.), *Marxism and Social Science*, London: Macmillan, pp. 259–79.

  (1999a) *Rethinking Green Politics*, London: Sage.

  (1999b) *Environment and Social Theory*, London: Routledge.

Bartlett, Robert (1997) 'Integrated Impact Assessment: The New Zealand Experiment', in Lynton Caldwell and Robert Bartlett (eds.), *Environmental Policy: Transnational Issues and National Trends*, Westport, CT: Quorum Books, pp. 157–71.

Bate, Roger (ed.) (1998) *Global Warming*, Cambridge: ESEF Publishing.

Baumgartner, Frank and Jones, Bryan (1993) *Agendas and Instability in American Politics*, University of Chicago Press.

Baxter, Brian (1999) *Ecologism*, Edinburgh University Press.

Beck, Ulrich (1992) *Risk Society*, London: Sage.

Beckerman, Wilfred (1995) *Small Is Stupid*, London: Duckworth.

Beetham, David (1977) 'From Socialism to Fascism: The Relation between Theory and Practice in the Work of Robert Michels', *Political Studies*, 25: 3–24, 161–81.

Bell, Daniel (1973) *The Coming Crisis of Post-Industrial Society*, New York: Basic Books.

Bell, Simon and Morse, Stephen (1999) *Sustainability Indicators*, London: Earthscan.

Benedick, Richard (1991) *Ozone Diplomacy*, Cambridge, MA: Harvard University Press.

Bennie, Lynn (1998) 'Brent Spar, Atlantic Oil and Greenpeace', *Parliamentary Affairs*, 51: 397–410.

Bennulf, Martin (1995) 'Sweden: The Rise and Fall of Miljöpartiet de Gröna', in Richardson and Rootes (eds.), pp. 128–45.

Benson, John (1978) 'Duty and the Beast', *Philosophy*, 53: 529–49.

Benton, Ted (1993) *Natural Relations*, London: Verso.

Beuermann, Christine and Burdick, Bernhard (1997) 'The Sustainability Transition in Germany: Some Early Stage Experiences', *Environmental Politics*, 6(1): 83–107.

Beuermann, Christine and Jäger, Jill (1996) 'Climate Change Policies in Germany: How Long Will Any Double Dividend Last?', in Timothy O'Riordan and Jill Jäger (eds.), *Politics of Climate Change*, London: Routledge, pp. 186–227.

Biehl, Janet (1991) *Rethinking Ecofeminist Politics*, Boston: South End Press.

Blowers, Andrew (1984) *Something in the Air: Corporate Power and the Environment*, London: Harper and Row.

(1997) 'Environmental Policy: Ecological Modernisation or the Risk Society?', *Urban Studies*, 34(5–6): 845–71.

Blühdorn, Ingolfur (1995) 'Campaigning for Nature: Environmental Pressure Groups in Germany and Generational Change in the Ecology Movement', in Ingolfur Blühdorn, Frank Kruse and Thomas Scharf (eds.), *The Green Agenda: Environmental Politics in Germany*, Keele University Press, pp. 167–220.

Boehmer-Christiansen, Sonja and Skea, Jim (1991) *Acid Politics*, London: Belhaven.

Bomberg, Elizabeth (1998a) *Green Parties and Politics in the European Union*, London: Routledge.

(1998b) 'Issue Networks and the Environment: Explaining European Union Environmental Policy', in Marsh (ed.), pp. 167–84.

Bookchin, Murray (1980) *Towards an Ecological Society*, Montreal: Black Rose.

(1982) *The Ecology of Freedom*, Palo Alto, CA: Cheshire.

(1989) *Remaking Society*, Montreal: Black Rose.

Bookchin, Murray and Foreman, Dave (1991) *Defending the Earth*, Boston: South End Press.

Bosso, Christopher (1997) 'Seizing Back the Day: The Challenge to Environmental Activism in the 1990s', in Norman Vig and Michael Kraft (eds.), *Environmental Policy in the 1990s*, 3rd edition, Washington, DC: CQ Press, pp. 53–74.

(1999) 'Environmental Groups and the New Political Landscape', in Vig and Kraft (eds.), pp. 55–76.

Botzler, Richard and Armstrong, Susan (eds.) (1998) *Environmental Ethics*, 2nd edition, London: McGraw-Hill.

Braadbaart, Okke (1998) 'American Bias in Environmental Economics: Industrial Pollution Abatement and "Incentives Versus Regulations"', *Environmental Politics*, 7(2): 134–52.

Bramwell, Anna (1985) *Blood and Soil: Walther Darré and Hitler's 'Green Party'*, Bourne End, Bucks.

(1989) *Ecology in the Twentieth Century*, New Haven: Yale University Press.

Brand, Karl-Werner (1999) 'Dialectics of Institutionalisation: The Transformation of the Environmental Movement in Germany', *Environmental Politics*, 8(1): 35–58.

Brennan, Andrew (1986) 'Ecological Theory and Value in Nature', *Philosophical Inquiry*, 8: 66–96 [reprinted in Elliot (ed.), (1995)].

(1988) *Thinking about Nature*, London: Routledge.

(1992) 'Moral Pluralism and the Environment', *Environmental Values*, 1: 15–33.

Brenton, Tony (1994) *The Greening of Machiavelli*, London: Earthscan.

Bressers, Hans, O'Toole, Laurence and Richardson, Jeremy (eds.) (1994) *Networks for Water Policy: A Comparative Perspective*, Newbury Park: Frank Cass.

Bryant, Raymond and Bailey, Sinead (1997) *Third World Political Ecology*, London: Routledge.

Bryner, Gary (2000) 'The United States: "Sorry – Not Our Problem"', in Lafferty and Meadowcroft (eds.), pp. 273–302.

Bryson, Caroline and Curtice, John (1998) 'The End of Materialism?', in Roger Jowell, John Curtice, Alison Park, Lindsay Brook, Katarina Thomson and Caroline Bryson (eds.), *British – and European – Social Attitudes: The 15th Report*, Aldershot: Ashgate, pp. 125–48.

Bullard, Robert (1990) *Dumping in Dixie*, Boulder: Westview Press.

Buller, Henry (1998) 'Reflections across the Channel: Britain, France and the Europeanisation of National Environmental Policy', in Philip Lowe and Stephen Ward (eds.), *British Environmental Policy and Europe*, London: Routledge, pp. 67–83.

Bulloch, John and Darwish, Adel (1993) *Water Wars: Coming Conflicts in the Middle East*, London: Victor Gollancz.

Bürklin, Wilhelm (1987) 'Governing Left Parties Frustrating the Radical Non-Established Left: The Rise and Inevitable Decline of the Greens', *European Sociological Review*, 3(2): 109–26.

Busenberg, George (1999) 'The Evolution of Vigilance: Disasters, Sentinels and Policy Change', *Environmental Politics*, 8(1): 90–109.

Cable, Sherry and Cable, Charles (1995) *Environmental Problems, Grassroots Solutions: The Politics of Grassroots Environmental Conflict*, New York: St. Martin's Press.

Caldecott, Leonie and Leland, Stephanie (eds.) (1983) *Reclaim the Earth: Women Speak Out for Life on Earth*, London: Women's Press.

Callenbach, Ernest (1978) *Ecotopia*, London: Pluto.

Callicott, J. Baird (1985) 'Intrinsic Value, Quantum Theory, and Environmental Ethics', *Environmental Ethics*, 7: 257–75.

(1986) 'On the Intrinsic Value of Nonhuman Species', in Bryan Norton (ed.), *The Preservation of Species: The Value of Biological Diversity*, Princeton University Press, pp. 138–172.

Carley, Michael and Christie, Ian (2000) *Managing Sustainable Development*, 2nd edition, London: Earthscan.

Carson, Rachel (1962) *Silent Spring*, Boston: Houghton Mifflin.

Carter, Neil (1992) 'The Greening of Labour', in Martin Smith and Joanna Spear (eds.), *The Changing Labour Party*, London: Routledge, pp. 118–32.

(1994) 'The Greens in the 1994 European Parliamentary Elections', *Environmental Politics*, 3(3): 495–502.

(1996) 'Worker Co-operatives and Green Political Thought', in Doherty and de Geus (eds.), pp. 56–75.

(1997) 'Prospects: The Parties and the Environment in the UK', in Michael Jacobs (ed.), *Greening the Millennium?*, Oxford: Blackwell, pp. 192–205.

(1999) 'The Greens in the 1999 European Parliamentary Elections', *Environmental Politics*, 8(4): 160–7.

Carter, Neil and Lowe, Philip (1995) 'The Establishment of a Cross-Sector Environment Agency', in Tim Gray (ed.), *UK Environmental Policy in the 1990s* London: Macmillan, pp. 38–56.

(1998) 'Britain: Coming to Terms with Sustainable Development?', in Hanf and Jansen (eds.), pp. 17–39.

Cater, Douglass (1965) *Power in Washington*, London: Collins.

Chatterjee, Pratap and Finger, Matthias (1994) *The Earth Brokers*, London: Routledge.

Christoff, Peter (1996a) 'Ecological Citizens and Ecologically Guided Democracy', in Doherty and de Geus (eds.), pp. 151–69.

(1996b) 'Ecological Modernisation, Ecological Modernities', *Environmental Politics*, 5(3): 476–500.

Church, Clive (1995) 'Switzerland: Greens in a Confederal Polity', in Richardson and Rootes (eds.), pp. 146–67.

Clapp, Jennifer (1998) 'Foreign Direct Investment in Hazardous Industries in Developing Countries: Rethinking the Debate', *Environmental Politics*, 7(4): 92–113.

Clark, Stephen (1977) *The Moral Status of Animals*, Oxford: Clarendon Press.

Cole, Alistair and Doherty, Brian (1995) 'France: *Pas commes les autres* – the French Greens at the Crossroads', in Richardson and Rootes (eds.), pp. 45–65.

Cole, H., Freeman, Christopher, Jahoda, Marie and Pavitt, K. (1973) *Thinking about the Future: A Critique of the Limits to Growth*, Brighton: Sussex University Press.

Collard, Andree (1988) *Rape of the Wild*, London: Women's Press.

Commoner, Barry (1971) *The Closing Circle: Nature, Man and Technology*, New York: Alfred Knopf.

Conca, Ken (1994) 'Re-thinking the Ecology–Sovereignty Debate', *Millennium*, 23(3): 701–11.

Connelly, James and Smith, Graham (1999) *Politics and the Environment*, London: Routledge.

Cotgrove, Stephen, (1982) *Catastrophe or Cornucopia?* Chichester: Wiley.

Cox, Graham, Lowe, Philip and Winter, Michael (1986) 'Agriculture and Conservation in Britain: A Policy Community under Siege', in Cox, Lowe and Winter (eds.), *Agriculture: People and Policies*, London: Allen and Unwin, pp. 181–215.

Crenson, Matthew (1971) *The Unpolitics of Air Pollution*, Baltimore: Johns Hopkins University Press.

Crepaz, Markus (1995) 'Explaining National Variations of Air Pollution Levels: Political Institutions and their Impact on Environmental Policy-Making', *Environmental Politics*, 4(3): 391–414.

Crosland, Tony (1971) *A New Social Democratic Britain*, London: Fabian Society.

Dahl, Robert (1961) *Who Governs?*, New Haven: Yale University Press.

Dalton, Russell (1988) *Citizen Politics in Western Democracies*, Chatham, NJ: Chatham House.

(1994) *The Green Rainbow: Environmental Groups in Western Europe*, New Haven: Yale University Press.

Dalton, Russell and Bürklin, Wilhelm (1996) 'The Two Electorates', in Russell Dalton (ed.), *Germans Divided*, Oxford: Berg, pp. 183–207.

Dalton, Russell and Rohrschneider, Robert (1998) 'The Greening of Europe', in Roger Jowell, John Curtice, Alison Park, Lindsay Brook, Katarina Thomson and

Caroline Bryson (eds.), *British – and European – Social Attitudes: The 15th Report*, Aldershot: Ashgate, pp. 101–23.

Daly, Herman (1992) *Steady State Economics*, 2nd edition, London: Earthscan.

Daly, Herman and Cobb, John (1990) *For the Common Good*, London: Green Print.

Daugbjerg, Carsten (1998) 'Linking Policy Networks and Environmental Policies: Nitrate Policy-Making in Denmark and Sweden 1979–95', *Public Administration*, 76: 275–94.

della Porta, Donatella and Diani, Mario (1999) *Social Movements*, Oxford: Blackwell.

Department of Transport (1989) *Roads for Prosperity*, London: HMSO.

Depledge, Joanna (2000) 'Rising from the Ashes: The Cartagena Protocol on Biosafety', *Environmental Politics*, 9(2): 156–62.

de-Shalit, Avner (1995) *Why Posterity Matters: Environmental Policies and Future Generations*, London: Routledge.

DETR [Department of the Environment, Transport and the Regions] (1998) *A New Deal for Transport: Better for Everyone*, London: The Stationery Office.

DETR [Department of the Environment, Transport and the Regions] (1999) *Quality of Life Counts*, London: The Stationery Office.

DETR [Department of the Environment, Transport and the Regions] (2000) *Climate Change: The UK Programme*, London: The Stationery Office.

Deudney, Daniel (1997) 'The Limits of Environmental Security', in Sheldon Kamieniecki, George Gonzalez and Robert Vos (eds.), *Flashpoints in Environmental Policymaking*, Albany: SUNY Press, pp. 281–310.

Devall, Bill (1990) *Simple in Means, Rich in Ends: Practising Deep Ecology*, London: Green Print.

Devall, Bill and Sessions, George (1985) *Living as if Nature Mattered*, Layton, UT: Peregrine and Smith.

Diani, Mario and Donati, Paolo (1999) 'Organisational Change in Western European Environmental Groups: A Framework for Analysis', *Environmental Politics*, 8(1): 13–34.

Dickens, Peter (1992) *Society and Nature*, Hemel Hempstead: Harvester Wheatsheaf.

Die Grünen (1983) *Programme of the German Green Party* (trans. Hans Fernbach), London: Heretic Books.

Dobson, Andrew (1998) *Justice and the Environment*, Oxford University Press.

(ed.) (1999) *Fairness and Futurity: Essays on Environmental Sustainability and Social Justice*, Oxford University Press.

(2000) *Green Political Thought*, 3rd edition, London: Routledge.

Doherty, Brian (1992) 'The Fundi–Realo Controversy: An Analysis of Four European Green Parties', *Environmental Politics*, 1(1): 95–120.

(1996) 'Green Parties, Nonviolence and Political Obligation', in Doherty and de Geus (eds.), pp. 36–55.

(1998) 'Opposition to Road-Building', *Parliamentary Affairs*, 51: 370–83.

(1999) 'Paving the Way: The Rise of Direct Action against Road-Building and the Changing Character of British Environmentalism', *Political Studies*, 47(2): 275–91.

Doherty, Brian and de Geus, Marius (eds.) (1996) *Democracy and Green Political Thought*, London: Routledge.

Dowding, Keith (1995) 'Model or Metaphor? A Critical Review of the Policy Network Approach', *Political Studies*, 43: 136–58.

Dowie, Mark (1995) *Losing Ground: American Environmentalism at the Close of the Twentieth Century*, Cambridge, MA: MIT Press.

Downs, Anthony (1972) 'Up and Down with Ecology – the "Issue Attention Cycle"', *The Public Interest*, No. 28.

Doyle, Timothy and McEachern, Doug (1998) *Environment and Politics*, London: Routledge.

Drengson, Alan (1989) *Beyond Environmental Crisis*, New York: Peter Lang.

Dresdner Kleinwort Wasserstein (2000) *Power Generation in the 21st Century*, London.

Dryzek, John (1987) *Rational Ecology*, Oxford: Blackwell.

(1990) *Discursive Democracy*, Cambridge University Press.

(1997) *The Politics of the Earth*, Oxford University Press.

Dudley, Geoffrey and Richardson, Jeremy (1996) 'Why Does Policy Change over Time? Adversarial Policy Communities, Alternative Policy Arenas and British Trunk Roads Policy 1945–95', *Journal of European Public Policy*, 3(1): 63–83.

Dunlap, Riley (1995) 'Public Opinion and Environmental Policy', in Lester (ed.), pp. 63–114.

Dunlap, Riley and Mertig, Angela (1992a) 'The Evolution of the US Environmental Movement from 1970–1990: An Overview', in Dunlap and Mertig (eds.), pp. 1–10.

(eds.) (1992b) *American Environmentalism: The US Environmental Movement 1970–1990*, New York: Taylor and Francis.

Dunleavy, Patrick and O'Leary, Brendan (1987) *Theories of the State*, London: Macmillan.

Duverger, Maurice (1954) *Political Parties*, London: Methuen.

Dworkin, Ronald (1993) *Life's Dominion*, New York: Alfred Knopf.

Eckerberg, Katarina (1997) 'Comparing the Local Use of Environmental Policy Instruments in Nordic and Baltic Countries – The Issue of Diffuse Water Pollution', *Environmental Politics*, 6(2): 24–47.

Eckerberg, Katarina and Brundin, P. (1999) *A Survey of Swedish Municipalities' Work with Agenda 21*, Swedish Ministry of Environment/Swedish Association of Local Authorities, Stockholm: Kommentus Förlag.

Eckersley, Robyn (1989) 'Green Politics and the New Class: Selfishness or Virtue?', *Political Studies*, 37: 205–23.

(1990) 'The Green Political Ball Park: An Overview of Positions and Players', unpublished paper.

(1992) *Environmentalism and Political Theory*, London: UCL Press.

(1993) 'Free Market Environmentalism: Friend or Foe', *Environmental Politics*, 2(1): 1–19.

(1996a) 'Greening Liberal Democracy: The Rights Discourse Revisited', in Doherty and de Geus (eds.), pp. 212–36.

(ed.) (1996b) *Markets, the State and the Environment*, London: Macmillan.

Economic and Social Research Council (Global Environmental Change Programme) (1999) *The Politics of GM Food: Risk, Science and Public Trust*, Special Briefing No. 5, Falmer: University of Sussex.

EEA [European Environment Agency] (1996) *Environmental Taxes: Implementation and Environmental Effectiveness*, Copenhagen: EEA.

(1997a) *Air Pollution in Europe 1997*, Copenhagen: EEA.

(1997b) *Environmental Agreements: Environmental Effectiveness*, Copenhagen: EEA.

(2000a) *European Community and Member States Greenhouse Emission Trends 1990–1998*, Copenhagen: EEA.

(2000b) *Recent Developments in the Use of Environmental Taxes in the European Union*, Copenhagen: EEA.

Ehrlich, Paul (1968) *The Population Bomb*, New York: Ballantine.

Ekins, Paul (1986) *The Living Economy*, London: RKP.

Ellerman, Denny, Joskow, Paul, Schmalensee, Richard, Montero, Juan-Pablo and Bailey, Elizabeth (2000) *Climate for Clean Air: The US Acid Rain Program*, Cambridge University Press.

Elliot, Robert (ed.) (1995) *Environmental Ethics*, Oxford University Press.

Elliot, Robert and Gare, Arran (1983) *Environmental Philosophy*, Milton Keynes: Open University Press.

Elliott, Lorraine (1994) *International Environmental Politics: Protecting the Antarctic*, London: Macmillan.

(1998) *The Global Politics of the Environment*, London: Macmillan.

ENDs [Environmental Data Services] (1997) *ENDs Report*, No. 274.

(1998a) *ENDs Report*, No. 281.

(1998b) *ENDs Report*, No. 283.

(1998c) *ENDs Report*, No. 282.

Environmental Audit Committee (1998–9) 6th Report, House of Commons, HC 426-I.

Enzensberger, Hans-Magnus (1974) 'A Critique of Political Ecology', *New Left Review* 84: 3–31.

Epstein, Leon (1967) *Political Parties in Western Democracies*, New York: Praeger.

Escobar, Arturo (1995) *Encountering Development*, Princeton University Press.

Eurobarometer (1992) *The Europeans and the Environment in 1992*, Brussels: European Commission.

(1995) *Europeans and the Environment*, Brussels: European Commission.

(1999) *What Do Europeans Think about the Environment?*, Brussels: European Commission.

European Commission (1992) *Towards Sustainability*, COM(92)23 final, Luxembourg: Office for Official Publications of the EC.

(1996) *Progress Report: Towards Sustainability*, COM(95)624 final, Luxembourg: Office for Official Publications of the EC.

(1997) *Directive 85/337/EEC: Update of 5-Years EIA Report*, Brussels (*www.europe.eu.int/ comm/environment/eia/eia-studies-and-reports/ 5years.pdf*).

European Communities (2000) *The Global Assessment. Europe's Environment: What Directions for the Future?*, Luxembourg: Office for the Official Publications of the European Communities (*http://europa.eu.int/comm/ environment/newprg/99543_en.pdf*).

Evans, Judith (1993) 'Ecofeminism and the Politics of the Gendered Self', in Andrew Dobson and Paul Lucardie (eds.), *The Politics of Nature*, London: Routledge, pp. 177–89.

Faucher, Florence (1998) 'Is There Hope for the French Ecology Movement?', *Environmental Politics*, 7(3): 42–65.

Flam, Helena (1994) *States and Anti-Nuclear Movements*, Edinburgh University Press.

Flynn, Andrew and Lowe, Philip (1992) 'The Greening of the Tories', in Wolfgang Rüdig (ed.), *Green Politics Two*, Edinburgh University Press, pp. 9–36.

Font, Nuria and Morata, Francesc (1998) 'Spain: Environmental Policy and Public Administration. A Marriage of Convenience Officiated by the EU?', in Hanf and Jansen (eds.), pp. 208–29.

Food Ethics Council (1999) *Novel Foods: Beyond Nuffield*, Southwell: Food Ethics Council.

Foreman, Dave and Haywood, Bill (1985) *Ecodefense: A Field Guide to Monkeywrenching*, Tucson: New Ludd.

Foster, John Bellamy (2000) *Marx's Ecology: Materialism and Nature*, New York: Monthly Review Press.

Fox, Warwick (1990) *Toward a Transpersonal Ecology*, Boston: Shambhala.

Francis, John (1994) 'Environmental Policy', in Gillian Peele, Christopher Bailey, Bruce Cain and Guy Peters (eds.), *Developments in American Politics 2*, London: Macmillan, pp. 271–88.

Frankel, Boris (1987) *The Post Industrial Utopians*, Cambridge: Polity Press.

Frankland, E. Gene and Schoonmaker, Donald (1992) *Between Protest and Power: The Green Party in Germany*, Oxford: Westview.

Freeman, A. Myrick (1999) 'Economics, Incentives and Environmental Regulation', in Vig and Kraft (eds.), pp. 190–209.

Freudenberg, Nicholas and Steinsapir, Carol (1992) 'Not in Our Backyards: The Grassroots Environmental Movement', in Dunlap and Mertig (eds.), pp. 27–37.

Friends of the Earth International (2001) *http://www.foei.org/*.

Gamson, William and Meyer, David (1996) 'Framing Political Opportunity', in McAdam et al. (eds.), pp. 275–90.

Garner, Robert (1993) *Animals, Politics and Morality*, Manchester University Press.

Gauthier, David (1986) *Morals by Agreement*, Oxford University Press.

Gee, David (1997) 'Economic Tax Reform in Europe: Opportunities and Obstacles', in O'Riordan (ed.), pp. 81–105.

Gelbspan, Ross (1997) *The Heat is On: The High Stakes over the Earth's Threatened Climate*, Reading: Addison-Wesley.

Georgescu-Roegen, Nicholas (1971) *The Entropy Law and the Economic Process*, Cambridge, MA: Harvard University Press.

Gibbs, Lois (1982) *Love Canal: My Story*, Albany: SUNY Press.

Gibowski, Wolfgang (1999) 'Social Change and the Electorate: An Analysis of the 1998 *Bundestagswahl*', *German Politics*, 8(2): 10–32.

Gilpin, Robert (1987) *The Political Economy of International Relations*, Princeton University Press.

Glasbergen, Pieter (1992) 'Agri-Environmental Policy: Trapped in an Iron Law? A Comparative Analysis of Agricultural Pollution Control in the Netherlands, the United Kingdom and France', *Sociologia Ruralis*, 32(1): 30–48.

Golding, Martin (1972) 'Obligations to Future Generations', *The Monist*, 56: 85–99.

Goldsmith, Edward, Allen, Robert, Allaby, Michael, Davoll, John and Lawrence, Sam (1972) *A Blueprint for Survival*, Harmondsworth: Penguin.

Golub, Jonathan (ed.) (1998) *New Instruments for Environmental Policy in the EU*, London: Routledge.

Goodall, Jane (1986) *The Chimpanzees of Gombe*, Cambridge, MA: Harvard University Press.

Goodin, Robert (1992) *Green Political Theory*, Cambridge: Polity Press.

Gore, Albert (1992) *Earth in the Balance*, New York: Houghton Mifflin.

Gorz, Andre (1980) *Ecology as Politics*, Boston: South End Press.

Gottlieb, Robert (1993) *Forcing the Spring: The Transformation of the American Environmental Movement*, Washington, DC: Island Press.

Gould, Carol (1988) *Rethinking Democracy*, Cambridge University Press.

Gould, Kenneth, Schnaiberg, Allan and Weinberg, Adam (1996) *Local Environmental Struggles*, Cambridge University Press.

Gouldner, Alvin (1979) *The Future of Intellectuals and the Rise of the New Class*, London: Macmillan.

Grant, Wyn (1995) *Pressure Groups, Politics and Democracy in Britain*, 2nd edition, Hemel Hempstead: Harvester Wheatsheaf.

Gray, John (1993) *Beyond the New Right*, London: Routledge.

Gray, Tim (1997) 'The Common Fisheries Policy in the European Union', *Environmental Politics*, 6(4): 150–8.

Gray, Tim, Gray, Mark and Hague, Rod (1999) 'Sandeels, Sailors, Sandals and Suits: The Strategy of the Environmental Movement in Relation to the Fishing Industry', *Environmental Politics*, 8(3): 119–39.

Greenaway, John, Smith, Steve and Street, John (1992) *Deciding Factors in British Politics*, London: Routledge.

Green Party (2001) *http://www.greens.org/elections/*.

Greenpeace (1999) *Annual Report 1999 (http://www.greenpeace.org/report99/ index2.html)*.

Grove, Richard (1995) *Green Imperialism*, Cambridge University Press.

Grubb, Michael (1995) 'Seeking Fair Weather: Ethics and the International Debate on Climate Change', *International Affairs*, 71(3): 463–96.

Grubb, Michael, Sebenius, James, Magalhaes, Antonio and Subak, Susan (1992) 'Sharing the Burden', in Irving Mintzer (ed.), *Confronting Climate Change*, Cambridge University Press, pp. 305–22.

Gruen, Lori (1993) 'Animals', in Peter Singer (ed.), *A Companion to Ethics*, Oxford: Blackwell, pp. 343–53.

Gruen, Lori and Jamieson, Dale (1994) *Reflecting on Nature: Readings in Environmental Philosophy*, Oxford University Press.

Grundman, Reiner (1991) *Marxism and Ecology*, Oxford: Clarendon Press.

Haas, Peter (1990) *Saving the Mediterranean*, New York: Columbia University Press.

(1999) 'Social Constructivism and the Evolution of Multilateral Environmental Governance', in Aseem Prakash and Jeffrey Hart (eds.), *Globalization and Governance*, London: Routledge, pp. 103–33.

Haas, Peter, Keohane, Robert and Levy, Marc (eds.) (1993) *Institutions for the Earth: Sources of Effective International Environmental Protection*, Cambridge, MA: MIT Press.

Hahn, Robert (1996) 'Economic Prescriptions for Environmental Problems: Lessons from the United States and Continental Europe', in Robyn Eckersley (ed.), pp. 129–56.

Haigh, Nigel (1998) *Manual of Environmental Policy*, London: Elsevier/Institute for European Environmental Policy.

Hajer, Maarten (1995) *The Politics of Environmental Discourse: Ecological Modernisation and the Policy Process*, Oxford University Press.

Hall, Peter (1993) 'Policy Paradigms, Social Learning and the State', *Comparative Politics*, 25: 275–96.

Ham, Christopher and Hill, Michael (1993) *The Policy Process in the Modern Capitalist State*, 2nd edition, Hemel Hempstead: Harvester Wheatsheaf.

Hanf, Kenneth and Jansen, Alf-Inge (eds.) (1998) *Governance and Environment in Western Europe*, Harlow: Addison Wesley Longman.

Hanf, Kenneth and van de Gronden, Egbert (1998) 'The Netherlands: Joint Regulation and Sustainable Development', in Hanf and Jansen (eds.), pp. 152–80.

Hanley, Nick and Spash, Clive (1993) *Cost–Benefit Analysis and the Environment*, Cheltenham: Edward Elgar.

Hardin, Garrett (1968) 'The Tragedy of the Commons', *Science*, 162: 1243–8.

(1977) 'Living on a Lifeboat', in Garrett Hardin and John Baden (eds.), *Managing the Commons*, San Francisco: W. H. Freeman, pp. 261–79.

Harrison, Kathryn (1999) 'Racing to the Top or the Bottom? Industry Resistance to Eco-labelling of Paper Products in Three Jurisdictions', *Environmental Politics*, 8(4): 110–37.

Harrison, Paul (1993) *The Third Revolution*, London: Penguin.

Harvey, David (1993) 'The Nature of Environment: The Dialectics of Social and Environmental Change', in Ralph Miliband and Leo Panitch (eds.), *Socialist Register*, London: Merlin, pp. 1–51.

Haward, Marcus and Larmour, Peter (eds.) (1993) *The Tasmanian Parliamentary Accord and Public Policy 1989–92*, Canberra: Federalism Research Centre.

Hayward, Tim (1995) *Ecological Thought*, Cambridge: Polity Press.

Heclo, Hugh (1978) 'Issue Networks and the Executive Establishment', in Anthony King (ed.), *The New American Political System*, Washington, DC: American Enterprise Institute, pp. 87–124.

Heilbroner, Robert (1974) *An Inquiry into the Human Prospect*, New York: Norton and Co.

Hempel, Lamont (1995) 'Environmental Technology and the Green Car: Towards a Sustainable Transportation Policy', in Frank Fischer and Michael Black (eds.), *Greening Environmental Policy*, London: Paul Chapman, pp. 66–86.

(1999) 'Climate Policy on the Installment Plan', in Vig and Kraft (eds.), pp. 281–302.

Hill, Michael, Aaronovitch, Sabrina and Baldock, David (1989) 'Non-Decision Making in Pollution Control in Britain: Nitrate Pollution, the EEC Drinking Water Directive and Agriculture', *Policy and Politics*, 17(3): 227–40.

HM Government (1994) *Sustainable Development: The UK Strategy*, London: HMSO.

Hoffman, Jürgen (1999) 'From a Party of Young Voters to an Ageing Generation Party: Alliance'90/The Greens after the 1998 Federal Election', *Environmental Politics*, 8(3): 140–6.

Holden Meehan (1998) *The Millennium Guide to Ethical and Environmental Investment*, London: Holden Meehan.

Hooghe, Mark and Rihoux, Benoît (2000) 'The Green Breakthrough in the Belgian General Election of June 1999', *Environmental Politics*, 9(3): 129–36.

Houghton, John, Jenkins, Geoffrey and Ephraims, J. (eds.) (1990) *Climate Change: The IPCC Scientific Assessment*, Cambridge University Press.

Hughes, Jonathan (2000) *Ecology and Historical Materialism*, Cambridge University Press.

Hukkinen, Janne (1995) 'Corporatism as an Impediment to Ecological Sustenance: The Case of Finnish Waste Management', *Ecological Economics*, 15: 59–75.

Humphreys, David (1998) 'The Report of the International Panel on Forests', *Environmental Politics*, 7(1): 214–21.

Hurrell, Andrew (1995) 'International Political Theory and the Global Environment', in Ken Booth and Steve Smith (eds.), *International Relations Theory Today*, Cambridge: Polity Press, pp. 129–53.

Hurrell, Andrew and Kingsbury, Benedict (1992a) 'The International Politics of the Environment: An Introduction', in Hurrell and Kingsbury (eds.), pp. 1–47.

(1992b) *The International Politics of the Environment*, Oxford University Press.

Inglehart, Ronald (1977) *The Silent Revolution*, Princeton University Press.

(1990) *Culture Shift*, Princeton University Press.

IPCC [Intergovernmental Panel on Climate Change] (2001) *Climate Change 2001: Impacts, Adaptation, Vulnerability*, Geneva: UNEP/World Meteorological Organisation.

IUCN/UNEP/WWF [International Union for the Conservation of Nature and Natural Resources/UNEP/WWF] (1980) *World Conservation Strategy: Living Resource Conservation for Sustainable Development*, Gland, Switzerland.

Jackson, Robert (1990) *Quasi-States: Sovereignty, International Relations and the Third World*, Cambridge University Press.

Jacobs, Michael (1991) *The Green Economy*, London: Pluto.

(1996a) *The Politics of the Real World*, London: Earthscan.

(1996b) 'Financial Incentives: The British Experience', in Eckersley (ed.), pp. 113–28.

(1997) 'Introduction: The New Politics of the Environment', in Michael Jacobs (ed.), *Greening the Millennium?*, Oxford: Blackwell, pp. 1–17.

Jahn, Detlef (1997) 'Green Politics and Parties in Germany', in Michael Jacobs (ed.), *Greening the Millennium?*, Oxford: Blackwell, pp. 174–82.

Jamison, Andrew, Eyerman, Ron, Cramer, Jacqueline and Laessoe, Jeppé (1990) *The Making of the New Environmental Consciousness*, Edinburgh University Press.

Jänicke, Martin (1991) *The Political System's Capacity For Environmental Policy*, Berlin: Free University.

Jänicke, Martin and Jörgens, Helge (1998) 'National Environmental Policy Planning in OECD Countries: Preliminary Lessons from Cross-National Comparisons', *Environmental Politics*, 7(2): 27–54.

Jansen, Alf-Inge and Mydske, Per Kristen (1998) 'Norway: Balancing Environmental Quality and Interest in Oil', in Hanf and Jansen (eds.), pp. 181–207.

Jansen, Alf-Inge, Osland, Oddgeir and Hanf, Kenneth (1998) 'Environmental Challenges and Institutional Changes: An Interpretation of the Development of Environmental Policy in Western Europe', in Hanf and Jansen (eds.), pp. 277–325.

Jehlicka, Petr (1994) 'Environmentalism in Europe: An East–West Comparison', in Chris Rootes and Howard Davis (eds.), *A New Europe? Social Change and Political Transformation*, London: UCL Press, pp. 112–31.

Jokinen, Pekka (1997) 'Agricultural Policy Community and the Challenge of Greening: The Case of Finnish Agri-Environmental Policy', *Environmental Politics* 6(2): 48–71.

Joppke, C. and Markovits, Andrei (1994) 'Green Politics in the New Germany', *Dissent*, Spring: 235–40.

Jordan, Andrew (1998a) 'Private Affluence and Public Squalor? The Europeanisation of British Coastal Bathing Water Policy', *Policy and Politics*, 26(1): 33–54.

(1998b) 'The Ozone Endgame: The Implementation of the Montreal Protocol in the United Kingdom', *Environmental Politics*, 7(4): 23–52.

(1998c) 'The Impact on UK Environmental Administration', in Lowe and Ward (eds.), pp. 173–94.

(2000) 'Environmental Policy', in Patrick Dunleavy, Andrew Gamble, Ian Holliday and Gillian Peele (eds.), *Developments in British Politics 6*, London: Macmillan, pp. 257–75.

(2001) 'Environmental Policy Integration in the UK: Efficient Hardware and Light Green Software', in A. Lenschow (ed.), *Environmental Policy Integration*, London: Earthscan.

Jordan, Andrew and O'Riordan, Tim (1999) 'Environmental Problems and Management', in Paul Cloke, Philip Crang and Mark Goodwin (eds.), *Introducing Human Geographies*, London: Arnold, pp. 133–40.

Jordan, Grant and Maloney, William (1997) *The Protest Business?*, Manchester University Press.

Kamieniecki, Sheldon (1995) 'Political Parties and Environmental Policy', in James Lester (ed.), pp. 146–67.

Kasa, Sjur (2000) 'Policy Networks as Barriers to Green Tax Reform: The Case of CO_2 Taxes in Norway', *Environmental Politics*, 9(4): 104–22.

Kemp, Ray (1992) *The Politics of Radioactive Waste Disposal*, Manchester University Press.

Keohane, Robert (1989) *International Institutions and State Power: Essays in International Relations Theory*, Boulder: Westview Press.

Kickert, Walter, Klijn, Erik-Hans and Koppenjan, Jap (1997) *Managing Complex Networks*, London: Sage.

King, Ynestra (1983) 'The Ecofeminist Perspective', in Leonie Caldecott and Stephanie Leland (eds.), *Reclaim the Earth*, London: Women's Press, pp. 9–14.

　(1989) 'The Ecology of Feminism and the Feminism of Ecology', in Plant (ed.), pp. 18–28.

Kingdon, John (1995) *Agendas, Alternatives and Public Policies*, 2nd edition, New York: HarperCollins.

Kitschelt, Herbert (1986) 'Political Opportunity Structures and Political Protest: Anti-Nuclear Movements in Four Democracies', *British Journal of Political Science*, 16: 58–95.

　(1988) 'Left-Libertarian Parties: Explaining Innovation in Competitive Party Systems', *World Politics* 40(2): 194–234.

　(1989) *The Logics of Party Formation: Ecological Politics in Belgium and West Germany*, Ithaca: Cornell University Press.

　(1990) 'New Social Movements and the Decline of Party Organization', in Russell Dalton and Manfred Kuechler (eds.), *Challenging the Political Order: New Social and Political Movements in Western Democracies*, Cambridge: Polity Press, pp. 179–208.

　(1994) *The Transformation of European Social Democracy*, Cambridge University Press.

Klandermans, Bert and Tarrow, Sidney (1988) 'Mobilization into Social Movements: Synthesizing European and American Approaches', *International Social Movement Research*, 1: 1–38.

Klinger, Janeen (1994) 'Debt-for-Nature Swaps and the Limits to International Cooperation on Behalf of the Environment', *Environmental Politics* 3(2): 229–46.

Konttinen, Annamari (2000) 'From Grassroots to the Cabinet: The Green League of Finland', *Environmental Politics* 9(4): 129–34.

Kraft, Michael and Vig, Norman (1999) 'Environmental Policy from the 1970s to 2000: An Overview', in Vig and Kraft (eds.), pp. 1–31.

Krasner, Stephen (1983) *International Regimes*, Ithaca: Cornell University Press.

Kriesi, Hanspeter (1993) *Political Mobilisation and Social Change: The Dutch Case in Comparative Perspective*, Aldershot: Avebury.

Kriesi, Hanspeter, Koopmans, Ruud, Dyvendak, Jan and Giugni, Marco (1995) *New Social Movements in Western Europe*, London: UCL Press.

Kronsell, Annica (1997) 'Sweden: Setting a Good Example', in Andersen and Liefferink (eds.), pp. 40–80.

Kütting, Gabriela (2000) *Environment, Society and International Relations*, London: Routledge.

Lafferty, William (1996) 'The Politics of Sustainable Development: Global Norms for National Implementation', *Environmental Politics*, 5(2): 185–208.

Lafferty, William and Eckerberg, Katarina (1998) *From the Earth Summit to Local Agenda 21: Working towards Sustainable Development*, London: Earthscan.

Lafferty, William and Meadowcroft, James (eds.) (2000a) *Implementing Sustainable Development*, Oxford University Press.

　(2000b) 'Patterns of Governmental Engagement', in Lafferty and Meadowcroft (eds.), pp. 337–421.

Laslett, Peter and Fishkin, James (eds.) (1992) *Justice between Age Groups and Generations*, New Haven: Yale University Press.

La Spina, Antonio and Sciortino, Giuseppe (1993) 'Common Agenda, Southern Rules: European Integration and Environmental Change in the Mediterranean States', in Duncan Liefferink, Philip Lowe and Arthur Mol (eds.), *European Integration and Environmental Policy*, London: Belhaven, pp. 217–36.

Lauber, Volkmar (1995) 'The Austrian Greens', *Environmental Politics*, 4(2): 313–19.

(1997) 'Austria: A Latecomer Which Became a Pioneer', in Andersen and Liefferink (eds.), pp. 81–118.

Lee, Kai (1993) *Compass and Gyroscope: Integrating Science and Politics for the Environment*, Washington, DC: Island Press.

Lees, Charles (1999) 'The Red–Green Coalition', *German Politics*, 8(2): 174–94.

Lele, Sharachchandra (1991) 'Sustainable Development: A Critical Review', *World Development*, 19(6): 607–21.

Leopold, Aldo (1949) *A Sand County Almanac*, Oxford University Press.

Lester, James (ed.) (1995) *Environmental Politics and Policy: Theories and Evidence*, 2nd edition, Durham: Duke University Press.

Lester, James and Loftsson, Elfar (1993) 'The Ecological Movement and Green Parties in Scandinavia: Problems and Prospects', in Sheldon Kamieniecki (ed.), *Environmental Politics in the International Arena*, Albany: SUNY Press, pp. 113–28.

Levy, Marc (1993) 'European Acid Rain: The Power of Tote-Board Diplomacy', in Haas et al. (eds.), pp. 75–132.

Lewanski, Rudolf (1998) 'Italy: Environmental Policy in a Fragmented State', in Hanf and Jansen (eds.), pp. 131–51.

Liberatore, Angela (1995) 'The Social Construction of Environmental Problems', in Pieter Glasbergen and Andrew Blowers (eds.), *Perspectives on Environmental Problems*, London: Arnold, pp. 59–83.

(1997) 'The Integration of Sustainable Development Objectives into EU Policy-Making: Barriers and Prospects', in Baker et al. (eds.), pp. 107–26.

Lindblom, Charles (1977) *Politics and Markets*, New York: Basic Books.

Lipschutz, Ronnie (with Judith Mayer) (1996) *Global Civil Society and Global Environmental Governance: The Politics of Nature from Place to Planet*, Albany: SUNY Press.

Lipset, Seymour Martin and Rokkan, Stein (1967) 'Cleavage Structures, Party Systems and Voter Alignments: An Introduction', in Seymour Martin Lipset and Stein Rokkan (eds.), *Party Systems and Voter Alignments: Cross-National Perspectives*, New York: Free Press, pp. 1–67.

Litfin, Karen (1994) *Ozone Discourses: Science and Politics in Global Environmental Cooperation*, New York: Columbia University Press.

(1998a) 'The Greening of Sovereignty: An Introduction', in Litfin (ed.), pp. 1–27.

(ed.) (1998b) *The Greening of Sovereignty in World Politics*, Cambridge, MA. MIT Press.

Lowe, Philip, Cox, Graham, MacEwan, Malcolm, O'Riordan, Timothy and Winter, Michael (1986) *Countryside Conflicts: The Politics of Farming, Forestry and Conservation*, Aldershot: Gower.

Lowe, Philip and Flynn, Andrew (1989) 'Environmental Politics and Policy in the 1980s', in John Mohan (ed.), *The Political Geography of Contemporary Britain*, London: Macmillan, pp. 255–79.

Lowe, Philip and Goyder, Jane (1983) *Environmental Groups in Politics*, London: George Allen and Unwin.

Lowe, Philip and Ward, Stephen (eds.) (1998) *British Environmental Policy and Europe*, London: Routledge.

Lucardie, Paul (1993) 'Why Would Egocentrists Become Ecocentrists? On Individualism and Holism in Green Political Theory', in Andrew Dobson and Paul Lucardie (eds.), *The Politics of Nature*, London: Routledge, pp. 21–35.

(1997) 'Greening and Ungreening the Netherlands', in Michael Jacobs (ed.), *Greening the Millennium?*, Oxford: Blackwell, pp. 183–91.

Lucardie, Paul, van der Knoop, Jelle, van Schuur, Wijbrandt and Voerman, Gerrit (1995) 'Greening the Reds or Reddening the Greens? The Case of the Green Left in the Netherlands', in Wolfgang Rüdig (ed.), *Green Politics Three*, Edinburgh University Press, pp. 90–111.

Luke, Tim (1988) 'The Dreams of Deep Ecology', *Telos*, 76: 65–92.

Lukes, Steven (1974) *Power: A Radical View*, London: Macmillan.

Lundqvist, Lennart (1980) *The Hare and the Tortoise: Clean Air Policies in the United States and Sweden*, Ann Arbor: University of Michigan Press.

(1998) 'Sweden: From Environmental Restoration to Ecological Modernisation', in Hanf and Jansen (eds.), pp. 230–52.

McAdam, Doug, McCarthy, John and Zald, Mayer (1996) *Comparative Perspectives on Social Movements*, Cambridge University Press.

McAdams, John (1987) 'Testing the Theory of the New Class', *Sociological Quarterly*, 28(1): 23–49.

McCormick, John (1989) *Reclaiming Paradise*, Bloomington: Indiana University Press.

(1991) *British Politics and the Environment*, London: Earthscan.

McCulloch, Alistair (1992) 'The Green Party in England and Wales: Structure and Development', *Environmental Politics* 1(3): 418–36.

MacDonald, Mary (1998) *Agendas for Sustainability*, London: Routledge.

McGinnis, Michael (ed.) (1998) *Bioregionalism*, London: Routledge.

McLaughlin, Andrew (1993) *Regarding Nature*, New York: SUNY Press.

McMichael, A. J. (1995) *Planetary Overload*, Cambridge University Press.

McNeish, Wallace (2000) 'The Vitality of Local Protest: Alarm UK and the British Anti-Roads Protest Movement', in Seel et al. (eds.), pp. 183–98.

Macrory, Richard (1986) *Environmental Policy in Britain: Reaffirmation or Reform?*, Berlin: International Institute for Environment and Society.

Maloney, William and Richardson, Jeremy (1994) 'Water Policy-Making in England and Wales: Policy Communities under Pressure?', *Environmental Politics*, 3(4): 110–38.

Markovits, Andrei and Gorski, Philip (1993) *The German Left: Red, Green and Beyond*, Cambridge: Polity Press.

Marsh, David (ed.) (1998) *Comparing Policy Networks*, Buckingham: Open University Press.

Marsh, David and Rhodes, R.A.W. (eds.) (1992) *Policy Networks in British Government*, Oxford University Press.

Marsh, David and Smith, Martin (2000) 'Understanding Policy Networks: Towards a Dialectical Approach', *Political Studies*, 48: 4–21.

Marsh, David and Stoker, Gerry (eds.) (1995) *Theory and Methods in Political Science*, London: Macmillan.

Martell, Luke (1994) *Ecology and Society*, Cambridge: Polity Press.

Maslow, Abraham (1954) *Motivation and Personality*, New York: Harper Row.

Mason, Michael (1999) *Environmental Democracy*, London: Earthscan.

Mathews, Freya (1991) *The Ecological Self*, London: Routledge.

Mathews, Jessica Tuchman (1989) 'Redefining Security', *Foreign Affairs*, 68(2): 162–77.

Mayer, Margit and Ely, John (1998) *The German Greens: Paradox between Movement and Party*, Philadelphia: Temple University Press.

Meadowcroft, James (2000) 'Sustainable Development: A New(ish) Idea for a New Century?', *Political Studies*, 48: 370–87.

Meadows, Donella, Meadows, Dennis, Randers, Jorgen and Behrens, William (1972) *The Limits to Growth*, London: Earth Island.

Meadows, Donella, Meadows, Dennis and Randers, Jorgen (1992) *Beyond the Limits: Global Collapse or a Sustainable Future?*, London: Earthscan.

Mellor, Mary (1992) *Breaking the Boundaries*, London: Virago.

(1997) *Feminism and Ecology*, Cambridge: Polity Press.

Melucci, Alberto (1989) *Nomads of the Present: Social Movements and Individual Needs in Contemporary Society*, London: Hutchinson Radius.

Merchant, Carolyn (1992) *Radical Ecology*, London: Routledge.

Michels, Robert (1959[1915]), *Political Parties*, New York: Dover.

Midgley, Mary (1983) *Animals and Why They Matter*, Harmondsworth: Penguin.

Milbrath, Lester (1989) *Envisioning a Sustainable Society*, Albany: SUNY Press.

Mill, John Stuart (1888) *Principles of Political Economy*, London: Longmans, Green and Co.

Miller, David (1999) 'Social Justice and Environmental Goods', in Dobson (ed.), pp. 151–72.

Miller, Marian (1995) *The Third World in Global Environmental Politics*, Buckingham: Open University Press.

Mitchell, Robert, Mertig, Angela and Dunlap, Riley (1992) 'Twenty Years of Environmental Mobilisation: Trends among National Environmental Organisations', in Dunlap and Mertig (eds.), pp. 11–26.

Mol, Arthur (1996) 'Ecological Modernisation and Institutional Reflexivity: Environmental Reform in the Late Modern Age', *Environmental Politics*, 5(2): 302–23.

Mol, Arthur, Lauber, Volkmar and Liefferink, Duncan (2000) *The Voluntary Approach to Environmental Policy*, Oxford University Press.

Mol, Arthur and Sonnenfeld, David (eds.) (2000) 'Ecological Modernisation around the World: Perspectives and Critical Debates', *Environmental Politics*, Special Issue, 9(1).

Mol, Arthur and Spaargaren, Gert (2000) 'Ecological Modernisation Theory in Debate: A Review', *Environmental Politics*, 9(1): 17–49.

Moran, Alan, Chisholm, Andrew and Porter, Michael (eds.) (1991) *Markets, Resources and the Environment*, North Sydney: Allen and Unwin.

Morgenthau, Hans (1978) *Politics among Nations*, 5th edition, New York: Alfred Knopf.

Morris, Julian et al. (eds.) (1997) *Climate Change*, London: Institute of Economic Affairs.

Morrison, Denton and Dunlap, Riley (1986) 'Environmentalism and Elitism: A Conceptual and Empirical Analysis', *Environmental Management*, 10(5): 581–9.

Mueller, Dennis (1989) *Public Choice II*, Cambridge University Press.

Müller-Rommel, Ferdinand (ed.) (1989) *New Politics in Western Europe*, Boulder: Westview Press.

(1990) 'New Political Movements and "New Politics Parties" in Western Europe', in Russell Dalton and Manfred Kuechler (eds.), *Challenging the Political Order: New Social and Political Movements in Western Democracies*, Cambridge: Polity Press, pp. 209–231.

(1998) 'Explaining the Electoral Success of Green Parties; A Cross-National Analysis', *Environmental Politics*, 7(4): 145–54.

Myers, Norman (1989) 'Environment and Security', *Foreign Affairs*, No. 74: 23–41.

Naess, Arne (1973) 'The Shallow and the Deep, Long-Range Ecology Movement', *Inquiry*, 16: 95–100.

(1989) *Ecology, Community and Lifestyle*, Cambridge University Press.

Nas, Masja (1995) 'Green, Greener, Greenest', in Jan van Deth and Elinor Scarbrough (eds.), *The Impact of Values*, Oxford University Press, pp. 275–300.

Nash, Roderick (1989) *The Rights of Nature: A History of Environmental Ethics*, Madison: University of Wisconsin Press.

Neale, Alan (1997) 'Organising Environmental Self-Regulation: Liberal Governmentality and the Pursuit of Ecological Modernisation in Europe', *Environmental Politics*, 6(4): 1–24.

Newell, Peter (1998) 'Who "CoPed" Out in Kyoto? An Assessment of the Third Conference of the Parties to the Framework Convention on Climate Change', *Environmental Politics*, 7(2): 153–9.

(2000) *Climate for Change: Non-State Actors and the Global Politics of the Greenhouse*, Cambridge University Press.

Newell, Peter and Paterson, Matthew (1998) 'A Climate for Business: Global Warming, the State and Capital', *Review of International Political Economy*, 5(4): 679–704.

Norton, Bryan (1991) *Towards Unity amongst Environmentalists*, Oxford University Press.

Nozick, Robert (1974) *Anarchy, State and Utopia*, Oxford: Blackwell.

Nussbaum, Martha (1986) *The Fragility of Goodness: Luck and Ethics in Greek Tragedy and Philosophy*, Cambridge University Press.

OECD (1989) *Economic Instruments for Environmental Protection*, Paris.

(1991) *Environmental Indicators: A Preliminary Set*, Paris.

(1997) *Environmental Taxes and Green Tax Reform*, Paris.

(1998) *Towards Sustainable Development: Environmental Indicators*, Paris.

Oelschlaeger, Max (1991) *The Idea of Wilderness*, New Haven: Yale University Press.

Offe, Claus (1974) 'Structural Problems of the Capitalist State', in Klaus von Beyme (ed.), *German Political Studies*, vol. 1, London: Sage, pp. 31–57.

(1985) 'New Social Movements: Challenging the Boundaries of Institutional Politics', *Social Research*, 52(4): 817–68.

Office for National Statistics (2000) *Social Trends 30: 2000 Edition*, London: The Stationery Office.

Ogle, Greg (2000) 'Accounting for Economic Welfare: Politics, Problems and Potentials', *Environmental Politics*, 9(3): 109–28.

Olson, Mancur (1965) *The Logic of Collective Action*, Cambridge, MA: Harvard University Press.

O'Neill, John (1993) *Ecology, Policy and Politics*, London: Routledge.

O'Neill, Michael (1997) *Green Politics and Political Change in Contemporary Europe*, Aldershot: Ashgate.

Ophuls, William (1977) *Ecology and the Politics of Scarcity*, San Francisco: Freeman and Co.

O'Riordan, Timothy (1981) *Environmentalism*, 2nd edition, London: Pion.

(1996) 'Democracy and the Sustainability Transition', in William Lafferty and James Meadowcroft (eds.), *Democracy and the Environment: Problems and Prospects*, Cheltenham: Edward Elgar, pp. 140–56.

(ed.) (1997) *Ecotaxation*, London: Earthscan.

O'Riordan, Timothy and Cameron, James (1994) 'The History and Contemporary Significance of the Precautionary Principle', in Timothy O'Riordan and James

Cameron (eds.), *Interpreting the Precautionary Principle*, London: Earthscan, pp.12–30.

O'Riordan, Timothy and Jäger, Jill (eds.) (1996) *Politics of Climate Change: A European Perspective*, London: Routledge.

O'Riordan, Timothy, Kemp, Ray and Purdue, Michael (1988) *Sizewell B: An Anatomy of the Inquiry*, London: Macmillan.

O'Riordan, Timothy and Voisey, Heather (eds.) (1997) 'Sustainable Development in Western Europe: Coming to Terms with *Agenda 21*', Special Issue of *Environmental Politics*, 6(1).

Ostrom, Elinor (1990) *Governing the Commons*, Cambridge University Press.

Ostrom, Elinor, Burger, Joanna, Field, Christopher, Norgaard, Richard and Policansky, David (1999) 'Revisiting the Commons: Local Lessons, Global Challenges', *Science*, 284: 278–82.

Oye, Kenneth (ed.) (1986) *Co-operation under Anarchy*, Princeton University Press.

Paehlke, Robert (1989) *Environmentalism and the Future of Progressive Politics*, New Haven: Yale University Press.

Paehlke, Robert and Torgerson, Douglas (eds.) (1990) *Managing Leviathan: Environmental Politics and the Administrative State*, Peterborough, Ont.: Broadview Press.

Panebianco, Angelo (1988) *Political Parties*, Cambridge University Press.

Papadakis, Elim (1993) *Politics and the Environment*, St Leonards, NSW: Allen and Unwin.

Parfitt, Derek (1984) *Reasons and Persons*, Oxford University Press.

Parsons, Wayne (1995) *Public Policy*, Cheltenham: Edward Elgar.

Pateman, Carol (1970) *Participation and Democratic Theory*, Cambridge University Press.

Paterson, Matthew (1996) *Global Warming and Global Politics*, London: Routledge.

Pearce, David (1998) 'Cost–Benefit Analysis and Environmental Policy', *Oxford Review of Economic Policy*, 14(4): 84–100.

Pearce, David, Markandya, Anil and Barbier, Edward (1989) *Blueprint for a Green Economy*, London: Earthscan.

Pearce, David (and 12 others) (1993) *Blueprint 3: Measuring Sustainable Development*, London: Earthscan.

Pearce, David and Turner, R. Kerry (1990) *Economics of Natural Resources and the Environment*, Hemel Hempstead: Harvester Wheatsheaf.

Pearce, Fred (1991) *Green Warriors*, London: Bodley Head.

Pehle, Heinrich (1997) 'Germany: Domestic Obstacles to an International Forerunner', in Andersen and Liefferink (eds.), pp. 161–209.

Pehle, Heinrich and Jansen, Alf-Inge (1998) 'Germany: The Engine in European Environmental Policy?', in Hanf and Jansen (eds.), pp. 82–109.

Pepper, David (1991) *Communes and the Green Vision*, London: Green Print.

   (1993) *Ecosocialism*, London: Routledge.

   (1996) *Modern Environmentalism*, London: Routledge.

Peters, B. Guy (1998a) 'Policy Networks: Myth, Metaphor and Reality', in Marsh (ed.), pp. 21–32.

   (1998b) 'Managing Horizontal Government: The Politics of Co-ordination', *Public Administration*, 76: 295–311.

Peters, B. Guy and Hogwood, Brian (1985) 'In Search of an Issue-Attention Cycle', *Journal of Politics*, 47: 238–53.

Peterson, John and Bomberg, Elizabeth (1999) *Decision-Making in the European Union*, London: Macmillan.

Pickering, Kevin and Owen, Lewis (1994) *An Introduction to Global Environmental Issues*, London: Routledge.

Plant, Judith (ed.) (1989) *Healing the Wounds: The Promise of Ecofeminism*, London: Green Print.

Plumwood, Val (1993) *Feminism and the Mastery of Nature*, London: Routledge.

(1996) 'Has Democracy Failed Ecology? An Ecofeminist Perspective', *Environmental Politics*, 4(4): 134–68.

Poguntke, Thomas (1993) *Alternative Politics: The German Green Party*, Edinburgh University Press.

Polsby, Nelson (1980) *Community Power and Political Theory: A Further Look at Problems of Evidence and Inference*, 2nd edition, New Haven: Yale University Press.

Ponting, Clive (1992) *A Green History of the World*, London: Penguin.

Porritt, Jonathon (1984) *Seeing Green*, Oxford: Blackwell.

Porter, Gareth and Brown, Janet Welsh (1996) *Global Environmental Politics*, 2nd edition, Boulder: Westview Press.

Porter, Michael (1990) *The Competitive Advantage of Nations*, New York: Free Press.

Pratt, Vernon, with Jane Howarth and Emily Brady 2000, *Environment and Philosophy*, London: Routledge.

Press, Daniel and Mazmanian, Daniel (1999) 'Understanding the Transition to a Sustainable Economy', in Vig and Kraft (eds.), pp. 257–80.

Princen, Thomas and Finger, Matthias (1994) 'Introduction', in Thomas Princen and Matthias Finger (eds.), *Environmental NGOs in World Politics*, London: Routledge.

Pross, Paul (1992) *Group Politics and Public Policy*, 2nd edition, Oxford University Press.

Pulido, Laura (1996) *Environmentalism and Social Justice*, Tucson: University of Arizona Press.

Rabe, Barry (1999) 'The Promise and Pitfalls of Decentralisation', in Vig and Kraft (eds.), pp. 32–54.

Radcliffe, James (2000) *Green Politics: Dictatorship or Democracy?* London: Macmillan.

Rawcliffe, Peter (1998) *Environmental Pressure Groups in Transition*, Manchester University Press.

Rawls, John (1973) *A Theory of Justice*, Oxford University Press.

Raz, Joseph (1986) *The Morality of Freedom*, Oxford: Clarendon Press.

RCEP [Royal Commission on Environmental Pollution] (1998) *Setting Environmental Standards*, 21st Report, Cm. 4053, London: Stationery Office.

(2000) *Energy – the Changing Climate*, 22nd Report, Cm. 4794, London: Stationery Office.

Redclift, Michael (1993) 'Sustainable Development: Needs, Values, Rights', *Environmental Values*, 2(1): 3–20.

Regan, Tom (1983) *The Case for Animal Rights*, London: RKP.

Reitan, Marit (1997) 'Norway: A Case of "Splendid Isolation"', in Andersen and Liefferink (eds.), pp. 287–330.

(1998) 'Ecological Modernisation and "Realpolitik": Ideas, Interests and Institutions', *Environmental Politics*, 7(2): 1–26.

Rhodes, Martin (1995) 'Italy: Greens in an Overcrowded Political System', in Richardson and Rootes (eds.), pp. 168–92.

Rhodes, R. A. W. (1988) *Beyond Westminster and Whitehall: The Sub-Central Government of Britain*, London: Unwin Hyman.

(1997) *Understanding Governance*, Buckingham: Open University Press.

Richardson, Genevra, Ogus, Anthony and Burrows, Paul (1983) *Policing Pollution*, Oxford University Press.

Richardson, Dick (1997) 'The Politics of Sustainable Development', in Baker et al. (eds.), pp. 43–60.

Richardson, Dick and Rootes, Chris (eds.) (1995) *The Green Challenge*, London: Routledge.

Richardson, Jeremy (ed.) (1982) *Policy Styles in Western Europe*, London: Allen and Unwin.

Ridley, Matt (1995) *Down to Earth: A Contrarian View of Environmental Problems*, London: Institute of Economic Affairs.

Rihoux, Benoît (2000) 'Governmental Participation and the Organisational "Transformation" of Green Parties: A Comparative Enquiry', paper presented at Political Studies Association conference, London School of Economics, April.

Ringquist, Evan (1995) 'Evaluating Environmental Policy Outcomes', in Lester (ed.), pp. 303–27.

Robertson, James (1985) *Future Work*, Aldershot: Gower.

Robinson, Mike (1992) *The Greening of British Party Politics*, Manchester University Press.

Robinson, Nick (2000) 'The Politics of the Car: The Limits of Actor-Centred Models of Agenda-Setting', in Seel et al. (eds.), pp. 199–217.

Rodman, John (1980) 'Paradigm Change in Political Science', *American Behavioral Scientist*, 24(1): 49–78.

Rohrschneider, Robert (1993) 'New Party versus Old Left Realignments: Environmental Attitudes, Party Policies and Partisan Affiliations in Four Western European Countries', *Journal of Politics*, 55(3): 682–701.

Rolston, Holmes (1988) *Environmental Ethics: Duties to and Values in the Natural World*, Philadelphia: Temple University Press.

(1991) 'Environmental Ethics: Values in and Duties to the Natural World', in F. Herbert Bormann and Stephen Kellert (eds.), *The Broken Circle*, New Haven: Yale University Press, pp. 73–96.

Rootes, Chris (1995a) 'A New Class? The Higher Educated and the New Politics', in Louis Maheu (ed.), *Social Movements and Social Classes: The Future of Collective Action*, London: Sage, pp. 220–35.

(1995b) 'Environmental Consciousness, Institutional Structures and Political Competition in the Formation and Development of Green Parties', in Richardson and Rootes (eds.), pp. 232–52.

(1995c) 'Britain: Greens in a Cold Climate', in Richardson and Rootes (eds.), pp. 66–90.

(1997) 'Environmental Movements and Green Parties in Western and Eastern Europe', in Michael Redclift and Graham Woodgate (eds.), *The International Handbook of Environmental Sociology*, Cheltenham: Edward Elgar, pp. 319–48.

(1998) 'Political Opportunity Structures: Promise, Problems and Prospects', *La Lettre de la Maison Française*, No. 10, pp. 75–97.

(1999a) 'Environmental Movements: From the Local to the Global', *Environmental Politics*, 8(1): 1–12.

(1999b) 'The Transformation of Environmental Activism: Activists, Organizations and Policy-Making', *Innovation*, 12(2): 155–73.

(1999c) 'Acting Globally, Thinking Locally? Prospects for a Global Environmental Movement', *Environmental Politics*, 8(1): 290–310.

Rootes, Chris and Miller, Alexander (2000) 'The British Environmental Movement: Organisational Field and Network of Organisations', paper at ECPR Joint Sessions, 14–19 April.

Rose, Adam (1992) 'Equity Considerations of Tradeable Carbon Emission Entitlements', in UNCTAD, *Combating Global Warming*, Geneva: UNCTAD.

Rose, Chris (1993) 'Beyond the Struggle for Proof: Factors Changing the Environmental Movement', *Environmental Values*, 2(4): 285–98.

Rosenbaum, Walter (1995) 'Bureaucracy and Environmental Policy', in Lester (ed.), pp. 206–41.

(1997a) 'Regulation at Risk: The Controversial Politics and Science of Comparative Risk Assessment', in Sheldon Kamieniecki, George Gonzalez and Robert Vos (eds.), *Flashpoints in Environmental Policy-making*, Albany: SUNY Press, pp. 31–61.

(1997b) 'The EPA at Risk: Conflicts over Institutional Reform', in Norman Vig and Michael Kraft (eds.), *Environmental Policy in the 1990s*, 3rd edition, Washington, DC: Congressional Quarterly Inc.

(1999) 'Escaping the "Battered Agency Syndrome": EPA's Gamble with Regulatory Reinvention', in Vig and Kraft (eds.), pp. 165–89.

Rowell, Andrew (1996) *Green Backlash: Global Subversion of the Environmental Movement*, London: Routledge.

Rowlands, Ian (1995) *The Politics of Global Atmospheric Change*, Manchester University Press.

(1997) 'International Fairness and Justice in Addressing Global Climate Change', *Environmental Politics* 6(3): 1–30.

Rucht, Dieter (1995) 'Ecological Protest as Calculated Law-Breaking: Greenpeace and Earth First! in Comparative Perspective', in Wolfgang Rüdig (ed.), *Green Politics Three*, Edinburgh University Press, pp. 66–89.

Rüdig, Wolfgang, Bennie, Lynn and Franklin, Mark (1991) *Green Party Members: A Profile*, Glasgow: Delta.

Rüdig, Wolfgang and Franklin, Mark (2000) 'Government Participation and Green Electoral Support: A Comparative Analysis', paper presented at Political Studies Association conference, London School of Economics, April.

Rüdig, Wolfgang and Lowe, Philip (1986) 'The Withered "Greening" of British Politics: A Study of the Ecology Party', *Political Studies*, 34: 262–84

Rydin, Yvonne (1998) *Urban and Environmental Planning*, London: Macmillan.

Ryle, Martin (1988) *Ecology and Socialism*, London: Radius.

Sabatier, Paul (1988) 'An Advocacy Coalition Framework of Policy Change and the Role of Policy-Oriented Learning Therein', *Policy Sciences*, 21: 129–68.

(1998) 'The Advocacy Coalition Framework: Revisions and Relevance for Europe', *Journal of European Public Policy*, 5: 98–130.

Sabatier, Paul and Jenkins-Smith, Hank (eds.) (1993) *Policy Change and Learning: An Advocacy Coalition Approach*, Boulder: Westview Press.

(1999) 'The Advocacy Coalition Framework: An Assessment', in Paul Sabatier (ed.), *Theories of the Policy Process*, Boulder: Westview Press, 117–66.

Sagoff, Mark (1988) *The Economy of the Earth*, Cambridge University Press.

Sairinen, Rauno (1996) *The Finns and Environmental Policy*, Helsinki: Central Statistics Office, Research Report 217.

Sale, Kirkpatrick (1980) *Human Scale*, London: Secker and Warburg.

(1991) *Dwellers in the Land: The Bioregional Vision*, 2nd edition, Philadelphia: New Society Publishers.

(1993) *The Green Revolution: The American Environmental Movement 1962–92*, New York: Hill and Wang.

Salleh, Ariel (1997) *Ecofeminism as Politics*, London: Zed Books.

Salt, Julian (1998) 'Kyoto and the Insurance Industry', *Environmental Politics*, 7(2): 160–5.

Sarkar, Saral (1999) *Ecosocialism or Ecocapitalism?*, London: Zed Books.

Saurin, Julian (1996) 'International Relations, Social Ecology and the Globalisation of Environmental Change', in Vogler and Imber (eds.), pp. 77–98.

Saward, Michael (1992) 'The Civil Nuclear Network in Britain', in Marsh and Rhodes (eds.), pp. 75–99.

(1996) 'Must Democrats Be Environmentalists?', in Doherty and de Geus (eds.), pp. 79–96.

Sbragia, Alberta (2000) 'Environmental Policy', in Helen Wallace and William Wallace (eds.), *Policy-Making in the European Union*, Oxford University Press, pp. 293–316.

Scharf, Thomas (1994) *The German Greens*, Oxford: Berg.

Schattschneider, E. E. (1960) *The Semi-Sovereign People*, New York: Holt, Rinehart and Winston.

Schlosberg, David (1999a) 'Networks and Mobile Arrangements: Organisational Innovation in the US Environmental Justice Movement', *Environmental Politics*, 8(1): 122–48.

(1999b) *Environmental Justice and the New Pluralism*, Oxford University Press.

Schumacher, E. F. (1975) *Small Is Beautiful*, London: Sphere.

Scott, Alan (1990) *Ideology and the New Social Movements*, London: Unwin Hyman.

Scruggs, Lyle (1999) 'Institutions and Environmental Performance in Seventeen Western Democracies', *British Journal of Political Science*, 29: 1–31.

Scruton, Roger (1984) *The Meaning of Conservatism*, London: Macmillan.

Seager, Joni (1993) *Earth Follies*, London: Earthscan.

Seaver, Brenda (1997) 'Stratospheric Ozone Protection: IR Theory and the Montreal Protocol on Substances that Deplete the Ozone Layer', *Environmental Politics*, 6(3): 31–67.

Seel, Benjamin (1997) 'Strategies of Resistance at the Pollok Free State Road Protest Camp', *Environmental Politics*, 6(4): 108–39.

Seel, Benjamin, Paterson, Matthew and Doherty, Brian (eds.) (2000) *Direct Action in British Environmentalism*, London: Routledge.

Seel, Benjamin and Plows, Alex (2000) 'Coming Live and Direct: Strategies of Earth First!', in Seel et al. pp. 112–32.

Sen, Amartya (1994) 'Population: Delusion and Reality', *New York Review of Books*, 22 September.

Sessions, George (ed.) (1995) *Deep Ecology for the 21st Century*, London: Shambala.

Shaiko, Ronald (1993) 'Greenpeace USA: Something Old, New, Borrowed', *The Annals*, July, pp. 88–100.

Shiva, Vandana (1989) *Staying Alive: Women, Ecology and Development*, London: Earthscan.

Singer, Peter (1976) *Animal Liberation*, London: Jonathan Cape.

(1979) *Practical Ethics*, Cambridge University Press.

Skea, Jim and Smith, Adrian (1998) 'Integrating Pollution Control', in Lowe and Ward (eds.), pp. 265–81.

Smith, Gordon (1996) 'The Party System at the Crossroads', in Gordon Smith, William Paterson and Stephen Padgett (eds.), *Developments in German Politics 2*, London: Macmillan, pp. 55–75.

Smith, Mark (1998) *Ecologism*, Buckingham: Open University Press.

(1999) *Thinking through the Environment*, London: Routledge.

Smith, Martin (1990) *The Politics of Agricultural Support in Britain*, Aldershot: Dartmouth.

(1993) *Pressure, Power and Policy: State Autonomy and Policy Networks in Britain and the United States*, Hemel Hempstead: Harvester Wheatsheaf.

Smith, Zachary (1995) *The Environmental Policy Paradox*, 2nd edition, Englewood Cliffs: Prentice Hall.

Soden, Dennis (ed.) (1999) *The Environmental Presidency*, New York: SUNY Press.

Spaargaren, Gert and Mol, Arthur (1992) 'Sociology, Environment and Modernity: Ecological Modernisation as a Theory of Social Change', *Society and Natural Resources*, 5(4): 323–44.

Spaargaren, Gert and van Vliet, Bas (2000) 'Lifestyles, Consumption and the Environment: The Ecological Modernisation of Domestic Consumption', *Environmental Politics*, 9(1): 50–76.

Spanou, Calliope (1998) 'Greece: Administrative Symbols and Policy Realities', in Hanf and Jansen (eds.), pp. 110–30.

Stirpe, Dave (1997) 'Smugglers Beware', *Our Planet*, UNEP, 9.2 (*http://www.ourplanet.com/*).

Stoett, Peter (1997) *The International Politics of Whaling*, Vancouver: UBC Press.

Strübin, M. (1997) 'Ecological Tax Reform in Germany', *German Politics*, 6(2): 168–80.

Sverdrup, Liv (1997) 'Norway's Institutional Response to Sustainable Development', *Environmental Politics*, 6(1): 54–82.

Sylvan, Richard and Bennett, David (1994) *The Greening of Ethics*, Cambridge: White Horse Press.

Szarka, Joseph (1999) 'The Parties of the French "Plural Left": An Uneasy Complementarity', *West European Politics*, 22(4): 20–37.

Szasz, Andrew (1994) *Ecopopulism: Toxic Waste and the Movement for Environmental Justice*, Minneapolis: University of Minnesota Press.

Tarrow, Sydney, (1994) *Power in Movement: Social Movements, Collective Action and Mass Politics*, Cambridge University Press.

Tatalovich, Raymond and Wattier, Mark (1999) 'Opinion Leadership: Elections, Campaigns, Agenda Setting and Environmentalism', in Soden (ed.), pp. 147–87.

Taylor, Bob Pepperman (1991) 'Environmental Ethics and Political Theory', *Polity*, 23: 567–83.

(1992) *Our Limits Transgressed: Environmental Political Thought in America*, Lawrence: University Press of Kansas.

Tilly, Charles (1978) *From Mobilization to Revolution*, Reading: Addison-Wesley.

Tokar, Brian (1992) *The Green Alternative*, San Pedro: R. & E. Miles.

Toner, Glen (2000) 'Canada: From Early Frontrunner to Plodding Anchorman', in Lafferty and Meadowcroft (eds.), pp. 53–84.

Touraine, Alain, (1981) *The Voice and the Eye: An Analysis of Social Movements*, Cambridge University Press.

Trainer, F. E. (1985) *Abandon Affluence!*, London: Zed Books.

Truman, David (1951) *The Governmental Process*, New York: Alfred Knopf.

Turner, R. Kerry, Pearce, David and Bateman, Ian (1994) *Environmental Economics: An Elementary Introduction*, Hemel Hempstead: Harvester Wheatsheaf.

Tyme, John (1978) *Motorways versus Democracy*, London: Macmillan.

UNCED [United Nations Conference on Environment and Development] (1992) *Agenda 21: A Programme for Action for Sustainable Development*, New York: United Nations.

UNDESA [United Nations Department of Economic and Social Affairs] (1999) *Comprehensive Review of Changing Consumption and Production Patterns*, Report of the Secretary-General.

UNDP [United Nations Development Programme] (1998) *Human Development Report 1998*, Oxford University Press.

UNEP [United Nations Environment Programme] (2000) *www.unep.org/ozone/PressBack/*.

Uranium Institute (2001) *http://www.uilondon.org/*.

Van der Heijden, Hein-Anton (1997) 'Political Opportunity Structure and the Institutionalisation of the Environmental Movement', *Environmental Politics*, 6(4): 25–50.

——— (1999) 'Environmental Movements, Ecological Modernisation and Political Opportunity Structures', *Environmental Politics*, 8(1): 199–221.

Van Muijen, Marie-Louise (2000) 'The Netherlands: Ambitious on Goals – Ambivalent on Action', in Lafferty and Meadowcroft (eds.), pp. 142–73.

Vig, Norman (1997) 'Presidential Leadership and the Environment: From Reagan to Clinton', in Norman Vig and Michael Kraft (eds.), *Environmental Policy in the 1990s*, 3rd edition, Washington, DC: CQ Press, pp. 95–118.

——— (1999) 'Presidential Leadership and the Environment: From Reagan to Clinton', in Vig and Kraft (eds.), pp. 98–120.

Vig, Norman and Kraft, Michael (eds.) (1999a) *Environmental Policy*, 4th edition, Washington, DC: CQ Press.

——— (1999b) 'Towards Sustainable Development', in Vig and Kraft (eds.), pp. 370–88.

Vincent, Andrew (1993) 'The Character of Ecology', *Environmental Politics*, 2(2): 248–76.

Voerman, Gerrit (1995) 'The Netherlands: Losing Colours, Turning Green', in Richardson and Rootes (eds.), pp. 109–27.

Vogel, David (1986) *National Styles of Regulation*, Ithaca: Cornell University Press.

——— (1987) 'Political Science and the Study of Corporate Power: A Dissent from the New Conventional Wisdom', *British Journal of Political Science*, 17: 385–408.

——— (1995) *Trading Up: Consumer and Environmental Regulation in a Consumer Economy*, Cambridge, MA: Harvard University Press.

Vogler, John (1992) 'Regimes and the Global Commons: Space Atmosphere and Oceans', in Anthony McGrew and Paul Lewis (eds.), *Global Politics*, Cambridge: Polity Press.

——— (1995) *The Global Commons: A Regime Analysis*, Chichester: Wiley.

Vogler, John and Imber, Mark (1996) *The Environment and International Relations*, London: Routledge.

Voisey, Heather and O'Riordan, Timothy (1997) 'Governing Institutions for Sustainable Development: The United Kingdom's National Level Approach', *Environmental Politics*, 6(1): 24–53.

Wall, Derek (ed.) (1994a) *Green History*, London: Routledge.

——— (1994b) 'Introduction', in Wall (ed.), pp. 1–15.

——— (1999) *Earth First! and the Anti-Roads Movement*, London: Routledge.

Wapner, Paul (1996) *Environmental Activism and World Civic Politics*, New York: SUNY Press.

Ward, Hugh (1999) 'Citizens' Juries and Valuing the Environment: A Proposal', *Environmental Politics*, 8(2): 75–96.

Ward, Hugh and Samways, David (1992) 'Environmental Policy', in David Marsh and R. A. W. Rhodes (eds.), *Implementing Thatcherite Policies*, Buckingham: Open University Press, pp. 117–36.

Ward, Neil (1998) 'Water Quality' in Lowe and Ward (eds.), pp. 244–64.

Ward, Neil, Lowe, Philip and Buller, Henry (1997) 'Implementing European Water Quality Directives: Lessons for Sustainable Development', in Baker et al. (eds.), pp. 198–216.

Ware, Alan (1996) *Political Parties and Party Systems*, Oxford University Press.

Warren, Karen (ed.) (1994) *Ecological Feminism*, London: Routledge.

WCED [World Commission on the Environment and Development] (1987) *Our Common Future*, Oxford University Press [The Brundtland Report].

Weale, Albert (1992) *The New Politics of Pollution*, Manchester University Press.

Weiss, Edith Brown and Jacobson, Harold (1998) *Engaging Countries: Strengthening Compliance with International Environmental Accords*, Cambridge, MA: MIT Press.

Wells, David (1978) 'Radicalism, Conservatism and the Environment', *Politics*, 13(2): 299–306.

Weston, Joe (1986) *Red and Green* London: Pluto.

White, Lynn (1962) *Medieval Technology and Social Change*, Oxford: Clarendon Press.

Whitelegg, John (1997) *Critical Mass: Transport, Environment and Society in the Twenty-First Century*, London: Pluto Press.

Wildavsky, Aaron (1995) *But Is It True?* Cambridge, MA: Harvard University Press.

Wilkinson, David (1997) 'Towards Sustainability in the EU? Steps within the European Commission towards Integrating the Environment into Other EU Policy Sectors', *Environmental Politics*, 6(1): 153–73.

Williams, Bernard (1973) 'A Critique of Utilitarianism', in J. J. C. Smart and Bernard Williams, *Utilitarianism: For and Against*, Cambridge University Press, pp. 75–150.

Williams, Marc (1996) 'International Political Economy and Global Environmental Change', in Vogler and Imber (eds.), pp. 41–58.

Williams, Marc and Ford, Lucy (1999) 'The World Trade Organisation, Social Movements and Global Environmental Management', *Environmental Politics*, 8(1): 268–89.

Williams, Marc (2000) 'The Changing Fortunes of the Austrian Greens', *Environmental Politics* 9(4): 135–40.

Williamson, Peter (1989) *Corporatism in Perspective: An Introductory Guide to Corporatist Theory*, London: Sage.

Wissenburg, Marcel (1998) *Green Liberalism*, London: UCL Press.

Wood, Christopher (1995) *Environmental Impact Assessment: A Comparative Review*, Harlow: Longman.

World Bank (1997) *Expanding the Measure of Wealth: Indicators of Environmentally Sustainable Development*, Washington, DC: World Bank.

(1999) *Environment Matters*, Washington, DC: World Bank.

Wright, Brian (2001) 'Environmental NGOs and the Dolphin – Tuna Case', *Environmental Politics*, 9(4): 82–103.

Yearley, Steven (1991) *The Green Case*, London: HarperCollins.

Young, Iris (1990) *Justice and the Politics of Difference*, Princeton University Press.

Young, Oran (1994) *International Governance*, Ithaca: Cornell University Press.

(ed.) (1999) *The Effectiveness of International Environmental Regimes*, Cambridge, MA: MIT Press.

Young, Stephen (2000) 'New Labour and the Environment', in David Coates and Peter Lawler (eds.), *New Labour in Power*, Manchester University Press, pp. 149–68.

Zald, Mayer and McCarthy, John (1987) *Social Movements in an Organizational Society*, New Brunswick: Transaction.

Zito, Anthony (2000) *Creating Environmental Policy in the European Union*, London: Macmillan.

Index